A-Z
HANDBOOK 4TH EDITION

Psychology

Mike Cardwell

DIGITAL EDITION

PHILIP ALLAN
UPDATES

Philip Allan Updates, an imprint of Hodder Education, an Hachette UK company, Market Place, Deddington, Oxfordshire OX15 0SE

Orders

Bookpoint Ltd, 130 Milton Park, Abingdon, Oxfordshire OX14 4SB
tel: 01235 827720
fax: 01235 400454
e-mail: uk.orders@bookpoint.co.uk

Lines are open 9.00 a.m.–5.00 p.m., Monday to Saturday, with a 24-hour message answering service. You can also order through the Philip Allan Updates website: www.philipallan.co.uk

ISBN 978-0-340-99103-9

First published 1996
Second edition 2000
Third edition 2003
Fourth edition 2010

Impression number   5   4   3   2
Year   2014   2013   2012

Typeset by Macmillan, India.

Printed and bound by CPI Group (UK) Ltd, Croydon, CR0 4YY.

Environmental information
Hachette UK's policy is to use papers that are natural, renewable and recyclable products and made from wood grown in sustainable forests. The logging and manufacturing processes are expected to conform to the environmental regulations of the country of origin.

Contents

A–Z entries

How to use this book

The *A–Z Psychology Handbook* is an alphabetical textbook designed for ease of use. Each entry begins with a one-sentence definition. This helps the user to add precision to essay writing and coursework projects.

Entries are developed in line with the relative importance of the topic covered. For example, *hysteria* is covered in a few lines, whereas an important topic area like *schizophrenia* receives more extended treatment. The latter would provide sufficient material around which to build an essay, or to clarify a difficult issue.

The study of psychology can be developed further by making use of the cross-referenced entries. The entry for *conformity (majority influence)*, for example, refers the reader to *innovation (minority influence)*. In this way the reader can appreciate how psychological knowledge is rarely confined to discrete subject matter categories. Cross-referenced entries are identified by the use of bold italics. These cross-references will help clarify understanding of an individual topic, and essay writing should benefit from the pathways to related topics that are indicated by italicised entries.

Psychology as a subject is notorious in its often confusing use of language, particularly as many words that have one meaning in common everyday language have quite a different meaning when used as specialist terms in psychology. Psychologists also have the frustrating habit of using more than one term to describe the same phenomenon. Although a book of this size could never even begin to draw together all the disparate ways that psychologists represent their knowledge, an attempt has been made to provide clarity of meaning from otherwise impenetrable jargon. Many of the terms that are in common use, not only in psychology, but also in everyday life, do tend to defy precise definition. *Personality*, *intelligence* and *self* are examples of terms used in psychology that have been used in so many different ways as to make the job of providing one all-embracing definition virtually impossible.

The *A–Z Psychology Handbook* is also a valuable revision companion. For many of the more central topic areas, commentary is included to assist the reader in acquiring a critical understanding of the topic in question. To aid the revision process, carefully selected lists are provided at the back of the book. Those facing examinations can use the lists to make the best use of the handbook during their revision time. You can also use the website that accompanies this handbook to access revision lists specific to your exam board unit. You should find these lists valuable when you come to do your revision.

A–Z Online

This new digital edition of the *A–Z Psychology Handbook* includes free access to a supporting website and a free desktop widget to make searching for terms even quicker. Log on to **www.philipallan.co.uk/a-zonline** and create an account using the unique code provided on the inside front cover of this book.

Once you are logged on, you will be able to:

- search the entire database of terms in this handbook
- print revision lists specific to your exam board
- get expert advice from examiners on how to get an A* grade
- create a personal library of your favourite terms
- expand your vocabulary with our word of the week

You can also add the other *A–Z Handbooks (digital editions)* that you own to your personal library on A–Z Online.

I hope that the *A–Z Psychology Handbook* proves an invaluable resource, fully relevant from the beginning of a psychology course right up to examinations and beyond.

Acknowledgements

In the previous editions of this text I wrote that it had been a daunting book to write, as psychology does not lend itself easily to simple definition. This fourth, updated, edition has been no less daunting, but has been made easier by the suggestions and constructive criticisms of colleagues and friends. I am indebted to John Gammon, Simon Green and Pam Prentice for their comments on the previous editions, and to all those other helpful souls who have corrected, criticised or in some other way influenced the writing of this fourth edition. My thanks also to my children Chris and Alex, who despite my attempts at parenting have grown into perfectly well-adjusted adults, and my wife Denise with whom I shall grow old and cantankerous!

There are bound to be errors in a text such as this, although I have not spotted them yet. If there are, I apologise, but hope that the rest of the book will be in some way helpful and informative.

Mike Cardwell

AA approach for substance misuse: Alcoholics Anonymous (and its sister organisation Narcotics Anonymous, or NA) is a group-based self-help programme. The AA and NA approach to substance abuse (such as alcohol or drugs) involves twelve steps that effectively encompass six stages. First there is an admission that alcohol or drugs have made life unmanageable, and the individual is powerless to change his/her substance abuse. The second stage involves acceptance of help from a 'higher power ' (i.e. AA or NA). Stage three involves becoming aware of the 'nature of our wrongs', and stage four concentrates of changing the 'defects of character' or personal shortcomings that led to the substance abuse. The fifth stage is about promising to make amends to those who have been most affected by the substance abuse (e.g. family), and the final stage aims for a 'spiritual awakening' and a commitment to help others who also want to recover.

ability refers to the qualities or skills that an individual possesses that enables them to carry out an activity without further training. For example, we may have athletic ability, intellectual ability, mathematical ability and so on.

ability grouping: the practice of placing children into groups with others of comparable academic level. This allows a teacher to provide a uniform level of instruction to an entire group.

ablation: the destruction or removal of a part of an organ using selective chemicals or surgical intervention. When used in the experimental study of the brain, a part of the brain is destroyed and the animal's subsequent behaviour evaluated. For example, if, as a result of destroying part of an animal's brain by means of a 'lesion', the animal is unable to accomplish tasks requiring vision, we may conclude that the site destroyed plays some role in vision.

abnormal behaviour is behaviour that departs from the norm or is harmful or distressing to the individual or to those around them. Abnormal behaviours are usually those that in some way violate society's ideas about what is an appropriate level of functioning. Different approaches within psychology have different views of the nature and origins of abnormal behaviour:
- *behaviour therapies* see abnormality as the development of maladaptive behaviour patterns established through the processes of *classical* and *operant conditioning*, and *modelling*
- *biological models of abnormality* see abnormal behaviour as being caused by either anatomical or biochemical problems in the brain
- *cognitive therapies* models stress the role of cognitive problems such as illogical thought processes and faulty assumptions about the world around us
- *humanistic therapies* models see abnormal behaviour resulting from blocks to an individual's potential for self-growth and development
- *psychodynamic* models see abnormal behaviour as being caused by underlying psychological forces of which the person is probably unaware, often originating from childhood experiences

- socio-cultural models focus on the social and cultural origins of abnormal behaviour through a consideration of dysfunctional family systems that 'reward' and maintain abnormal behaviour, and social stress systems that create specific problems for their members and therefore increase the likelihood of abnormal functioning.

One of the problems of having abnormality defined within a particular perspective is that what is or is not abnormal depends very much on the perspective taken. Thus within **psychoanalysis** (a psychodynamic approach), homosexuality would be considered an abnormality, whereas in the behavioural approach, it would not. Many psychologists now subscribe to the view that people must first have a biological, psychological or socio-cultural predisposition to a particular form of abnormal behaviour which is then activated and maintained by psychological stress (the **diathesis-stress paradigm** explanation of abnormal behaviour).

abnormal psychology is the scientific study of abnormal behaviour. By using scientific techniques, psychology attempts to describe, explain and predict abnormal behaviours. The ultimate aim of abnormal psychology is to **control** or prevent abnormal behaviours.

absolute threshold refers to the amount of energy necessary in a given stimulus for that stimulus to be detected. Anything below the threshold will not be detected, anything above it will be.

Abu Ghraib: In 2004, US media broke a story of torture and humiliation of Iraqi inmates at the Abu Ghraib prison in Baghdad by a small group of US soldiers. To psychologists this revelation was somewhat reminiscent of the findings of Zimbardo's Stanford Prison Study. Photographs depicted the torture of prisoners, including the use of dogs to scare prisoners as well as death threats and sexual abuse. The abuse of prisoners within Abu Ghraib resulted in a political scandal within the US and elsewhere. In 2006, the US military transferred the inmates to other prisons and handed over Abu Ghraib prison to the Iraqi authorities. In 2009, Iraq reopened Abu Ghraib under the new name of Baghdad Central Prison.

accommodation is a term normally associated with the developmental theory of Jean **Piaget** and refers to a type of adaptation in which a child develops new **schema** or modifies existing ones. This enables the child to better deal with the demands of the environment around them by constantly changing and updating the mental structures that are associated with it. For example, a child faced with a novel problem may not have the skills to deal with it. By experimenting with the problem, they may find a solution. In this way they **accommodate** the demands of the new problem and develop their existing schema in the process.

acetylcholine is a **neurotransmitter** found in the brain. Acetylcholine has been implicated in **Alzheimer's disease** in that a loss of this neurotransmitter is characteristic of the disease.

achievement goal theory: According to this theory, three factors interact to determine a person's motivation in sport: achievement goals, perceived ability and achievement behaviour. Some individuals have achievement goals that are task goal related, i.e. the focus is on improving performance relative to past performance rather than on comparison with others. Such individuals are more persistent and better motivated because the factors they focus on are internal and therefore more controllable. Other individuals have achievement goals that are more outcome goal related, i.e. they constantly compare themselves to others. Because such factors (e.g. the performance or skills of others) are external and uncontrollable, these individuals are less persistent and tend to give up more easily. Research suggests that task orientation is more conducive to positive behaviours in achievement settings such as sport.

achievement motivation is the tendency to persist at tasks that may be difficult or challenging for the individual. Differences in achievement motivation enable us to explain why less intelligent children may sometimes do better at school than their more intelligent classmates.

action potential is often referred to as a nerve impulse, and relates to the changes in electrical depolarisation that are transmitted along *neurons* and across *synapses*.

action research: a social psychological research technique pioneered by Kurt Lewin. Lewin believed that in order to gain insight into a problem, one must create a change and then see the effect. This type of research tends to be used in real-life situations, such as involving prisoners in community education programmes, or bringing together racially prejudiced people and the victims of their prejudice.

action slips: these are most commonly referred to as absent-mindedness, but are examples of *attentional* failure. Using evidence from diary accounts, the typical types of action slips appear to be:

- test failures – an inability to complete a planned sequence of activities because it is not monitored sufficiently at a critical point. For example, I frequently end up almost at my place of work because I have neglected to turn off the main road to go where I had originally intended to go
- storage failures – we forget earlier intentions or actions, e.g. putting a second spoonful of sugar in your coffee because you can't remember putting in the first
- sub-routine failures – when we insert or omit some stages in a sequence of activities. I remember once watching a chip shop owner throwing the freshly peeled potatoes straight into the fat (without putting them through the chipper first!)
- discrimination failures – where we fail to discriminate between two items, e.g. going into the wrong house or trying to open the door of the wrong car
- program assembly failures – when we use an inappropriate combination of things, such as putting salt in your coffee (or sugar on your chips).

What seems most odd about action slips is that they appear mostly during highly practised activities where you would expect to make the fewest errors. The answer appears to be in the type of *control* processes we use for different activities. In the early stages of learning an activity, it is under our conscious *attentional* control. As we become more skilled we switch to *automatic processing* of the activity. By relying on automatic processing, we occasionally lose the close control and monitoring that is only possible with attentional control. This is when we make our errors. The fact that action slips are fairly rare indicates that in real life we must switch between attentional and automatic processing.

activity theory is a theory of ageing. It maintains that activity and involvement in late adulthood is more likely to produce life satisfaction and psychological good health. Activity theory suggests that it is often desirable for individuals to carry through many of their middle adulthood roles and interests into later adulthood. As some of the major roles that people have (as parents and employees) are lost as they grow older, it is seen as important that they are replaced by new ones. The theory is often criticised as being rather simplistic in its suggestion that continued activity and involvement alone will ensure a high degree of life satisfaction and good health.

actor/observer differences: the tendency for people to attribute the behaviour of others to *dispositional* factors (i.e. something about the person), whilst frequently giving *situational* explanations for their own behaviour. One reason for the differences between an actor's (i.e. the person doing the action) and an observer's (i.e. a person watching) attributions is that they have different information available to them. The actor has more direct information available about the event than does the observer. The actor also knows more about their own previous behaviour than does the observer (i.e. they have more privileged information about the reasons for their behaviour than does an observer). The focus of attention is also different for the actor and observer. Actors focus outwards away from themselves towards the situation (and therefore cannot 'see' themselves behaving), and so are likely to locate the cause of their behaviour there (actor bias). Observers, on the other hand, focus their attention on the actor and are, therefore, more likely to bypass situational explanations and attribute the cause of behaviour to the actor (observer bias).

Although there is a great deal of support for the actor–observer effect, the evidence does not support a 'strong' view of this effect. However, a 'weak' form is consistent with the research findings. In this, observers do not make either a dispositional or a situational attribution, but use both dispositional and situational factors when determining the cause of events around them. They may rely on one relatively more than the other depending on their particular perspective of events.

addiction refers to the dependence that a person may develop towards a substance or an activity. Addiction may be characterised by tolerance (in that moderate amounts of stimulation no longer have an effect) and withdrawal symptoms (unpleasant feelings when not taking the substance or engaging in the activity). The consequences of addiction may be physical or psychological, in that a person may also develop an emotional addiction to the substance or activity (see *psychological dependence*).

adolescence: the period between puberty and adulthood. The concept of adolescence as a separate stage of development may well be a Westernised idea, with the transition from childhood to adulthood being marked by abrupt 'rites of passage' in many other cultures. The period of adolescence is viewed differently by different theorists. To *Freud* it was a stage where the upsurge of instincts following puberty leads to an emotional imbalance, and a period where adolescents must begin a process of *disengagement* from the family before taking their place in the adult world. Writers who are influenced by this way of thinking about adolescence often speak of adolescence as a period of *storm and stress*. Erik *Erikson* (a *neo-Freudian*) believed that adolescence was the most influential period in the development of adult personality. Erikson suggested that adolescents went through a psychological *moratorium* in which they tried out a number of different identities before committing themselves to the one stable identity with which they would enter adulthood. Social-psychological explanations of adolescence play down the role of internal factors and stress adolescents' concern with the changing roles and expectations that dominate their lives. From this perspective, adolescence is seen as being dominated by stresses and tensions, not so much because of inner emotional instability (the *Freudian* view) but because of conflicting pressures from outside.

adoption studies are used to illustrate a genetic role in some aspect of behaviour. If adopted individuals are found to be more similar to their biological parents than to their adoptive parents, this suggests the primacy of genetics over environment in whatever behaviour is being investigated (nature over nurture). Adoption studies have been used to support the role of genetic factors in a variety of disorders, including **schizophrenia**, *depression* and alcoholism.

adrenal glands: see *endocrine system*

advanced organisers: a concept associated with David Ausubel in the 1960s. Ausubel believed that, because the mind arranges and stores information in an orderly fashion, advanced organisers would allow students to understand how new information fits into their existing knowledge base. Examples of advanced organisers include the use of spider diagrams and concept maps.

advertising is essentially an attempt to change consumer behaviour. Research has established that change is more likely when advertisements contain attractive images and have an element of expert authority. The field of advertising is littered with claims and counter-claims concerning the role of psychology, but two fairly reliable findings are:
- messages linked with good feelings are more likely to be effective (e.g. drink this and you too will be happy and relaxed)
- appeals to fear can be effective, but only if the recipient of the message is given the chance to avoid it. The anti-drink-driving messages every Christmas are a case in point.

The discovery of **subliminal perception** added a new dimension to the subtleties of advertising. Advertisers were able to present adverts on cinema screens for very brief exposures (only about 1/3000th of a second). At this exposure **duration**, the message (such as 'Drink Coca-Cola') was below the threshold for visual perception. Arguments about the effectiveness or otherwise of subliminal advertising are largely academic, as it is banned both in this country and the USA.

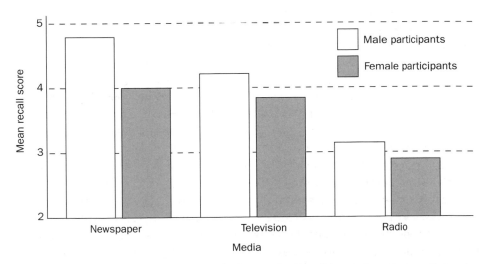

The effectiveness of political advertising in the media. Recall is greater when participants read the message than if they watch it on television, and is least when they listen to it on the radio (Gunter et al, 1986)

aetiology is a study of the causes of a particular behaviour or mental disorder.

affect is a generally loose term referring to our emotions or mood.

affectionless psychopathy is a clinical condition described by John **Bowlby** in which individuals display no guilt for their crimes, nor concern for their victims. In Bowlby's famous '44 Juvenile Thieves', a large proportion had been separated from their mother for more than six months before they were five years old. Of these, 14 had developed affectionless psychopathy, a result, Bowlby suggested, of the earlier separation.

affective disorder is another term for *mood disorder.*

affective filter: an emotional blockage to new learning. The affective filter is hypothesised to be a mental process whereby a learner's brain filters available input, letting in for processing only those items that were affectively (i.e. emotionally or attitudinally) acceptable to the learner. Certain emotions, such as anxiety, self-doubt, and mere boredom therefore interfere with the process of acquiring new information.

afferent neurons convey information from the senses (such as eyes or ears) to the *central nervous system (CNS)* for processing.

affiliation refers to the tendency for people to seek the company of others. It is also seen as a motivational variable, in that people differ in their need to affiliate. People may affiliate for a number of possible reasons:

- to avoid loneliness that may exist in the absence of a social network of friends and relatives
- to reduce anxiety, either because others provide a source of information that might reduce our anxiety, or because others provide emotional support
- to gain attention, where people seek the company of others so that they might be the centre of attention.

ageism is a form of *discrimination* where people are discriminated against purely because of their age. Although technically it could be applied to discrimination against any age group, it is more usually found in discrimination against the elderly. It can take many forms, ranging from legislative and social discrimination, to personal and relationship-oriented discrimination. It is also claimed that psychology itself discriminates against patterns of behaviour common in the later years, with many theories of human functioning appearing to see developmental change in old age as being somewhat dysfunctional. (See *social disengagement theory.*)

agency refers to the belief that human beings are free to make choices, show initiative and direct their own lives. Individuals may display this agency either socially or cognitively:

- social agency might be demonstrated if an individual participates actively and shows leadership in group activities, and is not passive or apprehensive in their interactions with others
- cognitive agency is characterised by a positive response to intellectual challenges and an originality in thought and action.

agentic state: the condition individuals are in when they see themselves as agents for carrying out another person's wishes. In Milgram's *obedience* studies, obedient participants were assumed to move from an *autonomous state*, where they made their own decisions about behaviour, to an agentic state where they simply obeyed the orders of the authority figure. The implication of this idea is that obedient individuals are not themselves evil but are products of situational forces that cause them to act in an evil way. This is the essence of the 'only obeying orders' defence heard from Nazi war criminals at the Nuremberg war trials following the Second World War.

aggression is any action or series of actions where the direct purpose is to cause injury or damage. Aggression is nearly always classed as an *anti-social behaviour*, being seen as a problem caused by biological deficiency, socialisation failure or the frustration caused by poor environmental conditions. There are instances where aggression has positive consequences, for example where it may be used to bring about positive social change or withstand oppressive forces in our life. The major explanations of aggressive behaviour are:

- biological – for example, aggression may be a product of over-crowding and the need to establish a territory (there is little evidence for this). Whereas non-human animals are more able to restrict their aggression to ritualistic displays, human beings appear less able to do the same. Recent research has established the possible role of the *neurotransmitter serotonin* in the aggressive behaviour of chimpanzees, with a suggestion that the same role may be observed in humans
- psychological theories such as the *frustration-aggression theory* see aggression as an inevitable consequence of a blocked, or frustrated goal. A typical example would be the driver who gets stuck in traffic and takes it out on other road users, the so-called 'road rage'
- social (or social-psychological) theories, such as the *social learning theory*, recognise the importance of *imitation* in the acquisition of aggressive behaviour. Children pick up their aggressive behaviour through watching the aggression of others who are then rewarded in some way (e.g. getting what they want) for their aggression.

All these different typologies of aggression have consequences for the reduction of aggressive behaviour. Biological and psychological theories, with their emphasis on biological inevitability or psychological abnormality, might marginalise aggressive behaviour and draw attention away from other factors in everyday life that might contribute to its development and reduction. Social-psychological theories, on the other hand, are far more optimistic about the *control* and reduction of aggressive behaviour. What has been learned, after all, can always be changed.

agoraphobia is a type of *anxiety disorder* that makes people fearful of public places. Agoraphobia is often accompanied by a panic attack when the sufferer enters crowded streets, shopping centres, public transport and so on. As a result, severe agoraphobics become virtual prisoners in their own homes. Many sufferers of agoraphobia are less concerned that the symptoms (such as dizziness or nausea) of the disorder might occur, but rather that they might be overwhelmed by the anxiety that these symptoms produce. The commonest treatments for agoraphobia involve one of the exposure therapies. In some cases, therapists offer support, reasoning or persuasion to encourage agoraphobics to venture further and further from home. Other therapists use *reinforcement* techniques (such as praising the client for spending increasingly longer periods of time in the feared situation). Up to 80 per cent of sufferers who receive exposure treatment tend to improve, although these improvements are often only partial and relapses often occur.

AIDS (acquired immune deficiency syndrome) is caused by a virus known as the 'human immunodeficiency virus' (HIV). The virus attacks the helper T-cells of the *immune system*. These cells identify infections and stimulate the production of other cells that fight them.

The virus invades and kills these cells and thus eventually disables the entire immune system. The AIDS patient is then open to attack from any infections. In other words, HIV is never the cause of death; it weakens the immune response and therefore allows other infections to do their harm.

HIV is associated primarily with the high-risk sexual and drug-taking behaviours of homosexual/bisexual males and intravenous drug-users. It is important to remember, however, that it is specific behaviours that put these people at risk rather than some underlying characteristic of the groups themselves. High-risk behaviours include any unprotected sexual behaviour (such as anal and oral intercourse) that directly exposes a sexual partner to the body fluids (blood, semen, etc.) of an HIV-infected individual. HIV is also passed on as a result of needle-sharing in intravenous drug users. The high incidence of AIDS among intravenous drug-users is thought to account for the growing number of people with AIDS in the prison system.

The AIDS epidemic has had a profound impact on the gay community. Gay men without AIDS may develop acute psychological reactions that include panic attacks and generalised anxiety. People with AIDS must also endure the stigma of the disease as well as the physical suffering. As the perceived threat of AIDS increases, people become keener to impose social restrictions. AIDS patients may face the loss of employment and housing because of the stigma attached to the disease. This was powerfully illustrated in the film *Philadelphia* starring Tom Hanks. The fear of contracting AIDS from infected persons had led to a great deal of public hysteria, but research consistently reassures us that the risk of contracting AIDS from casual contact is 'minimal to non-existent'.

aims: broad general statements of what a researcher wants to find out in a study, for example, whether exercise can decrease feelings of depression.

alarm call: a vocalisation used by animals to alert other group members to the presence of a predator. Animals that produce these may draw attention to themselves and so put themselves in danger. However, this behaviour may be beneficial in that it may distract the predator or cause it to abandon its attack. Alternatively, the calling animal may be taken by the predator but, through its self-sacrifice, may help to save the lives of genetically related animals around it (*kin selection*).

alarm reaction: see *general adaptation syndrome*

algorithm: a problem-solving procedure requiring repetition in order to eliminate possible answers until only the correct one remains. An algorithm will always come up with the solution to a task if one exists. Because algorithmic reasoning can be long-winded, we often rely on mental short-cuts and 'rules of thumb' to reach the answer to problems in a more time-efficient way.

alienation: in its common usage it refers to a feeling of separation from others. In its existentialist usage, the term refers to a separation of a person from their real self, which may come about because of their preoccupation with doing the right thing and conforming to the wishes of others.

allele: the two forms of a *gene* that are located at the same point on an autosome (non sex-linked chromosomes). If the alleles (for example, for eye colour) are the same, the individual is described as homozygous, and will display the trait. If the alleles are different, the individual is described as heterozygous, and the relationship between the alleles (i.e. the one which is dominant) will determine which trait is displayed.

alpha bias is the traditional view of gender differences that sees real and enduring differences between men and women. Some alpha bias theories are used to heighten the value of women (e.g. Nancy Chodorow's conception of women as more relational and caring) and some are used to devalue women such as *Freud's* theory of psychosexual development (see also *beta bias*).

alpha male: observers of monkeys and other apes have used this term to describe the dominant male in a social hierarchy. The alpha male is not necessarily the most aggressive or the most sexually active, although he does appear to assume responsibilities to monitor and *control* fighting within the group, as well as protecting the group from outside threats.

alpha rhythm: the brainwave pattern of a person who is in a relaxed and wakeful state.

altered states of awareness: a reference to the belief that there are different states or levels of awareness (or consciousness). The state under which a person is operating can be changed artificially (e.g. through *hypnosis*), or naturally, through sleep. It is believed that a person's state of awareness has an effect on their psychological functioning, for example, their motivational state.

alternative hypothesis: see *hypothesis*.

altricial species: animal species that are relatively helpless at birth and therefore need substantial parental care and protection if they are to survive. Although normally contrasted with *precocial species*, the terms refer more to points on a continuum rather than distinct classifications. Thus, some animals require more parental care than others, although both may be described as altricial. For example, birds that nest in trees are usually altricial, whereas many ground-nesting birds, such as ducks and geese, are precocial. The former must stay in their nests until fully fledged and rely on their parents for food and survival. The latter follow their mother shortly after hatching and feed themselves, although they still need parental care until they are fledged.

altruism (biological): literally, any act of one organism which increases the chances of survival of another organism whilst decreasing its own. Mothers who place themselves between their young and a predator, and vampire bats who share their food with a hungry non-relative, are both examples of what appears to be altruistic behaviour. The fact that some animals would engage in self-sacrificing or self-endangering behaviours posed an apparent threat to Darwin's theory of evolution by *natural selection*. This theory proposed that only behaviours that caused their bearers to have more offspring would be favoured by the process of natural selection. Altruistic behaviour would not appear to do this, and therefore surely would not be favoured by natural selection. The two major explanations of altruistic behaviour that still allow it to fit within the broad framework of natural selection are:

- *kin selection* – animals may leave behind more copies of their *genes* by helping close genetic relatives. According to this explanation, self-sacrifice may profit an animal if by so doing it can preserve a greater number of its genes in the next generation
- reciprocal altruism – an animal may exhibit self-sacrificing behaviour in the expectation that this 'favour' will be returned in the future. As the altruist benefits in the long term, there is no real disadvantage to them.

Altruism (biological)

Fitness change to recipient

Fitness change to donor animal		Gain	Loss
	Gain	Cooperative	Selfish
	Loss	Altruistic	Spiteful

Different types of behavioural interaction in animals (after Hamilton, 1964)

altruism (human): a type of *pro-social behaviour* in which a person will voluntarily help another at some cost to themselves. The primary motivation for altruistic behaviour is seen as a desire to improve the welfare of another person rather than the anticipation of some reward (compare this with the previous section on *altruism (biological)* or for any other reason that might be seen as self-interest. Explanations for human altruism are as follows:

- we may be motivated to help others because of our *empathy* for them. We thus help others because we share their emotional pain (the *empathy-altruism hypothesis*)
- we help others because it overcomes the negative state we are in. Seeing others in distress or in need makes us upset, and we want to rid ourselves of this negative state. By helping the person concerned we can escape from our own negative state (the negative-state relief model)
- *sociobiological* theories stress that although helping behaviour may not *appear* to be in the altruist's self-interest, it often can be. Altruistic behaviour is seen as a strategy that has evolved through the process of *natural selection.* By behaving altruistically toward close genetic relatives (such as children), we help in the survival of our own genes (*kin selection*). By helping someone today (e.g. letting another car in front of us in a queue) we anticipate a return of the favour at a later date (*reciprocal altruism*)
- cultural theories stress the development of norms of altruism such as the social-responsibility norm (help those who need it) and the reciprocity norm (help those who have helped you). Such theories argue that cultural evolution is a far greater influence in human altruism than the biological evolution suggested by sociobiology.

Alzheimer's disease: a form of *dementia* which is characterised by a gradual loss of memory, a decline in intellectual ability and a deterioration in personality and social behaviour. The disorder starts with the destruction of brain tissue in the limbic system and *cortex* which leads to *anterograde amnesia*. In this state, Alzheimer's sufferers may forget what they are doing half way through an activity and find it difficult to suppress other thoughts and plans that are irrelevant to the task they are trying to complete. As the disease progresses, degeneration of the brain tissue spreads and a general deterioration of cognitive skills sets in. Typically, patients seem unable to carry out even the simplest and most familiar of tasks, such as dressing themselves or making a cup of tea. In the final stages of the disease they may be unable to recognise family members, a characteristic that sets Alzheimer's disease apart from other forms of dementia, where it is mainly the learning of new information rather than the recall of past memories that is disrupted. There is often a regression to an earlier age (usually mid-adulthood) as if memories after this have been wiped out. This may be why sufferers don't recognise close family members, such as their spouse, because they expect to see the person as they were many years ago. Alzheimer's disease is linked particularly to the degeneration of **acetylcholine neurons** in the brain. In post-mortems of the brains of Alzheimer's sufferers, up to three-quarters of acetylcholine pathways are found to be destroyed.

ambiguous figures: any figure that is open to different perceptual interpretations. Examples include the **Rubin's vase** illusion and the **Necker cube**.

American Sign Language: a system of gestures and finger spelling used by hearing-impaired people in the USA; it is also known as Ameslan. Most students come across the use of this system in early studies of chimpanzee 'language' where these animals were taught to communicate with their trainers using Ameslan.

amnesia: a loss of memory due either to brain damage or psychological **trauma**. The two major types are **anterograde amnesia** (the inability to remember new information) and **retrograde amnesia** (the loss of memories from the period leading up to the amnesic episode).

amnesic syndrome refers to a severe impairment of memory, which is a product of organic damage caused by chronic alcohol abuse (**Korsakoff's syndrome**) or as a result of brain infection or stroke. It is characterised by a marked impairment in episodic memory, although other types of memory such as working memory, semantic memory and procedural memory may remain relatively intact.

anaclitic depression: the deep and often progressive depression experienced by infants who are separated from or have lost their mother and do not have a suitable substitute to take her place.

anaclitic identification: a tendency for the child to **identify** with the primary love object such as a parent who is supportive and caring.

anal personality: a **psychoanalytic** term which refers to an adult who has been **fixated** during the anal stage of psychosexual development. This fixation can develop either through excessive gratification of the **id** impulses (through very lax attitudes to toilet training, for example) or inadequate gratification (e.g. through very strict attitudes to toilet training) during early childhood. The anal retentive personality (developed as a result of strict attitudes to toilet training) is described as being obsessively clean and perhaps stingy with money, and the anal expulsive personality (developed as a result of lax attitudes to toilet training) poorly organised and perhaps aggressive.

analysand: a term given to somebody who is undergoing **psychoanalysis**. The term was originally coined because trainee psychoanalysts who were undergoing analysis as part of their training objected to being called 'patients'.

analysis of variance (ANOVA): see **covariation principle**

analyst: a general term, which most typically refers to a practising **psychoanalyst**.

androcentric theories: any theory that offers an interpretation of the lives of women based on the study of men. As a result of this, ideas of 'normality' may be drawn exclusively from studies of the development of males, and so many aspects of female development may be seen as 'abnormal' or 'deficient'.

androgen: a naturally occurring hormone, such as **testosterone**, produced in the testes. Androgens control the development and maintenance of masculine characteristics.

androgyny: a type of **gender-role** identity where the person scores highly on both masculine and feminine personality characteristics. Research has shown that androgynous children may possess a higher sense of **self-esteem**, and are generally more adaptable in their behaviour. They can show masculine independence or feminine sensitivity as the situation demands. It also appears to be the case that it is the masculine component of androgyny that is most related to psychological well-being, with androgynous females in particular enjoying superior psychological health compared to those with more traditional identities. Females without androgynous characteristics may experience adjustment difficulties because their **traits** appear not to be as highly valued by society. As society increasingly values what are traditionally labelled as feminine characteristics, the androgynous personality may well become the norm for both sexes.

anger management: a set of strategies intended to control constructively the emotional feelings and expression of anger. Individuals with a 'bad temper' or with a tendency to let anger overpower them can benefit from the strategies of anger management. In anger management, such people are encouraged to learn how to control their anger and channel it properly. Strategies include simple relaxation methods, communicating more effectively (e.g. by slowing down and thinking before speaking), or even using the defusing affects of humour. Because **stress** is a causal factor in excessive anger, management techniques may also include strategies for reducing stress, including stress-relieving techniques such as yoga or meditation.

animal intelligence is a notoriously difficult concept. It may be seen as a hierarchy of learning processes, with **habituation**, the most basic form of learning, being shared by all species. As we move 'up' the phylogenetic hierarchy, animals acquire the ability to learn by association (**classical** and **operant conditioning**), complex learning abilities such as problem-solving and learning sets, and finally, the acquisition of language (considered unique to humans).

However, this view of intelligence is criticised by many comparative psychologists as being unacceptably narrow. If intelligence is seen as the ability to solve problems that have ecological relevance in the animal's own environment, then all species must be seen as equally intelligent in their own ways. There has been considerable comparative interest in species differences in **self-recognition** and **theory of mind**, although the relevance of such cognitive abilities to animals is still uncertain.

Intelligence may be simply a product of brain size, which present humans and the cetaceans (whales, dolphins and porpoises) as among the most intelligent species. Relative brain size (i.e. brain size relative to body size) is considered to be a better indicator of animal intelligence, although such a view also has problems (see **brain size and intelligence**).

Intelligence may also be seen as a product of how animals solve social problems as well as physical problems, a form of intelligence that social psychologists call **social cognition**. Primates that form large and stable social groups are assumed to have the most highly developed social cognition of all animals. Repeated interactions over a prolonged period allow these animals to learn each other's identities and to build up altruistic or antagonistic relationships. According to evolutionary psychologists, reasoning ability evolved largely out of the need to detect cheaters in social relationships (i.e. animals which take the benefits of social relationships must also pay a cost), a cognitive adaptation for *social exchange*.

animal language has two major meanings. It refers to attempts to teach human language to non-human animals, and also to the study of 'natural' animal language in the wild. Until the 1970s, it was generally accepted that *language* was solely the province of human beings. Early attempts to teach *American Sign Language* (ASL) to chimpanzees did have limited success, but were criticised as demonstrating little more than the chimps' skills at imitating the signs made by their trainers.

The most famous of these studies involved a female chimp, Washoe, who was able to sign simple sentences, respond to questions and even use signs in a supposedly novel way. Analysis of film footage of Washoe and her trainers showed that they would often provide unintentional cues that helped Washoe respond with the correct sign. Other studies were criticised because the chimps showed little evidence of basic language skills such as syntax (the rules of word order) or generativity (combination of words into novel sentences). Recent research using a bonobo (pygmy chimpanzee) called Kanzi has overcome most of the methodological criticisms of the earlier studies and has provided astonishing evidence of complex language skills in a non-human animal. As well as being able to communicate through a symbol board connected to a voice synthesiser, Kanzi can also understand several hundred words in spoken English. Marine mammals may also be able to learn a form of human language. Research with a female dolphin called Akeakamai has shown that she can respond accurately to an artificial language where hand gestures stand for the words. Each gesture stands either for an object (a ball or hoop, for example), an action (fetch, throw, etc.) or a position (left, right, etc.). Not only does Akeakamai appear to understand the importance of word order and syntax, but can also respond appropriately when familiar 'words' are rearranged into novel sentences of up to five gestures.

Other studies have attempted to see if animals in the wild can communicate with each other in a language-like manner. A number of different species have been reported to give different alarm calls according to the type of predator (eagles, leopards, pythons, for example). The 'words' used by adult vervet monkeys pass on information that enables other vervets to respond in the most appropriate manner for that particular predator. Evidence suggests that perhaps language is not a uniquely human skill, but rather a continuum of skills that different species exhibit, or can be taught to exhibit, in varying degrees.

animal navigation and migration: see *homing*

animal research: the use of non-human animals in psychological research. Animals are used for a variety of different reasons, both in the study of animals themselves (*ethology*) and in the pursuit of knowledge that would be beneficial to humans. It is this latter area that has attracted the greatest controversy. Animals are used for a variety of reasons:
- they offer the opportunity for greater experimental *control* and objectivity
- animals have been used in situations where it would be impossible to use humans
- animals and humans have sufficient of their physiology and evolutionary history in common to justify conclusions drawn from the one to the other (i.e. some primates share over 95 per cent of their genetic makeup with humans).

Supporters and opponents of animal research disagree over some of the fundamental issues underlying the relevance and morality of this avenue of research interest. The basic argument that animals and humans differ extensively in their brain physiology does not really stand up to critical scrutiny, with all mammals sharing the same kind of brain structure and mechanisms of **neuronal transmission**. Similarly, the basic classification of behaviour (as affective, cognitive and motivational) is present even in the humble laboratory rat.

The area that provokes the most passionate debate is in the ethics of animal research. The term **speciesism** has been coined to describe the way in which we ignore the rights of animals in research projects. Some opponents of animal research have taken an absolute moral stance on this issue and claim that the use of animals for our ends could never be justified on moral grounds. Others have taken a more relative view of the debate, and argue that good-quality research that involves minimal stress for the animal and has clear medical benefits should be allowed. The Animals (Scientific Procedures) Act of 1986 sets clear guidelines for the use of animals in research in the UK, although recent surveys have established that this type of research is very much on the decline in this country. Although most interest appears to centre around the use of animals in laboratory research, it should also be remembered that animals are frequently studied in their own natural habitat. Such studies place special responsibilities on the researcher to minimise the impact of the research on the natural ecology of the animals being studied.

animism: the belief that inanimate objects are alive and as such have life-like qualities such as feelings and intentions. A child may get angry and smack his bicycle because it 'made him get hurt'. Animism is a characteristic found in children in **Piaget's** second stage of intellectual development, the pre-operational stage. Piaget believed that animism was a characteristic of the child's **egocentric** reasoning – if the child has feelings and intentions, then so must all other things.

anomalous experience: an event that cannot easily be explained using conventional laws of science, therefore is explained as being caused by **paranormal** influences such as **extrasensory perception (ESP)** or an **out-of-body experience (OBE)**.

anorexia nervosa refers to a type of **eating disorder** in which the person fears that they might become obese and therefore engages in self-starvation. As a result of this disorder, the sufferer finds it difficult to maintain a minimal body weight and may feel fat even when emaciated. The **DSM-IV-TR** classification for this disorder lists the following as symptoms of anorexia:

- refusal to maintain body weight at or above minimal normal weight for age and height, or failure to make expected weight gain during period of growth leading to body weight of less than 85 per cent of that expected
- intense fear of becoming fat, even though underweight
- disturbance in the way that one's body weight or shape is experienced; undue influence of body weight or shape on self-evaluation; denial of seriousness of current low body weight
- in post-menarcheal girls (those who have begun to menstruate) the absence of three consecutive menstrual cycles.

Anorexics appear preoccupied with becoming thin and tend to set weight limits for themselves that are well below the acceptable weight for their age and height. Despite this drive for thinness, anorexics may be preoccupied with food, possibly a result of their food deprivation. Anorexics exhibit various kinds of cognitive dysfunctions such as a distorted body image or a need to be perfect in every way. Other features of this disorder include personality and mood problems and medical problems that develop as a result of the starvation diet imposed by the sufferer.

anoxia means deprivation of oxygen. Anoxia due to birth complications can cause brain damage in the baby.

ANS: see *autonomic nervous system.*

antabuse is a drug that is relatively harmless when taken on its own, but produces nausea and sickness when taken with alcohol. It is commonly used as part of a programme with people who are trying to give up alcohol.

antagonistic: in its general use, anything that acts in opposition to something else.

antecedent variables: something in an experiment that happens before some other event, and might possibly explain it. These can be planned or unplanned. An *independent variable* can act as an antecedent variable for some behaviour change in an experiment, as can other factors such as how rude or friendly the experimenter is when they introduce the *participant* to the experimental procedure.

anterograde amnesia refers to a person's inability to remember new information, perhaps as a result of some shock or trauma, or brain damage.

anthropomorphism: attributing human feelings and emotions to non-human animals. We frequently do this when we say that a cat is 'enjoying itself' or that our dog is 'happy' to see us. It is a tendency that those who work with or observe animals try to avoid.

anti-bullying strategies: effective strategies for dealing with bullying involve both preventing bullying incidents and responding to them. Strategies include developing *empathy* and an appreciation for diversity within a school or other collective institution as well as considering the types of sanction or support available to the bully.

anti-depressants: a type drug that elevates the mood of people suffering from *depression*. The major types of anti-depressant drugs are the tricyclics, MAO (monoamine-oxidase) inhibitors and the selective *serotonin* re-uptake inhibitors (SSRIs). During the process of *neuronal transmission*, transmitter substances such as nor-epinephrine and serotonin are released by one neuron and then activate the next neuron. These transmitter substances may then be re-absorbed by the releasing neuron or deactivated by an enzyme such as monoamine oxidase. Tricyclic drugs interfere with the reabsorption of transmitter substances and MAO inhibitors, as the name suggests, prevent enzymes from deactivating them. As a result, transmitter substances remain active for longer, and the person experiences an elevation of mood. Tricyclic drugs are prescribed more often than the MAO inhibitors nowadays because of the dangerous side-effects that may occur with the latter (for example, they may cause a dangerous rise in blood pressure, and if combined with other drugs, could be fatal). Second generation anti-depressants include SSRIs such as Prozac (fluoxetine).

anti-psychiatry: a radical *therapy* movement that was a spin-off from *existential therapies* and was popularised by R D Laing and David Cooper. This movement was opposed to traditional psychiatric conceptions of *mental illness*. The movement was quite broad in its beliefs and alternative practices, but had four central beliefs to which most anti-psychiatrists subscribed:

- in the absence of oppression, human beings would live in harmony with each other
- everything that was diagnosed psychiatrically, unless clearly organic in origin, was a form of alienation
- this alienation is seen as a consequence of oppression. Those who are diagnosed as mentally ill are prevented from understanding the origins of the oppression. They come to believe that the alienation they experience is their own fault
- psychiatry is all about deceiving people about their oppression.

Although some of the ideas of anti-psychiatry have been incorporated into modern therapeutic practices, the movement is largely of historical interest today.

anti-psychotic drugs: drugs that are effective in treating the most disturbing forms of psychotic illness, such as schizophrenia and manic depression (*bipolar disorder*). Anti-psychotic medication helps individuals function as well as possible in their lives, as well as increasing their feelings of subjective well-being. Conventional anti-psychotics are used primarily to combat the positive symptoms of *schizophrenia* – such as *hallucinations* and thought disturbances. Atypical anti-psychotic drugs also combat these *positive symptoms* of schizophrenia, but there are claims that they have some beneficial effects on *negative symptoms* as well.

anti-Semitism: discrimination against Jews. Many famous psychologists such as Sigmund *Freud* had been victims of anti-Semitism in their original countries.

anti-social behaviour refers to any behaviour that is considered harmful or disruptive within a group or society. The label 'anti-social' is in itself a subjective term, but there is general agreement that aspects of behaviour such as *aggression* or *discrimination* would fall into this category.

anti-social personality: a personality disorder that is characterised by a lack of regard for the rights and feelings for others, an absence of shame following violation of moral codes and an inability to form emotional relationships or take responsibility for actions. Explanations of the anti-social personality (also sometimes referred to as the psychopathic personality) vary according to the psychological perspective adopted. *Psychodynamic* theorists tend to explain it through an absence of parental love during infancy. As a result of this, children fail to form a basic trust with others. They respond to such inadequacies by becoming emotionally detached, and thus show less awareness of others, which in turn leads to a poorly developed *superego*. *Behaviourists* suggest that this disorder may be acquired through the process of *modelling* and point to the fact that many parents of people with the anti-social personality also have the disorder. More recently research has suggested a biological link with the evidence that the *autonomic* and *central nervous systems (CNS)* of people with this disorder appear to act more slowly that normal. Their anti-social acts may then be interpreted as a continual search for excitement in an attempt to increase the activity of their nervous systems. A variety of different treatments is used for this disorder, but only a minority volunteer for or complete treatment programmes. *Cognitive-behavioural therapy* (where clients are guided toward thinking at a more abstract and higher level of moral functioning) and wilderness programmes (to develop individual and group commitment in a challenging environment) are two examples of treatments used.

anxiety: feelings of fear and apprehension which are accompanied by increased and prolonged physiological *arousal*. These may be normal and transitory, or abnormal and long lasting. As such, the symptoms of anxiety may be present in many of the psychological disorders. Anxiety may be measured in a number of different ways, by self-report, by measuring arousal using the *galvanic skin response (GSR)*, or by the observation of overt behaviour (such as agitated movements, rapid speech or sweating, for example).

anxiety disorder: a classification of disorders that are characterised by severe anxiety. The most common of adult mental disorders, examples are *phobic disorders (phobias), post-traumatic stress disorder* and *obsessive-compulsive disorder*.

anxiety-neurosis is a term for what are now referred to as *panic disorders* or generalised anxiety disorders.

APA: the American Psychological Association

aphagia: a condition thought to be caused by a *lesion* in the lateral *hypothalamus*, and which causes the organism to stop eating.

aphasia refers to impairment of spoken language as a result of brain injury. There are many different types of aphasia.

aphonia: an inability to produce speech sounds. The term is used when the reasons are other than brain damage and may be due, at least in part to psychological *trauma.*

apnoea: obstructive sleep apnoea (OSA) is a condition where muscles in the throat relax and cause a total blockage of the airway. The term 'obstructive' is used to distinguish OSA from less common forms of apnoea, such as central sleep apnoea, which is caused by the brain 'forgetting' to breathe during sleep. The lack of oxygen in OSA causes a person to come out of deep sleep into a brief period of wakefulness, in order to restore normal breathing. However, once back in deep sleep, further episodes of apnoea can occur. These repeated interruptions to sleep can lead to the person feeling very tired during the day.

approach-approach conflict refers to the conflict experienced when an organism is faced by two equally attractive but incompatible (i.e. they can't do both) choices. As the organism moves closer to one of the two, its attractiveness increases and the conflict is resolved.

approach-avoidance conflict refers to the conflict shown by an organism when a specific behaviour is associated with both pleasant and unpleasant consequences. If a rat is trained to run through a maze for food and is then subsequently given an electric shock for reaching the same goal, it will show conflict behaviour, perhaps by getting half way around the maze, stopping, going back, stopping and going forward again. Animals who experience approach-avoidance conflict also engage in *displacement* behaviour where appropriate activities appear at inappropriate times. For example, during courtship, the male bird is both attracted to the female and also fears her (she may attack him). He may then displace his conflict into the displacement activity of courtship preening, an activity that over time becomes established as part of the courtship ritual in that species.

ARAS: ascending reticular activating system. See *reticular formation*.

aromatherapy is the study of scents used in a therapeutic manner. It involves the skilled and controlled use of essential oils (liquids that are distilled from plants, shrubs, flowers, trees, bushes and seeds) for emotional and physical health and well-being. The practice of aromatherapy goes beyond smell, though. It involves 'pure' essential oils and treatments that many believe have a chemical effect on the body. They can be applied with massage, in the bath, in the air, and in hair-care. As a holistic medicine, aromatherapy is claimed to be both a preventative approach as well as an active treatment during acute and chronic stages of illness or disease. The history of aromatherapy goes back thousands of years. Aromatic plants and essential oils were used in biblical times. Ancient Greeks and Romans used the oils in their medical treatments and the Egyptians used aromatic plant essences to treat both physical and mental health problems. A French chemist, Rene-Maurice Gattefossè first coined the term 'aromathèrapie' in the 1920s. He was convinced that the oils had antiseptic properties – more powerful than the antiseptics that were used at that time, and also suspected that they had other important healing abilities.

The actual mode of action of essential oils is still far from known, although there is strong evidence that they can have a pharmacological effect on various tissues. Studies have shown that essential oils have an effect on brainwaves and can also alter behaviour. It is possible that most of the effect of the oils is transmitted through the brain via the olfactory system. Used professionally and safely, aromatherapy has been shown to have beneficial effects on a range of psychological states and behaviours, including EEG activity, alertness, and mood.

arousal refers to a state of readiness in which an organism is prepared for '*fight or flight*'. This involves changes at sensory, hormonal, glandular and muscular levels. A person's state of arousal varies from being alert to being in a state of deep sleep. The ascending reticular activating system (ARAS) (see *reticular formation*) is able to detect the arrival of an external stimulus. If it is of potential significance to the organism it activates the whole brain. Stimulation of the ARAS will cause a sleeping animal to wake and will increase alertness in an animal that is already awake. The arousal levels of an organism are also affected by the daily cycle (*circadian rhythms*) and in humans, by the use of stimulant drugs (such as caffeine) and *depressant* drugs (such as alcohol). Although most smokers believe that smoking calms them, nicotine in cigarettes actually has an arousing effect. This is one of the reasons why so many people smoke in pubs. The stimulating effects of nicotine counteract the depressant effects of the alcohol, and thus enable them to remain good humoured and sociable.

artificial intelligence (AI): a combination of expertise from *cognitive psychology* and computer science which focuses on the development of computer programs that are able to perform complex tasks. The essence of this approach is that operating systems are then described as possessing human-like reasoning ability or *intelligence*. The degree to which AI programs accurately mimic human cognitive functioning is open to question. Human cognition involves an interaction between the cognitive system and the biological system. Much of the former is a response to the demands of the latter. Computers, on the other hand, operate purely within a cognitive domain. Human cognitive processing is affected by all manner of different motivational and emotional factors whereas computer programs are 'single-minded' in the way they tackle problems.

Asch effect: see *conformity (majority influence)*.

assimilation: a term used by Jean **Piaget** in his theory of intellectual development, it refers to the child's interpretation of the world around him in terms of existing **schema**. For example, a young child who calls all men 'daddy' is demonstrating a belief that all men are daddies. His interpretation of the social world of grown-ups is based on that premise. Together with the process of **accommodation,** assimilation allows the child the means to adapt to the world around him.

associative play: a classification of social play where a child plays alongside another child and may offer 'advice' or 'criticism' on the other child's play. The important distinction between this type of play and truly co-operative play is that in the former children are interested in each other's play but are not yet co-operating to achieve a common goal in their play.

assortative mating refers to the tendency for animals (including human beings) to seek out and mate with other animals that are similar, although not identical, to themselves. This is seen as a biological tendency to maximise the benefits of inbreeding (maintaining existing genetic stock) with outbreeding (introducing genetic variety). It is in the interests of animals to avoid excessive inbreeding (as it increases the risk of disorders caused by **recessive genes**) as well as excessive outbreeding (the genetic lottery). Assortative mating is a suitable compromise, and retains some of the advantages of each.

asymmetrical order effects: a type of **order effect** in an **experiment** where the effect is greater in one direction than it is in the other. For example, if the difference in performance between **participants** carrying out a task under condition A followed by condition B is greater than the difference between the order B followed by A, then the order effect is described as asymmetrical. In such cases it is normally appropriate to use different participants for the two conditions.

Atkinson and Shiffrin's model of memory: also known by various other names such as the multi-store model of **memory**, this proposes the existence of three separate but sequentially linked memory systems, the sensory memory, **short-term memory** and the **long-term memory.** The sensory memory contains a fleeting impression of a sensory stimulus (a sight or a sound); the short-term memory a limited recollection of recently perceived stimuli (a telephone number or an order of drinks); and the long-term memory a more or less permanent store of memories for later retrieval (e.g. our telephone number). Each of these memory systems is seen as differing in the way they process information, how much information they can hold and for how long they can hold that information.

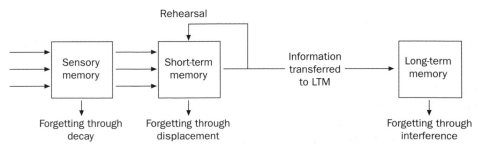

The multi-store model of memory (adapted from Atkinson and Shiffrin, 1971)

attachment is a close emotional bond between two people characterised by mutual involvement and affection, and a desire to maintain proximity. The term is more usually used to refer to the bond that forms between a caregiver (normally the mother) and the infant. Early explanations of attachment saw the mother as a *secondary reinforcer* with food as the *primary reinforcer*. Later explanations stressed the importance of physical contact in the development of the attachment bond. John *Bowlby* argued that the formation of this bond is pre-programmed into the infant. Taking his inspiration from insights derived from *imprinting* research, Bowlby believed that babies that stayed close to their mother would be more likely to survive in a harsh and unfriendly environment. Mary Ainsworth's work using the *strange situation test* has identified a number of different attachment types.

attention: a term used in *cognitive psychology* to refer to the tendency of an organism to focus on selected features of the environment. Attention can be usefully classified as either focused or divided.

Using focused attention, the organism selects (or focuses) on only one input from the environment. More experimental work has been carried out on focused auditory attention (attending to auditory messages) than on focused visual attention (attending to visual material). Early filter theories of focused auditory attention proposed that only one input was selected for processing, with non-selected inputs awaiting their turn in a sensory buffer. Later theories suggested that all inputs were processed but that those not originally selected by an attentional filter were processed in an attenuated (weakened) form. Explanations of focused visual attention have likened attention to a spotlight beam. Material presented within this beam is subjected to detailed processing, whereas outside this beam there is little or no processing of the visual stimulus. Depending on the nature of the task, this 'beam' of attention can be either very narrow or very broad. Feature integration theories suggest that objects outside the attentional beam might be processed in a limited way. Processing would be limited to their physical characteristics, but not their meaning. The combination of these features to form objects requires focused attention.

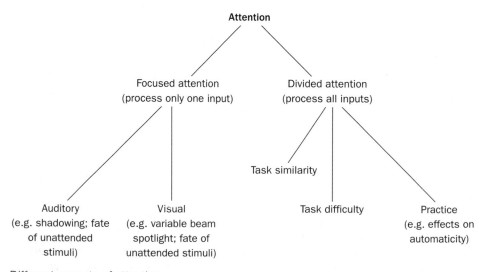

Different aspects of attention

Divided attention is what happens when we try to do more than one thing at once. We are all familiar with the trials and tribulations of splitting our attention between two or more tasks, for example driving a car and holding a conversation at the same time. Experienced drivers have no difficulty in driving and talking at the same time, whereas people learning to drive find this combination of activities far more tricky. The effectiveness of divided attention is determined by:

* task similarity – if tasks are dissimilar (as in the example above), there is a greater chance that they can be performed well together. If both tasks make use of the same sensory modalities (i.e. both are visual or both auditory tasks) then this puts limitations on the processing *capacity* of the organism
* task difficulty – as might be expected, the difficulty of tasks is crucial in the ability to perform both successfully. This is particularly problematic when one task requires an increase in resource allocation. Consider the driving and talking example given earlier. Under normal driving conditions both tasks can be performed adequately. If the driving conditions become more demanding (overtaking, negotiating a roundabout, etc.), then intelligent conversation becomes more difficult
* practice – as we become more practised at tasks, we are better able to perform them both together. This may be due to a number of reasons. We may develop better strategies for performing the tasks without one interfering with the other (for example, talking only when driving in a straight line). The demands made on our attentional resources may be reduced as tasks become more practised. As processing becomes more automatic, fewer specific processing resources are needed (compare the intense concentration of the learner driver with the far more relaxed attitude of the experienced driver).

attention-deficit hyperactivity disorder (ADHD): a childhood disorder characterised either by an inability to concentrate on tasks, or hyperactive and impulsive behaviour, or both of these together. Approximately 3–5 per cent of children are thought to have ADHD, although there is a tendency for normally hyperactive or distractible children to be wrongly diagnosed as having the disorder. A child who has ADHD may also experience learning or communication difficulties at school. This isn't surprising given the inattentiveness and possibly disruptive behaviour of ADHD children, but it is important to stress that ADHD and learning disabilities are separate disorders. The causes of ADHD are not clear. Some theorists suggest the possibility of neurological dysfunctions as the main cause, whereas others point to family stress as the main reason for its development. Given the uncertainty about its origins, most researchers are now of the opinion that it has multiple and interactive causes. There is similar disagreement about the best treatment for the disorder. Stimulant drugs such as *ritalin* have the effect of increasing attentiveness and decreasing activity in ADHD children. Behavioural treatments may involve parents rewarding attentiveness and good behaviour, whereas cognitive therapies may emphasise self-instruction and heightened self-awareness.

attenuator model of attention was able to offer an explanation for the finding that we are frequently able to perceive some information even when we do not appear to be paying attention to it. This model, proposed by Anne Triesman, states that unattended messages are processed more thoroughly than was previously thought. At the first stage, in which stimuli are selected for further processing, the rejected message is not lost but is weakened (attenuated). The rejected message does receive some processing, but may not reach consciousness. Very important information (such as your name) has a low threshold for selection and will trigger a switch of processing if it is heard. Because of the value of this type of selective processing in social gatherings, it was known as the '*cocktail party effect*'

attitude: a hypothetical construct (i.e. something that cannot be measured directly, and whose existence must be inferred) which refers to a state of readiness, based on past experiences, which guides, biases or otherwise influences our behaviour. Attitudes may also be seen as having three components: the cognitive – what we believe about an object; the affective – our feelings toward an object; and the behavioural – how we might actually behave toward an object. With less firmly entrenched attitudes we may rely more on the affective component, and summarise our attitude simply in terms of whether we like or dislike something. Attitudes serve a number of motivational functions:

- ego-defensive functions – attitudes protect us from experiencing negative feelings about ourselves as we *project* negative feelings onto others (see *prejudice*)
- value-expressive functions – attitudes are the ways in which we express those things that are important to us
- instrumental functions – attitudes may be adopted and expressed because they enable us to gain social acceptance or avoid social disapproval
- knowledge functions – attitudes help us to organise our social world along evaluative dimensions (e.g. things I like and things I don't like) and allow us to make predictions about events in it.

attraction: see *interpersonal attraction*

attractiveness of defendant: research suggests that juries trying criminal cases are likely to be more lenient when the defendant is physically attractive.

attribution: the way in which we assess the causes of a behaviour or personal characteristics of a person from the way they behave. The term is more commonly used nowadays in the former sense. In this usage, a person (the observer) sees the behaviour of another (the actor) and draws an *inference* as to what they feel has caused the behaviour in question. The choice for the observer is between an attribution based on *dispositional* factors (such as ability or effort) or *situational* factors (some aspect of the environment or luck). Social psychologists have developed a number of theories of attribution which explain the rules people use when making attributions about their own or the behaviour of others (see, for example, the *covariation principle* and *correspondent inference model*). Attribution is not always an accurate and objective process as there are a number of *attributional biases* which influence the way in which people judge the behaviour of themselves and others. When personal goals, motives or perhaps strong attitudes get in the way of the attributional process, it is said to be biased.

attribution retraining: a cognitive approach that attempts to redirect or correct maladaptive attribution styles. For example, individuals may attribute another person's actions to their hostile intent or to interpersonal rejection. Similarly, individuals may believe that they cannot alter the course of events around them, so no longer try to do so (see *learned helplessness).*

attributional biases: the tendency to depart from the rules of *attribution* in establishing the causes of behaviour. Attributional biases are essentially faults in this normally orderly process and can lead to errors in the interpretation of our own and others' behaviour. An example of an attributional bias is the fundamental attribution error in which observers of behaviour have a tendency to overuse *dispositional* explanations of the behaviour of others despite these attributions often being groundless. (See also *actor-observer/differences*; *hedonic relevance*; *self-serving attributional bias*.)

audience effect: the effect of others watching on our performance of some task. Research has produced results which are often seemingly contradictory. Sometimes the effect of an audience improves our performance (*social facilitation*) and sometimes it causes the opposite effect (*social inhibition*). Early analysis by Zajonc (1965) showed:
- if the tasks were easy and well learned, then the presence of others would have a facilitating effect
- if the tasks were difficult or not well learned, the presence of others would have an inhibitory effect.

Audiences appear to increase the production of dominant responses in those performing a task. Dominant responses are those which are more likely to be produced at any given time. On a simple task this would probably mean an increase in the right responses (doing the task well), on a difficult task it would mean an increase in the wrong responses (making more mistakes).

There are a number of possible explanations for these results:
- audiences create *arousal* in those participating on a task. This is an innate response to the presence of others, and increases the overall activation (or *drive*) level of the person
- audiences create *evaluation apprehension* which increases arousal and therefore the overall drive level of the person. This is a learned response to the possibility of evaluation in a task
- audiences serve as a distraction and so increase arousal. As distraction always impairs performance (it divides our attention between the task and the audience), the beneficial effects from the increased arousal must be greater than the negative effects of the distraction. They are in simple tasks but not in difficult tasks
- cognitive-motivational explanations stress that being watched by an audience creates an awareness of the possible negative effects of failure (embarrassment or disapproval) or the possible positive effects (admiration or approval, for example). The possibility of negative consequences increases task-irrelevant processing (such as worrying) which leads to increased effort. In simple tasks the beneficial effects of the increased effort outweighs the negative effects of the task irrelevant processing and performance is facilitated. In difficult tasks the task-irrelevant processing is harmful (it divides attention) and performance is inhibited. This is represented in the diagram overleaf.

auditory system: the sensory system concerned with hearing. The sensation of hearing involves the transformation of the vibration of air molecules into the perception of loudness, pitch and timbre (the subjective experience of tone and resonance) in the auditory cortex.

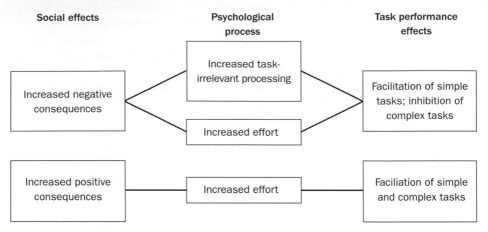

Social effects	Psychological process	Task performance effects

A cognitive–motivational model of SFI effects

augmentation principle refers to part of the ***attribution*** process, whereby the role of a specific cause is increased if it has an effect despite the presence of inhibitory factors. For example, someone who does well in an examination despite poor teaching, dodgy textbooks and prolonged illness is more likely to have their success attributed to ability or hard work (***dispositional attribution***) than someone who has had none of these disadvantages.

authoritarian childrearing: see *child rearing styles*

authoritarian personality: an individual who is intolerant of ambiguity, overly respectful of authority and hostile to any group that appears to challenge the status quo. The idea of the authoritarian personality is attributed to Adorno, himself a victim of **anti-Semitism.** Following extensive interviews with people with these personality ***traits***, Adorno discovered that they had the following in common:
- they tended to idealise their parents, speaking of them as 'paragons of virtue'
- they had experienced a very strict upbringing
- they had a ***repressed*** hostility towards their parents.

The repressed hostility is ***displaced*** onto others (e.g. minority groups) who are perceived as having the hostility to authority that has been repressed in the person with the authoritarian personality. In this way parents are seen as passing on their own authoritarian personality indirectly, with ***prejudice*** toward minority groups being a consequence of the authoritarian personality of their children. As an explanation of prejudice, the authoritarian personality is rooted in a particular set of childrearing experiences within a specific cultural context. It is rarely quoted as an acceptable explanation of prejudice today.

authoritative childrearing: see *child rearing styles*

autistic disorder (autism): a disorder of childhood which is classified under ***DSM-IV-TR*** as a pervasive developmental disorder. Children suffering from an autistic disorder are generally unresponsive to others, have poor communication skills and may react to the environment in bizarre ways. The majority of autistic children are male, and two thirds of sufferers remain impaired throughout adulthood. This figure may not reflect the true status of autism in adulthood as research findings are limited to those adults who did not have the benefit of extensive therapy programmes. The major characteristics of autism are:

- unresponsiveness – autistic children display both a lack of responsiveness and a lack of interest in other people. Social activities, where they are evident, tend to be superficial and passive
- language and communication deficits – many autistic children fail to speak, and those who do may show peculiarities in their speech (see *echolalia*)
- limited imaginative play and deviant responses to the environment – autistic children play and interact with the environment in unusual ways, such as over-reacting to small changes in their routine. They are thus said to have an 'obsession with sameness'.

There are a number of different explanations that have been offered for autistic disorders, including the following:

- perceptual-cognitive views – autism stems from an inability to comprehend sounds or from the overselectivity of specific parts of a stimulus. The autistic child has perceptual or cognitive disturbances that make normal communication or relationships impossible
- biological views stress a multitude of possible causes including *genetic* factors, birth complications and neurological dysfunction
- family and environmental views – now falling more into disfavour, these views claim that autism may be caused, or at least triggered, by the personality characteristics of the parents or by a pattern of abnormal parent–child interaction
- a more recent explanation for autism is *theory of mind* deficit, a theory that the child cannot develop a theory that people (themselves and others) have a mind. Thus, they cannot imagine the thoughts or anticipate the behaviour of others.

There are problems in trying to treat autistic children because they do not adjust easily to changes in their routine, and their behaviour difficulties may interfere with effective therapy. Particularly in *behaviour therapies*, it is difficult to find an effective *reinforcer* that works with autistic children. There is no one wonder-cure that can totally reverse the pattern of autism, although the following techniques can help the sufferer to at least function more effectively:

- *behaviour therapies* – can increase desirable behaviours by selectively *reinforcing*(*shaping*) appropriate behaviours, and (sometimes) punishing inappropriate ones
- *drug treatments* – although little use on their own, *psychotropic drugs* used in conjunction with other therapies can have positive effects
- communication training – makes use of non-vocal communication techniques such as sign language and symbol boards to enable autistic children to at least communicate with the therapist.

autistic hostility: a term used to describe the tendency of many prejudiced people to form their *prejudices* in the absence of any actual interaction with the objects of their prejudice. Without information to the contrary, they tend to develop the idea that the group they are prejudiced against are a mirror-image of themselves. This perceived difference thus justifies their hostility and their prejudice becomes more deeply entrenched.

autobiographical memory: a personal and unique representation of general or specific events and personal facts, autobiographical memory can be described as the 'psychological history of the self'. Remembering that you spent a muddy few days at Glastonbury during the summer, plus the experiences you had there, is part of your autobiographical memory.

Autobiographical memory is an aspect of *episodic memory*, our ability to recall specific past events about what happened where and when. The study of autobiographical memory poses problems, because it is often difficult to prove whether the events took place as reported.

autogenic training is a self-regulation method in which people listen to special phrases (such as 'I am beginning to feel quite relaxed' and 'Deep within my mind I can visualise and experience myself as relaxed, comfortable and still'). These create the physical sensations of warmth and heaviness associated with muscle relaxation. There is some evidence that this technique is beneficial for migraine sufferers and people being treated for hypertension.

autokinetic effect: a type of apparent motion where a small, stationary point of light appears to move in an otherwise dark room. The movement is apparent rather than real and is caused by eye movements.

automatic processing: a type of mental *operation* that is normally rapid, does not require *conscious* awareness, and is generally a result of prolonged practice. A familiar example of automatic processing is the Stroop effect, where *participants* are presented with colour words (red, blue, etc.) but with the words written in a different colour ink (i.e. red written in blue ink, blue in red ink, etc.). They are then asked to name the ink colour of the word. The fact that they find this difficult to do is taken as evidence of automatic processing, i.e. participants find it difficult not to recall the name of the word rather than its colour. Although there are a number of explanations for automatic processing, there is significant support for the view that as people become more practised at responding to a stimulus, they store a considerable amount of information about the stimulus including its meaning (this explains the inability to suppress the meaning of the words in the Stroop effect). As a result of this, future presentations of the stimulus activate these stored representations without needing to proceed to a second conscious stage of attentional processing. This flexibility means that we no longer have to waste conscious effort on routine operations.

autonomic nervous system: a division of the nervous system comprising the *sympathetic nervous system* and the *parasympathetic nervous system* (see diagram opposite). Many of its functions are self-regulating rather than being under the conscious *control* of the organism. The main control for the activities of the autonomic nervous system lies in the *hypothalamus.* The ANS controls a number of glands, the heart muscle and the muscle of the gut.

autonomous morality: an aspect of *moral development* which is characterised by children's movement from an unquestioning acceptance of adult rules to a view of fairness which is based on co-operation and reciprocity. Children learn to solve moral conflicts in ways that are beneficial to themselves and their *peers*. They begin to express the same concern for others as they do for themselves. Rules are no longer seen as inflexible but can be changed to suit the will of the majority. Unquestioning obedience to adult rules is no longer sufficient for an action to be judged morally right.

autonomous state: the state individuals are in when they see themselves as 'acting on their own', i.e. their behaviour is determined by their own free will, and without situational influences. In Milgram's *obedience* studies, obedient participants are assumed to shift from an autonomous state to an *agentic state*.

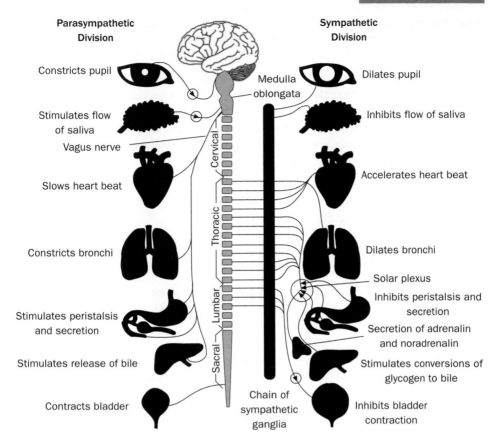

Parasympathetic Division — Sympathetic Division

Constricts pupil — Dilates pupil

Medulla oblongata

Stimulates flow of saliva — Inhibits flow of saliva

Vagus nerve

Cervical

Slows heart beat — Accelerates heart beat

Thoracic

Constricts bronchi — Dilates bronchi

Solar plexus

Inhibits peristalsis and secretion

Lumbar

Stimulates peristalsis and secretion

Secretion of adrenalin and noradrenalin

Stimulates release of bile — Stimulates conversions of glycogen to bile

Sacral

Contracts bladder — Chain of sympathetic ganglia — Inhibits bladder contraction

The autonomic nervous system

autosomes: the non-sex linked *chromosomes*.There are 46 chromosomes in a human body cell, arranged in 23 pairs. Of these, 22 are autosomes, and the remaining pair is the XX or XY sex chromosomes.

average: a measure or indication of what is typical or central in a set of scores. More exactly it is used in its mathematical sense, where, as the *mean*, it is calculated by dividing the sum of all the scores by the total number of scores.

aversion therapy: a therapeutic technique which uses an unpleasant stimulus to change a deviant behaviour. The deviant behaviours in question are usually alcoholism and drug abuse, although the technique has also been more controversially used for sexual perversions and aggressive behaviour. Aversion therapy works by pairing together the stimulus that normally invites the deviant behaviour (such as an alcoholic drink or a sexual image) with an unpleasant (aversive) stimulus such as an electric shock or a nausea-inducing drug. With repeated presentations, the two stimuli become associated and the person develops an aversion toward the stimulus that formerly gave rise to the deviant behaviour (i.e. tries to avoid it). The use of such aversive stimuli has been controversial to say the least, and the images of Stanley Kubrick's film *A Clockwork Orange* present a view of aversion therapy that to many people smacks of coercion and *control* rather than therapeutic gain.

aversive: something that is unpleasant. This may be a stimulus or event (such as a drug which causes sickness) or a situation (such as being exposed to a loud noise or painful electric shock).

avoidance learning: an aspect of *operant conditioning* where the organism learns to avoid some situation by responding to a stimulus (a light or a tone) that typically precedes it. In this way the organism prevents the *aversive* event that would otherwise occur. The avoidance response might be active in that the organism must make a response to avoid the aversive situation or passive, in that they must refrain from making a response in order to prevent the aversive situation happening.

awareness: a subjective state in which we are conscious of something. The term has a number of meanings, ranging from being aware of stimuli in our physical world, to being aware of our inner self and its influence on our behaviours.

A–Z Online

Log on to A–Z Online to search the database of terms, print revision lists and much more. Go to **www.philipallan.co.uk/a-zonline** to get started.

babbling: a repetitive type of infant vocalisation (words such as dadada, mamama) which has no special meaning (it is a repetition of consonant sounds), but ends up having meaning given to it by others in the infant's social world. Thus, if when the infant makes the dadada sounds, the father reacts in a positive way, this acts as a ***reinforcer*** and makes it more likely that the sounds will appear again. Deaf children also babble, but in the absence of feedback to their babbling, this soon ceases.

bad genes theories: any explanations of differences between racial, gender or class divisions as being predominantly due to genetic inferiority of one group compared to the other. This kind of belief was extremely common in the period up to the twentieth century (e.g. Herbert Spencer's application of Darwin's theory of ***natural selection*** to divisions of strong and weak, and rich and poor). Similar ideas still exist today despite the more liberal tradition of modern psychology. Arthur Jensen's research into intelligence differences between white and black Americans created a controversy that extended far beyond its original psychological context.

balance theory: first formulated by Fritz Heider in 1946, it proposes that people strive to maintain consistency in their attitudes to themselves, other people and events in their social world. Heider proposed that the relations among P (the person), O (another person) and X (an object or event) can be either balanced or unbalanced. For example, if you are a member of an anti-vivisection group and you find that your new psychology teacher is a keen supporter of animal research, this poses a problem for your relationship with that teacher. You may well feel uncomfortable at liking someone who holds such a fundamentally different view to such an important issue. The only ways to achieve cognitive balance would be to dislike the teacher or change your own attitude to animal research.

Examples of balanced states   Examples of unbalanced states

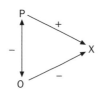

P likes something, so does O, so P likes O.

P likes something, O does not, so P dislikes O.

P likes O, but dislikes something that O likes.

P dislikes O but they share a liking for something else.

bar chart: a way of graphically representing scores on some *discrete variable*. For example, we may want to represent the number of cars of different nationalities in the college car park. The resulting bar chart might look something like this.

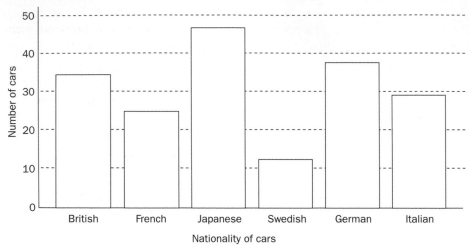

Example of a bar chart

baseline: a point of comparison against which the effect of some treatment can be assessed. For example, the effectiveness of a drug can be determined by comparing behaviour after taking the drug to behaviour before. In *experiments,* the *control group* is commonly used as a baseline against which to assess the effectiveness of the *independent variable.*

basic trust (vs mistrust): the first stage in the psychosocial theory of Erik Erikson. If infants in the first year are given warm and responsive care, they develop a trust and confidence both in the person who cares for them and also in the world around them. If the infant does not receive such favourable treatment, they develop a mistrust of the world around them and are less confident in the developmental stages to come.

Bayley Scales: a sort of infant *intelligence* test, designed for children aged between 2 and 30 months. Infants are scored on three criteria: the motor scale, consisting of skills like throwing a ball; the mental scale, which includes tests on the child's ability to follow directions, or find a hidden toy; and the behavioural record, which measures things like social responsiveness and fearfulness. On the basis of these tests the child is given a developmental quotient (DQ) which in turn enables the practitioner to assess whether s/he is at the appropriate level for their age or whether they are showing signs of slower or accelerated development.

BBC prison study: a study carried out by social psychologists Alex Haslam and Stephen Reicher and broadcast on the BBC in 2002. The BBC Prison Study explored the social and psychological consequences of putting people in groups of unequal power, examining when people accept inequality and when they challenge it. Unlike in Zimbardo's Stanford Prison Study, Haslam and Reicher discovered that, when prisoners identified together, it gave them the power to resist, challenge and, ultimately, to defeat the guards.

behaviour: a general term which refers to any response of an *organism* that can be measured. The argument over what is and what is not behaviour has developed from the early days of *behaviourism* with its emphasis on only those responses which were overt and observable. Over the years the term has been broadened, and is now used to represent a whole range of responses which are neither overt, nor directly observable. For example, the workings of human *memory* or problem-solving might be thought of as behaviour, even though they cannot be observed directly but must be inferred from their product.

behaviour genetics: a field of study that is concerned with the *genetic* bases of behaviour. It is a central belief of this approach that differences in the genetic constitution of human beings can account for much of their variation and the differences in how they respond to their environments.

behaviour modification: any technique of behaviour change that is based on the procedures of *operant conditioning.* This would include *modelling*, *token economies* and *shaping*.

behaviour therapy: any technique of behaviour change that is based on the procedures of *classical conditioning*. This would include *aversion therapy*, *implosion therapy* and *systematic desensitisation*.

behavioural categories: during an *observational* study, a researcher records the number of instances of behaviour that fit into a number of predetermined categories of behaviour, e.g. aggressive behaviours, helping behaviours and so on.

behaviourism: an approach to psychology that accounts for *behaviour* in terms of observable events and without reference to mental concepts such as '*mind*' or '*emotion*' Behaviourism has gone through many transformations in the years since it was developed by John Watson in the early part of the twentieth century. One more recent extension of this approach has been the development of *social learning theory*, which emphasises the role of plans and expectations in people's behaviour. Under social learning theory, people were no longer seen as passive victims of the environment, but rather they were seen as self-reflecting and thoughtful. In radical behaviourism (the original form of this approach), however, the relationship between the environment and the organism is seen as a straight line, in that organisms act on their environment, which in turn provides rewards and punishments to determine the future *probability* of a response occurring:

Behaviour --▶ Environment
◀----------------------------- (rewards and punishments)

Behaviourism offered explanations for all manner of different aspects of a person's life. Such accounts were always centred around the idea of *learning.* Behaviours were acquired (learned) in one of two main ways – classical conditi conditioning. Examples of *classical conditioning* applied to real lif

- taste aversion – using derivations of classical conditioning, it is p people develop aversions to particular foods
- learned emotions, such as love for parents, were explained as p the stimulation they provide
- advertising – we readily associate attractive images with the pro

32

- development of **phobias** – classical conditioning is seen as the mechanism by which we acquire many of these irrational fears.

The use of **operant conditioning** techniques is referred to as **behaviour modification**. Behaviour has been 'modified' in a number of different ways and settings such as:

- in classroom management – teachers have been able to change the behaviour of disruptive children
- in **therapy** – behavioural modification treatments have been applied in a variety of different contexts, from the treatment of phobias to the teaching of **autistic** children.

Evaluation of behaviourism includes:

- behaviourism might be seen as under-estimating the importance of inborn tendencies. It is clear from research on **biological preparedness** that the ease with which something is learned is partly due to its links with an organism's potential survival
- the behaviourist emphasis on single influences on behaviour is a simplification of circumstances where behaviour is influenced by many factors. When this is acknowledged, it becomes almost impossible to judge the action of any single one
- this over-simplified view of the world has led to the development of 'pop behaviourism', the view that rewards and punishments can change almost anything. This was never what behaviourists such as **Skinner** intended. Skinner was at pains to emphasise the importance of intrinsic rewards such as a person's pride and initiative in their choice of activities.

Bem Sex-Role inventory: a measurement scale that presents males and females with 20 characteristics that are commonly judged as being more desirable for males (such as being forceful, ambitious and aggressive) and 20 that are judged as being more desirable for females (such as compassionate, loyal and gentle). **Respondents** are asked to rate themselves on a scale of 1 to 7 on each of the 40 entries, ranging from 'almost always true of me' to 'almost never true of me'. They are then given a score on a masculinity scale and on a femininity scale. Classification of scores is as follows:

Scores	Classification
High masculine & low feminine	Masculine
High feminine & low masculine	Feminine
High feminine & high masculine	Androgynous
Low feminine & low masculine	Undifferentiated

Bem's original suggestion that **androgynous** people were better adjusted and enjoyed more positive **self-esteem** has not stood up well to research evidence. Most research has established that those who score high in terms of masculinity tend to enjoy a higher level of self-esteem. Recent theorists have tended to abandon these rather simplistic notions of masculinity and femininity as measured in simple personality traits, and have suggested a much more global view of male and female differences that cannot be reduced in this way.

ereavement describes the state where a person survives the death of a close friend or
on. The death of a spouse (husband or wife) is generally considered to be the most

behaviour: a general term which refers to any response of an *organism* that can be measured. The argument over what is and what is not behaviour has developed from the early days of *behaviourism* with its emphasis on only those responses which were overt and observable. Over the years the term has been broadened, and is now used to represent a whole range of responses which are neither overt, nor directly observable. For example, the workings of human *memory* or problem-solving might be thought of as behaviour, even though they cannot be observed directly but must be inferred from their product.

behaviour genetics: a field of study that is concerned with the *genetic* bases of behaviour. It is a central belief of this approach that differences in the genetic constitution of human beings can account for much of their variation and the differences in how they respond to their environments.

behaviour modification: any technique of behaviour change that is based on the procedures of *operant conditioning.* This would include *modelling*, *token economies* and *shaping*.

behaviour therapy: any technique of behaviour change that is based on the procedures of *classical conditioning*. This would include *aversion therapy*, *implosion therapy* and *systematic desensitisation*.

behavioural categories: during an *observational* study, a researcher records the number of instances of behaviour that fit into a number of predetermined categories of behaviour, e.g. aggressive behaviours, helping behaviours and so on.

behaviourism: an approach to psychology that accounts for *behaviour* in terms of observable events and without reference to mental concepts such as '*mind*' or '*emotion*' Behaviourism has gone through many transformations in the years since it was developed by John Watson in the early part of the twentieth century. One more recent extension of this approach has been the development of *social learning theory*, which emphasises the role of plans and expectations in people's behaviour. Under social learning theory, people were no longer seen as passive victims of the environment, but rather they were seen as self-reflecting and thoughtful. In radical behaviourism (the original form of this approach), however, the relationship between the environment and the organism is seen as a straight line, in that organisms act on their environment, which in turn provides rewards and punishments to determine the future *probability* of a response occurring:

Behaviourism offered explanations for all manner of different aspects of a person's life. Such accounts were always centred around the idea of *learning.* Behaviours were acquired (learned) in one of two main ways – classical conditioning and operant conditioning. Examples of *classical conditioning* applied to real life are:

- taste aversion – using derivations of classical conditioning, it is possible to explain how people develop aversions to particular foods
- learned emotions, such as love for parents, were explained as paired associations with the stimulation they provide
- advertising – we readily associate attractive images with the products they are selling

- development of **phobias** – classical conditioning is seen as the mechanism by which we acquire many of these irrational fears.

The use of **operant conditioning** techniques is referred to as **behaviour modification**. Behaviour has been 'modified' in a number of different ways and settings such as:

- in classroom management – teachers have been able to change the behaviour of disruptive children
- in **therapy** – behavioural modification treatments have been applied in a variety of different contexts, from the treatment of phobias to the teaching of **autistic** children.

Evaluation of behaviourism includes:

- behaviourism might be seen as under-estimating the importance of inborn tendencies. It is clear from research on **biological preparedness** that the ease with which something is learned is partly due to its links with an organism's potential survival
- the behaviourist emphasis on single influences on behaviour is a simplification of circumstances where behaviour is influenced by many factors. When this is acknowledged, it becomes almost impossible to judge the action of any single one
- this over-simplified view of the world has led to the development of 'pop behaviourism', the view that rewards and punishments can change almost anything. This was never what behaviourists such as **Skinner** intended. Skinner was at pains to emphasise the importance of intrinsic rewards such as a person's pride and initiative in their choice of activities.

Bem Sex-Role inventory: a measurement scale that presents males and females with 20 characteristics that are commonly judged as being more desirable for males (such as being forceful, ambitious and aggressive) and 20 that are judged as being more desirable for females (such as compassionate, loyal and gentle). **Respondents** are asked to rate themselves on a scale of 1 to 7 on each of the 40 entries, ranging from 'almost always true of me' to 'almost never true of me'. They are then given a score on a masculinity scale and on a femininity scale. Classification of scores is as follows:

Scores	Classification
High masculine & low feminine	Masculine
High feminine & low masculine	Feminine
High feminine & high masculine	Androgynous
Low feminine & low masculine	Undifferentiated

Bem's original suggestion that **androgynous** people were better adjusted and enjoyed more positive **self-esteem** has not stood up well to research evidence. Most research has established that those who score high in terms of masculinity tend to enjoy a higher level of self-esteem. Recent theorists have tended to abandon these rather simplistic notions of masculinity and femininity as measured in simple personality traits, and have suggested a much more global view of male and female differences that cannot be reduced in this way.

bereavement describes the state where a person survives the death of a close friend or relation. The death of a spouse (husband or wife) is generally considered to be the most serious threat to the health and well-being of the survivor. The degree of stress experienced as a result of bereavement depends on several factors:

- the timing of the death – unexpected death creates a far greater stress in the survivor than an expected death
- the number of other stressors being encountered by the survivor (such as health and financial stressors)
- the distress of the 'arrangements' that must be dealt with after the death (such as the funeral, dealing with financial and personal matters of the deceased).

It is usual for survivors to go through a period of grief. Grief may be expressed physically (by a lack of energy), cognitively (through confusion and disbelief), emotionally (with guilt and depression) and behaviourally (by crying). It is also common for the bereaved to go through stages of grieving, during which they may experience numbness and disbelief, turning to a full realisation of the loss and eventually a more constructive and positive stage in which the experience is incorporated into their life rather than dominating it.

beta bias: a term used to classify any theory or research that ignores or minimises differences between men and women. Beta bias theories tend either to ignore questions about the lives of women, or assume that insights derived from studies of men will apply equally well to women.

beta rhythm: also known as beta activity, this occurs when the organism is awake and alert, possibly thinking actively or attending to events in the environment. When measured on an *EEG*, beta activity is characterised by irregular, low-amplitude waves.

bias: a tendency to treat one individual or group in a different way to others. Bias can be positive or negative. With positive bias, we show favourable behaviour toward the recipient of the bias, whilst with negative bias, we show unfavourable behaviour towards them. In research design, we may have biased *samples,* such that the underlying *population* is not appropriately sampled. In psychological research and theory there is evidence of *gender* and *cultural biases*. *Intelligence* tests are often accused of having a cultural bias, with some test constructors claiming to have developed *culture-free tests* that eliminate the kinds of cultural and sub-cultural biases found in other tests.

biased sampling refers to the over-representation of one category of *participant* (males, females, students, people of a certain age, etc.) in a sample so that the sample fails to adequately represent the *population* from which it was taken. There are many ways in which we might introduce sampling bias, such as:

- giving insufficient thought to the sampling technique being used, e.g. only picking people who happen to be in the refectory during your psychology lesson (think, why weren't *they* in a lesson?)
- only using volunteers – what sort of people volunteer for research; are they typical?
- only using students – a large majority of social psychology research projects in the USA involved only students, most of these being *psychology* students.

bilateral ECT: see *electroconvulsive shock treatment (ECT)*

bimodal distribution: a type of frequency distribution where there are two *modes,* i.e. two high points on the graph. For example, if we were to mix together two groups of students, one French and one English, and give them a test of French history, the resulting graph might look something like this:

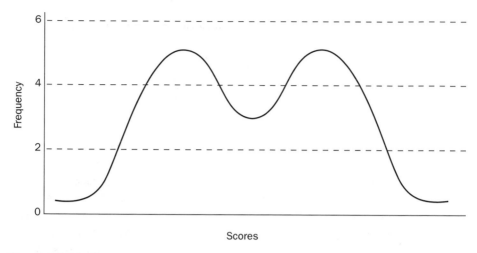

Bimodal distribution

biofeedback: a technique for controlling physiological responses by receiving information about those responses as they occur. Monitoring devices track physiological responses such as heart rate, blood pressure and muscle tension, and provide the person with feedback in the form of a light or tone whenever they change the response in the desired direction.

With practice, a person can learn to **control** all sorts of bodily functions, predominantly through relaxation. By relaxing, the person might be able to cause a change in the response, and the light or tone then acts as **reinforcement** that their efforts are causing a change.

It is also claimed that biofeedback techniques can have significant positive effects in the reduction of generalised **anxiety disorders**. Through the use of an electromyograph (EMG), clients can receive feedback concerning the state of muscle tension in their body (for example, in the facial muscles). By controlling this, they can reduce the tension in their body and the accompanying anxiety.

Techniques such as this and the related efforts to reduce heart rate in sufferers of anxiety disorders have had only limited success. In tests of the technique, clients seemed able to reduce their heart rate only slightly, but rather than enjoying a reduction of anxiety when that happened, they became even more anxious when they saw how easily it went up! It is similar to the trend for some car manufacturers to build in mpg feedback displays that constantly tell you the present miles per gallon related to current driving conditions. While it is encouraging to see 55 mpg while descending a hill, the sight of 10 mpg whilst crawling in traffic is enough to make any heart race!

This limited effectiveness of biofeedback techniques applied to anxiety disorders has led one critic to observe that in teaching an anxious client how to slow down their heart rate, we would end up with an anxious client whose heart beat slower!

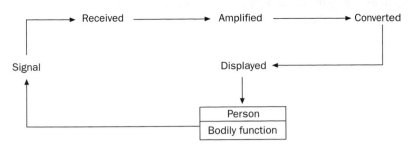

A biofeedback system

biological model of abnormality is a view that mental disorders are caused by abnormal physiological processes. Often referred to as the biomedical or medical approach, the biological approach is broader and focuses very much on the role of **genetic** and biochemical factors in the onset of mental disorders. A quote from Maher (1966) summarises the essence of this approach: 'Behaviour is considered pathological and is classified on the basis of symptoms, classification being called **diagnosis**. Processes designed to change behaviour are called **therapies**, and are sometimes applied to patients in mental hospitals. If the deviant behaviour ceases, the patient is described as cured.'

Examples of the biological approach applied to mental disorders include:
- **anxiety disorders** are explained by a defect in the **autonomic nervous system** that causes a person to become too easily aroused
- **depression** is seen as being caused by a dysfunction in the normal processes of **neuronal transmission**
- **schizophrenics** inherit a predisposition to develop a brain abnormality that produces the symptoms of schizophrenia.

Important research areas in this approach include:
- **genetics** – by using **concordance** studies, it is possible to investigate the possible influence of genetic factors in any specific disorder. They show, for example, that if one member of a **monozygotic twin** pair develops schizophrenia, there is a 50 per cent chance that the other twin will also develop the disorder. In most disorders that have a genetic influence, people inherit the **genotype**, whereas the symptoms of a disorder are the **phenotype**. Whether or not the person develops the symptoms of the disorder is determined by a number of other factors
- biochemistry – different explanations of disorders propose too many or too few specific **neurotransmitters**. For example, in **schizophrenia**, an excess of dopamine is thought to be responsible for many of the symptoms (see **dopamine hypothesis**).

An implication of the biological approach is that alterations in bodily functioning will be effective in the treatment and prevention of disorders. The major type of treatment associated with this perspective are the **drug treatments**. In attempting to correct the symptoms of schizophrenia, for example, anti-psychotic drugs will restore the balance of dopamine to its appropriate level. Stimulants such as **ritalin** are used in the treatment of **attention-deficit hyperactivity disorder (ADHD)**, and sedatives such as valium can reduce the tension in **anxiety disorders**. Other forms of biological intervention include **electroconvulsive shock treatment (ECT)** which can be used in conditions of severe depression. Some critics of the biological approach point out that whereas the symptoms of physical illness are objective (it is hard to argue that someone does not have chicken pox if they have all the physical symptoms), the symptoms of mental illness are subjective. When we describe some aspect of a person's behaviour as **abnormal**, we are inevitably making a value judgement that is rooted within a specific cultural context. Likewise, whereas the causes of chicken pox are well established, the causes of the majority of mental illnesses are not.

biological preparedness: see *preparedness*

biological rhythms: like the seasons of the year and the rhythm of the tides, the body also has its rhythms. Some of these are obvious, such as the female menstrual cycle and the alternation of sleeping and waking; others are less obvious, such as the variations in body temperature over a single day. Many of these rhythmic activities appear to be in-built, or **endogenous**, so that they persist even when the environmental stimuli are absent. Many such rhythmic activities are controlled by endogenous pacemakers in the brain, which act as a form of 'body-clock'. However, even with these endogenous pacemakers, behaviour in the real world has to be adapted to external events such as the day-night cycle. Where external events (such as the amount of light) have a role in rhythmic activities, they are called **zeitgebers**.

There are four major types of bodily rhythm:
- **ultradian rhythms** have a frequency of more than one complete cycle every 24 hours (e.g. sleep stages in a single night's sleep)
- **infradian rhythms** occur less often than once every 24 hours (e.g. the human menstrual cycle)
- **circadian rhythms** occur once every 24 hours (e.g. the sleep–waking cycle)
- circannual rhythms occur on a yearly basis (e.g. hibernation in squirrels).

biomedical model of abnormality: see *biological model of abnormality*

biopsychology: a term given to the scientific investigation of the relationship between biology and behaviour. Biopsychologists normally study the brain and nervous system in an attempt to establish their impact on behaviour at all levels.

biopsychosocial model: a model of heath and illness that moves away from the narrowness of the **biomedical model of abnormality**, and acknowledges that health and illness are determined as much by social, cultural and psychological factors as they are by biological factors. The biopsychosocial model does not look for single causes but sees health and illness as having many causes and also many effects. Cancer is known to have a number of precursors (i.e. something that signals the approach of something else), some of which are biological, some psychological and some social. For example:
- oncogenes are cancer-causing genes that produce uncontrolled growth in cells when they are activated by other genes, viruses or carcinogens
- carcinogens are cancer-producing agents that are present in many different aspects of our environment, including the by-products of environmental pollution, soil and tobacco
- approximately one-third of deaths from cancer are estimated to be related to tobacco use, and a further one-third to dietary factors.

It is sometimes difficult to separate out individual behaviours from behaviours that reflect important cultural values. For example, the incidence of cervical cancer among Mormon and Amish women is far lower than the average for other American women. It is believed this is due to their strict codes of sexual behaviour – women who become sexually active earlier and have multiple partners appear to be more at risk for cervical cancer than those who do not.

Cancer is also acknowledged to have many different effects, some biological (such as the appearance, in some cancer sufferers, of psychological problems that are a direct product of organic changes in the central nervous system), and some social (such as the effects on the families of cancer sufferers).

biosocial approach to gender development: Money and Ehrhardt (1972) argued that sex of rearing is the pivotal point in gender development. Biology is likely to determine sex of rearing as a baby is sexed at birth and everything else follows from that. Once a child is born, social labelling and differential treatment of boys and girls interact with biological factors to steer development. Money and Ehrhardt predicted that, if a genetic male is mislabelled as a girl and treated as a girl before the age of three, he would acquire the gender identity of a girl. Thus the key to gender development, according to Money and Ehrhardt, is the label that a person is given, and the subsequent sex-typed rearing he or she receives.

bipolar depression: see *bipolar disorder*

bipolar disorder: a less common category of *mood disorder* which has symptoms of both *mania* and *depression*. A formal diagnosis of a bipolar disorder is made if the symptoms below are severe enough to cause a serious impairment of functioning or to require hospitalisation, and if the client shows evidence of elaborated or irritable mood, plus three of the following symptoms:
1. Increase in activity level.
2. Unusual talkativeness.
3. An impression that thoughts are racing.
4. Sleep loss.
5. Inflated self-esteem.
6. Distractibility.
7. Excessive involvement in activities with undesirable consequences (e.g. risk taking).

Bipolar disorders affect about 1 in 100 of the population and are recurrent. Explanations of the depressive aspect of a bipolar disorder are similar to those of major depression. The manic phase of the disorder is thought to be a defence against the depressive state of the individual. (See *depression*.)

bobo doll: a round-bottomed inflatable toy made famous by Albert Bandura's studies of the imitation of aggression.

body image in sport: body image is the way a person thinks about his or her body and how it looks to others. Generally both men and women who participate in sport have a more positive body image than those who do not. However, research suggests that male bodybuilders experience greater dissatisfaction with their body image, often suffering from low self-esteem combined with high perfectionism. By way of contrast, women who take part in sport (bodybuilders, rowers and netballers) tend to have a more positive body image despite their divergence from cultural ideals of slimness and femininity.

bonding: the term has a number of meanings within psychology, but in its most common usage it refers to the feelings that parents have for their children (compared to the term *attachment* which refers to the feelings that children have for their parents). Bonding has a special role in the maintenance and care of children, and in safeguarding them from abuse or abandonment.

bottom-up processing: explanations of perceptual processing that see perception being directly influenced by the sensory input. (See *direct theories of perception*.)

Bowlby, J (1907–1990): John Bowlby was made famous by his views on the importance of the **attachment** bond that forms between caregiver and child, and the effects that the deprivation of that bond may have both in the short-term and long-term development of the child. Bowlby believed that the infant should experience a warm, intimate and continuous relationship with his or her mother. Drawing upon evidence gathered from a variety of sources, including studies of hospitalised children, institutionalised children and evacuees, as well as experimental work with motherless monkeys, Bowlby suggested that prolonged separation from the primary caregiver (usually the mother) or the failure to form an attachment bond (**privation**) would lead to adverse effects in later life, including the possible development of **affectionless psychopathy** and difficulties in forming intimate relationships with others. Bowlby claimed that children who were deprived of maternal love would nearly always be retarded in some way, physically, socially or emotionally.

BPS: a common abbreviation of the **British Psychological Society**.

BPS code of ethics: a set of guidelines published (and updated regularly to reflect developments within the subject) by the British Psychological Society (BPS). Adherence to the code of ethics ensures that research is carried out in a way that is in the best interests of the participants, and is also morally defensible to those outside the research context.

brain: part of the **central nervous system (CNS)**. The brain can be conveniently divided into the forebrain, midbrain and the hindbrain:

Major division	Sub-division	Principle structures
forebrain	telencephalon	cerebral cortex
		basal ganglia
		limbic system
	diencephalon	thalamus
		hypothalamus
midbrain	mesencephalon	tectum
		tegmentum
hindbrain	metencephalon	cerebellum
		pons
	myelencephalon	medulla oblongata

- telencephalon – contains two symmetrical hemispheres that make up the cerebrum. This consists of the **cerebral cortex** and the sub-cortical regions of the basal ganglia and the limbic system. The basal ganglia is involved in the **control** of movement. **Parkinson's disease** is caused by a degeneration of **neurons** in the midbrain that have their axons in the basal ganglia. Parts of the limbic system (most notably the hippocampus) are involved in learning and memory, whilst other areas appear to have a role in emotional behaviour
- diencephalon – contains the thalamus and the **hypothalamus**. The thalamus relays sensory input to the **cerebral cortex**, whilst the hypothalamus controls the **autonomic nervous system** and the **endocrine system,** and organises behaviours that are essential to the organism's survival

- mesencephalon – consists of the tectum and tegmentum. The tectum contains the superior and inferior colliculi, which are part of the visual and auditory systems respectively. The tegmentum contains a number of structures, the most important of which is the reticular formation, which plays an important role in *sleep*, movement and *attention*
- metencephalon – contains the pons and the *cerebellum*. The pons has a role in sleep and *arousal*, while the cerebellum receives sensory information and integrates it with information about movement to produce co-ordinated movements
- myelencephalon – has one major structure, the medulla oblongata which, through its *control* over the reticular formation, plays a part in regulation of the cardiovascular system and the respiratory system.

brain dysfunction and crime: some scientists believe that a biological dysfunction, combined with a particular pattern of socialisation, can lead to violent crime. Research using *positron emission tomography (PET)* scanning has shown, for example, that some people are born with brains that may make them prone to violence, perhaps because the part of their brains involved in creating a sense of conscience is dysfunctional.

brain lateralisation: see *lateralisation of function*

brain size and intelligence: the idea that brain size is related to *intelligence* was widespread among neuroanatomists around the turn of the century. This received a severe blow when it was found that the brains of several distinguished people (who had bequeathed their bodies to science) showed no outstanding characteristics whatever and were, in fact, disappointingly ordinary. This was just as well, as elements of such work were being badly misused to justify repressive racist, anti-feminist and colonial attitudes. The advent of more reliable measures of 'intelligence' coupled with the development of sophisticated brain-scanning methods (such as the MRI) has suggested that such a relationship, albeit a fairly moderate one, may actually exist. It is important to remember that this moderate relationship between absolute brain size and intelligence still allows for the role of many additional important factors in the determination of intelligence.

It is widely believed that cetaceans (the whales, dolphins and porpoises) are also highly 'intelligent'. The major historical basis for this belief is the size and complex surface appearance of cetacean brains. If 'intelligence' were simply determined by absolute brain size, there would be no difficulty in deciding which species was top. The brain of a sperm whale is nearly 8 kg, the brain of an African elephant 7.5 kg and the brain of a human is a miserly 1.5 kg. But as the species with the biggest brains also tend to be the ones with the biggest bodies, it might be that large animals just need larger brains to *control* and maintain their larger bodies. A simple way to make allowance for different body-weights is to express brain-weight as a percentage of body-weight. In this way of determining 'intelligence', humans are seen to have a great advantage over other mammals, and we also have a very different view of the large whales. However, research suggests that relative brain size is not necessarily related to intelligence either, as there are too many anomalies. A particular example is the spiny anteater with a neocortex (greatly developed in primates and humans) relatively much larger than that of a human. Despite this endowment, nobody has so far put forward any claims for superior 'intelligence' in spiny anteaters.

British Psychological Society (BPS): the professional body for practising psychologists in the United Kingdom. As well as overseeing the training of psychologists in this country (through BPS approval of recognised degree courses in psychology), the BPS also guides and monitors the professional conduct of its members through the BPS guidelines (see *codes of practice*).

Broca's aphasia: a disruption of speech production that is caused by damage to *Broca's area*. The disruption is largely restricted to the production of speech, with comprehension of language being much less impaired. Some aspects of this aphasia, such as agrammatism, do also create problems in the comprehension of language. Broca's aphasia produces three major speech deficits:

- agrammatism – difficulty in using various grammatically important words such as the, a, some, in, as well as problems with grammatical markers such as -ed or have as in the sentence 'I have been'
- anomia – a difficulty in finding words, which adds to the lack of fluency and general slowness of speech
- articulation difficulties – the mispronunciation of words with the sounds often being in the wrong order.

Broca's area: an area in the frontal lobe of the cortex which is the centre for speech production. Damage to this area disrupts a person's ability to speak and can lead to Broca's aphasia.

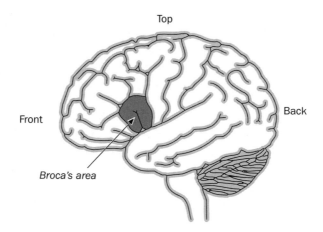

Broca's area

Bruce and Young's theory of face recognition: Bruce and Young (1986) described face recognition as a series of stages that are accessed one after the other. There are two paths through the model – one for familiar faces and one for recognising facial expressions (unfamiliar faces). The first path is concerned with the recognition of familiar faces. Face recognition units contain information about familiar faces. If the encoded information has a reasonable match with this information then the appropriate node is activated, which then triggers the personal identity node. The personal identity nodes contain information about a person's identity, e.g. their temperament, their friendliness and so on. Once a person's identity is established, then the name can be retrieved using the name recognition unit. Names can be accessed only once the person has been identified; there is no direct link from face to name. The second path of the model is concerned with the other kinds of information provided by faces, such as information about emotional state or information related to what a person is saying. Encoded data is used to work out the meaning of facial expressions in the expression analysis node, and lip movements help to understand what someone is saying (facial speech analysis).

Bruner, J (1915–): a cognitive psychologist who believed that intellectual development in the child depends very much on the way in which the mind uses the information that it receives. Bruner believed that children develop different ways of representing the environment around them:

- enactive – they represent the world through their sensori-motor actions. If you have ever attempted to describe a spiral staircase without resorting to physical actions then you are probably aware of the nature of this type of representation
- iconic – thinking based on the use of mental images
- semantic – the representation of the environment through language. This enables the child to access much of the knowledge available in their surroundings and to go beyond the information given. For Bruner, language is the vital ingredient that opens up new horizons of intellectual development.

bulimia nervosa: an eating disorder in which a person habitually engages in episodes of uncontrollable eating (bingeing) followed by self-induced vomiting or other compensatory behaviours. As with *anorexia nervosa,* bulimics have an abnormal concern with body size, having a morbid fear of being or becoming fat. The *DSM-IV-TR* diagnosis of bulimia nervosa applies if the following criteria are present:

- recurrent episodes of binge eating
- recurrent and inappropriate compensatory behaviours to prevent weight gain. These include vomiting and the use of laxatives (purging-type bulimia nervosa) or excessive exercise (non-purging type bulimia nervosa)
- binge eating and compensatory behaviours occur on average at least twice a week for a period of three months or more
- self-evaluation is unduly influenced by body shape and weight
- the disturbance is not part of a larger pattern of anorexia nervosa.

Bulimia is predominantly a problem of adolescence and early adulthood. The majority of bulimics are female (approximately 90 per cent of cases), typically beginning around the late teens or early twenties. In the early stages the disorder tends to be triggered by an upsetting event or a depressed mood. Later the bingeing may become carefully planned, with foods bought especially for the purpose.

Bingeing normally begins with feelings of extreme tension, which may be temporarily displaced by the eating. It is then followed by feelings of self-reproach and guilt, together with a fear of weight gain. Vomiting and other compensatory behaviours relieve the uncomfortable physical feelings and reduce the feelings of guilt associated with bingeing. A cycle of bingeing and purging quickly develops with the bulimic becoming increasingly depressed and guilty over his or her secret life. Treatments for bulimia include:

- individual insight therapies – such as *cognitive therapy* – which attempt to alter the bulimic's attitude to their weight and body shape, and eliminate the type of thinking that raises their levels of anxiety and leads to the binge-purge cycle
- behaviour therapies – may involve exposure and response prevention. Vomiting is seen as a *compulsive* behaviour that helps to deal with the guilt after bingeing. The bulimic may be allowed to eat the 'forbidden' foods but then be prevented from vomiting
- *anti–depressant drugs* are often used in conjunction with other types of treatment.

The vast majority of bulimics show significant improvement as a result of treatment. Some do not, however, and even when they do, they may later relapse back into the binge–purge cycle. Factors influencing the rate and nature of recovery include:
- binge–purge patterns of long **duration** are more difficult to change
- recovery is more difficult when the binge–purge patterns have taken the place of other more 'normal' activities such as socialising, leisure activities or sex
- change is more difficult when the sufferer is severely **depressed** or experiences some other emotional distress.

burnout and withdrawal: the psychological, emotional and physical withdrawal (e.g. from an occupation) resulting from chronic stress.

bystander behaviour: sometimes known as the bystander effect or bystander apathy to indicate the tendency of people witnessing an emergency to ignore the problem. Normal episodes in everyday life tend to involve familiar **scripts,** but emergencies are unplanned, unfamiliar and often require instant action. The single most important factor that determines whether someone will help in an emergency appears to be whether they are alone or in the company of others. When in the company of other potential helpers, people are far less likely to help than when they are on their own.

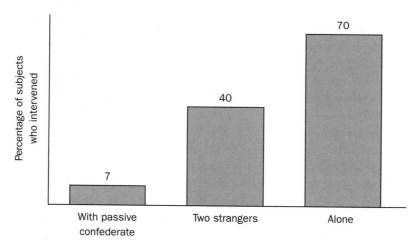

The bystander effect: the effect of a second bystander on emergency intervention (based on Latané and Rodin)

Three social processes appear to account for this phenomenon:
- **social influence** processes – people look to others in order to correctly interpret a situation. If others don't react, it cannot be a true emergency. As we are often taught to stay calm in an emergency, this inactivity is seen as the most appropriate response (see **pluralistic ignorance**)
- audience inhibition – the risk of being embarrassed by acting inappropriately may inhibit possible helping behaviour (see **evaluation apprehension**)
- diffusion of responsibility – when there are several people present, the responsibility for helping is spread so that each individual feels less responsible to take action.

These three processes tend to reinforce each other and suppress the likelihood of any one member or any one person helping.

capacity: a measure of the amount of information that can be held in memory. This is measured in terms of separate items of information, such as a list of digits. ***Long-term memory*** has potentially unlimited capacity. ***Short-term memory***, on the other hand, has a very limited capacity (usually 5–9 items, or '7-plus-or-minus-two'). Beyond this capacity, new information can 'bump' out other items from STM.

cardinal traits are characteristics that have an overwhelming effect on almost everything that we do. We may say that Mother Theresa of Calcutta has the cardinal trait of ***altruism***, or that Margaret Thatcher had the cardinal trait of self-belief. It is arguable whether the rest of us have such overwhelmingly significant single characteristics. It is more likely that we have a small number of central traits, such as generosity, impulsiveness and warmth, that reflect the way in which we typically relate to others.

cardiovascular disorder: refers to any disorder of the heart (e.g. coronary heart disease) and circulatory system (e.g. hypertension – high blood pressure). Research suggests a relationship between prolonged exposure to stressors and the risk of cardiovascular disorders. Acute and chronic stress may affect the cardiovascular system (i.e. the heart and circulatory system) in many different ways, including the following:
- hypertension (high blood pressure)
- coronary heart disease caused by atherosclerosis (narrowing of the coronary arteries)
- stroke (brain damage caused by disruption of blood supply to the brain).

caregiver: a term used in the ***attachment*** literature referring to those who have ***bonded*** with the child and fulfil its psychological needs as well as its physical needs. The term 'primary caregiver' is often synonymous with 'mother', but the term is used in deference to the fact that the primary caregiver may not be the mother, as indeed the caregivers may not necessarily be the parents.

carpentered environment: a reference to the perceptual world in which children of industrial societies develop. We are exposed to buildings and other structures that are essentially man-made (hence the term carpentered) and this defines the perceptual experiences of our early years. The majority of man-made structures make use of straight lines and angles, and thus we become used to perceiving our world in this way. Perception theorists use this fact as a possible explanation for why we are liable to many perceptual ***illusions*** (such as the Müller–Lyer illusion) that people in non-carpentered environments do not experience. Because the term carpentered is less culturally familiar to modern-day students, there is a frequent misreading of the word as carpeted which may raise quite different issues!

case study: an attempt to explore, in some considerable depth, the behaviour and experiences of an individual. Case studies involve detailed descriptions of those aspects of the behaviour which are of interest to the person carrying out the study, as well as their interpretations of what they have found. This is inevitably a somewhat subjective exercise, because what is selected as being important as well as the interpretations that are put on them, is very much a decision for the person carrying out the study. Case studies differ from other approaches to the study of behaviour and experience in a number of ways:

- they are far more detailed than experiments and observations and give the researcher a far greater depth of insight into the individual
- they are highly focused methods which concentrate not only on an individual, but also on one narrow area of that individual's psychological functioning
- they tend to use *qualitative research* rather than traditional tests and measurements (*quantitative data*)
- they acknowledge the importance of subjective reports (e.g. what the individual feels or believes) as well as the more objective data that might be obtained by other means
- they are an example of the *idiographic* approach to research as opposed to the more *nomothetic* approach of the experimental methods.
- they provide a much richer account of behaviour than could ever be obtained by using more quantitative methods
- they do not try to sweep *individual differences* under the carpet; instead they acknowledge and emphasise the uniqueness of each individual's makeup and experiences
- because of this uniqueness, there are problems in trying to generalise findings to other people. It is safer to say that although it is possible to learn much about the behaviour of all humankind from the use of techniques such as case studies, their primary aim is to explore the behaviour and experiences of a unique individual
- the subjectivity implied in a case study means it is often difficult for an outside observer to disentangle what is information and what is *inference* on the part of the researcher.

castration anxiety: a *psychoanalytic* term which is used to refer to the anxiety experienced by the young boy as a result of his rivalry with his father for the affections of the mother. As a part of the *Oedipus complex*, castration anxiety is thought to arise when young boys, on seeing a naked female, perhaps for the first time, realise that women do not have a penis. Because of the rivalry the child experiences with his father at the time, he develops a fear that the same thing could happen to him (an understandable fear given the importance of the penis during the phallic stage of psychosexual development). By *repressing* his desire for the mother and *identifying* with his father (*identification with the aggressor*), he averts the possibility of this terrible event. The fact that few of us have any recollection of this episode was no problem to *Freud*. First of all, he claimed that the whole drama was acted out at an *unconscious* level, and second, when we reach the age of six or so, we develop infantile *amnesia* which causes many of the experiences of the early years to be forgotten.

catastrophe theory: predicts that an increase in arousal beyond an optimal point leads to a dramatic decline in performance. When an athlete goes beyond the optimal point, a large and dramatic decline in performance ensues, a 'catastrophe' from which it is very difficult for them to recover.

catatonic schizophrenia: a form of *schizophrenia* where the person may alternate between a state of rigid immobility and a state of agitated excitement. In the former state, the limbs of the catatonic schizophrenic become stiff for extended periods of time, and they appear extremely apathetic and withdrawn. In the latter state, they typically talk, shout and gaze about in a greatly agitated manner. Nowadays these symptoms are effectively controlled by drug treatments.

catharsis: the expression of formerly *repressed* feelings in order to overcome the problems associated with them. The term is commonly used in connection with *psychodynamic* therapies where it is believed that underlying problems cannot be resolved unless the emotions connected with them are also discharged.

causal attribution: a statement of what we believe caused a particular behaviour. If, for example, you believe that the reason for you passing an examination is the quality of teaching you received, you would be making a causal attribution, attributing your success to the teaching (a *situational attribution*).

causal schemata: an aspect of attribution theory in which a person has a number of preconceived ideas about the sort of things that might lead to a particular effect, or the possible inter-relationships between them. For example, failing an examination might be associated with lack or revision, poor ability, poor teaching and so on. Any one of these might be responsible for the examination failure. With knowledge of the presence of one of these possible causes, the person may discount the role of others (the *discounting principle*).

causation: an important characteristic of scientific psychology, the belief that events do not just happen, they are caused by something else. If we offer one (often simple) cause for an observed event, such as an excess of *dopamine* for *schizophrenia*, this may not adequately reflect the numerous other possible causes that might contribute to the onset of this event. Thus, most psychologists believe in the principle of multiple causes for events, rather than just one single cause.

cause and effect: as above, a belief that a cause can be established for every event. In an *experiment*, the *independent variable* that is manipulated is hypothesised as the cause, and the resultant change in behaviour (the *dependent variable*) is the effect. An absence of cause–effect inferences is often quoted as the major disadvantage of *non-experimental approaches*.

ceiling effect: refers to what might happen if, when behaviour is measured in an *experiment*, the measurement device being used fails to discriminate adequately between the different *participants*. For example, if on a test of mental arithmetic the highest possible score was 50 and nearly all the participants were gaining 49 or 50, the test would obviously be too simple, and the performance of the participants would be constrained by the ceiling (see also *floor effect*).

celebrity (attraction to): most explanations of our attraction to celebrities revolve around the formation of parasocial relationships that we form with celebrities we see regularly on television or in the movies. Evolutionary explanations might emphasise the selective development of skills that enhance survival, including minds prone to creativity and fantasy, which would be favoured through the process of *sexual selection*. As celebrities represent this world of fantasy we become attracted to them.

central coherence deficit: central coherence describes the use of context in processing sensory information. This 'global processing' becomes more important than local, detailed processing when determining the meaning of events. It has been suggested that, in autism, there may be a deficit of central coherence, which causes individuals with autistic disorder to focus more on local detail than on the context of the material. This would explain why many such individuals display skills that require specific and highly detailed attentional processing.

central nervous system (CNS): comprises the *brain* and spinal cord. The CNS is surrounded and protected by cerebrospinal fluid which both supplies nutrients and also cushions the CNS from movements of the skull and spinal column.

central tendency: a typical value in a set of scores, normally calculated as either the *mean*, *median* or *mode*. The nature of the *data* tends to determine which of these measures is the most appropriate to use. The mean might be seen as the most informative measure, in that its calculation makes use of all values, but it does tend to be distorted by the odd unusual score in a set of data (outliers). The median may be used in such cases, or where the data is in the form of ranks. The mode is a crude impression of what is typical in that it is the commonest score in a set of data.

central trait: see *cardinal traits*

centration: a characteristic of the reasoning of young children, in which they focus (or centre) on only one aspect of a problem, and neglect other important features. For example, in the *conservation* of volume, the child may say that water poured into a small, narrow glass increases in volume because they focus only on the height and ignore the fact that this is compensated by the decrease in the diameter of the glass.

cerebellum: the part of the brain whose main function is to co-ordinate muscular activity, without any need for conscious supervision on the individual's part.

cerebral cortex: the convoluted surface of the cerebral hemispheres of the brain. The cortex is divided into four lobes: the frontal, parietal, temporal and occipital lobes.

The part of the cortex that covers the greater surface of the cerebral hemispheres is called the neocortex, so-called because it is part of our more recent evolutionary history. The neocortex can be divided into areas according to their functions. Different parts of the neocortex deal with sensory and motor functions. Association areas in the cortex are involved in the planning of movements (frontal lobes) and in perception and memory (posterior lobes).

chemotherapy: a form of *therapy* where a mental disorder is treated by drugs (chemicals) rather than by psychological, behavioural or any other means. The use of such drugs is based on the belief among some biomedical psychologists that most, if not all, mental or behavioural disorders are caused by a form of chemical imbalance. The use of chemotherapy restores the balance, and, it is reasoned, rids the client of their symptoms. Sometimes these drugs are given as a direct treatment (e.g. *anti-depressants*), sometimes they are used as a 'chemical strait-jacket' whilst other forms of treatment are applied.

child rearing styles: a reference to the distinct ways in which parents interact with their children. Different styles of parenting can be distinguished by the degree to which they are demanding of the child (e.g. setting high standards and demanding obedience to parental authority) and/or responsiveness to the rights and needs of the child:

- authoritative parenting – both demanding and responsive. Parents make reasonable demands for maturity and obedience in the child, but also express warmth and affection and show an appreciation of the rights of the child in decision-making
- authoritarian parenting – demanding but not responsive. Children are expected to obey parents at all times, and parents may resort to punishment if this is not forthcoming. Little regard is given to the needs of the child in this approach
- permissive parenting – responsive but not demanding. Children are given every opportunity for making their own decisions, and parents do not attempt to impose their own rules and routines upon them
- uninvolved parenting – neither responsive nor demanding. Basically a 'hands off' approach to parenting where minimal parental interaction is evident. At its extreme this may border on neglect.

children as witnesses: an area of research interest that examines the credibility of children's memories of traumatic experiences. This area is particularly important when dealing with children's recollections of sexual abuse. Until the 1970s, children's accounts of sexual abuse were generally regarded as unreliable. From the 1980s onwards, the courts have been more willing to accept the accuracy of children's memories of events. Psychological investigations of this difficult area cannot be accomplished using traditional *experimental* methods, but *interview* research has established that children are able to remember events with as much accuracy as adults, but like adults, are susceptible to other factors that influence the accuracy of their recollections. Wade and Tavris (1995) list the following research findings:

- like adults' memories, children's recollections can be influenced by leading and misleading questions
- the recollections of children, like those of adults, are often influenced by their *stereotypes* or preconceptions about people
- children usually know the difference between reality and fantasy, but in emotionally intense situations the boundary may blur
- when children are questioned by adults, they will sometimes give answers that they think the adult wants rather than answers based on their own knowledge of an event
- the emotional tone of an interview can influence the accuracy of the child's report. A coercive or urgent interviewing manner may influence the child to say what they feel the adult wants them to say.

chi-squared test of association: a statistical test which assesses the association between two *variables*. For example, the test may assess whether there is an association between gender and newspaper preference, or whether any observed tendencies for men to buy one type of paper and women another is simply due to chance.

Chomsky, N (1928–): a *psycholinguist* who proposed that human beings have an innate ability for *language*. Language acquisition is facilitated by the *language acquisition device*, or LAD, which operates on the speech that we hear as infants. Chomsky believed that the LAD was pre-programmed with the universal rules of grammar. By hearing speech in a specific language (such as English), the LAD is able to extract from its universal rules those which are appropriate for that language. Chomsky suggested that children quickly develop transformational rules which enable them to extract the same meaning (deep structure) from different word orders (surface structure). For example, in the sentences 'The dog chased the boy' and 'The boy was chased by the dog', the surface structures are different, but the deep structures are the same.

chromosome abnormalities: normally arise when there is an extra **chromosome** or a chromosome missing. An example of a disorder where there is a chromosome missing is Turner's syndrome, where there is only one sex chromosome, an X chromosome, and an absence of ovaries. Normal **secondary sexual characteristics** develop, but the person remains sterile. An example of a disorder where there is an extra chromosome is **Down's syndrome** (or Trisomy 21), where there are three chromosomes instead of two at the 21st pair.

chromosomes carry our genes. Human beings have 46 chromosomes in each cell, arranged in 23 pairs, of which 22 are the **autosomes** and one is the sex-linked X or Y chromosome. During fertilisation, when the male chromosomes in the sperm combine with the female chromosomes in the ovum, an XX arrangement will produce a female and an XY a male.

chronic schizophrenia: a diagnostic label used for a pattern of **schizophrenia** which has lasted for a considerable period of time without showing significant improvement after therapy or treatment.

chronological age: a child's actual age. This is sometimes divided into their **mental age** in order to calculate an **intelligence quotient** or **IQ**.

chunking: a method of increasing the **capacity** of **short-term memory** by combining units of information (usually numbers) into chunks. Impressive feats of memory can then result. For example, the numbers 3, 5, 2, 7, 5, 8, 5, 1, 0, 4, 3, 9 would normally overload our short-term memory (see **magic number seven (plus or minus 2)**), but if they are arranged into chunks 352, 758, 510, 439, they become a lot more manageable.

circadian rhythm: a 24-hour cycle which shows a repeating pattern of physical changes. Research has shown that many biological functions conform to this daily cycle, including sleep/waking, temperature, hormone secretion and blood pressure. If an organism is isolated from the normal **cues** of light and dark, they are still able to maintain their circadian rhythm with remarkable accuracy. The pervasive influence of these rhythms means that variations in working patterns, such as in shift work, create problems of adjustment that may cause significant performance decrements in the initial stages of the shift period. These rhythms are controlled by the body's biological clock which is most probably located in the **hypothalamus**. The night-and-day cycle keeps the clock regulated, but is not necessary to drive it.

clairvoyance: the ability to perceive objects or events even though they do not directly stimulate the sensory organs. Being able to describe what is inside a sealed envelope would be an example of clairvoyance.

classical conditioning: also known as Pavlovian conditioning after Ivan Pavlov, who is generally credited with discovering it, this is an explanation of **learning** in which one **stimulus** or event comes to predict the occurrence of another stimulus or event.

What is actually learned in classical conditioning is a new association between an originally neutral stimulus (NS) and an existing response. Using the 'language' of the classical conditioning *paradigm*, the neutral stimulus is paired with a stimulus (the unconditional stimulus, or UCS) that already produces the response in question (the unconditional response or UCR). With repeated presentations of the neutral stimulus and the unconditional stimulus, the neutral stimulus (now known as the conditional stimulus, or CS) takes on the properties of the unconditioned stimulus and is now able to produce the same response (although this is referred to as the conditional response, or CR). We may think of the UCS–UCR association as being a natural one, and the CS–CR association as a learned one that has come about because of the association between the new and the old stimuli. For example, we normally salivate when we have food in our mouths. This is a *reflex* action that aids the digestion of food. If something precedes the food (a dinner bell perhaps), we may eventually end up salivating to the sound of the bell. In this example, the bell would be the neutral stimulus, the food in the mouth the unconditional stimulus and the salivation the unconditional response.

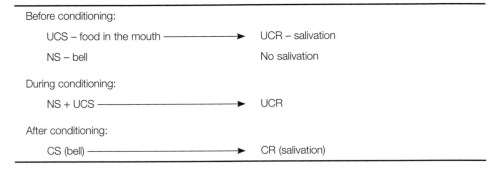

The order in which the NS and the UCS are paired together is important. The most effective learning comes about if the NS precedes the UCS and it is weaker if they occur simultaneously. In some cases, conditioning may take place if the NS occurs after the UCS, but this normally disappears quite quickly. The most important aspect of the conditional stimulus is that it helps the organism to predict the coming of the unconditional stimulus. This is most effectively accomplished when it occurs before, rather than at the same time as or after the UCS. Because the CS–CR association is an acquired one, it can also be lost if the CS no longer predicts the coming of the UCS. If the bell were constantly being rung without being followed by the presentation of food, the association would be extinguished. If the bell is then rung again some time in the future, we may salivate a little (spontaneous recovery), but if the whole procedure (CS + UCS, etc.) is repeated, learning will now be much more rapid than it was previously. Once an organism is conditioned to respond to one CS, they may then show the same response to similar stimuli (stimulus generalisation). This might be seen as a safety feature of learning. The more alike two stimuli are the more likely that the same response would be appropriate. When this is not appropriate, organisms can be trained to respond to only one of a class of similar stimuli (stimulus discrimination).

class inclusion: the relation between two classes in which all members of one class are included in the other, as in the proposition 'All students are humans'. This skill is not as simple as it sounds. *Piaget* used a hypothetical scenario in which a child says to his three sisters 'a portion of my flowers is yellow', and the task was to identify the colour of his bunch of flowers. Children were then asked which of the following three answers was correct –

(1) all your flowers are yellow; (2) none of your flowers is yellow; or (3) some of your flowers are yellow. Many of the children and adolescents asked picked the first answer, thus making the wrong inference based on the information they were given. Class-inclusion tasks such as this one were regarded by Piaget as a measure of the child's grasp of hierarchical classification.

claustrophobia: an unreasonable and intense fear of closed spaces such as lifts, small rooms and other confined spaces. It is one of a class of phobic disorders known as specific phobias (see *phobic disorders (phobias)*).

client-centred therapy: see *person-centred therapy*

clinical interview: a research method in which the interviewer uses flexible and open-ended questions to probe the way in which a participant reasons about something. Because of the flexibility of the technique, it is able to extract a great deal of information from the participant, and because of its probing sensitivity, it can uncover insights into the participant's reasoning that would be less likely to be uncovered using other methods. Because of the flexible questioning procedures, each interview tends to be unique, the interviewer being guided by the responses of the participant. This means that it is difficult, even inappropriate, to compare the responses of one participant directly with the responses of another.

clinical psychologist: a psychologist who has completed post-graduate training in the assessment and treatment of psychological problems, and also completed a period of supervised clinical practice.

clinical psychology: that area of psychology that deals with the assessment and treatment of abnormal or maladaptive behaviour.

cluster sampling: a particularly economical way of selecting participants for an investigation. A hall of residence, or members of one specific town might be considered sufficiently representative that researchers can draw their 'clusters' from these groups, trying to include as many people from the group as possible.

CNS: see *central nervous system (CNS)*

coaching effectiveness training: training people in how to create a coaching environment that promotes both enhanced performance and psychological growth of athletes.

co-action effect: refers to the effect produced when people work alongside each other on the same task. When people work together in this way, they use each other as a *social comparison* to evaluate their own performance. This comparison may lead to increased attention to performance in order to compete, thus producing a *social facilitation* effect (see also *social loafing*).

cocktail party effect: a term used in early *attention* research to describe the ability of people to be able to switch their attention rapidly to a non-processed message. This posed great problems for the early 'single-channel' models of attention which suggested that rejected messages would be lost before any significant processing took place. The cocktail party effect showed that certain types of stimuli would elicit this switching between messages (such as the physical location of the speaker, the pitch of the voice or the use of familiar stimuli such as the listener's name). As a result of findings such as this, the *attenuator model of attention* was developed. This proposed that all stimuli are processed, but rejected stimuli are processed in a weakened form. Note that as few students go to cocktail parties nowadays, some textbooks have renamed this effect as the 'lunch-queue effect'.

codes of language: see *restricted code*

codes of practice: a reference to the ethical guidelinespublished by psychological organisations such as the *BPS* and the *APA*. These contain prescriptive advice on the conduct of psychologists in research and practice. The codes of practice reflect those issues that are seen as most important within the context of cultural, religious and professional concerns, and are constantly updated to reflect the changing priorities within the society in which they are used. Each country has its own code of practice, although in Europe, there is a move towards developing a common code that reflects the priorities of member states.

coding systems: usually used in *qualitative research*, a coding system is a way of *operationalising* a particular behaviour or behaviours. For example, in an *observational* study of shyness (Asendorpf et al, 2002), six distinct behaviours were coded as manifestations of shyness. These included speech duration, gaze aversion and bodily tension.

coercive power: refers to the power that one person has over others because they have the power to punish them for non-compliance. This type of social power can be found wherever the behaviour of a person is influenced by the threat of punishment from someone else.

cognition: any thought, attitude or belief about the world around us. When used in *cognitive dissonance* theory, it may also refer to a perception about a behaviour.

cognitive-affective stress model: a model of stress management that takes into consideration the stressful nature of the situation, the stressed person's cognitive appraisal of the situation (i.e. feelings and thoughts), physiological responses, and behaviour.

cognitive behavioural therapy: an approach to the treatment of psychological disorders which combines cognitive and behavioural techniques. For example, in the treatment of *anxiety disorders*, therapists might use *habituation* training. In this technique, clients might be asked to call their *obsessive* thoughts to mind for a prolonged period. With such intensified exposure to the threatening thoughts, they gradually lose their ability to cause anxiety, and so fewer obsessive thoughts (and their related *compulsive* acts) are present in the future.

cognitive consistency theories are theories of *attitude* organisation that have as their central theme the fact that people strive for consistency in what they believe, the attitudes that they possess and the way in which they act. Any inconsistency (such as doing something you don't believe in) produces an unpleasant feeling (*cognitive dissonance*) which the individual is motivated to reduce by changing (in this example) either the attitude or the behaviour in order to restore consistency.

cognitive dissonance: an unpleasant feeling which arises when two or more of our *cognitions* are inconsistent. The main causes of cognitive dissonance are as follows:

- when two attitudes are inconsistent in some way such as, 'I like this person' and 'I don't like this person's political views'
- when people say or do things they don't mean, or behave in ways that are inconsistent with their underlying attitudes, perhaps arguing the merits of vegetarianism then ordering a beefburger at the local burger bar, for example (*counter-attitudinal behaviour*).

The weaker the reasons for the person behaving in this attitude-discrepant way, the greater will be their experience of dissonance, and the stronger will be their motivation to alter the underlying attitude in order to restore the consistency between attitude and behaviour. For example, the burger-eating vegetarian might have had plenty of choice in what to eat, but chose a burger (a weak reason) or was forced at gunpoint to eat it (strong reason). The former is more likely to cause dissonance than the latter. As an explanation of attitude change, cognitive dissonance theory argues that doing things that are inconsistent with our attitudes may cause us to change those attitudes to overcome the negative feelings of dissonance.

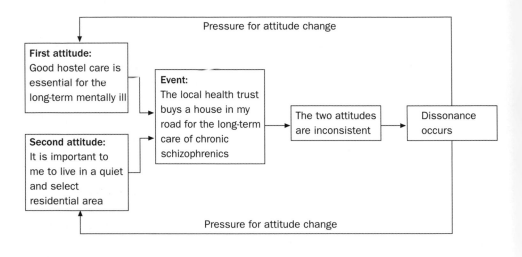

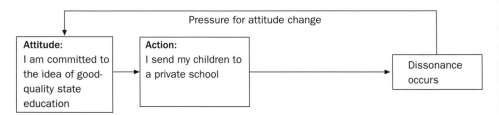

Cognitive dissonance. Two examples of change as a result of cognitive dissonance

cognitive evaluation theory: associated with Deci (1975), this theory attempted to explain the relationship between external rewards and intrinsic motivation. The theory describes two main ways in which such rewards affect intrinsic motivation. First, the reward may be perceived as the primary reason why an individual participates in a given activity (i.e. a controlling aspect). Second, an external reward may also have an informational aspect that affects individuals' opinions of their own competence (i.e. whether they are 'doing it right'). Most rewards have both a controlling aspect and an informational aspect. The combined effects of these two aspects may either increase or decrease an individual's intrinsic motivation. External rewards that have mainly a controlling aspect tend to decrease intrinsic motivation.

cognitive interview: this was first developed in the USA in the 1980s and represented the alliance of two different fields of study within psychology applied to the problem of eyewitness testimony. Insights about managing face-to-face interaction from social psychology were combined with insights from cognitive psychology concerning how we remember things.

The cognitive interview incorporates a number of different cognitive strategies that have quite distinct theoretical bases.

- It is assumed that a retrieval cue will be more effective if there is an overlap between it and the encoded information. Based on the *encoding* specificity principle, the cognitive interview encourages witnesses to recreate the original encoding context so as to increase the accessibility of stored information.
- Because our memories are made up of a network of associations rather than discrete and unconnected events, there are a number of ways that these memories can be accessed. The cognitive interview exploits this by using multiple retrieval strategies – witnesses may be asked to recall information from different starting points (beginning, middle, end, backwards as well as forwards).
- According to *schema* theory, familiar events have a schema (or script) that guides the encoding of an event by organising information into a hierarchy of slots. A witness's prior expectations may allow them to fill some empty slots with 'default' (or anticipated) information. Recall, according to this theory, is prone to the inclusion of information that is assumed on the basis of prior expectations. This gives us a way of explaining errors and *confabulations* (inserted details) during recall.

More recent developments of the cognitive interview have tended to transfer the *control* of the interview to the witness, using the witness's replies as a basis for subsequent questioning. This 'enhanced' version of the cognitive interview also encourages witnesses to create an image of the scene during questioning. Interviewers then probe this image, focusing on the witness's explicit memory of the event. This enhanced version of the cognitive interview has been extensively evaluated in a number of countries, including the UK. Research studies suggest significant increases in recall over eyewitness accounts without the aid of cognitive interviewing procedures. However, recent research suggests that, particularly with children, this increase may be achieved together with a significant number of confabulations.

cognitive labelling theory proposes that *stimuli* provoke non-specific *arousal* that is cognitively labelled on the basis of situational cues (i.e. knowledge about the context of the emotional event). An emotional experience requires both autonomic arousal and a relevant cognition about the environment. A particular emotion cannot be ascribed to the effects of physiological arousal alone. Nor can an emotional experience be triggered by the mere presence of an environmental event. However, the combination of sympathetic arousal and an appropriate environmental situation can produce a complete emotional reaction.

The results of research in this area add a new dimension to understanding the effects of drugs that are designed to stabilise emotions or reduce anxiety. The effects of these drugs could be either on the central interpretation of the environment (i.e., the cognition) or on the peripheral arousal aspects. It is very likely that the autonomic stabilising effects play an important role in changing an individual's interpretation of the environment. It is possible that an individual whose autonomic nervous system has been stabilised by an anti-anxiety drug may conclude that the situation is not anxiety provoking because there is little autonomic arousal.

cognitive map: a term used to describe the belief that an animal is able to develop and internalise a spatial representation of its immediate location. This was in contrast to the *behaviourist* belief that animals such as rats were only able to learn their way through a maze because they were being **reinforced** for making the right responses. Evidence from experiments demonstrating **latent learning** does seem to support this notion.

cognitive processes: those aspects of mental 'behaviour' that involve the manipulation of material in an abstract way. The term is usually used to refer to operations such as **thinking, memory** and **perception.**

cognitive psychology: that branch of psychology that attempts to study and understand the way in which **cognitive processes** work. Cognitive psychologists use such knowledge to explain many aspects of our everyday behaviour, from traffic accidents (**perception** and **attentional** explanations) to study skills (**memory** explanations).

cognitive rational non-adherence: an explanation of why some people decide not to adhere to prescribed medical treatment. Sometimes the side effects of a treatment can be so unpleasant or undesirable that the patient decides, quite rationally, not to proceed with the treatment. For example, Bulpitt (1988) found that a number of men taking a drug for hypertension experienced increased sexual problems (e.g. impotence) as a side effect and so as a result discontinued their treatment.

cognitive restructuring therapy: a form of cognitive therapy in which the therapist helps the patient to recognise, challenge and change cognitive distortions and negative thought patterns. Repetitive practice with this exercise trains people to become aware of and reject cognitive errors that creep into their thoughts, causing them to become depressed.

cognitive science: any scientific discipline that studies the human mind and how it might work. It includes computer models of thought, **artificial intelligence (AI)**, linguistics and neuropsychology among others.

cognitive skills programmes: any programme designed to change the way that individuals think or solve problems, with the aim of making them more effective members of society. For example, it is assumed that the thinking skills of an offender, including ways of reasoning and solving problems, is an important factor in his or her criminal behaviour (see **criminal thinking patterns**). The use of cognitive skills programmes in this context is designed to change these characteristic patterns of thinking and, consequently, reduce repeat offending.

cognitive styles: a term used to describe the different and characteristic ways in which individuals think, perceive and remember information, or their preferred approach to using information to solve problems.

cognitive therapies: any of a group of therapies that are based on the assumption that people's emotions and behaviour are heavily influenced by the way they reason about their experiences. By giving people insight into their faulty thought patterns, they are able to change the way they think and thus eliminate their problems. Rational-emotive therapy, as developed by Albert Ellis, is based on the idea that people's emotional and behavioural disorders develop because of their irrational beliefs. The therapist confronts the client about these irrational beliefs as they appear in therapy, and directs them into more effective styles of thinking and acting. Aaron Beck's cognitive therapy is commonly used for the treatment of **depression** and **anxiety disorders**. It assumes that these psychological disorders develop because of irrational thinking, which Beck calls 'cognitive distortions'. The therapist attempts to make the client aware of their distorted and irrational thinking, and shows them how to substitute more constructive patterns of thinking and behaving.

cohesion: a term commonly used when talking about groups, it refers to the tendency of group members to 'stick together' with relation to important issues such as rules, behaviours or general camaraderie. There is a belief that the more cohesive a group, the happier and ultimately the more effective and influential the group will be on its members.

cohort effects: children born within the same cultural or historical conditions will show similarities of thought and behaviour that can be directly attributed to the common cultural-historical influences. For example, a study of the social development of adolescents would yield quite different results if it were to compare adolescents growing up in the 1940s, 1960s and 1980s because of the significant differences between those periods.

coincidence: if two events happen at about the same time, we may (wrongly) assume that one event has caused the other. This may be explained in terms of probability misjudgement – some people have a greater desire for causal explanations for coincidences because they believe that such events are not likely to co-occur by chance. For some people, a causal explanation for coincidental events may provide them with a sense of order in their world and increase their feelings of control.

cold-parenting: an early (and largely discredited) view of the causes of autism. Autism was thought to be a developmental consequence of being raised in an environment where parents were cold, rigid and rejecting toward the child.

collective unconscious: a term usually attributed to Carl *Jung*, and meaning that part of a person's unconscious that is common to all members of their race. It is supposedly inherited and contains the remnants of our ancestral past.

collectivism: a type of social arrangement where the good of the group is considered more important than the good of the individual. In a comparison of 53 different national and regional *cultures*, Hofstede (1983) found that the cultures that demonstrated most evidence of collectivism were Guatemala, Ecuador and Panama, whereas the countries that demonstrated the most evidence of *individualism* were Australia, the USA and Great Britain.

colour blindness: an inherited defect whereby a person is unable to distinguish between two or more colours. Trichromats have normal colour vision, dichromats are unable to distinguish between two colours (either red-green or blue-yellow), and monochromats have total colour blindness. Of the different kinds of colour blindness, red-green dichromacy is the commonest. Colour blindness is a sex-linked genetic *trait* and affects far more males than it does females.

colour constancy: the tendency for a familiar colour to maintain its colour even though the viewing conditions have changed. We may recognise our own car as maintaining its colour at night whereas the ones around it tend to lose theirs.

common-sense psychology: a set of views shared by 'ordinary folk' that are the product of sound reasoning and logic. Common-sense theories tend not to be tested against reality in the same way that psychologists might test their own predictions and are frequently contradictory ('out of sight, out of mind' and 'absence makes the heart grow fonder' are two popular examples). There is also a popular belief that all psychology is common sense. Psychologists, however, frequently turn up findings that are counter-intuitive and could not have been predicted by relying on common sense.

common traits: a characteristic found in all members of a *culture*. Although such traits are possible, it is more likely that we attribute common traits to members of another culture in the form of cultural *stereotypes*.

communication network: this may be either physical or organisational and determine the distribution of communication within a group. In the 'wheel', for example, all members on the periphery of the group must communicate through a central person, whereas in the 'all-channel' network, any person can communicate with any other without relying on their message going through an intermediary.

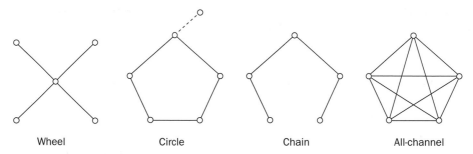

| Wheel | Circle | Chain | All-channel |

Some communication networks

companionate love: feelings of love and affection that are based on mutual attraction, respect, friendship and general concern for each other's interests and feelings.

comparative psychology: in the strictest definition of the term, comparative psychology is the study of non-human animals with a view to drawing insights and comparisons concerning the behaviour of human beings. This does draw on a very wide range of different academic approaches, including ethology, learning theory and sociobiology. Note that to be truly comparative the emphasis of the approach should be on the comparisons that may be drawn with humans. However, much of the academic study of this area at A-level tends to stress the study of non-human animals in their own right, an area more accurately referred to as animal behaviour.

competence: an *ethical* requirement by which all psychologists must ensure that they work within their limits of competence. This also necessitates referring people who may seek advice to those better able to provide it.

competition by exploitation: an arrangement among animals competing for resources whereby competitors are distributed between different habitats according to the quality of resources available in each. Imagine two separate habitats. One has more resources (food for example) than the other. Assuming that there is no aggression or territorial limitation, animals that are free to choose would choose the better habitat. The resources in this habitat would gradually become depleted as they were shared among more and more individuals. At this point, any new animals would be better off choosing the poorer habitat where, despite the fact that the resources are in shorter supply, there is less competition and therefore more to go around. Theoretically the two different habitats would be filled in such a way as to ensure that each animal has the same resources regardless of which habitat they are in.

competition for resources: refers to an inference that might be drawn from Darwin's theory of *natural selection*. Darwin believed that all species had the potential for producing far more offspring than would ever be able to survive, yet population sizes remain more or less stable over time. Given that resources (such as food, mates or nesting sites) are limited, he believed that animals must compete for access to them. Those who were successful in attaining those resources would be able to reproduce more successfully than those who were less able to accumulate resources.

complex: when used in its psychopathological sense, this term refers to a cluster of ideas or dispositions that carry with them a certain emotional investment. In other words, the person who possesses a particular complex gets 'hung up' on the ideas or feelings that characterise the complex, and experiences some degree of emotional disturbance as they attempt to deal with them. The most well known (to students of psychology) are the **Oedipus complex** and **Electra complex**. The best known (to non-psychology students) is the inferiority complex, a term coined by Alfred Adler.

compliance: a form of *social influence* in which one person attempts to influence another in order to get them to comply with a request. This may take several forms:
- ingratiation – we attempt to make ourselves more attractive to another so that they will be more likely to let us have what we want. For example, many people apply flattery liberally when trying to get around somebody else
- multiple requests, such as the **foot in the door** and the **door in the face techniques.** In the former, a small request is followed by a larger request. In the latter, a large request is followed by a smaller request (as a climb down)
- the 'that's not all' technique, where (normally) a seller will add extras to a deal before the recipient has made up their mind whether to buy. This is common practice in market trading, where quite fantastic deals seem to be put together before our eyes, thus magnifying the bargain. ('There's the full dinner service and the casserole dishes and the free tea set and that's not all....')

compulsion: repetitive behaviours which the individual feels compelled to perform in order to stop something terrible from happening. The connection between the compulsive behaviour and its apparent purpose tends to be unreasonable and the behaviour tends to be excessive in itself. To the person with the compulsion, however, despite the fact they may be aware of this fact, the act must be performed with great regularity, otherwise there will be dire consequences. The compulsive behaviour does relieve anxiety for a short while, but no other pleasure is derived from the performance of the act itself.

computed tomography (CT) involves moving an X-ray source in a circular arc around a patient's head. At each position a small amount of X-ray radiation passes through the head. The amount of this radiation that is absorbed depends upon the density of the brain tissue. A ring of detectors opposite the X-ray source analyses the amount of radiation that has passed through the head. The X-ray source and detectors are then moved to a new position, and in this way a composite picture can be built up of the brain through an amalgamation of horizontal sections.

computer analogies: within cognitive psychology, information processing models, such as the **multi-store model of memory**, were influenced by analogies with the working of computers. Parallels have been drawn between the workings of the human mind and the information processing of a computer. For example, like the human mind, a computer is not restricted to carrying out just one specific function. It can, in principle, carry out any instruction that its human programmer can specify exactly, the only limitation being the time it may take or the amount of storage space available.

computerised axial tomograms (CAT): see *computed tomography (CT)*

conative: a mental process, specifically part of an attitudinal process, that is to do with movement or volition. When applied to *attitudes,* it refers to that part of the attitude that predisposes us to act in a certain way. For example, if we are prejudiced against America and Americans, we are unlikely to want to go there for our holidays.

concept: an internal representation of something. For example, we may understand the concept of honesty if we can somehow represent that idea to ourselves. Infants are said to have the object concept when they understand that an object continues to exist even when it is out of sight.

concordance: the degree to which two things are in agreement or harmony. Examples would include agreement of opinion between two people, or perhaps the *genetic* similarity between two individuals. Concordance studies use individuals of known genetic similarity (for example, *monozygotic twins*; father–son; first cousins; etc.) and tests for their similarity in other areas such as *intelligence* or *personality*. In this way it is possible to obtain an idea of the genetic influence on these areas of functioning.

concrete operational thought: see *Piaget, J*

concurrent validity: see *validity*

conditional positive regard: see *unconditional positive regard*

conditional reinforcer: see *secondary reinforcement*

conditional response: see *classical conditioning*

conditional stimulus: see *classical conditioning*

conditioning: see *classical* and *operant conditioning*

conditions of worth: a term used by *humanistic* psychologist *Carl Rogers* to describe social influences on the self-concept. Rogers believed that it is crucial for children to receive positive regard – affection and approval – from the important people in their lives, particularly their parents. However, Rogers believed that this regard is often conditional, i.e. it comes with strings attached. For example, for children to be loved and approved of, they must be well mannered, quiet, boyish, girlish or whatever. These characteristics, which lead to the desired approval, become the child's conditions of worth. If these are severely limiting then the process of *self-actualisation* will be severely impeded. Children's conditions of worth come to control more and more of their behaviour as they begin to apply them to themselves. Rogers referred to the pattern of self-acceptance and self-rejection based on conditions of worth as conditional self-regard.

conduct disorders: a diagnostic classification for a wide variety of different behaviours (such as destructive behaviour and theft) that are expressed frequently and with intensity. Thus, while telling the odd lie may be considered wrong, it is not really indicative of an underlying conduct disorder. However, persistently telling large and often malicious lies may be. There is some evidence that conduct disorders may be transmitted *genetically*, although there is also a large body of evidence that abnormal family circumstances and the effects of parental discord and divorce also have a strong impact on their development. Conduct disorders are primarily disorders of childhood and adolescence, and in adulthood may develop into an *anti-social personality disorder.*

cones: the receptor cells in the *retina* that enable us to see colour. The majority of our cones are found in the *fovea*, with a thinner scattering over the periphery of the *retina*. Because of the higher threshold (compared to the monochromatic rods) of cones, they only operate under good light conditions. Cones enable us to maximise our visual acuity (the sharpness of our vision) and we automatically fixate on a point in such a way as to focus the light from that point onto the fovea. As we move the point of fixation away from the fovea we bring about a corresponding decrease in visual acuity.

confabulation: the *conscious* or sometimes *unconscious* process by which we fill in gaps in our memory of an event. This has led many psychologists to believe that memory is essentially reconstructive, in that we add, delete or change aspects of a memory so that it makes sense to us.

confederates: those people who take part in a piece of *research* who are not real *participants*, but who are playing a part in order to elicit some behaviour from the real participants in the study. In Asch's famous work on *conformity*, confederates were used to create the false majority effect, and the real participants were then studied to see how they reacted to this. The term 'stooge' is also used to describe this role in a research study.

confidentiality: an *ethical* requirement of both *research* and *therapy*, in which *participants* or clients have the right to expect that information gathered during the research or therapy session will not be made public without their consent. This is not quite as simple as it sounds when applied to therapeutic situations. Therapists believe that without the client's belief that sessions will remain confidential, they cannot be as open with their thoughts and feelings, and some of the benefits of therapy will be lost. However, therapists working in the UK are obliged to let their clients know at the outset of the therapy session that they must pass on any information that for legal reasons cannot stay confidential to that session.

conflict: a term that has a very wide variety of uses in psychology, but generally refers to any situation where the organism (person or animal) experiences antagonistic feelings or impulses. For example, a person may experience a conflict over whether to approach an attractive stranger at a party (and risk rejection) or whether to stay in the safety of their friends (and lose the opportunity). This is referred to as the *approach-avoidance* conflict. The term may also be used in its Freudian sense, where the most famous of the Freudian-inspired conflicts is the *Oedipus complex*.

conformity (majority influence): a form of *social influence* which results from exposure to the opinions of a majority. The term is often used in a seemingly negative way, as if conformity were an unthinking acquiescence to the views of a deviant majority. Recognising and acting within the *pro-social norms* of a group may be seen as a desirable act; unthinking conformity to a deviant group opinion may be considered less so. The two major reasons why people appear to conform are because of:

- normative influence – we conform in order to belong, to be liked and to be approved of by others
- informational influence – we conform because of uncertainty and out of a desire to be correct.

The most famous studies of conformity were carried out in the 1950s by Solomon Asch. To this day, any situation which involves a majority exerting its effect on the opinions of an aberrant individual is known as the Asch effect. Asch found that when faced with a majority opinion, individuals showed a tendency to contradict the evidence of their own senses and agree with the majority. Later research showed that the tendency to conform dropped sharply under certain circumstances, such as if the individual was joined by another who shared the minority opinion.

We should, perhaps, distinguish between public **compliance** (doing or saying what those around us do and say) and private acceptance (changing our underlying attitudes and beliefs). What often happens in both experimental studies of conformity and also in real-life conformity is that we comply with the wishes of others without actually changing what we really believe (normative influence). Some critics argue that conformity research is rooted in a particular cultural and historical context. The need to conform, they claim, would not be as great today (see also **innovation (minority influence)**).

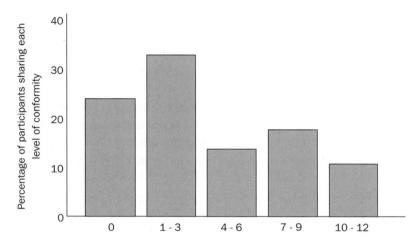

The major findings from Asch's research. Participants were required to report aloud which three lines were the same as a reference line. On twelve of the eighteen trials, the other participants (accomplices of the experimenter) unanimously gave the wrong answer. If the single naïve participant joined them in giving the same wrong answer, they were said to have conformed

confounding variables: refers to the possible influence of other uncontrolled factors on the behaviour being measured (the **dependent variable**) in an experiment. For example, a study some years ago established a body strength difference between Catholics and non-Catholics. Close examination of the experimental procedures showed that this difference could be put down not to religious affiliation or the athleticism of the Catholic mass, but to occupational differences in the participants used (the Catholic participants were all taken from a **population** of motorway construction workers who just happened to be building a motorway close to the university concerned ... !). In this example, occupation was seen as the confounding variable.

congenital means present at birth. The term is often (wrongly) used synonymously with the term **innate**, yet need not imply that something is inherited. If the foetus is exposed to a harmful influence whilst still in the womb, it may be born with a congenital malformation.

conscience: a set of moral principles that guide us in our decisions regarding right and wrong. In Freudian theory, the conscience is, specifically, that part of the **superego** which is the internalised abstraction of parental *control* which punishes errant behaviour with feelings of guilt or shame.

conscious: see *consciousness*

consciousness: in the most general sense of the word, this refers to a state of awareness that is felt or experienced by the individual, yet is hidden from others. The term is used in more specialist ways by different theorists:

- in *cognitive psychology* it is interpreted as a form of *attention*
- in the *psychoanalytic* theory of Sigmund *Freud*, consciousness is the level at which the *ego* operates, and is the rational, decision-making part of the mind. The preconscious, on the other hand, is that part of the mind which contains information of which we are unaware. We could, however, change the status of this information by directing our attention towards it, i.e. we would bring it into *consciousness.* The *unconscious* mind contains material that we can access with only the greatest difficulty, if at all. Part of the reason for this is that it has been *repressed* into the unconscious, so we are motivated to keep it there.

The important functions of consciousness include the monitoring of ourselves and our environment, and the sifting of important from unimportant information. From the information we gather during this monitoring process, we are able to engage in the conscious planning of our behaviour. In this function, consciousness has an important role in our survival.

consensus refers to our knowledge of the attitudes or behaviour of others. If we discover that most people feel or behave in the same way that we do with respect to some object or issue, then we experience high consensus. If we stand alone in that most people have different attitudes or actions, then we experience low consensus. Within *attribution* theory we are more likely to make a *situational attribution* if we experience high consensus. Even if we do not have this information, there is still a tendency to assume that people similar to ourselves will think and act in the same way as ourselves (the *false consensus bias*).

consent: an *ethical* requirement which demands that all participants or clients should agree to the procedures which are to take place. Within a research context this also implies that participants should be free to withdraw from the study at any time without undue pressure being put upon them to continue. A key issue in this consideration is whether the participants or clients have sufficient information about the procedures, and understand that information when giving their informed consent. We might assume that if someone were to volunteer for an *experiment*, they would be doing so because they knew exactly what was going to happen to them.

This is not necessarily the case. Some research studies have found that only about one third of *participants* volunteering for an experiment really understand what is involved. If we were to extend this reasoning to *therapy* and treatment, the problem of informed consent becomes even more worrying. Failure to fully understand the nature and consequences of a psychological treatment may be due to a number of different factors. These would include the inability of the client to make a balanced judgement of the possible costs and benefits of the treatment being offered, and also the fact that for some therapies to be fully effective, all aspects cannot be explained to the client in advance. The therapist must strike a balance between providing appropriate information to the client about the type of treatment and creating appropriate conditions for it to be effective.

conservation: the understanding that the physical characteristics (such as weight, volume, etc.) of objects remain the same even though the appearance of them may change. This is a characteristic of pre-operational reasoning in *Piaget's* theory of intellectual development. For example, a child is shown two rows of coins. There is an equal number of coins in each row, and they are evenly spaced. One row is then spaced out, and the pre–operational child claims that there are now more coins in that row than in the other. Conservation failure demonstrates a number of characteristics of the pre-operational child's reasoning:

- it is perceptually based rather than logically based. They are distracted by the fact that something looks different, and do not appear to grasp that logically it cannot be different
- they are liable to **centration**, focusing on only one aspect of the problem, and neglecting to take into account other important features that would affect the outcome
- by focusing on the end results of conservation, they see them as unrelated rather than a transformation of one to the other. The two rows of coins in the example below are seen as different rows of coins rather than the same one transformed
- they lack reversibility, in other words, the inability of the child to mentally reverse an operation (i.e. move the coins back together).

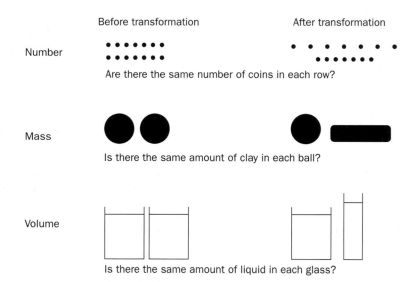

Some examples of conservation problems

conspecific: any animal that is a member of the same species as the animal to which it is being compared. For example, my cats are conspecifics of my neighbour's cat.

constancy: the tendency for familiar objects to give rise to the same perceptual experiences despite changes in the viewing conditions. Thus, an opening door will continue to appear rectangular, despite the fact that the stimulus that falls upon our *retina* is transformed from the original rectangular shape to a trapezoidal shape (*shape constancy*). See also *colour constancy* and *size constancy*.

construct: in its most common usage in psychology it refers to something that cannot be observed directly but is assumed to exist on the basis of some observable behaviour. An example is the notion of *intelligence*, which is assumed to exist in that it would then explain differences in intelligent behaviour between individuals.

constructive theories of perception are explanations of *perception* that are essentially top-down in nature. Perception is seen as a set of constructions that enable the perceiver to make sense of the sensory input they receive. This is accomplished through inferences and guesses based on previous experience and memories. Although there are differences in the various constructive theories, they share the following assumptions about the perceptual process:
- perception is both active and constructive
- perception is not the direct equivalent of sensory data. This is the basis for expectations and hypotheses about what is being experienced
- because of the necessity of *hypothesis* and inference, perception is prone to error. Perceptual illusions arise when we apply our previous knowledge and expectations inappropriately to the sensory input received.

This last assumption is one of the main weaknesses of the approach. That is, perception is usually accurate, therefore sensory data must carry a great deal more information than might be anticipated in this approach.

construct validity: see *validity*

content analysis: a general term, which refers to the fact that sometimes people are not studied directly, but indirectly, through what they produce (political speeches, literary works and so on). It is possible to obtain some understanding of a person's psychological state or perhaps evidence of some more general behaviour within a culture by looking closely at the content of such artefacts. A detailed examination of the speeches of ex-president of the USA, Ronald Reagan, gave psychologists evidence of the speech errors typically associated with the progressive mental disorder Alzheimer's disease. Similarly, an analysis of television advertisements may give us interesting insights into gender *stereotyping*.

context dependency: the tendency to encode features of the immediate environment in which a stimulus is learned or perceived. Subsequent presentation of these contextual cues may trigger the memory or vice-versa.

contingency theory of leadership refers to an explanation of the effectiveness of a leader being determined both by the leader's *traits* and the features of the situation. This theory proposes that leaders who rate their least preferred co-worker (LPC) in negative terms (lazy, incompetent, etc.) are more concerned with task accomplishment than with relations with the people that work under them. They are referred to as Low LPC leaders. High LPC leaders, on the other hand, remember their LPC in more favourable terms which betrays more of an interest in maintaining good relations with those with whom they work. The extent to which either of these leadership styles is effective in a given task situation depends on the amount of situational *control* evident in the task. Situational control is measured along three dimensions:
- the amount of support the leader receives from the followers. The more the support, the better the relations between leader and follower
- the degree of structure in the task – measured by the extent to which everyone knows what they are trying to achieve and how they are going to achieve it

- the position of power of the leader, demonstrated by their ability to enforce co-operation and compliance in the followers.

The situational control in a given task varies from high (good relations with followers, highly structured task, high position power of the leader) to low (poor relations, unstructured task and low position power). Low LPC leaders are more effective when situational control is either high or low. High LPC leaders, on the other hand, appear more effective when situational control is only moderate.

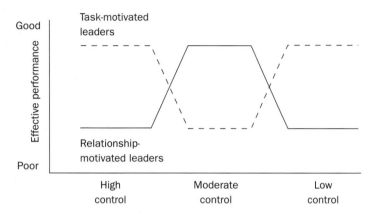

Situational control and performance of leaders

control: a person's actual ability to anticipate and influence events that might occur in his or her environment, as well the perception that one is able to control those events when they do happen. Stress occurs as a result of an interaction between the perceived demands of the environment and the individual's perceived ability to cope. When perceived demands exceed perceived ability to cope we feel out of control. Lack of control is distressing (stressful) because the individual is at the mercy of outside forces.

control group: in an experiment, this is a group of participants, matched as closely as possible to the *experimental group*, that does not receive the *independent variable*. If the performance of the experimental group is significantly different to that of the control group, the experimenter can attribute the difference to the effect of the independent variable. To test the therapeutic effects of a new drug, psychologists may employ a control group that does not receive the drug but receives a *placebo* instead. If the group that receives the drug shows a significant improvement but the placebo group does not, then the improvement is attributed directly to the effect of the drug.

conventional morality: see *Kohlberg, L*

convergent thinking: a form of thinking normally associated with problem-solving and intelligence, or any other type of task where the individual works towards the one right answer. This is normally contrasted with *divergent thinking* where the individual moves toward a more novel and original line of thought that may yield any of a number of possible answers to a problem.

co-operative learning: see *Vygotsky, L*

correlation coefficient: a mathematical representation of the degree of relatedness of two sets of measurements. A coefficient of +1 indicates a perfect positive correlation, in that high values of one measure (such as height) might relate perfectly to high values of another (such as foot size). A coefficient of –1 indicates a perfect negative correlation (also known as an inverse relationship), in that high values of one measure (such as miles per hour) might relate perfectly to low values of the other (such as miles per gallon). A coefficient of 0 would indicate no relationship at all between the two sets of measurements. Coefficients of +1, –1 and 0 are extremely rare in psychology, but a tendency towards one rather than another gives us valuable information concerning the nature (positive or negative) and the strength (between 0 and 1) of the relationship between the scores.

correspondent inference model: an aspect of *attribution* theory whereby we use information about the behaviour of others to infer that they possess specific *traits* that would be stable over time. This seems a deceptively simple thing to do, but the process is not all that clear-cut. In order to gain useful information (correspondence) for an inference about stable traits to be made, three factors are considered:
- the behaviour must be voluntary. If someone is forced to behave in a certain way, it tells us very little about them as a person
- the behaviour should produce non-common effects (i.e. consequences that would be produced by this behaviour but not by others). For example, we assess a business person as being generous and philanthropic if they donate money anonymously, but not if they do so in a blaze of publicity where there are other possible consequences (e.g. free advertising for their company). In this example, our assessment of them as being generous could only have come about if we felt they had nothing else to gain
- actions that are low in social desirability tell us more about a person than actions that conform to a social norm. Thus, if someone is loud and argumentative during a class discussion, we are more likely to see this as a stable trait of the person than if they were quiet and agreeable.

cortex: see *cerebral cortex*

counselling: essentially counselling is a purposeful relationship in which one person helps another to help themselves. It is a way of relating and responding to another person so that the other person is helped to explore their thoughts, feelings and behaviour, to reach a clearer self-understanding and then to find and use their strengths, draw on their resources so that they can cope more effectively with their life, making appropriate decisions by taking relevant action (British Association for Counselling definition).

counter-attitudinal behaviour: when we behave in a way that is contrary to an established attitude. For example, if we disliked a particular band yet bought a ticket for one of their concerts, our behaviour would be contrary to our attitude to that band. This inconsistency of attitude and behaviour can lead to a state of *cognitive dissonance*.

counterbalancing: an experimental technique used to overcome *order* and *practice effects*. If experimental conditions are always carried out in the same order (condition A followed by condition B), then it makes it possible that *participants* might improve or get worse simply as a result of the order in which they carry out the two conditions (due to the effects of learning, fatigue, boredom, etc.). Counterbalancing does not get rid of this effect, but does seek to balance it out so that any difference due to order is the same for the A–B order as it is for the B–A order.

	Conditions			Conditions
Participant no. 1	A–B		Participant no. 1	A–B
Participant no. 2	A–B		2	B–A
Participant no. 3	A–B		3	A–B
Participant no. 4	A–B		4	B–A
A non-counterbalanced design			A counterbalanced design	

counter-conditioning: a procedure whereby an animal is trained to respond in a different way to a stimulus that is already conditioned, but produces an incompatible response. This is the principle behind *systematic desensitisation* where the presence of a feared stimulus (such as a spider) produces a fear response. Through counter-conditioning, the fear response can be replaced by a relaxation response, so that in future presentations of the feared stimulus, the fear and the relaxation are incompatible and so (hopefully) the client feels more relaxed and less fearful.

counter-transference: as part of *psychoanalytic* therapy, the therapist may transfer feelings or conflicts they may have about their own life, or significant others in it, onto the client. It is imperative that the therapist recognises this possibility and guards against it.

covariation principle: an aspect of *attribution* theory which claims that if two events occur together (for example having migraine headaches when we do not have our customary three cups of coffee in the morning), we are tempted to see one event as causing the other, particularly if the migraines are absent when we do drink coffee. This basic proposal has been elaborated in the Analysis of Variance (ANOVA) model which looks at how we use covariation information across three dimensions which are relevant to the behaviour and its context:

- consensus – does everybody react in the same way? If they do, there is high consensus; if the behaviour in question is only found in this person (the actor), there is low consensus
- consistency – does the person normally react like this in this situation? If they do, there is high consistency; if they do not, there is low consistency
- distinctiveness – do they only react like this in this situation or across lots of situations? If it is only in this situation, there is high distinctiveness; if they react in a similar way in different situations, there is low distinctiveness.

Depending on the combination of information we are then able to explain an event by attributing it to either the actor (a *dispositional attribution*), the person or object to which it was directed (an *external* or *situational attribution*) or the situation in which the behaviour was observed (a *situational attribution*).

Attribution made to:	the actor	the object	the situation
Consensus	low	high	–
Consistency	high	high	low
Distinctiveness	low	high	–

An alternative to the ANOVA approach is the Abnormal Conditions Focus Model which rejects the logical rules of inference that characterise ANOVA. It proposes a simpler, non-logical, almost common-sense view that we look for abnormal events that might have caused a behaviour. If there is something unusual or abnormal that has happened, this is seen as the probable cause of a behaviour, and other information is seen merely as background. Thus many people will attribute success or failure, good fortune or bad fortune to all manner of what is for them abnormal events. Prior to the abnormal event occurring, the effect was absent, therefore the two things must be related. An example of this would be a family that goes on holiday to France and they all become ill. As this had never happened on their normal holidays in the West Country, they reason, it must be due to the fact that they had gone abroad. This may well stop them going abroad again because they connect illness and foreign travel.

criminal thinking patterns: ways of thinking that might distinguish criminals from law-abiding citizens. Criminals may, for example, attempt to play down the seriousness of their conduct by blaming problems on external circumstances, pointing out the unfairness in the world or devaluing their victims. Other criminals may feel weak and helpless when not in control of a situation and attempt to alleviate this feeling by manipulating, intimidating or assaulting others. For lifestyle criminals (e.g. those who burgle or shoplift), experience has taught them that they get away with most of their crimes. This leads to a sense of overconfidence and a feeling of invulnerability.

criminological psychology is that branch of psychology that is concerned with all aspects of criminal behaviour – from the study of crime, criminals and the victims of crime, through to the study of police, jurors and the rest of the legal process.

critical life event: any event in our life that necessitates a major life adjustment. These are normally taken to be events such as *bereavement*, divorce, retirement, etc. (See *life events*.)

critical periods: a term which refers to a fixed and crucial time during the early development of an *organism* when it is able to learn particular things that will be essential for survival (such as staying close to the parent) and later social adaptation (such as picking a mate of the right species). The term is most often experienced in the study of *imprinting*, where it used to be thought that young birds could only develop an attachment to the mother (or another *conspecific*) at a fixed time soon after hatching. The term *sensitive period* is used more often nowadays, indicating that many organisms are most susceptible to learning certain things at certain times, but these periods are not as critical as they were once thought to be.

cross-cultural research is a comparative technique used by social psychologists, sociologists, anthropologists etc. It involves studying different cultures (such as Japan, Kenya and Guatemala) with respect to some particular process or pattern of behaviour such as child-rearing. This provides a setting for a natural *experiment* that allows researchers to study the behaviour in question in quite different cultural settings. For example, cultures that allow their children little time for free play can be compared with cultures that encourage a great deal of free play. If there is a significant difference in later social and cognitive development between the two cultures, this suggests an important role for play in the development of social and cognitive competence.

cross-sectional method: a type of research design where groups of people of different ages are studied at the same point in time. For example, a researcher wanting to find out how children of different ages reason about a moral dilemma might choose cross-sections of children at different ages and measure the differences in their performance.

PROS: • the cross-sectional design enables the investigator to gather valuable information concerning the norms (i.e. what is typical) for different age groups
   • because participants are usually seen only once, the research design does not suffer from the 'drop-out' effect characteristic of the *longitudinal study*.

CONS: • in drawing conclusions about what is typical for one age, we must make what may be an unwarranted assumption, that the behaviour of younger children reflects what the older children were like when they were that age. This is particularly problematic when there is a wide age range being studied, and raises the possibility of cohort effects being responsible for the behaviour
   • cross-sectional designs only yield information about age-group changes, and tell us nothing about the reasons for those changes. It is not enough to dismiss them as simply being 'age-related'.

crowd: apart from the obvious definition – an aggregation of people – the term has a special meaning within the study of *adolescence*. Here it refers to a large and loosely organised group which may afford the adolescent an identity based on the stereotype of the group while they are still developing their own personal sense of identity.

crystallised intelligence: acquired skills and knowledge that a person has about the world, for example knowing how to ride a bike, read a book or translate this book into Polish. This is the type of intelligence that is being assessed in tests that measure factual knowledge and the application of factual knowledge (see also *fluid intelligence*).

cue: this may refer either to some aspect of a stimulus that enables the observer to discriminate between it and another stimulus (for example, the subtle differences in female markings that enable male ducks to discriminate between females of different species), or alternatively something that 'cues' or guides behaviour in a certain way. For example, in *cue-arousal theory*, the presence of certain cues (such as weapons, antagonistic chants or just plain rudeness) may cue or guide people toward responding in an aggressive manner.

cue-arousal theory: a theory of *aggression* that sees aggressive behaviour as being elicited by the presence of *cues* in the environment. This explanation is an extension of the *frustration-aggression theory* of aggression, and claims that people who are *aroused* through frustration are likely to store that arousal until something in the environment causes its release. This explanation of aggressive behaviour is often put forward to explain the 'weapons effect'. Societies that have a more relaxed attitude to the carrying of guns inevitably have a higher incidence of violent crime involving guns. Rather than acting as a deterrent, guns are seen as stimulating aggressive behaviour. Canada and the United States differ not only in the number of gun-related violent crimes (the US has far more) but also in their laws concerning the carrying and ownership of guns (Canadians are not allowed to carry guns 'for personal protection').

cue-dependent memory (forgetting): information is stored in the memory system but may be inaccessible unless there is a specific cue to trigger the memory. For example, a sound or smell can trigger quite detailed memories from our childhood.

cult: a highly cohesive group that shares the same beliefs or practices that differ significantly from those of mainstream social groups. Many cult groups have developed conversion techniques to exploit the vulnerabilities of potential converts and, once in the group, cult leaders and their trainers exert a systematic social influence that can produce significant behavioural and ideological change. Not all cults are destructive, and many of those who join and remain in cults do so out of a quest for some sort of spiritual connection. Whether or not a cult is destructive is usually determined by the morality of the cult leader and the nature of his or her dream.

cultural anthropology: normally distinguished from physical anthropology (the study of humankind from a biological or evolutionary perspective), cultural anthropology is concerned with the different social systems that make up communities, societies and nations.

cultural bias is the interpretation of other cultures using the perspective of one's own culture. Cultural bias occurs when people of one culture make assumptions about the behaviour of people from another culture based on their own cultural norms and practices (see *ethnocentrism* and *Eurocentrism*). Cultural bias occurs in many different areas of psychology, including the diagnosis of abnormal behaviour, the construction and interpretation of intelligence tests, and our understanding of interpersonal relationships.

cultural blindness: the belief that colour and culture make no difference and that all people are essentially the same, and that what is appropriate for one culture (e.g. an educational practice) should be appropriate for all.

cultural determinism: the belief that patterns of behaviour are determined more by cultural than biological or psychological factors. Cultural determinism emphasises the continuity of patterns of behaviour over time as learned behaviour is handed down from one generation to the next.

cultural diversity: a term which implies recognition that the members of different cultures, ethnic groups, socio-economic groups and genders are socialised to behave in ways that are considered 'culturally correct' for those groups of people. Recognising the importance of cultural diversity in psychology is vital if we are really to understand the complexities of the behaviour we are studying. At its simplest level, for instance, social psychologists have noted that in many Eastern cultures, the 'group' appears to have primacy over the individual in motivating behaviour. In most Western cultures, however, individual needs tend to be emphasised over group needs (see *individualism* and *collectivism*).

cultural relativism: the view that patterns of understanding and behaviour found in different cultures are as good as each other. One of the implications of this view is that it is impossible to judge the superiority of a particular set of values outside the specific cultural context in which they are set. Likewise, judgements of normality or abnormality depend very much on the cultural experiences and biases of the person doing the judging.

culture: literally, the human-made part of the environment. In its simplest definition, it refers to the products of socialisation within any organised group, society or nation and involves a set of rules, norms and customs that are agreed by the members of that group. It is also used to describe the people that make up that group. In this sense it is more appropriate to think of culture as an active rather than a passive thing. Each of us contributes to the culture of the next person, and in turn are affected by them.

culture-bound syndromes are defined by *DSM-IV-TR* as 'recurrent, locality-specific patterns of aberrant behaviour and troubling experience that may or may not be linked to a particular DSM category. Many of these patterns are indigenously considered to be "illnesses", or at least afflictions, and most have local names'. Culture-bound syndromes (CBSs) can be classified into several different types.

A psychiatric illness (not organically caused) which is locally recognised as an illness and does not resemble a Western category. An example of this type of CBS is amok (found in Malaysia and Indonesia), characterised by a period of brooding followed by wild, aggressive behaviour.

A psychiatric illness (not organically caused) which is locally recognised as an illness and does resemble a Western category. An example is taijin kyofusho (Japan), an intense fear that one's body, body parts or bodily functions are embarrassing or offensive to other people.

A psychiatric illness not yet recognised in the West. An example is kuru (New Guinea), a progressive **psychosis** and **dementia** indigenous to cannibalistic tribes in the region. This organic disorder (i.e. having a physical cause) has been identified with a form of Creuzfeldt–Jakob disease (CJD).

A psychiatric illness that is found in many cultures but only recognised as an illness in one or a few. An example is koro (China), a belief that the penis is retracting into the abdomen, and when fully retracted will result in death. Panic attempts to keep the penis from retracting can lead to severe physical damage.

Culturally accepted classifications of illness that would not be regarded as acceptable in the West. An example would be 'evil eye' (Mediterranean and Middle East), which is a common idiom for disease, misfortune or social disruption throughout these areas.

A syndrome allegedly occurring in a given culture, but which does not, in fact, exist. An example is windigo (Algonkian Indians), involving distaste for ordinary food and feelings of depression and anxiety leading to possession by a giant man-eating monster, often resulting in homicide and cannibalism.

Although some of these CBSs do appear to be specific to one particular culture (e.g. amok and koro), others such as kuru, caused by an aberrant protein in the brain which replicates itself by deforming other proteins, do not appear to be quite so culture bound.

culture-free tests: the ideal that tests (most specifically tests of **intelligence**) are free from any bias towards members of one culture rather than another. Many of the well-known intelligence tests (such as the Stanford-Binet and the **WISC**) have been criticised for being Anglo-centric (they are biased towards English-speaking peoples). Other tests have been criticised for their bias towards 'WASP' (White, Anglo-Saxon, Protestant) American children. It is doubtful whether tests can ever be truly free of culturally acquired knowledge. The majority of such tests measure **crystallised intelligence**, and as such are measuring skill in a cultural context.

cupboard-love theory: a popularised term for the behaviourist explanation of **attachment.** In this explanation, the mother acts as a source of **primary reinforcement**; that is, she provides the child with the nourishment s/he needs. Because of consistent associations (mother and food), she gradually becomes a **secondary reinforcer** to the child. Eventually the presence of the mother becomes reinforcing, and the child seeks to maintain proximity at all times. Following the experimental work by Harry Harlow with rhesus monkeys, this theory gradually fell out of favour.

curiosity drive: a supposedly *innate* tendency for organisms to seek out that which is novel in their environment.

Curry's onion model: Curry (1983) proposed her 'onion' model for categorising different *learning* styles. Learning behaviour is seen as controlled by the central personality dimension, translated through the middle layer of information processing, and given a final twist by interaction with environmental factors such as instructional styles.

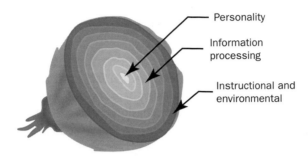

Personality

Information processing

Instructional and environmental

custodial sentencing: a form of sentencing where an individual's liberty is restricted, e.g. through a prison sentence or a stay in a youth justice centre. Remand prisoners may be detained in custody until the charges against them have been heard, whereas sentenced prisoners will, following conviction for an offence, have been directed by the judge to spend a certain amount of time in prison.

Do you need revision help and advice?

Go to pages 298–312 for a range of revision appendices that include plenty of exam advice and tips.

daily hassles: those frustrating, irritating everyday experiences that occur regularly in our work, home and personal life. Examples of stressors include being stuck in traffic, having an argument with a friend or close relative, or rude behaviour. There are many possible reasons why we find daily hassles so stressful. Hassles may prevent us from pursuing current behavioural goals, so we must invest additional effort and develop new action plans to deal with the hassle. This extra effort expenditure creates a temporary loss of resources so that fewer resources are available for pursuing the primary task. The side effects of this would then include increased fatigue and negative mood. The situation can deteriorate even further if attempts to cope with the hassle are not completely successful so that dealing with it remains costly in terms of energy resources. A second explanation considers hassles to be stressful because they affect the rate at which we progress toward our primary goal. According to this model, it is not merely the discrepancy between current state and the eventual goal that creates stress and negative emotional reaction, but the reduction of this discrepancy as a function of time. Because hassles create obstacles, which result in slower progress than anticipated, they cause negative mood regardless of the effort needed to cope with any disruption.

dark adaptation: the process by which the eyes adjust to a low light intensity. *Cones* do not function at all in low light. *Rods* are bleached in bright light and therefore have to readjust in order to reach their maximum sensitivity. For total dark adaptation, the process takes as long as four hours, but the dark-adapted eye is then one million times more sensitive than the normally adjusted eye.

Darwinism: an explanation of the evolution of *genetically* acquired *traits* that is based on the work of Charles Darwin. The central proposition of Darwinism is the principle of *natural selection*. Darwin believed that the variations in form between different organisms meant that there was a 'struggle for survival'. Those traits which had survival value for the organisms that possessed them would eventually be passed on to their offspring. This process means that over time, organisms may become better adapted to their ecological niche with the eventual consequence that new species gradually appear. True Darwinism stresses the gradual change over generational time rather than the sudden changes proposed by alternative explanations of evolution. This explanation of evolutionary change is often confused (by some) with the view of evolution put forward by Lamarck, in which animals adapt during their lifetimes and then pass on those acquired characteristics to their offspring. Giraffes stretching their necks to reach the higher leaves is the normal example put forward to support the now discredited Lamarckian view of evolutionary change.

data: information or measurements gathered during the course of a study. The interpretation of data allows the research psychologist to draw conclusions about the event under study.

day care is not a precise concept but generally refers to a form of temporary care (i.e. not 24 hours), given by someone other than a family member, and usually taking place outside the home. Leaving a child with a childminder is seen as a preferable form of day care for many parents, because the care the child receives is more likely to be similar to the care they would receive in their own home. Another commonly used form of day care is the day nursery. Day nurseries can be found in a variety of locations including; schools, churches, women's shelters, and so on. One of the most rapidly growing forms of day care is the nursery within the workplace. This is gaining popularity because employers recognise that providing onsite day care is not only a good benefit for employees but it also makes good business sense.

Evidence suggests that the more time children spend in day care across their infant, toddler, and pre-school years (combined), the more likely they are to behave in aggressive and disobedient ways as 4–8 year olds. Children who experience better quality day care (i.e. where caregivers are attentive, responsive, affectionate and stimulating) tend to benefit, especially in terms of their cognitive and language development, relative to those who experience poorer quality care.

debriefing: a post-experimental interview in which the experimenter tries to restore the **participant** to the same psychological state they were in when they entered the experiment. Sometimes it is seen as sufficient to inform the participant of the true nature and purpose of the experiment; at other times debriefing has a more involved and important purpose. In Stanley Milgram's experimental studies of **obedience** to authority, effective debriefing was vital. To start with, participants had to be reassured that they had not really killed the other person. Those who had withdrawn during the study had to be reassured that they had actually behaved in a socially desirable way (i.e. by refusing to be coerced into destructive obedience), whereas those who had obeyed right up to the full shock limit had to be reassured that what they had done was very much the majority response. Debriefing is especially vital when participants have been deceived in any way during the experiment.

decay: information that is not rehearsed disappears (i.e. decays) as time passes. Information is physically represented as a **memory trace**, but this is fragile and disintegrates if not constantly refreshed. Without this rehearsal, the trace decays completely within a very short time, meaning that recall is no longer possible.

The original version of **Atkinson and Shiffrin's model of memory** (**multi-store model of memory**) emphasised decay as the main cause of forgetting in short-term memory, although their later version emphasised displacement rather than decay.

decentration: refers to the child's increasing ability to view events from the perspective of others rather than from within his or her own perspective (**egocentricity**). Thus, a five-year-old boy who has a sister may reply that he has a sister, but when asked if she has a brother will reply 'no'. An older child who is able to put himself in the place of his sister would answer 'yes, she has a brother'. The term has an alternative use in **Piagetian** theory, where it refers to the ability of the child to move away from their concentration on the perceptual properties of a stimulus in **conservation** tasks. The child who can decentrate is less likely to be fooled by the same volume of liquid being presented in two different shaped containers (despite the fact they look different) and instead bases his or her response on more logical reasoning.

deception: the deliberate misleading of *participants* during a research study, either through telling them lies or by omitting to tell them some important detail of the research such that they are unable to give their full *informed consent*. By deceiving participants we may make them cynical and distrustful about psychology and psychologists. The amount of anger or discomfort expressed by participants when the deception is revealed is normally a good guide to the damage it has caused. In some cases deception is understandable and to a certain degree, acceptable (the study simply would not work if participants knew everything about the design) but deception in investigations of a trivial nature is clearly less acceptable than deception in investigations that make a significant contribution to psychological knowledge.

declarative knowledge: a term that refers to any knowledge to which an individual has conscious access and that can be stated in some way. Thus, when we learn to type we rely on our knowledge of where the keys are to direct our fingers (declarative knowledge), but as we become more skilled we no longer need to think where the keys are and we move our fingers to the appropriate position seemingly without conscious thought (*procedural knowledge*). The representation of knowledge within these two systems has been demonstrated by studies of amnesic patients who may show a total loss of their declarative memory but their procedural memory remains intact.

deductive reasoning is a process of moving from reasoning about the general to reasoning about the particular. If something is true (e.g. a theory or set of premises), then it follows that some more particular truth must also be true. If we believe our car to be empty of petrol, then it follows that the petrol gauge would register empty. This is an example of deductive reasoning. Inferences drawn from accepted truths may be valid, e.g.:

>	All mammals are warm-blooded

>	Humans are mammals

>	Therefore humans are warm-blooded

or invalid:

>	All criminals are evil

>	Some criminals are men

>	Therefore all men are evil

The accuracy of our deductive reasoning, as any great detective will confirm, lies in the appropriateness of the leap from what is known to be true, to what, logically, must also be true as a result.

deep structure: the underlying meaning of a sentence. For example, the sentence 'They are eating apples' has two possible deep structures. Most sentences can be understood by listeners without knowledge of the deep structure, but by using information in the surface structure of the sentence (i.e. information contained in the grammar of the sentence). Thus, the sentence 'This is an eating apple' elicits only the one meaning (unless you have a particularly bizarre mind) so the surface structure is adequate for it to be understood. Only when the meaning is ambiguous, as in the former example, does the listener require information about the deep structure of the sentence.

defence mechanism: an *unconscious* strategy that protects our conscious mind from *anxiety*. According to *Freudian* theory, defence mechanisms involve a distortion of reality in some way so that we are better able to cope with a situation. The defence mechanisms include *displacement*, *projection*, *reaction formation*, *regression* and *repression*.

defiance of authority: resisting the orders of an authority figure. In Milgram's studies of obedience to authority, several factors increased the likelihood of defiance, including the proximity of the victim, the absence of the authority figure and the presence of disobedient peers.

Defining Issues Test (DIT): a test of moral reasoning where participants read a series of *moral dilemmas* and rate the importance of a number of different statements concerning the dilemma. Each statement presents a particular moral issue. For example, in response to the *Heinz dilemma*, participants may rate the statement: 'Heinz should steal the drug because he owes it to his wife to try and save her' as the most important, and 'Heinz should not steal the drug because he might get caught and get into trouble' as less important. By scoring the ratings that participants give to a range of these statements, an investigator can assess at which of *Kohlberg's* stages of moral development the individual is currently functioning, as well as the relative importance (how highly they rate it as being an important moral issue) of Kohlberg's most advanced form of moral reasoning, *post-conventional morality*.

degeneration: the destruction of neural tissue as a result of injury or a lack of chemical nutrients.

dehumanisation: human beings usually have moral inhibitions about killing fellow humans, but this changes if the target group is dehumanised so that its members are seen as worthless animals and therefore not worthy of moral consideration. In the Rwandan genocide, the influential Hutu-controlled 'hate' radio station RTLM encouraged Hutu listeners to murder their Tutsi neighbours by referring to the minority Tutsi as 'inyenzi' (cockroaches).

deindividuation: a process where people lose their sense of socialised individual identity and resort to unsocialised and antisocial behaviours. People normally refrain from acting in an aggressive and selfish manner in part because they are easily identifiable in societies that have strong norms against such 'uncivilised' behaviour. In certain situations such as in crowds, these restraints may become relaxed and people may engage in antisocial behaviour. Conditions that increase anonymity serve to minimise concerns about evaluation by others and weaken normal controls based on guilt, shame or fear. The larger the group, the greater the anonymity and the greater the difficulty in identifying a single individual. In a large crowd, each person is faceless and anonymous. The concept of deindividuation has been used to explain the behaviour of crowds who have 'baited' potential suicide victims to jump. The fact that these incidents tended to occur at night, when the crowds were large and physically removed from the jumpers meant that deindividuation was more likely to occur.

More recent developments of the concept of deindividuation have distinguished between the effects of reduced public self-awareness (being anonymous to others) and reduced private self-awareness. A person who is self-focused tends to act according to internalised attitudes and moral standards. If the person submerges themselves within a group, they may lose this focus and become less privately self-aware. It is this reduction in private self-awareness that is associated with increased antisocial behaviour rather than the anonymity of public self-awareness.

Although the concept of deindividuation is supported by a great many research studies, researchers have often failed to distinguish between the effects of anonymity of victims (e.g. in the case of aggression against a 'faceless' enemy) and of the aggressor (e.g. as in the case of hooded terrorists who cannot be identified by their victims). It also raises the question of whether 'identifiability' is in respect to the **in-group** or the **out-group**. In other words does the likelihood of aggression increase if our in-group cannot recognise us, or when the out-group cannot recognise us?

delirium: a state of great mental confusion where consciousness becomes cloudy, the person experiences great difficulty focusing their attention, and may also experience delusions, **hallucinations** or **illusions**. The literal meaning of the word delirium is a deviation from a track, and this is exactly what is involved: the sufferer deviates from their normal state. The sufferer has great trouble concentrating or maintaining a coherent train of thought and they may develop perceptual disturbances, often mistaking unfamiliar objects as familiar. Mood swings are also common in the delirious state, with dramatic swings from one emotion to another. Delirium is thought to be caused by a number of possible factors, with drug intoxications, neurological disorders and the stress of a change in surroundings being some of them.

For most sufferers of delirium, this is very much a temporary state; it is estimated, for example, that between 10 and 15 per cent of patients become delirious after general anaesthetic. The most vulnerable age group is the elderly, especially those who already have another organic brain disorder. One of the most important features in the management of delirium in the elderly is the education of family members. A client with a progressive disorder such as **Alzheimer's disease** may develop an infection which in turn causes the symptoms of delirium. Family members may over-react to these new symptoms, believing that they are a sign that the client is losing ground fast and their deterioration is irreversible.

delusional disorders: a psychotic disorder which is not part of a **schizophrenic** diagnosis, yet is also characterised by the presence of one or more delusions. Relatively rare amongst the general population, its incidence increases slightly with age. For example, some people may be convinced that their neighbours are trying to poison their cat or are plotting against them.

demand characteristic: any aspect of the experimental situation that prompts the **participant** to interpret the study in a specific way and adjust their behaviour accordingly. By adjusting their behaviour to what they see as the 'demands' of the experiment, participants introduce a bias that may contaminate the results of the study.

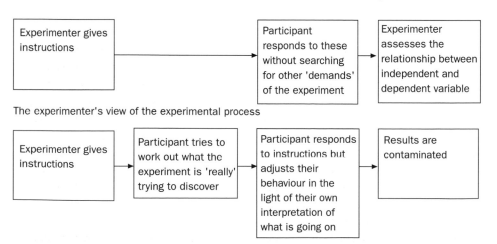

The experimenter's view of the experimental process

The role of demand characteristics in the experimental process

dementia: a disorder that is characterised by a serious decline in mental faculties, particularly in the loss of memory, as well as impairment of at least one other cognitive function. This group of disorders may impair what we know or even who we are. There are a number of different dementias, but the commonest division is into cortical dementias and sub-cortical dementias:

- cortical dementias – as well as memory impairment, sufferers may also experience *aphasia*, *personality* changes such as impulsiveness, and progressive deterioration of a number of other faculties. *Alzheimer's disease* is the best known of the cortical dementias
- sub-cortical dementias – memory impairment here is experienced as an inability to retrieve information from long-term storage. Aphasia is not present, but personality deterioration is. An example is Huntington's disease – a degeneration of cognition, emotion and movement. This has a dramatic effect on personality, and leads to depression, instability and anxiety.

Other dementias have been associated with HIV and AIDS, meningitis, drug abuse and advanced cases of syphilis. Treatment for the dementias is tricky because they affect so many different areas of the brain and involve so many different neurochemicals. Diagnosis involves taking a complete history of the patient (for example checking for alcohol abuse or a family history of Alzheimer's disease); checking for specific cognitive impairments; and using brain imaging techniques to look for obvious physical causes such as brain *lesions.* The main type of treatment for dementias is drug treatments, which focus on the *neurotransmitters* that seem central to the action of the dementia concerned. Recent research has attempted to develop chemicals that will stimulate the development of neural pathways to replace those that have been destroyed.

dendrites: processes near the cell body of a *neuron* that receive an incoming impulse from the adjacent neuron.

denial: a *defence mechanism* in which a person may deny some aspect of reality. For example, someone who cannot come to terms with the death of a loved one may still talk to them, lay the table for them and even wash and iron their clothes.

deoxyribonucleic acid (DNA): the molecule which is the chemical basis of heredity. DNA carries all genetic information on the *chromosomes*.

dependent personality disorder: a type of *personality disorder* where a person becomes so reliant on others that they cannot make even the smallest decision for themselves. People who have this disorder experience profound feelings of inadequacy and helplessness. They may go to great lengths to avoid being alone and need constant reassurance from others. In extreme cases of the disorder they may be unable to tolerate any physical separation from their partner. If a relationship ends, the person may be devastated and seek to find another relationship as quickly as possible. Maintaining a relationship is so important that they may continue in abusive partnerships rather than be alone. People who have dependent personality disorder are also more vulnerable to other disorders such as *depression* and *phobias*. Possible explanations of dependent personality disorder are:

- psychoanalytic explanations suggest that it reflects a *fixation* at the oral stage, a childlike wish to be cared for
- behaviourist explanations revolve around the idea of faulty learning experiences that overly reward dependent behaviour while punishing independent behaviour

- cognitive explanations stress the role of maladaptive thought patterns. People with dependent personality disorder believe they are inadequate and need another person to help them cope. They develop the mistaken belief that being independent means being alone.

Because of the nature of this disorder, clients may shift responsibility for their condition onto the therapist and adopt a very passive role in the therapy sessions. **Psychodynamic** therapies attempt to bring the repressed memories that are causing the disorder into consciousness. A particular issue in these therapies is the almost inevitable **transference** that takes place from client to therapist. **Cognitive therapies** and **cognitive-behavioural therapies** try to change assumptions of incompetence and may provide assertiveness training for clients to better express their needs and wishes within a relationship.

dependent variable: some aspect of behaviour that is affected by the action of the **independent variable** in an **experiment**. An experimental effect is produced if the independent variable causes a change in the dependent variable. For example, the provision of feedback in a task (independent variable) may cause an increase in the overall accuracy of performance (dependent variable).

depressants: substances that slow down the activity of the **central nervous system (CNS)**, and, if taken in large enough doses, may reduce inhibitions and impair judgement and concentration. The commonest forms of depressant are alcohol, sedatives (such as valium and librium) and the opiods (such as morphine and heroin).

depression: a type of **mood disorder** in which the person experiences feelings of great sadness, worthlessness and guilt, and finds the challenges of life overwhelming. Within the **DSM-IV-TR** classification of mental disorders, there are two categories of depression: major depression (or **unipolar disorder**) and **bipolar disorder**. Major depression is by far the more common form of the disorder. The formal diagnosis of major depression requires the presence of five of the following symptoms (including either depressed mood or loss of interest and pleasure):

- Sad, depressed mood.
- Loss of interest and pleasure in usual activities.
- Difficulties in sleeping (insomnia) or, in some patients, a desire to sleep all the time.
- Shift in activity level, becoming either lethargic or agitated.
- Poor appetite and weight loss, or increased appetite and weight gain.
- Loss of energy and great fatigue.
- Negative self-concept, feelings of worthlessness and guilt.
- Difficulty in concentrating, slowed thinking and indecisiveness.
- Recurrent thoughts of death or suicide.

Major depression is probably the most widespread of the mental disorders, affecting about 1 in 20 people. The average age at which it is first diagnosed is between 40 and 50, and it is more common in women than men. Explanations of depression include the following:

1. Biological theories which see depression as an inherited disposition and therefore stress the contribution of genetic factors (more important in bipolar depression than in unipolar depression) and, more recently, research has found a possible link between

the *neurotransmitters serotonin* and noradrenaline and the development of both categories of depression.

2. Cognitive theories emphasise the role of irrational thoughts and beliefs as major factors influencing the emotional state of the individual. Aaron Beck's theory sees depression in adulthood as being caused by a bias toward negative interpretations of events. These are a legacy of childhood experiences such as the loss of a parent, social rejection by peers or the depressive attitude of a parent. These biases are activated whenever the individual encounters situations that are in some way similar.

Treatments for depression include:

1. Psychological *therapies*, such as those based on Beck's cognitive therapy, attempt to expose the negative and illogical ways of thinking of the depressive, and help them toward a new and more realistic way of viewing themselves and events around them.

2. Biological therapies include the use of *electroconvulsive shock treatment (ECT)* and *drug treatments*, most notably the use of *anti-depressants* of the tricyclic and fluoxetine categories (such as Prozac).

Clinical evidence has shown that drug therapies have a quicker effect on reducing depressive symptoms, although psychological therapies such as the cognitive therapy mentioned above are increasingly able to match drug therapies, particularly after the initial stages of the disorder. An increasing number of studies have shown that cognitive therapies have a better record for preventing the recurrence of depression, although the combined advantages of cognitive therapy and drug therapy appear more helpful to depressed patients than either type of therapy alone. (See also *bipolar disorder*.)

deprivation: see *maternal deprivation*

depth perception: our ability to comprehend that some objects are 'deeper' or more distant than others. Depth may be perceived using binocular cues (from both eyes) such as retinal disparity (the closer an object is to the viewer, the more disparate the images from the two eyes will be). However, most depth perception is based on monocular cues (from one eye), including relative size (smaller objects appear further away), occlusion (if one object partially blocks another it appears to be closer) and linear perspective (parallel lines appear to converge in the distance).

desensitisation: a term used to refer to a decrease in sensitivity towards a stimulus. For example, an organism will react to a sudden noise the first few times, but gradually the reaction will disappear.

determinism: see *free will vs determinism*

development: in its most common form of usage in psychology, the sequence of changes over the life span of an individual.

developmental norms: the average or typical skills and behaviours that might be present in a child of a particular age. These are established by studying large numbers of children at different ages (the *cross-sectional method*).

developmental psychology: the branch of psychology that is concerned with change and development over the lifespan. The term is often used synonymously with the term 'child psychology', to reflect the preoccupation with that period of development. Because of this, other terms, such as *life-span development* and gerontology, are often used for the study of later development.

deviation from ideal mental health: a definition of abnormality that explains *abnormal behaviour* in terms of deviation from one or more of the major criteria of positive mental health proposed by Jahoda (1958). These are:
1. positive attitude to the self (i.e. having self-respect and self-acceptance)
2. self-actualisation of one's potential
3. resistance to stress (i.e. having developed good coping strategies for stress)
4. personal autonomy (i.e. being able to make decisions on the basis of what is right for ourselves rather than others)
5. adapting to the environment (i.e. being flexible and able to adjust to change).

deviation from social norms: a definition of abnormality that defines abnormal behaviour as being any behaviour that is considered 'deviant', i.e. behaviour that is antisocial or undesirable. What is considered abnormal is any behaviour that deviates from a social (rather than a statistical) norm. These are implicit 'rules' about how we ought to behave (e.g. talking to ourselves in public), and violation of these rules is considered 'deviant' or 'abnormal'. These rules reflect the moral standards of a particular culture; therefore, under this definition, what is considered abnormal will differ from culture to culture.

diagnosis: refers to the identification and classification of a psychological disorder. The term is used in much the same way as it is used in physical medicine, i.e. a person who is referred to a *psychiatrist* or *clinical psychologist* might be diagnosed as suffering from *depression* or *schizophrenia*. Effective diagnosis depends on the existence of clearly defined and distinct diagnostic categories. In psychology, these do not exist in quite the same way as they do in physical illness. Because of this, mental health professionals focus more on the pattern of symptoms shown by the client, rather than attempting to categorise them into one distinct disorder. This avoids some of the problems that might arise from misdiagnosis of a disorder.

Diagnostic and Statistical Manual (DSM): a classification, definition and description of over 200 mental health disorders. DSM is regularly updated, the most recent (2004) being DSM-IV-TR.

PROS: • classification systems such as DSM provide a diagnostic shorthand for mental health professionals. With agreed terms and categories of disorder, effective communication concerning patients and their treatment is possible

• they provide an understanding of *aetiology* – a diagnosis of a disorder should allow the practitioner to suggest the causes of the symptoms (unfortunately the disagreement about causes of mental disorders makes this very difficult)

• they provide a plan for treatment – once diagnosed, the most appropriate course of treatment can be prescribed. Clinical research has established that certain treatments work most effectively with specific disorders.

CONS: • humanistic psychologists argue that classification systems depersonalise clients by reducing them to a set of medical diagnostics

• they may suffer from a lack of *reliability* in that not all practitioners will arrive at the same diagnosis when presented with the same symptoms and information about a condition. The greater precision of the categories of DSM-IV-TR has reduced this problem, although it is still evident, especially in certain disorders

- they give insufficient information about the causes of different disorders. Within the diagnostic category of **schizophrenia** for example, there are many different subtypes. The problem is whether these are best treated as variations of the same basic disorder, or as quite different disorders with different causes and therefore requiring different treatments.

diathesis–stress paradigm: a belief that individuals may have a predisposition (the diathesis) towards developing a particular disorder which then makes them more vulnerable to later environmental events (the stress). If an individual possesses the diathesis for a disorder (e.g. they may have inherited a particular biological dysfunction), this may not necessarily mean they will develop the disorder. This would be determined by the life stresses (such as the effects of psychological **trauma**) that the person later encounters. It is fairly well established that **schizophrenia** involves an inherited predisposition that makes some people more likely to develop the disorder than others, but whether they do or they don't develop schizophrenia may be determined by the later difficulties that they face in their life.

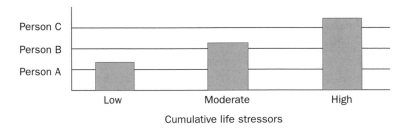

Cumulative life stressors

Person A is vulnerable at low levels of stress, person B at moderate levels and person C is only vulnerable at high levels of stress

Individual differences in stress tolerance thresholds

Dibs: a book written by psychologist Virginia Axline, *Dibs: In Search of Self* tells the story of an emotionally disturbed yet gifted child (given the pseudonym Dibs to preserve anonymity) who is perceived as being 'mentally defective' by his parents because of his reclusive and autistic behaviour.

dichotic listening: as used in **attention** research, this involves presenting one message to the left ear, and a different message to the right ear. In the dichotic listening task, participants are asked to repeat back one of the messages whilst ignoring the other. The fact that they are generally able to do this means that they were using the direction of a message (right or left ear) to make attentional decisions.

diencephalon: a major division of the forebrain, containing the **thalamus** and the **hypothalamus**.

dieting: the act of restricting food intake (or the intake of particular foods) in order to achieve or maintain a certain weight.

difference threshold: the minimum difference in the intensity of two stimuli necessary to detect that they are different. For example, two lights may be illuminated at the same time. The difference threshold is reached when an observer can tell that one is brighter than the other.

differential association hypothesis: the view that people learn patterns of criminal behaviour in the same way as they learn normal behaviour, i.e. through interaction with others. By interacting with other people, individuals learn the values, techniques and motives for criminal behaviour.

differentiation: the practice of teaching in such a way as to accommodate different ability levels within a single classroom.

diffusion of responsibility: is the tendency for multiple bystanders to be less likely to help in the event of an emergency than if they were there alone. In such cases, the responsibility for action is shared (or diffused) among all of the bystanders present. Because of the other people present, each individual feels less personal responsibility to help, and therefore is less likely to do so.

digit span: a test of *short-term memory* in which a participant is given a series of digits (such as 3, 6, 1, 9, 5, 6, 4) and is then asked to repeat them back. The average digit span is generally felt to be around 7 ± 2 digits.

dimorphic: literally meaning having two forms, this term is likely to be encountered in the phrase *sexually dimorphic* where it describes the fact that in many species (most notably ducks) the sexes are physically quite different. The bright and conspicuous colouring of male ducks appears to have been shaped by *sexual selection*, with the sole purpose of attracting females. The drab colouration of females, on the other hand, has been fashioned by *natural selection*, and serves the purpose of camouflage against predators whilst sitting on the nest. Where there are no major discernible differences between the sexes, they are described as sexually *monomorphic*.

direct fitness: the reproductive gain that can be achieved by measuring only the direct descendants of an animal (i.e. its offspring).

direct theories of perception: see *perception*

disclosure: see *self-disclosure*

discounting principle: the role of other causes can be discounted if we can attribute an action to a single, plausible cause. For example, if we know that there has been a recent heavy snowfall, we are less likely to attribute someone's late arrival to laziness, bad timekeeping or mechanical breakdown.

discourse analysis: refers to the ways in which psychologists attempt to extract the meanings of everyday communications between people. The central idea of discourse analysis is that the content of a communication is an important influence on the behaviour of the people taking part in the conversation, or those who are exposed to it. Discourse analysis can take place on several levels, such as:

- deconstructionism – an attempt to unravel what is actually said, and the underlying assumptions and biases that lurk behind the communication. We often hear people say things like 'I'm not prejudiced, but ...'
- interpretative repertoires – the terms and styles of language that are used in the communication. For example, the term 'friendly fire' was often quoted during the Gulf War as a metaphor for being mistakenly attacked by your own side. Somehow the former did not have the same sense of tragic incompetence as the latter.

Discourse analysis has the obvious advantages of being a rich and often subtle source of insight into lay explanations of behaviour and experience, and it addresses issues of high natural interest.

discovery learning: a *Piagetian* belief that children should learn by doing. Instead of presenting facts and knowledge verbally to the children, the role of the teacher is to provide the right sort of setting and materials and allow children to choose freely among them. In this way, children experience the intrinsic satisfaction of discovering something for themselves. *Piaget* believed that a discovery-based education was critical because the primary aim of education is to create people who can do new things, people who are creative, inventive and discoverers.

discrete variable: a measurement of something which is a discrete category rather than a continuous score. For example, males and females are discrete variables, as are particular brands of car. Height, weight and IQ are examples of continuous variables.

discrimination refers to a set of behaviours toward members of a categorised group which are unfair in comparison to members of other groups. They can occur at several levels, from simple avoidance to active and hostile attacks on the target group or individual. Discriminatory behaviours may be linked to underlying *prejudiced* attitudes, or may be a product of the social forces present at the time. Alternatively, they may reflect the discriminator's belief in a *just world* where the targets of discrimination are seen as deserving such treatment.

discriminative stimulus: an aspect of *operant conditioning* whereby the organism is *reinforced* for a response when a particular stimulus is present, but not when it is absent. For example, a pigeon may learn to peck at a green disc, and avoid discs of other colours. To accomplish this, the experimenter would have reinforced the former response and not the latter responses.

disease model: a term that refers to the *biomedical model of abnormality*. Within this model there is a belief that psychological malfunctions are a product of a physical malfunction or disease. Within this context, people with an abnormal behaviour are described as patients, and their abnormality a disease. Although adherents of the biomedical approach to abnormality believe that it is only a matter of time before we find a physical cause for most disorders, the fact remains that there are very few where there is incontrovertible proof. The development of more psychologically oriented approaches to abnormal behaviour has led to a general abandonment of the terms 'patient' and 'disease', preferring instead the more psychologically neutral terms 'client' and 'disorder'.

disengagement: a gradual increase in self-absorption and a corresponding decrease in involvement with the outside world that is thought to accompany the process of ageing. Disengagement theory suggests that this gradual decrease in activity levels for older people is a natural part of the ageing process. Disengagement is often a two-way process, with society also easing older people more onto the sidelines (through retirement ages and general marginalisation of older people). This gradual disengagement of the person from society can lead to a sense of psychological well-being, and can therefore be seen as an adaptive process.

disorganised speech: one of the *positive symptoms* of *schizophrenia*, this refers to the incoherent and wandering speech patterns that make it difficult for a listener to follow the schizophrenic's line of thought. These speech disturbances used to be regarded as one of the major diagnostic symptoms of schizophrenia, but this presents two problems:

- many schizophrenics do not show these disorganised speech patterns
- disorganised speech is also symptomatic of other disorders (e.g. *mania*) so is insufficient to discriminate between schizophrenia and other mental disorders.

displacement has two major meanings in psychology, although the idea behind the definitions is broadly the same:

- if one goal is blocked, an organism may displace its response energy onto some other behaviour. A bird that is being defeated in a dispute may suddenly start preening or pecking at the ground
- in *psychoanalysis,* displacement refers to the transfer of repressed desires or impulses onto a substitute person or object. For example, if we are reprimanded by our boss, we may 'take it out' on a less dangerous substitute (e.g. shouting at our children or slamming a door).

displacement (memory): refers to existing information being displaced (i.e. 'pushed out') from memory by newer information. In the *multi-store model of memory*, loss of information from short-term memory is thought to be due to displacement.

disposition: an assumed mental or physical organisation within an individual that produces stable and consistent patterns of behaviour over time and across different situations.

dispositional attribution: when we attribute the cause of our own or someone else's behaviour to factors that are under the direct control of the person. Thus, a dispositional attribution is being made when we reach a conclusion that the behaviour in question is being caused by the effort or ability of the person concerned rather than some external influence such as the weather, other people or sheer bad luck (see *situational attributions*). Biases in this process, such as the *actor/observer* effect, mean that the correct attribution of dispositional factors is not necessarily guaranteed. In this type of bias we have a tendency to overuse dispositional attributions when we observe the behaviour of others, and *situational attributions* when we judge our own behaviour. Thus; 'He is clumsy, I was tripped …' is a classic actor/observer effect.

disrupted families: a broad term used to describe families that have been subjected to various types of disruption such as separation/divorce, widowhood, step-parenting and so on.

disruption of attachment: Bowlby's theory of attachment suggests that attachment with a mother figure is essential for healthy social and emotional development. Disruption of this attachment, therefore, is thought to have a negative effect on development. A number of studies have supported this idea, particularly if disruption is in the early years, but other studies have shown that the ill effects of disruption can be minimised if the child is provided with appropriate emotional care during any separation from the primary attachment figure.

dissociative disorders: a type of disorder in which one part of a person's identity becomes dissociated from another. These may include:

- dissociative amnesia, where a person is unable to recall information about a particularly traumatic period in their lives

- dissociative fugue, where a person may forget their true identity and attempt to establish a new one
- *multiple personality disorder (MPD)*, where the person may display a number of different identities each with their own distinct memories.

dissociative identity disorder (DID): formerly known as multiple personality disorder (which is the name still used on the ICD classification system), is a condition where a patient appears to split into two or more separate personalities or 'alters'. A diagnosis of DID requires that at least two personalities routinely take control of the individual's behaviour with an associated memory loss that goes beyond normal forgetfulness. These different personalities may not know about the existence of each other, and in extreme cases they may argue with or subvert the activities of each other. The phenomenon is relatively new and largely unheard of in the UK. That it might exist at all has raised a number of strange moral and legal conflicts. Some murderers in the USA have claimed that the crime was committed by an alter (another of their personalities), therefore they cannot be held responsible. The growth of DID as a phenomenon has been closely tied to the increase in reported cases of child abuse. During therapy, many people have reported incidents of abuse that have not been verified by objective report. This led to accusations that these memories had been unwittingly planted in the minds of vulnerable patients by the therapists themselves (see *recovered memories*). This discovery tended to discredit the widespread preoccupation with early abuse, and with it the possibility of DID as a distinct condition. Cynics of DID started to see it as a clinical invention rather than a real mental disorder.

dissonance theory: see *cognitive dissonance*

distortion illusions: An illusion that distorts an image's shape and/or size by making it look larger, smaller or just a different shape. Examples include the Müller–Lyer illusion and the café wall illusion (see below).

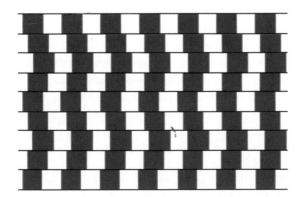

Café wall illusion

distraction-conflict theory: a theory suggesting that when people are working alongside or in front of other people, they are distracted by having to pay attention to both the tasks and the other people. The conflict that this produces (do I pay more attention to the people or the task?) increases *arousal*, which in turn increases the tendency to perform certain dominant responses. If these are appropriate to the task (e.g. increased concentration), they enhance performance, if they are not (e.g. trying to show off to the onlookers), they may have the opposite effect.

distributed practice: see *massed practice*

distribution: a graphical representation of the frequency with which certain scores are found. This can be represented in a number of different ways, including **histograms** and **bar charts**.

distributive justice: the allocation of resources (both benefits and burdens) among members of a community in a manner that is considered fair or socially just.

divergent thinking: see *convergent thinking*

divided attention: see *attention*

dizygotic twins: another term for non-identical twins. Literally, it means two zygotes, or eggs, have been fertilised, rather than in the case of **monozygotic twins** where just one egg is fertilised and goes on to split into identical twins.

DNA: see *deoxyribonucleic acid (DNA)*

dominance hierarchy: a set of relationships among a group of animals in frequent contact, such that an established social order is formed. Dominance hierarchies are made up of a set of individual dominance relationships. There are a number of different types of hierarchy. In the simplest, the linear hierarchy, animal A dominates animal B who dominates animal C and so on. Sometimes triangular relationships form, where animal A is dominant over animal B who is dominant over C who is dominant over A. Triangular hierarchies normally arise where status within a family group is not reflected in the troop as a whole. For example, in a troop of rhesus monkeys, A (a female) may be dominant over her younger brother (B). Because of his age, he may in turn be dominant over another younger, non-related male (C). Because in this troop males are generally dominant over females, C is dominant over A.

A further complicating arrangement in dominance hierarchies is the development of coalitions. These form when two animals (B and C) come together to dominate a third (A) who would normally be dominant to both. Once dominance is established between the coalition and the single animal, in future encounters the single animal will defer to either member of the coalition in disputes over resources. Although the existence of dominance hierarchies is well documented, they are by no means universal. African green monkeys, for example, show little or no evidence of a dominance hierarchy, whereas their close relative, the vervet monkey, has a pronounced linear hierarchy. Some animals that are naturally territorial may change over to a dominance hierarchy when crowded in captivity. This is believed to be a reaction to the stress of captivity. There are several advantages of dominance:

- dominant animals are better fed and healthy as they obtain a greater share of resources
- higher rank is normally associated with greater reproductive success
- in many animals, seniority in the hierarchy is age-related, therefore there is little need for aggression as animals work their way up the system
- dominance hierarchies are also advantageous to subordinate animals who are able to benefit from the advantages of group living (such as defence against predators) rather than living in isolation
- subordinate animals may develop a variety of tactics for 'sneaking' resources so they do not have to compete directly with the more dominant animals in the group.

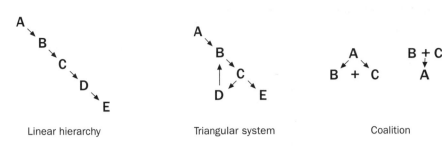

Linear hierarchy   Triangular system   Coalition

door-in-the-face technique: a *compliance* technique, where people are asked a large favour first (which they probably refuse) and are then asked a second, much smaller favour. For example, if you wanted to borrow £5 from one of your parents, you will be more successful if you start at £20 (which they will probably refuse) and then ask for £5. As you have made a concession to them by scaling down your request, they will feel duty-bound to reciprocate!

dopamine: a chemical *neurotransmitter* found in the brain. Dopamine is produced from tyrosine, an amino acid which can be found in various foodstuffs or may be manufactured in the liver. Through the action of various enzymes, tyrosine is eventually converted to dopamine which is then stored in the synaptic vesicles to be used in the process of *synaptic transmission*.

dopamine hypothesis: excessive activity of the *neurotransmitter* dopamine has been linked to schizophrenia. In those suffering from schizophrenia, neurons that use dopamine fire too often and transmit too many messages; as a result, the symptoms associated with schizophrenia appear. Evidence for the role of dopamine comes from two main sources:
- anti-psychotic drugs that reduce the symptoms of schizophrenia block receptor sites for dopamine, and therefore reduce its activity. Similarly, drugs which increase psychotic-like symptoms, such as amphetamines, indirectly increase dopamine activity
- levels of dopamine in the brain can be assessed from levels of homovanillic acid (HVA), a chemical by-product of dopamine. From concentrations of HVA in the brains of schizophrenic patients, it is found that they have much higher levels of dopamine than do normal controls. Autopsies of the brains of schizophrenic patients have also shown that they have far more dopamine receptors than do non-schizophrenics.

From this evidence it was claimed that the symptoms of schizophrenia could be controlled by reducing the levels of dopamine activity in the brain. There are several problems with the dopamine hypothesis:
- only about 50–60 per cent of patients respond to anti-psychotic drugs
- it is now believed that excessive dopamine activity may only be implicated in Type I schizophrenia (characterised by the positive symptoms, such as delusions or hallucinations) and not in Type II schizophrenia (characterised by negative symptoms, such as flatness of affect and loss of personal volition)
- it is also puzzling that drugs which reduce dopamine activity (such as phenothiazines) have to reduce the levels of dopamine to below normal if they are to be effective. According to the theory, reducing levels of dopamine to normal should be sufficient for the client to experience a significant therapeutic effect, but apparently this is not so.

double-bind theory refers to the contradictory messages that an individual receives from another person who has influence over them. Examples would include the adolescent who is criticised by their parents for their independence and rebellion but is also criticised when they show excessive dependence on the parents. The adolescent is thus caught in a 'double-bind', in that nothing they do will be satisfactory to the parents. It is thought that double-bind conflicts such as this might be instrumental (as life stresses) in the development of some mental disorders.

double-blind procedure: a procedure within an experiment which is designed to reduce the biases that may occur through either the participant or experimenter knowing under which condition of the experiment the participant is operating. If neither knows this information, then they cannot adjust their behaviour to achieve the results they may expect to find under that condition.

Down's syndrome: a chromosomal disorder that leads to mental retardation. It is estimated that 1 in every 1000 children born has a form of Down's syndrome, although this figure can rise to as many as 1 in 40 in mothers over 45. In the commonest type of Down's syndrome (trisomy 21), the individual has a third chromosome at the 21st pair. Most Down's children have an *IQ* of between 35 and 55, although some of the claims for specific personality characteristics are merely unwarranted stereotypes.

dream analysis: *Freud* believed that all dreams were the unconscious fulfilment of wishes that could not be satisfied in the conscious mind. Dreams therefore protect the sleeper but also allow some expression to these latent urges. According to Freud, although dreams represent unfulfilled wishes, their contents are expressed symbolically. The real meaning of a dream (the latent content) is transformed into a more innocuous form (the manifest content), which may be meaningless to anybody but a psychoanalyst trained to interpret these symbols. In order fully to understand the meaning of dream symbols, Freud believed it was necessary to consider them in the context of a person's life. Freud did not support the idea of dream dictionaries because symbols are personal. He also believed that sometimes there was no hidden meaning in a dream.

dreams: a form of visual imagery experienced during *rapid eye movement (REM) sleep*. Research has shown that people woken during REM sleep typically report that they had been dreaming. Dreaming is also found in non-REM sleep, although not as regularly. The exact function and nature of dreams is one of the oldest debates in psychology. *Freud* claimed that they were *wish fulfilment*, in that urges that were unacceptable to the conscious mind could be exercised in the unconscious world of dreams. Cognitive explanations of the nature of dreams are far less exciting, with dreams representing a sort of mental filing system. As we sleep, our brains continue to process the day's activities. Dreams simply represent our brain's attempt to form some sort of order out of a chaotic cognitive world of images left over from the day.

drive: a term which describes the motivational state of an animal arising directly from some specific need (e.g. a need for food, a need to escape and so on). If we have a need for food then we experience the motivational state of hunger.

drive theory: the idea that individuals are born with a number of basic physiological needs and that a negative state of tension (e.g. feelings of hunger or thirst) is experienced if these needs are not satisfied. When a need is satisfied (e.g. the hungry person eats), the associated drive is reduced and the organism returns to a state of homeostasis. According to this theory, all behaviour can be explained in terms of the pleasure gained when such drive-induced tensions are reduced.

drug treatments: an approach to the treatment of psychological disorders that is based on biological explanations of abnormal behaviour. Drug treatments cover four major types:

- anti-anxiety drugs – these do have a beneficial effect in reducing *anxiety* but can be over-used and may produce dependence if they are used for a prolonged period of time
- anti-psychotic drugs – used to alleviate the symptoms of the *psychoses.* They are commonly used in the treatment of *schizophrenia.* When used in the treatment of this disorder, they are more effective than any other form of treatment used on its own, but may appear insufficient unless combined with other forms of *psychotherapy*. Anti-psychotic drugs may also cause unwanted side-effects which are not always reversible when the treatment ceases. Anti-psychotic drugs are popular for the simple reason that they offer hope and improvement for clients that might otherwise exist in a state of hopeless misery
- *anti-depressant* drugs – relieve the symptoms of *depression.* These include the MAO inhibitors, tricyclics and the second generation anti-depressant drugs such as 'Prozac' The latter two types are prescribed more often than the MAO inhibitors, which have a number of potentially dangerous side-effects. Although anti-depressants are only marginally more effective than *cognitive therapies*, when used together they are more effective than either used alone
- anti-bipolar drugs, such as lithium (in the form of lithium carbonate), are used as a treatment for people suffering from a *bipolar disorder*. These people have mood swings from *mania* to *depression*,and these drugs stabilise their mood states.

DSM: see *Diagnostic and Statistical Manual (DSM)*

DSM-IV-TR: the most recent (2004) update of the *Diagnostic and Statistical Manual (DSM)*.

dualism: a philosophical position which is normally encountered in the mind–body debate. Dualism draws a distinction between the mind and body in one of two ways. Parallel dualism sees the mind and the body as fundamentally different parts of the same organism. They co-exist, but in separate and parallel forms. Interactive dualism, on the other hand, acknowledges the separate nature of mind and body, but sees them as constantly interacting.

Duck's model of relationship breakdown: Duck's original model of relationship breakdown was extended by Rollie and Duck in 2006. Rather than expressing the breakdown of a relationship in terms of distinct stages, Rollie and Duck emphasised the different communication processes that characterised different phases of a relationship breakdown. In the first (breakdown), one partner realises his or her dissatisfaction with the relationship. In the second (intrapsychic processes), the partner broods on faults of the other and re-evaluates alternatives to the relationship. The third (dyadic processes) is characterised by a discussion of the relationship with the other partner, and a reassessment of goals, possibilities and commitments. The fourth (social processes) involves others outside the relationship, and alliance building. In the penultimate phase (grave-dressing), stories are prepared for different audiences in order to save face. The final phase (resurrection) prepares the individual for a different relational future.

duration: a measure of how long a memory lasts before it is no longer available. The duration of memories in the **short-term memory** is a matter of seconds unless it is rehearsed. The duration of memories in **long-term memory** is anywhere from 2 minutes to 100+ years – i.e. anything that isn't short-term.

dyscalculia: a difficulty with mathematics. There are very strict criteria that determine if a student has a learning disability as it is defined by educational psychologists. When a child's maths difficulties are severe enough to meet these criteria, special educational intervention is appropriate. On the other hand, 'dyscalculia' has no clearly defined criteria. A child with any degree of maths difficulty may be considered to have 'dyscalculia' by some educational specialists. Being identified as having 'dyscalculia', therefore, may or may not indicate the need for special educational intervention. However, the term is seldom used within schools because of the lack of any strict or measurable criteria.

There are a number of possible causes of dyscalculia. The most common reason for maths difficulties lies with a weakness in the visual processing of numbers. Some children also experience sequencing problems: if they have difficulty sequencing or organising detailed information, they often have difficulty remembering specific facts and formulae for completing maths calculations. Some children simply develop a 'maths phobia' either because of negative experiences in the past, or lack of self-confidence. Sometimes maths phobia can cause as much difficulty as a learning disability.

dysfunction: any breakdown in normal functioning, either of the person or of some physical or mental structure within the person.

dysfunctional behaviour: an inappropriate action or response in a given situation that is a problem for the individual and may be an indication of underlying psychopathology.

dyslexia: a term with two distinct meanings. In the more familiar case the term 'developmental dyslexia' is used to describe difficulties with written and spoken language that are believed to be a product of anomalies of development. It is assessed that some 2–4 per cent of ten year olds are significantly affected by dyslexia. The second, and less familiar use of the term dyslexia is in 'acquired dyslexia', where, as a result of a stroke or related injury, language skills have become impaired. Only the former (developmental) type of dyslexia will be elaborated here. Specific developmental dyslexia (often referred to as a 'specific learning difficulty') typically involves the following:

- difficulties in learning to read or spell that are not due to lack of intelligence or opportunity
- uncertainty over right and left
- confusion between the letters b and d
- difficulties in learning arithmetic tables
- difficulties in recalling items (such as the months or the year or the seasons) in sequence.

Difficulties have typically been experienced in distinguishing those poor readers and spellers who display the dyslexia syndrome, and those who do not. A person is more likely to be diagnosed as dyslexic if they are unusually weak in these areas compared to other skills (notably **intelligence**).

ear acupuncture: a controversial form of complementary therapy that is claimed to help alleviate a variety of conditions including stress, drug withdrawal, eating disorders and depression.

eating disorder: a term which refers to a serious disruption of the eating habits or the appetite. The main types of eating disorder are *anorexia nervosa* and *bulimia nervosa*.

echolalia: a condition often found in *autistic* children, whereby they show a pathological repetition of the words of others. This is sometimes immediate and sometimes delayed for hours or even days (delayed echolalia). Echolalia is also a symptom of *catatonic schizophrenia*.

ecological accounts of sleep: see *evolutionary explanations of sleep*

ecological demands and human intelligence: explanations of the evolution of human intelligence that focus on the adaptive demands of finding and extracting food, and dealing effectively with the demands of the environment rather than the demands posed by living with other humans (see *Machiavellian intelligence*).

ecological validity refers to the degree to which the results of an investigation can be generalised beyond the immediate setting in which they were gathered to other settings and other situations. Laboratory *experiments* are frequently criticised for lacking ecological validity because it is doubted whether their findings would apply outside the contrived conditions of the laboratory. In a sense, ecological validity refers to the need for more *naturalistic* settings for research. A natural setting does not, however, make a study ecologically valid. To discover a particular sort of social behaviour on an oil rig or a desert island does not necessarily tell us that such behaviour would be universal across all situations and settings. Something is only ecologically valid if it can be shown to occur outside the immediate setting in which it was observed. Social psychology is riddled with such problems, as so many of the investigations we read about in the text books have used the laboratory as a research setting. Milgram's classic experiments on *obedience* to authority have been criticised because of the artificiality of the highly academic setting in which they were carried out. There has been considerable dispute over whether such findings really can tell us anything useful about the sort of atrocities that take place during wartime, for example, which have frequently been attributed to obedience to authority. Cognitive psychologists such as Neisser have also criticised much of established theory on *attention* and *perception* because they have been based on laboratory research that is far removed from the way we use our cognitive faculties in real life.

ECT: see *electroconvulsive shock treatment (ECT)*

educational psychology: a broad-based discipline concerned with the application of psychological knowledge in educational settings. Educational psychologists are involved in applying the principles of learning in classroom settings, in classroom management, *psychometric testing*, teacher training and other aspects of child and adolescent development that are directly linked to the educative process. In this country, educational psychologists are employed by local authorities. They usually possess an honours degree in psychology (or equivalent), a teaching qualification and appropriate experience, and finally a postgraduate qualification (masters degree) in educational psychology.

EEG: see *electroencephalogram (EEG)*

effect: literally, something that happens as a direct result of something else. In *experiments*, it is possible to establish a cause-and-effect relationship between two measured *variables*. For example, if giving alcohol to *participants* causes them to fall over, then the falling over is the effect.

efferent neuron: a nerve cell that that carries nerve impulses away from the *central nervous system (CNS)* to the muscles and glands of the body. Also known as a motor neuron.

E-FIT: a computerised method of synthesising images in order to produce a composite face. This system enables a trained operator to produce an accurate likeness based on a witness's description. E-FIT is claimed to be unique because it recognises, and was developed to include, the psychological factors that affect our ability to recall and recognise faces.

ego: that part of the personality which, according to *Freud*, operates on the *reality principle* (i.e. keeps us in touch with reality) and must mediate between the demands of the pleasure-seeking *id* and the moralistic *superego.* The ego uses *defence mechanisms* to protect the individual from *unconscious* anxiety. The term is also used in psychology in a more general way, meaning anything to do with one's self.

egocentricity: means viewing the world only from one's own perspective, and apparently being unaware that another person might have a different perspective. In the developmental theory of Jean *Piaget,* this is seen as a characteristic of the pre-operational child. In Piaget's original three mountains experiment, young children were asked how the mountains would look to a child with a different observational point than their own. The fact that they seemed unable to do this (choosing instead the view that they themselves had) appeared to indicate their egocentricity. Later research using culturally more familiar tasks (such as the naughty boy/policeman task) showed that children could *decentre* much earlier than originally suggested by Piaget.

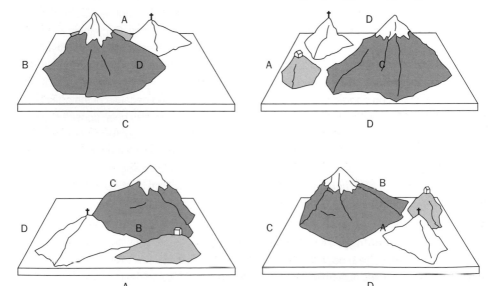

The model of the mountain range used by Piaget viewed from four different sides

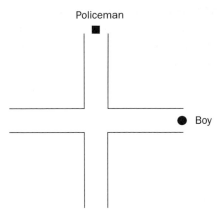

The naughty boy and policeman problem. Children who can 'decentre' are able to position the boy where he cannot be seen by the policeman

egocentric speech: a term used by Jean **Piaget** to describe the 'speech for self' of young children. Young children frequently chatter away as they play, despite the fact that there is no one else playing with them. This type of speech is not really intended as a form of social communication and gradually declines as the child develops more social speech.

ego-defence mechanisms: see *defence mechanism*

ego-ideal: see *superego*

egoism: the tendency for people to behave largely out of self-interest.

eidetic imagery refers to the ability to still 'see' an image despite the fact that it is no longer present. The mental image is a true representation of the objective image, rather than a reconstruction through memory. This skill is rare in adults, but reasonably common in children (about 1 in 20 children has this ability).

Eisenberg's model of pro-social reasoning: Eisenberg identifies the emergence of *empathy* as an important point in the development of prosocial reasoning. Young children experience personal distress when they see that someone else is unhappy, but their distress is not because they are experiencing someone else's emotions, it is because it is personally distressing for them. Eisenberg believes that the key to the development of empathy lies in the ability of the child to take the perspective of another person. An emotional response is turned into empathic concern when the child understands the distress of others and feels concern for them. Eisenberg devised a set of **moral dilemmas** to assess children's development of prosocial reasoning. From these responses she identified five stages of prosocial reasoning, from a hedonistic, self-focused orientation (level 1) found in young children, through to strongly internalised principles (level 5), found in some adolescents and most adults. Older children are capable of more mature levels of reasoning, but may sometimes revert to earlier levels.

elaborated code: see *restricted code*

elaboration-likelihood model: this suggests two different routes to persuasive communication depending on whether the audience is likely to focus on the message itself or on other 'peripheral' factors such as how attractive or credible the source appears to be. If an audience focuses on the arguments themselves (for example they are likely to be of interest to them), then a central route to persuasion is more effective. If people focus more on the context of the message than the message itself, then a peripheral route is more likely to be effective.

Electra complex: the female version of the *Oedipus complex* in which girls between the ages of four and six envy their father for possessing the penis that they have been denied. When the girl discovers that she lacks a penis, she is thought to blame the mother, and thus transfers her affections from the mother to the father. Because (according to *Freud*) both boys and girls value the penis, daughters choose their fathers as their primary love object. He does, after all, possess the penis they lack. As they realise the unequal struggle to possess the father, they must renounce these feelings and identify with their mother. This is the fundamental problem. Boys renounce their feelings for the mother because of the fear of castration, yet Freud suggested that this would not be the case with girls, who had already been castrated by their mother. Freud suggested that the Electra complex would simply fade away as girls realised that they would never possess their father. However, because the threat of punishment through castration is not present for girls, they are not under the same pressure to renounce these feelings and identify with the moral standards of the mother. The consequences of this, Freud felt, would be that girls develop a weaker *superego* and are therefore seen as morally deficient. (See also *alpha bias*.)

electrical self-stimulation of the brain: pulses of electrical current delivered through electrodes implanted in the brain, which act as a reward when an animal presses a lever. It is thought to be a more powerful *reinforcer* than the more natural reinforcers like food or drink, because the animal does not seem to become satiated (i.e. does not stop pressing the lever when it reaches a certain optimum level).

electrical stimulation of the brain (ESB) involves the application of a weak electrical current to a specific area of the brain. Within psychology, this technique has been used to study the relationship between areas of the brain and the different functions that they control.

electroconvulsive shock treatment (ECT): a treatment sometimes used in cases of severe depression. An electric current of between 65 and 140 milliamps is passed through electrodes attached to each side of the client's forehead. This causes loss of consciousness and a convulsive seizure that lasts from 30 seconds to a few minutes. It is these convulsions rather than the electric shock itself that appears to be the key to the effectiveness of ECT. The main reason why ECT is used is because some patients do not seem to respond to *anti-depressant* drugs but do respond to ECT.

PROS:
- it is claimed that ECT reduces depression more rapidly than drugs. This is particularly important in suicidally depressed patients
- ECT's effectiveness is supported by well-documented research evidence, especially in chronic drug-resistant patients
- the side-effects of ECT are less troublesome than from many forms of medication and are usually only temporary.

CONS:
- there is no data to support the view that ECT saves lives in suicidally depressed patients
- there is an equally large body of contradictory evidence that challenges the effectiveness of ECT
- the side-effects of ECT may be more serious than claimed by its users. They may involve cognitive dysfunctions (such as amnesia) and permanent organic changes if used regularly.

electroencephalogram (EEG): a method of recording changes in the electrical activity of the brain.

emic: an analysis of human behaviour that focuses on the many varied ways in which behaviours are enacted in different cultures.

emotion: although everybody knows what emotions are, the term itself is notoriously difficult to define. Definitions can be broad, in that emotions are seen as multi-faceted responses that involve interaction between subjective feelings and objective experiences, or narrow, in that emotions are simply how we 'feel' (for example, happy, angry, sad, etc.) In the former use of the term, emotions can be seen as giving rise to:

- affective experiences such as those which are experienced as pleasurable or unpleasurable. These can be external (such as meeting a dangerous animal) or internal (such as a particular thought or image)
- *cognitive processes* where we label the affective experience (e.g. as happiness or sadness) and appraise our reactions to it. For example, seeing a dangerous animal at the zoo will not produce quite the same emotional reactions as seeing the same dangerous animal blocking our path in the wild
- physiological adjustments to whatever it is that is arousing us. That is, our body prepares us to deal with the situation, and then after the situation has passed, attempts to return our body to a state of equilibrium
- behaviour that tends to be goal directed and adaptive, e.g. we attempt to remove ourselves from whatever is causing the unpleasurable feelings, or prolong whatever is causing us the pleasurable feelings.

There are a number of characteristics of emotions that set them apart from other experiences such as feelings or sentiments:

- they are acute – being more momentary than prolonged
- they are experienced as an intense state – i.e. they are more than just a passing sentiment
- they are characterised by behavioural disorganisation – behaviour tends to become random and chaotic when the organism is in an emotional state
- emotions tend to be a product of the *evolutionary* adaptation of that species – they reflect survival strategies, although the causes of that response may no longer be contemporary
- emotions are non-habitual – i.e. they are not habits in that they do not express themselves as part of some regular cycle, but are reactions to specific experiences.

emotion-focused coping: the use of coping strategies that deal only with the emotional distress associated with stressful events rather than dealing directly with the event itself (see *problem-focused coping*). Examples of emotion-focused coping include focusing on and venting emotions (e.g. crying or getting angry) and wishful thinking (e.g. dwelling on what might have been). Emotion-focused coping may reduce arousal prior to a more constructive problem-focused approach or may help people to deal with stressful situations where there are few options to change the situation itself.

emotional intelligence: a type of social intelligence that involves the ability to monitor one's own and others' emotions, to discriminate among these emotions and to use this information to guide one's thinking and actions (Salovey and Mayer, 1990). Salovey and Mayer claim that emotional intelligence has five principal features:

1. Being aware of one's own emotions.
2. Being able to manage one's own emotions.
3. Being sensitive to the emotions of others.
4. Being able to respond to and negotiate with other people emotionally.
5. Being able to use one's own emotions to motivate oneself.

empathy: this term refers to our awareness of the emotional state of another person, and our ability to share the experience with them. In this latter sense, we vicariously experience the same emotions. It is common to share emotions with our children, so that we feel pride when they feel pride, we share their sadness and their loneliness. Having empathy with another is more than 'feeling sorry' for them or 'pleased for them', it is a common sharing of the same pain, pleasure, anger, etc. When these emotions are painful, we are frequently motivated to act to relieve them. The empathy-altruism theory, for example, explains human *altruism* in terms of the shared pain we have with somebody in need. We are thus seen as helping them to overcome our own empathic pain.

empathy-altruism hypothesis: a theory which explains altruistic behaviour as a consequence of our empathy with another person in need. Witnessing another person in distress will create empathic concern (e.g. sympathy) and helpers would then be motivated to help alleviate the other person's distress. Empathy consists of a number of different components, including perspective-taking (seeing things from the other person's point of view), personal distress (experiencing emotions such as alarm or sadness) and empathic concern. It is perspective-taking that leads to empathic concern. If the perspective of the other person is not taken, this does not happen, and we experience personal distress rather than empathetic concern (see *negative-state relief* model). Any actions we take to reduce this will be based on egoistic motives (i.e. to reduce our own personal distress).

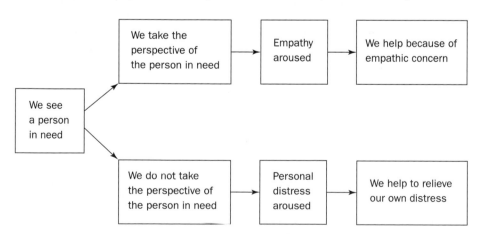

Research in this area has consistently found that people high in empathic concern are more likely to help another person even when they are in a position to escape from the responsibility of helping. Research has also cast doubt on the suggestion that people who show empathic concern only help others in order to escape social or self-disapproval. It therefore contradicts the underlying assumption that human nature is fundamentally self-serving.

empirical research: research that results in the collection, analysis and evaluation of data. The term 'empirical' is frequently (although not altogether accurately) used synonymously with experimental.

enactive representation: see *Bruner, J*

encephalisation: the characteristic of some species (human beings among them) having brains that are larger than we would predict for an animal of that species' body-mass. Such species are said to be 'encephalised'. Other species that share this characteristic are dolphins and porpoises, elephants, gorillas and chimpanzees. Animals who do not classify as being encephalised include the rat, lion and blue whale.

encoding: the way information is changed so it can be stored in memory. We can compare the way that information is stored in **short-term memory** (STM) and **long-term memory** (LTM) in terms of the encoding of the **memory trace**. Acoustic coding involves coding information in terms of the way it sounds, and semantic coding involves coding information in terms of its meaning. STM involves acoustic coding – when we try to keep information active in STM we repeat it over and over to ourselves – in other words we maintain an acoustic memory trace. LTM, on the other hand, involves semantic coding. That is, we encode information according to the *meaning* of words, rather than the way they sound.

endocrine system: a system of internal glands that produce hormones and release them into the bloodstream. Hormones are then distributed to the rest of the body through the bloodstream. Hormones affect physiological and behavioural functions by acting on receptors in the various target sites. For example, the male sex hormone **testosterone** causes the growth of facial hair by stimulating testosterone receptors in the skin, which then activate hair growth. Hormones that affect behaviour act upon receptors in the brain. When these receptors are activated, they cause an increase in the activity levels of the **neurons** that contain the receptors. For example, the action of testosterone upon specific receptor sites in the brain can cause an increase in the aggressive behaviour of males of most species. Castration (and thus stemming the production of testosterone) causes a decrease in the amount of aggressive behaviour. This does not mean that human aggression is entirely a product of testosterone, nor would castration necessarily be an appropriate remedy for it! It is clear that human aggression is a complex interaction of physiological, experiential and social factors.

endogenous: a general term meaning 'from within'. Development that is a product of internal **maturation** is described as endogenous, whilst development that is caused by outside influences (such as teaching or **conditioning**) is described as **exogenous.**

endogenous depression: *depression* which is thought to be caused by internal factors such as physiological dysfunction. The term is used when there are no identifiable external causes (such as bereavement or redundancy) that might have precipitated the disorder.

endogenous pacemakers: sometimes referred to as 'biological clocks', these are most probably an inherited genetic mechanism. Human bodily rhythms of activity and rest must respond to **zeitgebers** (such as light) if the behaviour they control is to be fully co-ordinated with the external world. The presence of light as a zeitgeber is also necessary to re-set the clock every day so that the biological rhythm is perfectly co-ordinated with the external world. In birds and reptiles, the most important pacemaker is the pineal gland. This structure contains light receptors that respond to light penetrating the thin layer of skull that lies above the pineal gland. These light receptors influence the activity of neurons in the pineal gland, which have a natural rhythmic activity and also convert the neurotransmitter serotonin into the hormone melatonin. Melatonin is then released into the general circulation, acts on many of the body's organs and glands, and seems to be responsible for the rhythmic nature of many activities. The manufacture and release of melatonin is regulated by the amount of light falling on the pineal, decreasing as light increases.

In mammals, the pathways are more complicated. The main biological clock seems to be a small area in the hypothalamus, the suprachiasmatic nucleus (SCN), whose neurons have an inbuilt *circadian* rhythmic firing pattern. This nucleus regulates the manufacture and secretion of melatonin in the pineal gland via an inter-connecting pathway. Another pathway connects the retina of the eye to the SCN. This allows the amount of light falling on the retina to influence the activity of SCN neurons and, indirectly, the release of melatonin from the pineal. The pineal and the SCN function jointly as endogenous pacemakers or biological clocks in the brain. The sensitivity of the pineal and SCN to light, and the role of melatonin in controlling sleep and activity amongst other things, mean that despite the endogenous nature of the clocks, their activity is synchronised with the light–dark rhythm of the world outside. Occasionally, studies have allowed us to look at the effects of removing light as a zeitgeber and allowing these biological clocks to 'run free'. Such studies show that subjects with free-running biological clocks settle to a rhythmic sleeping–waking pattern of about 25 hours, i.e., slightly longer than under normal conditions.

endorphins: a term used to refer to any morphine-like substance that is manufactured naturally in the brain. The discovery of endorphins (an abbreviation of endogenous morphine) suggested that pain-controlling drugs such as morphine work on the same neural systems that are normally activated by the brain's own naturally produced endorphins.

enrichment: see *hothousing*

enuresis: a term for incontinence. Although generally used to describe bed-wetting in children, the term has a much wider application than in just describing this disorder.

environment: a term which usually implies an organism's surroundings, although it can also apply to our internal (i.e. physiological) environment. The term also carries with it the implicit suggestion that the identified environment has a modifying influence on the organism. Thus we say that someone is 'a product of their environment'.

environmental stressors (aggressive behaviour): these are those aspects of the physical environment that are thought to contribute to antisocial behaviour. They may cause an increase in *arousal*, which may in turn evoke negative emotions and thus hostile thoughts and then, perhaps, aggressive behaviour. Several stressors in the environment have been shown to relate to aggressive behaviour.
- The effects of high temperatures on aggression have been demonstrated in a number of studies, both in the laboratory and also in the natural environment. In hotter regions of the world, people tend to show more aggression than cooler regions, and hotter years, seasons and days tend to have more incidents of violent crimes than cooler ones. Laboratory studies of the relationship between heat and aggression have found evidence for an 'inverted U' relationship between heat and aggression. As temperature rises, so does aggression, but only to a certain level, after which it begins

to decline. Research on the effects of heat on aggressive behaviour does not tend to show a consistent relationship between the two. Perhaps the most important general conclusion that can be drawn is that high temperatures can change the way in which people interpret ambiguous situations, and may, therefore predispose a person towards an aggressive response.

- Intense levels of noise may also act as antecedents of aggression. Noise may adversely affect the ability to deal with frustration, and may increase aggression simply because it raises arousal levels. This is particularly evident if the noise is experienced after a person has become ready to aggress because of some prior provocation. Research suggests that under circumstances in which noise might be expected to increase arousal (e.g. when it is both unpleasant and uncontrollable), aggression responses become more frequent. However, when the noise does not appreciably increase arousal (as when the individual has control over it), noise appears to have little or no effect on aggression.

- Crowding is the psychological experience of discomfort and stress associated with the limited space. If our expectations of the use of space are violated by the presence of others, the feeling of crowding is induced. An increase in the number of people or decrease in the amount of available space (indicating social and spatial density respectively) leads to high-density situations in which an individual may feel uncomfortable. Research into this area has produced inconsistent results suggesting only a weak relationship between high densities and aggressive behaviour. Researchers have also found that the effects of changes in social density are more aversive than changes in spatial density.

EPI: see *Eysenck Personality Inventory (EPI)*

epinephrine: a term used in the USA for what we in Europe refer to as adrenaline.

episodic memory: a distinction between episodic memory (memory for personal events or episodes) and *semantic memory* (memory for facts) was suggested by Tulving in 1972. Episodic memory is claimed to hold information relating to episodes in a person's life, such as events at college or childhood experiences. Semantic memory, on the other hand, would contain more factual information such as our memory of algebra or of a particular aspect of psychology. Although this is a useful distinction to make, and it is clear that the type of information stored in these two memories differs, it is less clear that the processes involved are equally distinctive. Memories of factual knowledge tend to be stored within an episodic context, in that when recalling some aspect of psychology, we may also recall the context (the day, the situation, etc.) in which we learned it.

What this means in practice is that whilst we may have two different memories for facts and events, they usually work together. Evidence supporting this distinction comes from studies of *amnesic* patients (people suffering a temporary or permanent memory loss). They are typically reported as having intact semantic memories but poor episodic memories, being unable to remember conversations taking place or meeting new people. Eysenck and Keane (1990) suggest that, despite the immediate appeal of this evidence, it does have its flaws. Most studies of amnesic patients have discovered a loss of memory for episodes *after* the onset of amnesia, whereas the intact semantic memory concerns information acquired *before* the onset of amnesia. Recent studies have found that amnesics can recall episodes prior to their amnesia, yet cannot retain factual knowledge that they have acquired after their amnesia. It is clear from such findings that the initial claims for episodic/semantic differences in amnesic patients may have been overstated.

equilibration: a term used in the *cognitive-developmental* theory of Jean *Piaget* to describe the child's movement between a state of equilibrium, when they are mostly *assimilating*, to a state of disequilibrium, when they are mostly **accommodating**. When children are not changing a great deal, their existing understanding of the world is sufficient to solve most of the problems they have to face. This is a state of equilibrium. When they are forced to face new challenges such that they realise that this new information does not match their current understanding, they are forced into a state of transition, or disequilibrium. By changing their present level of understanding or ability (accommodation), they are able to restore the former state of equilibrium. Each time that equilibrium occurs, the child produces more effective schemata (mental structures).

equity theory: a theory which suggests that people try to maintain a balance between what they put into a relationship and what they get out of it. Most people would expect to receive rewards from a relationship which are roughly proportional to the contributions they put into it. If there is inequity in the relationship, then members may feel motivated to end it. Research with married couples has shown that those who thought their rewards were more or less equal to their contributions were happy with the relationship. Those who felt that their rewards were less than their contributions were less happy, but so too were those who felt their rewards were greater than their contributions.

Erikson's 'Eight ages of man': Although Erikson accepted the basics of *Freud's* psychoanalytic theory, he believed that we should place a stronger emphasis on the lifelong relationship between the individual and the social system in which he or she develops. Erikson believed that there are eight distinct stages to a person's life. Each stage presents particular challenges that are characteristic of that time of the person's life. For example, in the first year of life, the infant must face the challenge of 'trust versus mistrust'. Successful resolution of the challenges of this stage results in the development of trust, failure leads to mistrust in others. In midlife, a person faces the challenge of 'generativity versus stagnation' In this stage, individuals may express themselves as caring and productive members of their own generation or perhaps in terms of their ability to help members of the next generation unlock their potential and achieve success. Those without children and without jobs or lifestyles that have significant meaning to them may experience a feeling of stagnation. Psychologically healthy individuals meet the challenges of each stage and are thus prepared for the challenges of the next stage. Psychologically unhealthy individuals may fail to meet the challenges of a particular stage and therefore must deal with the conflicts that emerge from this failure in the stages that follow.

erogenous zones: areas of the body which produce sexual sensations when they are stimulated.

Eros: in Freudian theory, the term used for the life instincts. Most notable of these is the sex or reproductive instinct.

ESB: see *electrical stimulation of the brain (ESB)*

ESP: see *extrasensory perception (ESP)*

ethics/ethical issues: a consideration of what is acceptable or right behaviour in the pursuit of a particular personal or scientific goal. The study of ethics has traditionally been a branch of philosophy rather than of science, but with increasing accountability within the field of scientific enquiry, it is clear that the morality of a particular endeavour must be as important as its practical considerations. When applied to research with human beings, the relevance of ethics becomes paramount. Most psychologists subscribe to a relative view of the ethical responsibilities of psychologists, in that the ends are seen as justifying the means. The publication of clear guidelines (for example those produced by the **British Psychological Society (BPS)**) ensure that research is carried out in a way that is both in the best interests of the participants, and is also morally defensible to those outside the research context. These guidelines include reference to the importance of **informed consent** and the avoidance of deception. Simple rule-following may not always produce the most ethically correct research. In the view of many social psychologists, the role of research scientists is a wider one, and may include responsibilities within a far wider social context than the immediate responsibilities toward their research participants. Research into areas such as **obedience** and **bystander behaviour** has been defended by such reasoning. The use of non-human animals has provoked especially fierce argument over such a point (see **animal research**).

ethnocentrism: a term which refers to the use of our own ethnic group as a basis for judgements about other ethnic groups. There is a tendency to view the beliefs, customs and behaviours of our own group as 'normal' and those of other ethnic groups as 'strange' or deviant. There is the implicit assumption in all of this that our own ethnic group is somehow superior to the others that we are judging it against.

ethnomethodology: a technique devised by Garfinkel to discover hidden **norms** by violating them. Most societies have formal rules and norms that are enforced by legislation. For example, bank robbery is quite clearly a crime punishable by fine or imprisonment. Other norms differ from culture to culture, and may be quite invisible to people who are 'visitors' to that culture. These norms are never formally stated, yet are often of vital importance in our social interactions. For example, pointing out to your teacher that your classmate failed to complete her lab report because she had been at a rave the night before is not a crime, yet anyone who acted this way would be violating one of the implicit rules of friendship, i.e. never snitch on a friend. By violating these norms, we can become aware of their existence, and can draw people's attention to them.

ethology: literally, the biological study of behaviour. Ethologists spend a great deal of their time studying animals in their feral (wild) state. As a result of painstaking observation of different species, ethologists are able to produce a detailed description (ethogram) of the patterns of behaviour of the animals concerned. For example, observations of the behaviour of the male stickleback during the breeding season shows stereotypical movements and activities that are common to all males within the same species. They gather weed and glue it together to form a nest. If another male approaches, they show a special 'head down' posture which is a threat display to the intruder. If a female approaches, he leads her to the nest with a 'zig-zag' dance. After she has laid her eggs in his nest, he follows her into the nest and fertilises the eggs. As part of his responsibility to his newly acquired nest of eggs, he fans them to keep them supplied with oxygen. The ethologist Niko Tinbergen suggested that there were four main questions that could be asked in the study of animal behaviour:

- development – does the behaviour change over the lifetime of the animal?
- causes – is the behaviour a product of internal states or external stimuli?
- functions – why does the animal behave in that way? What are the advantages to the animal?
- evolution – what are the evolutionary origins of the behaviour?

Early ethological theories about animal behaviour were based more on careful observation and intuition than on the experimental evidence more typically associated with scientific psychology.

Although the ethological study of animal behaviour tends to be found under the heading of **comparative psychology** in A-level syllabuses and textbooks, there are significant differences between the two disciplines. Ethologists have an interest in many different species and the different behaviours characteristic of those species. Comparative psychologists, on the other hand, study a restricted number of species with the assumption that they can develop general laws of behaviour that would apply to all species. This study of species-specific behaviour is very important in ethology. Patterns of stereotyped behaviour in these species led ethologists to believe that such behaviour was **innate** or instinctive. The controversy between ethology and comparative psychology has led to important changes in thinking in both disciplines. Psychologists came to acknowledge the evolutionary influences and constraints on **learning**, and ethologists began to see the value of a carefully controlled experimental approach in the understanding of animal behaviour.

etic: a form of analysis that focuses on the universals of human behaviour. Many theories have claimed universality in their application (see **Kohlberg's** theory of moral development as an example) without, it appears, sufficient evidence for so doing. In this sense, they become examples of an 'imposed etic'.

etiology: see *aetiology*

eugenics: a programme of **selective breeding** with the aim of 'improving' human abilities through careful transmission of inherited characteristics. Impractical, immoral and largely outdated as an idea.

Eurocentrism is a form of cultural bias whereby psychologists place more emphasis on European (or Western) theories and ideas, at the expense of other cultures. Implicit in this definition is the assumption that Western concepts are fundamentally different (and most probably superior) from those in other cultures. The term may also be used in a somewhat contradictory way to reflect the assumption that Western theories and ideas are, in fact, universal (see *etic*).

evaluation apprehension: refers to the concerns that a participant has when they feel they are being judged within an experiment. Because of this concern, they may attempt to alter their behaviour so they are seen in a favourable light.

event sampling: an aspect of **observational** studies, where an event is recorded every time it occurs. For example, if we were recording the intricacies of a football match, we might record every time a particular player passed the ball, tackled, hurled abuse at the referee, and so on. Event sampling rarely involves more than a simple recording of the incidence (i.e. whether it occurred or not, and if so how many times) of a particular behaviour.

evolution: refers to the change over successive generations of the genetic make-up of a particular animal population. The central idea of an evolutionary perspective to animal *traits* is that animal species are changeable rather than fixed, and that this change is likely to be caused by the process of *natural selection.* Given that genetic variation can be caused or increased by a number of different factors, including *mutation* and migration (movement of animals from one group to another), natural selection serves the purpose of selecting and stabilising particular gene patterns. Although it is still widely believed that natural selection is the main cause of evolutionary change, there are other possible influences including genetic drift, where gene frequencies change at random, and the founder effect, where the founders of a population of animals are not representative of their original population. This latter explanation is analogous to a desert island being colonised by two members of the 6ft 9in and over, red-headed club. Although the colony might very quickly grow to a substantial size, the members of that population would be quite different genetically to the rest of the human species, yet this difference would not have been caused by natural selection.

evolutionary explanations of mental disorders are attempts to explain why those disorders, if genetic, still persist in the gene pool and have not been weeded out by *natural selection*. One possibility is that some disorders (such as *depression* or *schizophrenia*) give rise to behaviours that profit the individual either directly (e.g. personal survival) or indirectly (e.g. increasing the survival of genetic relatives). The *rank theory of depression* is an example of the former. The major attraction of this field of psychology is that it gives us an insight into the 'normal' functions of many disorders rather than seeing them as biological or psychological aberrations.

evolutionary explanations of sleep: also referred to as 'ecological' explanations, evolutionary explanations emphasise the selective advantage of sleep to animals. These advantages include energy conservation, foraging requirements and predator avoidance. Sleep provides a period of enforced inactivity and therefore is a means of conserving energy. Herbivores have a diet that is relatively poor in nutrients and so must spend a great deal of time eating. Consequently they cannot afford to spend time sleeping. Carnivores, on the other hand, have a diet high in nutrients and so do not need to eat continuously. Consequently they can afford to rest for much longer. Sleep may also be constrained by predation risk. Predators can sleep for longer whereas, for prey species, sleep time is reduced as they must remain vigilant to avoid predators. The more dangerous an animal's world, the less time it can afford to spend sleeping and being vulnerable.

evolutionary psychology is a branch of science that believes that human beings adapted to a relatively stable ancestral environment, the 'environment of evolutionary adaptedness' (EEA), over a period of approximately 100,000 years. Humans evolved highly specific mental mechanisms to cope with the challenges of the EEA, and those same 'hard-wired' instincts persist in modern humans. Under this perspective, humans have innate areas in their brains that are highly specialized, and only activated when specific problems (such as choosing a mate) are faced. These areas give the brain specific 'instructions' that have evolved from our ancestral past to help us adapt to all situations, even though in recent times the environment (and therefore the problems we face) has changed rapidly.

evolution of intelligence refers to the debate concerning how and why human intelligence has developed as it has. One argument focuses on the relationship between *brain size and intelligence* and the increasing evidence of *encephalisation* among the higher primates. However, larger brains are also very 'expensive' in terms of the increased need for energy to run them efficiently, so clearly they must equip us with significant advantages that outweigh the costs of maintaining such an extravagant organ. The two most commonly suggested factors thought to have necessitated the evolution of large human brains and the corresponding increase in intelligence are:

- *foraging* demands: the ability to find food would have presented early man with significant challenges that would demand sophisticated cognitive skills
- group living: the increasing social complexity of social living and the need to maintain group cohesion and minimise group conflict is thought to correlate positively with the increased development of the neocortex in particular.

ex post-facto study: a type of *research* study in which the *independent variable* is some aspect of the participant (such as their age, gender, political persuasion or whatever). As the researcher has no control over the independent variable in that s/he cannot manipulate it, the independent variable can only be varied by selecting participants that differ in the chosen feature (e.g. different age groups). Because manipulation of the independent variable is not possible and participants cannot be randomly assigned to different conditions (such as age groups), the relationship between independent variable and *dependent variable* cannot be established as a causal one. Thus we may say that people of different age groups perform differently in some way, but we cannot say that these differences in behaviour were caused by age.

excitation: in physiology this term is taken to mean a pattern of change within a receptor produced by stimulus energy. Away from this quite specific usage, it means any increase in tension such as might be produced by *arousal*.

excitation-transfer theory: an explanation of how *arousal* that is generated in one situation can be transferred to another and added to the arousal generated in the second. The resultant effect is that the experience of arousal in the second situation is more intense as a direct result of the addition of the arousal from the first situation. For example, you have just finished a bout of physical exercise, and whilst cooling off, someone passes a derogatory comment about you. There are three possible interpretations of the arousal that you feel:

1. If you have only just finished the exercise you would attribute the arousal to the exercise. As a result, there is no need to look for another cause.
2. If the arousal caused by the exercise has passed, and provided the comment was not *too* derogatory, very little arousal is produced by the new situation, so nothing happens.
3. If the time interval between exercise and comment is long enough for the person to *think* the arousal from the exercise has passed but not long enough to get rid of all its residual effects, then these are transferred to the new situation, where together with the arousal from that may produce an aggressive reaction.

exercise and well-being: exercise has long been regarded in popular culture as an effective way of coping with stress and recent research suggests it may also have beneficial effects on alleviating depression. However, excessive exercise may also lead to problems for some people. Exercise dependency syndrome is a form of addictive behaviour that can lead to a state in which individuals continually increase the amount of exercise they perform, as they build a tolerance to exercise. This may result in the individual making other daily activities and responsibilities secondary to exercise.

existential therapies: see *humanistic therapies*

exogenous: refers to anything whose origins are outside the organism. For example, exogenous depression is caused by events in a person's life rather than anything to do with their biological make-up.

exogenous zeitgebers: see *zeitgebers*

experiment: an experiment involves the manipulation of an *independent variable* in order to see its effect on a *dependent variable*. In simple terms, an experimenter will manipulate some aspect of a situation and then observe the effect that this has on some aspect of behaviour. There are three main types of experiment:

1. **The laboratory experiment.** The main characteristic of the laboratory experiment is the investigator's ability to control and alter the variables being tested. Because of this control the investigator is able to eliminate many of the *extraneous variables* that might otherwise affect the results of the experiment. Examples might include heat, noise, distractions or the nature of the participants themselves.

PROS: • because of the experimenter's ability to control the effect of extraneous variables, cause-and-effect relationships can be established
• the laboratory offers the experimenter the opportunity to measure behaviour with a greater precision than would be possible in the natural environment
• the laboratory also allows the research scientist to simplify the complex events of the natural world by breaking them down into simpler component parts (experimental *reductionism*).

CONS: • it is claimed that the laboratory lacks relevance to real life, in that tasks explored in the laboratory may not generalise to the outside world
• participants may react to the laboratory setting either by acting in the way they feel the experiment requires (*demand characteristics*) or by displaying artificial behaviour because of their concern that they are being judged in some way (*evaluation apprehension*)
• avoiding demand characteristics and evaluation apprehension often involves the use of deception in laboratory research. This raises serious questions concerning the *ethics* of such investigations.

2. **The field experiment.** This type of experiment replaces the artificial setting of the laboratory with a more natural one. Participants are not aware that they are taking part in an experiment. Instead of investigating the impact of an independent variable in a contrived environment, or simply waiting for the variable concerned to occur naturally, the investigator creates the situation of interest and then records people's reactions to it. An example would be to observe whether passers-by react differently to an 'emergency' when the 'victim' is smartly or untidily dressed.

PROS: • by focusing on behaviour in its natural setting, the experimenter increases the external validity of the findings
• because participants are unaware of their participation in an experiment they are less likely to display *demand characteristics* or *evaluation apprehension*

- the experimenter maintains control over the ***independent variable***, therefore decisions regarding cause–effect relationships are still possible.

CONS:
- because many manipulations of the independent variable may be quite subtle, they may go unnoticed by the participants. Similarly, the reactions of the participants may also be subtle and may go unnoticed by the experimenter
- in contrast to the laboratory setting, the experimenter has less control over the effect of ***extraneous variables*** which might interfere with the purity of the cause–effect relationship
- because participants are not aware of their participation in an experiment, there are ***ethical*** concerns such as invasion of privacy and lack of informed consent.

3. **The natural experiment.** This is not regarded as a 'true' experiment because the ***independent variable*** is not under the direct control of the experimenter, and it is not possible to exert control over the allocation of ***participants*** to the various conditions of the experiment. In the natural experiment, the independent variable is manipulated by some outside agent (such as a school or hospital) and the psychologist is then able to study the resulting change.

PROS:
- because of the real-life context of these studies, they enable psychologists to explore issues of high natural interest which might have important practical implications
- there are fewer ***ethical*** problems (because of the absence of direct manipulation), although such methods have their own ethical problems such as invasion of privacy

CONS:
- as the experimenter has little control over the variables under study, any questions of cause and effect become increasingly speculative
- because participants' behaviour is influenced by many factors of which the investigator has no knowledge or control, natural experiments are extremely difficult to replicate.

experimental designs: a procedure used to control the influence of participant variables in an ***experiment.*** There are three major types of experimental design:
- the repeated measures design – all participants take part in all conditions. For example, in an experiment to test the effect of alcohol on mental arithmetic, the same participants would be used in the alcohol condition and in the no alcohol (***control***) condition
- matched subjects (participants) design – an attempt is made to relate the participants in some way. They are matched in terms of whatever the experimenter feels might have an effect on their performance and thus mask the effect of the ***independent variable.*** For example, age, gender and personality type may have pronounced effects on a number of different tasks, and so can be matched across the different conditions
- the independent subjects (participants) design – participants are randomly allocated to different conditions, so that if participant variables do have an effect on performance on the task, they do not do so in any systematic manner.

experimental group: those participants in an ***experiment*** who receive the ***independent variable*** under study. In an experiment to test the effects of music on ability to perform mathematical calculations, the group of participants who listened to music while they performed maths calculations would be the experimental group. A comparison group who performed the same calculations without the music would then act as a **control group.**

experimenter effects refer to some aspect of the experimenter's make-up or of their behaviour that has an effect on the behaviour of the **participant** in an investigation. Experimenters that are friendly, or who are rude and patronising, may create a situation where the participants do not act as they would normally have done simply because they are reacting to the influence of the experimenter's behaviour. Similarly experimenters may influence the research by virtue of their age, sex, race, physical attractiveness, etc. and the interactive effect that this has on the participants. Through unintentional bias during the recording of data, and the general procedural details of the investigation, researchers may also obtain results that are consistent with their expectations.

expert witnesses: those considered to have specialist knowledge or training in a specialist field. Expert witnesses are permitted to state their opinion in court concerning aspects of their field of expertise even though they were not present at the event in question. For example, a psychologist might testify about the possible causes of a defendant's behaviour.

explicit memory: normally contrasted with implicit memory, this is a type of memory that requires a conscious attempt to remember something previously learned. When you sit an examination and attempt to recall the labours of your last two years' work, you will be using your explicit memory. Implicit memory involves the repetition of previously learned activities without any apparent conscious attempt to retrieve them. Studies of **amnesic** patients have shown that typically they have impaired explicit memories but largely intact implicit memories.

external attribution: see **situational attribution**

external validity: an experiment is externally valid if the results can be generalised beyond this specific situation (i.e. to other people, other settings and over time). External validity concerns what goes on outside the experiment. If we are confident that an experimental effect has good **internal validity**, we might then ask how far we can generalise this beyond the immediate experimental setting. This involves a consideration of ecological validity, **population validity** and validity over time.

extinction: a term used in **classical** and **operant conditioning** to refer to the loss of a learned response. In classical conditioning, the conditioned stimulus (CS) is no longer accompanied by an unconditioned stimulus (UCS). Repeated presentations of the conditioned stimulus without the unconditioned stimulus will result in the loss of the conditioned response. For example, ringing a bell (CS) just before giving food (UCS) to your dog will eventually result in it getting very excited whenever the bell is rung on its own. After a while, this excitement disappears as the bell no longer predicts the coming of food. In operant conditioning, the response is no longer followed by a **reinforcer** or the reinforcer used is no longer effective. For example, giving your dog a biscuit every time it fetches the paper will eventually have your dog fetching and carrying everything from the parish newsletter to *The Sunday Times*. When the biscuits run out though, it will only be a matter of time before you are back to fetching your own paper. In its more widely used definition, the term extinction also means 'loss of a species', such as in the extinction of already lost species (e.g. the dodo) and other species that are thought to be threatened by extinction.

extraneous variable: in an experiment, any variable other than the *independent variable* that may influence the behaviour being studied. In an ideal experiment, the experimenter controls all variables except the one being manipulated, and then observes the outcome of this one variable on the dependent variable. An extraneous variable is considered to be an additional plausible explanation for any subsequent change in the dependent variable, therefore researchers must attempt to minimise their influence. For example, in an experiment to test the effect of background music on performance of a task, a plausible extraneous variable is loudness, in that any loud noise, musical or not, is likely to be distracting and therefore influence performance.

extrasensory perception (ESP) refers to perception which is thought to occur without stimulation of the normal sensory channels such as vision and hearing. It includes telepathy (thought transfer), clairvoyance (perception of an object removed from our normal sensory awareness) and precognition (perception of events yet to come).

extrinsic motivation: motivation to engage in a task as a means to an end, i.e. because it is likely to lead to an external reward, rather than engaging in a task for personal satisfaction or a sense of accomplishment (intrinsic motivation).

extroversion: a dimension of *personality* which is characterised by a variety of *traits* such as impulsiveness and sociability. In the EPI (*Eysenck Personality Inventory (EPI)*), Eysenck developed a method of testing people along the continuum of *introversion–extroversion.* The more sociable, impulsive and willing to take risks a person was, the higher they scored on extroversion. Eysenck believed that extroversion was largely due to heredity. Compared to introverts, extroverts have a lower level of cortical activity, and therefore must seek stimulation (hence their sociability and impulsiveness) to maintain an optimum level of *arousal*.

eyewitness testimony: the role of witnesses in the legal process is an important one. The testimony of an eyewitness can mean the difference between the police achieving a valid outcome, or a culprit getting away with a crime. It might also mean the conviction of a guilty person or the release of an innocent one. With the exception of a defendant's guilty plea, testimony from eyewitnesses is the most influential determinant of the outcome of a criminal trial.

However, research has shown that eyewitness memory can be prone to error. A witness sees the perpetrator of a crime at one time and later makes an identification of a suspect from memory. Unlike video recorders, however, memories are subject to fading and fabrication; they become both 'less' (through fading) and 'more' (through fabrication) over time. Eyewitness memory goes through three stages.

- First, during a crime, the witness encodes into storage details of the event and culprit(s). *Encoding* may be only partial and distorted – most crimes happen very quickly, often at night and can be accompanied by lots of rapid, complex action, some of it violent.
- Second, the witness retains the encoded information for some length of time. Memories can be lost or modified during retention – most forgetting takes place within the first few minutes of a retention interval, and other activities between encoding and retrieval can significantly colour the memory itself.
- Third, the witness retrieves it from storage. The witness has to dig back into memory and pull out details of something that might have happened some considerable time before.

At each phase of this process, therefore, error can creep in. Also, the answers that police and other interviewers get are affected both by their retrieval format and the questions they ask. Recent developments such as the *cognitive interview* are claimed to considerably improve the amount and accuracy of information that can be retrieved by eyewitnesses, although even this method has been called into question.

Eysenck Personality Inventory (EPI): a way of measuring personality along the dimensions of extroversion–introversion, and neuroticism–stability. Clients are asked a series of questions such as 'Do you tend to enjoy yourself at parties?'. By responding yes or no to these questions, the person filling out the inventory is providing information for the psychologist to construct a profile which will give them a score for extroversion and for neuroticism. As some people who fill out the inventory may fake their answers and try to respond in a way that is socially desirable, the inventory also includes a lie scale of questions that can only be answered in one way. If the client scores over a certain number on the lie scale, the overall test results are discarded.

A–Z Online

Log on to A–Z Online to search the database of terms, print revision lists and much more. Go to **www.philipallan.co.uk/a-zonline** to get started.

F scale: a measuring instrument used by Adorno in his investigations of the ***authoritarian personality***. The F scale measures the extent to which people agree or disagree with statements such as: 'Obedience and respect for authority are the most important virtues children should learn'. A high degree of agreement with statements such as this indicates the presence of an authoritarian personality.

face recognition involves comparing a perceived stimulus pattern with stored representations of familiar faces. One suggestion is that our store of familiar faces might act as a series of templates so that the face we perceive is matched against each template in turn until an acceptable match is made. An alternative explanation is based on an analysis of the features of the perceived face and the comparison with a list of features that we associate with a particular face. If the features of the new face match the list associated with someone familiar, a match is made, and the face recognised. Seeing face recognition in this way should mean that rearranging the features would make no difference to the likelihood of face recognition – they are the same features after all. However, scrambled faces are far more difficult to recognise than normally arranged faces.

More recent attempts to explain face recognition have focused on the typical errors made when trying to recognise a familiar face. These include failing to recognise a familiar person, misidentifying one person as another, and failing to remember someone's name. This has led to the development of models of face recognition that see it as part of a simultaneous sequence of cognitive processing that converges on the successful recognition and identification of a person and their usual context.

face validity: see *validity*

failure of executive functioning: executive functions allow the individual to plan, initiate and execute goal-directed behaviour. Impairment (e.g. through frontal lobe damage) can substantially disrupt daily functioning. Individuals who suffer failure of executive functioning may, for example, display impulsivity, an inability to control emotional expression and a lack of awareness or concern about the impact of their behaviour on others.

failure to function adequately: is a definition of abnormality based on a person's inability to function within broadly defined limits of 'normal behaviour', (e.g. being able to look after oneself, or being able to carry on normal social discourse). If a person's behaviour interferes with their ability to operate within those limits, then it may be classified as abnormal. Behaviour that is bizarre (such as having hallucinations) or inefficient (such as being unable to leave the house because of our obsessions) or which might be considered unpredictable or incomprehensible to others, might be defined as abnormal.

false-belief test: when used with children, these tests indicate that children who have developed a theory of mind are able to understand false beliefs in others (i.e. that other children do not necessarily have the same knowledge that they have, therefore would not be able to make the same judgements). See *Sally-Anne test* and *Smartie tube test*.

false confessions: an admission of guilt when the person confessing is not responsible for the crime. Innocent people may confess to a crime for a number of reasons. These include coercive questioning, diminished capacity, fear of violence or a misunderstanding of the situation. Some false confessions can be explained by the mental state of the individual. For example, people with mental disabilities may falsely confess because they feel compelled to agree with authority figures. Mentally capable individuals may give false confessions because of a belief that they will be released after confessing and prove their innocence later. One thing in common to most explanations of false confessions is people's belief that confessing will be more beneficial to them than continuing to maintain their innocence.

false consensus bias: the tendency to see our own attitudes, beliefs and behaviour as being typical. For example, students who smoke typically believe that the majority of other students also smoke. Non-smoking students, on the other hand, believe that the majority of other students do not smoke. Possible reasons for the false consensus bias are:
- if others are perceived as sharing our opinions and beliefs, this enhances our confidence that our own opinions and beliefs are normal
- the way we process information about others means that we are often more likely to remember and recall more instances of the agreement of others than of their disagreements.

false memory debate: see *recovered memories*

false memory syndrome: see *recovered memories*

family dysfunction: a situation within a family where conflict, lack of empathy toward family members and even abuse occur continually. Children of such families may grow up believing such behaviour is normal. Dysfunctional families are often characterised by one parent being psychologically dependent (i.e. co-dependent) in an unhealthy way on another who is addicted to a drug or self-destructive behaviour, such as chronic gambling. They may also be the result of alcoholism, substance abuse, parents' untreated mental illnesses, or parents emulating their own dysfunctional parents and dysfunctional family experiences.

family studies: a method used within the field of behavioural genetics. For example, a family study may be used to identify the degree of risk of relatives developing a mental disorder that other family members suffer from. In such studies, family studies can be used to determine the risk of passing down mental disorders to offspring within families. Family studies are also used to determine the genetic contribution for a particular characteristic such as *intelligence*. A stronger similarity in terms of that characteristic for relatives who share more of their genes is taken as an indication of the importance of genetic factors in the development of that characteristic. However, because of the problems posed by shared environment among close biological relatives, researchers tend to make more use of *twin* and *adoption studies* when studying the inheritance of intelligence in particular.

family therapy: therapy that involves the whole, or part, of a family. The aim of the therapy is to produce change in the systems of interaction between family members. Family relationships are seen as an important factor in psychological health.

fear appeals: the use of fear in a persuasive message in an attempt to change a person's attitude or behaviour. Results of the effectiveness of using fear as a trigger for attitude change have often appeared contradictory, but the following factors seem to be important:

- how unpleasant is the event described?
- how likely is it that the unpleasant circumstances will occur if the recommended action is not taken?
- how effective is the recommended action in avoiding the unpleasant circumstance?
- how able is the recipient of the message to carry out the recommended action?

So, a person is more likely to change if they believe something unpleasant will happen if they don't change and that they are able to carry out what appears to be an effective remedial action to avoid the circumstances described in the fear appeal.

fear arousal and health: fear arousal has been suggested as a way of raising awareness of risk behaviour (e.g. unsafe sex, smoking and alcohol abuse), and of changing these risky behaviours into more healthy behaviours. Research suggests that fear is a motivator to behaviour change, i.e. without fear there is little likelihood of action. Fear may also motivate health-promoting behaviour, but only in conditions where individuals have high outcome expectations (i.e. they expect any change to make a significant difference) and high *self-efficacy* expectations (i.e. they are confident in their ability to make the change).

feature analysis: an aspect of bottom-up processing, whereby we can recognise an object because our sensory systems analyse stimuli into basic features before higher centres of the brain recombine these features to create a full perceptual experience. Colour, motion and spatial orientation are some of the features that our perceptual system analyses in this way.

feature detection theories: see *pattern recognition*

feedback: a general term that has a multiplicity of meanings. It means the information from muscles that helps to guide movement (kinaesthetic feedback), or the information that follows performance of a task (feedback of results), or it can mean the information we receive from others as we operate within our social world. In this last usage, the term feedback is taken to mean social approval or disapproval in the form of smiles, frowns, comments from others and so on.

feminism: a personal position that stresses a high regard for women as human beings, and a belief that men and women should be socially, economically and legally equal.

field dependence/independence refers to the degree to which an individual's *perception* is influenced by the background environment (the field). The simplest demonstration of this has been to show a *participant* a rod, and then rotate the frame surrounding the rod. The participant then has to rotate the rod until s/he believes it is truly vertical. Those participants who find it hard to do this, and are influenced in their perceptual judgement by the orientation of the frame (the field in this case), are described as field dependent, and those who are able to correctly judge when the rod is vertical regardless of the orientation of the frame are judged as field independent. People lie on a continuum between these two descriptions. Field dependence has also been linked with differences in other areas of psychological functioning such as *personality* and mental health.

field experiment: see *experiment*

field studies: literally any piece of research that takes place outside of the laboratory, and within the context in which a behaviour normally occurs.

fight or flight: a description of the way in which animals prepare themselves to deal with danger. A sequence of activity is triggered which prepares the body for the possibility of defending or attacking (fight) or running away to safety (flight). This activity involves changes in the nervous system and the secretion of hormones which are necessary to sustain *arousal*.

figure ground: these terms describe the perceptual relationship between the figure (whatever is in the foreground or is focused upon by the observer) and the background (i.e. the rest of the perceptual field).

filial imprinting: refers to the attachment of a young animal to its parent. Many birds imprint, as do nearly all herd animals. This is an early form of learning, and ensures the survival of young animals who might otherwise die of exposure or be taken by a predator (see *imprinting*). Filial imprinting is a two-way process, since parents also exhibit attachment behaviours to offspring. Farmers often experience difficulties in getting orphaned lambs adopted by another ewe for precisely this reason.

fixation: an aspect of *Freudian* theory, this refers to an abnormal state of development where the child becomes frozen at that particular stage. Subsequent development will be affected by this fixation, as it sets up personality *traits* that last throughout life (see, for example, *anal personality*). If a person is excessively gratified or under gratified in a particular stage, they can become fixated and will *regress* back to that stage whenever they are in a state of stress as an adult.

fixed-interval reinforcement: see *schedules of reinforcement*

fixed ratio reinforcement: see *schedules of reinforcement*

Flanders' interaction analysis: a form of coding system used by educational researchers to investigate classroom transactions. This system divides all the talk that takes place in the classroom into ten categories. Seven are devoted to teacher talk, two to pupil talk and a tenth, silence or confusion, covers all other conditions (see table overleaf). An observer builds up a picture of a lesson by categorising classroom talk into these ten different categories. To do this they note every three seconds what type of verbal activity is going on. It is largely the use of the Flanders' system that has led to the suggestion of a 'two-thirds rule', i.e. that teachers tend to talk for two thirds of all classroom talk.

flashbulb memory: a term given to the memories that accompany a particularly significant emotionally arousing event. The analogy of a flashbulb describes the way we can often remember where we were, what we were doing, who we were with and so on, as if the whole scene had been 'illuminated' by a flashbulb. The most famous examples of this phenomenon are the deaths of John F. Kennedy, John Lennon and Princess Diana. Many people are able to remember very clearly what they were doing when they heard news of these events.

flooding: a therapeutic technique similar in nature to *implosion therapy*, except that unlike implosion, the client is actually put into the *phobic* situation. For example, someone with a fear of heights is taken to the top of a tall building, an *agoraphobic* is taken to a public place. The therapy works through confronting the client with the feared situation until the fear subsides. The situation itself may be preceded by the client listening to a tape recording of an account of their most feared situation. This is played over and over again until the client no longer fears the same degree of terror. They are then exposed to the situation themselves. This therapy can work quite quickly for specific phobias (such as fear of snakes or spiders),

Flanders' interaction analysis

		Categories
Teacher talk	Indirect influence	1 Accepts feelings of participants in non-threatening manner
		2 Praises or encourages
		3 Accepts or uses ideas of others
		4 Asks questions
	Direct influence	5 Lectures – giving facts or opinions
		6 Gives directions
		7 Criticises or justifies their authority
Student talk		8 Pupil's respond to teacher
		9 Talk by pupils which they initiate
		10 Silence or confusion

but is less rapid for agoraphobia. Not surprisingly, the therapy is one of the least popular with clients, but is one of the most effective. It is only ever carried out with the full consent of the clients involved.

floor effect: the opposite to a ***ceiling effect***, this refers to the possibility that when measuring some aspect of performance in an ***experiment***, we use a measuring device that fails to adequately discriminate between the participants in the study. If, on a test of mental arithmetic, the maximum mark were 50 and nearly all the participants scored 1 or 2 out of 50, the test would obviously be too difficult. The performance of participants is constrained by the difficulty of the test, hence the floor effect. It thus becomes difficult to assess the impact of the ***independent variable*** because the measuring device being used is inappropriate.

fluid intelligence: an abstract form of intelligence which involves reasoning and the ability to find solutions to novel problems. It is believed by many to peak before the age of 20 (see also ***crystallised intelligence***).

follow-up study refers to the process of maintaining contact with ***participants*** after an investigation in order to see what long-term effects have been caused by their participation in the study. Follow-up studies are useful for a number of reasons. They enable the investigator to check for any ill effects caused by participation in the study, and they occasionally establish the existence of ***sleeper effects*** that would otherwise be undetected.

food caching: the tendency for animals to store food outside their bodies. Food can then be gathered when it is reasonably plentiful, and stored for later consumption. They may do this in a number of ways, including burying and hiding. The advantages of doing this are:

- it creates a store of resources for times when resources are likely to be scarce (such as in winter)
- resources can be hidden from competitors
- the animal has to spend less time foraging, releasing it to engage in other behaviours.

Food caching also carries a number of risks, including:

- resources may be discovered and stolen by competitors
- the animal must form a mental map of the cache area in order to retrieve it, and if the landmarks forming the map are disturbed by other animals for example, the cache may not be re-discovered.

Because of the potential risks of thieving and loss, optimal caching behaviour may involve spreading food over a number of small sites rather than storing it all in one large store. This advantage has to be balanced against the cost in terms of time and energy of establishing and remembering more than one site.

foot-in-the-door technique: a *compliance* technique which is based on the idea that if people agree to a small request initially, they are more likely to agree to a much larger request later on. For example, asking a neighbour to feed your cat whilst you are away for the weekend will lead to a greater chance of them saying yes to feeding the cat, walking the dog and chatting to the plants whilst you are on a month's holiday in South America (see also *door-in-the-face technique)*.

foraging: a term used to describe the ways in which animals satisfy their nutritional requirements. Foraging types can be classified in various ways.

WHAT THEY EAT:

- herbivores – that consume living plant tissue
- carnivores – that consume the tissue of living animals
- omnivores – that consume a mixture of plant and animal tissue
- detritovores – that consume dead organic matter

THE EFFECT ON THE ORGANISM EATEN:

- predation – the prey is killed and then eaten
- parasitism – part of the prey is consumed but it is not killed

MODE OF ACTIVITY:

- searchers – who actively move through their environment in search of food. These include grazers, whose food is abundant, and hunters, whose food is more patchily distributed
- sit-and-wait foragers – who establish a position in their environment and then wait for prey to come to them.

115

forced-choice item refers to any test where respondents have to choose one of a number of alternative responses. For example, they may be asked to choose between two statements, neither of which really reflects their true feelings. Although this may seem like a pointless thing to ask people to do, it does have the advantage that it largely overcomes the tendency to produce socially desirable responses and enables the investigator to look for consistent trends in the responses given.

forebrain: see *brain*

forensic psychology: a branch of psychology that is concerned with the application of psychology in the criminal and civil justice field. Forensic psychologists work for prison services, the National Health Service, probation services, police services and social services. Key tasks of forensic psychology include implementing treatment programmes, crime analysis and giving expert evidence in court.

forgetting: as a general idea in psychology, this refers to a person's loss of the ability to recall or recognise that which they have previously learned. The exact nature of this loss depends very much on the theory being discussed. Explanations of forgetting can be divided into trace-dependent forgetting, where the *memory* trace is actually lost from memory, and cue-dependent forgetting where, although the trace still exists in a person's *long-term memory*, it can no longer be retrieved. Some of the major explanations of forgetting are:

- interference – the existing memory is distorted in some way, either by something learned in the past (proactive interference) or something learned in the future (retroactive interference)
- *repression* – normally taken to mean motivated forgetting, in that people unconsciously repress painful or disturbing memories
- retrieval failure – more recent explanations of forgetting have emphasised the importance of *cues* in the processes of remembering and forgetting. These might be internal (such as psychological or physiological states – being nervous, drunk, etc.) or contextual (aspects of the environment). We are more likely to remember information if we recall it in the same state and context that it was learned in the first place. This has tremendous implications for study skills.

formal operational thought: see *Piaget, J*

fovea: a small area on the *retina*. When we fixate an object, we focus the light from that object onto the fovea. This small area is packed with *cones* and is the area of the sharpest vision.

fraternal twin: see *dizygotic twin*

free association: a *psychoanalytic* term used to describe the free association of ideas that can give an insight into the *unconscious* mind of the *analysand*. Typically, the analyst gives the analysand a word or an idea and they respond in an unconstrained way, saying effectively whatever comes into their mind. The analyst then offers interpretation of the relationship observed.

free-rider effect: a free-rider is someone who takes advantage of a shared resource but does not contribute to the costs involved. Examples of the free-rider effect are car tax dodgers, who use the roads but do not pay for their upkeep, and colleagues who drink your tea and coffee but never cough up for the kitty. There is a difference between the free-rider effect and *social loafing*, as the latter only involves a decrease in effort, not a total absence as in the free-rider effect.

free will vs determinism: refers to the debate between those who believe that behaviour is determined by external or internal factors acting upon the individual (determinism), and those who believe that people respond actively to events around them (freedom). A belief in science as a route to knowledge is essentially a vote for the determinist side of the debate, in that one of the assumptions of psychological science is that all events are caused. The notion of pure free will suggests that events are uncaused or completely random. This is not what psychologists mean by free will. An individual's behaviour is seen not as being determined by external events (such as **conditioning**) but rather that they act consistently with their character (soft **determinism**). Free will is thus seen as any act which is free from external coercion. Handing over all our money to someone in the street may be a sign of our generous character, but not if we were being held at gunpoint. Both actions are determined, but the first is seen as an act of free will, whereas the second is an act of coercion.

ARGUMENTS IN FAVOUR OF FREE WILL:
- the main argument concerns the idea of moral responsibility. We must be seen to be in control of our actions to be held responsible for them
- humanistic therapies such as **client-centred therapy** are based on the assumption of free will. The therapist helps the client to exercise free will in such a way as to maximise the rewards in their life.

ARGUMENTS AGAINST FREE WILL:
- belief in free will is inconsistent with the assumptions of science, i.e. all physical events have a cause
- there is a good deal of uncertainty about what is meant by free will. To imply that all behaviour is uncaused or random is unacceptable; to imply that free will has an effect on behaviour opens up questions that science has yet to answer.

ARGUMENTS IN FAVOUR OF DETERMINISM:
- ideas of determinism are compatible with the success of science. Science is seen as a successful route to knowledge. With this knowledge comes the ability to predict and ultimately control behaviour.

ARGUMENTS AGAINST DETERMINISM:
- determinism is essentially unfalsifiable. If a cause cannot be found for some aspect of behaviour, this is not to say that a cause does not exist, but simply that it hasn't yet been discovered.

frequency graph: a graphical representation of how often certain events or scores occur. Frequency distributions can be represented in a number of different ways including *histograms*.

Freud, S: (1856–1939) the founder of *psychoanalysis*, hailed by many as the greatest genius of the century, by others as an intellectual confidence trickster. Freud's major contribution to psychology was in the structure and development of *personality.* To Freud, the personality was made up of three major interacting systems:

- the *id* – present at birth, and energised by biological and psychic energy. The id operates according to the pleasure principle, i.e. it seeks pleasure and avoids pain. It is constantly driving for expression
- the *ego* – has to arbitrate between the demands of the id and the superego. It operates according to the reality principle, controlling the id's drive for immediate satisfaction until an appropriate outlet can be found
- the *superego* – the moral part of the personality (a product of *socialisation*) which contains the ego-ideal (standards of good behaviour that we aspire to) and the conscience (an 'inner voice' that tells us when we have done something wrong). The superego is seen as the purveyor of rewards (feelings of pride and satisfaction) and punishments (feelings of shame or guilt) depending on which part (ego-ideal or conscience) is activated.

The demands of the id ('I want it, and I want it now') and the demands of the superego ('No, it's wrong') frequently conflict. The ego deals with this conflict by operating unconscious *defence mechanisms*. These deny or distort reality in such a way that we are protected from the anxiety that would otherwise result from unresolved conflicts. Freud believed that we are constantly in a state of conflict between the id and superego, and the wishes of the individual against the demands of the environment. Freud believed that this latter conflict was also inevitable, as cultures (and their rules) come and go, but human characteristics, being *innate*, go on forever. Freud believed that the personality developed through five stages. These are referred to as *psychosexual development* stages to emphasise that the most important driving force in development is the need to express sexual energy. At each stage this energy is expressed in different ways and through different parts of the body:

1. The oral stage (0 to 2) – the mouth is seen as the focal point of sensation, and is the way in which the child expresses early sexual energy.
2. The anal stage (2 to 3) – the beginnings of ego development as the child becomes aware of the demands of reality and the need to conform to the demands of others. The major issue at this stage is toilet training as the child learns to control the expulsion of body waste.
3. The phallic stage (3 to 6) – sexual energy is now focused on the genitals. The major conflict of this stage is the *Oedipus complex* in which the child unconsciously wishes to possess the parent of the opposite sex and rid themselves of the parent of the same sex. As a result of this desire, boys would experience *castration anxiety* which would drive them to identify with their fathers (*identification with the aggressor*). Freud was obviously more puzzled by the course of female development, claiming that they would experience penis envy (a realisation that they do not have a penis) which they would overcome by eventually achieving motherhood and having their own baby (a male

baby who would have the sought-after penis). Any other course of female development was then seen as deviant.

4. The latent stage (6 to 12) – the child develops their confidence and mastery of the world around them. Freud believed that during this stage, the 'experiences and excitations' of the previous stages are repressed and children develop infantile *amnesia*, being unable to remember much of their early years.

5. The genital stage (12+) – the culmination of psychosexual development and the fixing of sexual energy in the genitals. This eventually directs us towards sexual intercourse and the beginnings of the next cycle of life.

There are a variety of comments which can be made about Freudian theory:

- Freud's pessimistic view of humankind sees conflict, destructive drives, selfishness and lust as inevitable human characteristics. **Neo-Freudians** have emphasised creativity, love, *altruism* and hope
- Freud felt that when girls discovered that they lacked a penis, they would fear and envy those that possessed one (men), accepting their inferior status because of this deficiency. An alternative interpretation might propose that men envy women their ability to create and nurture life within their bodies, therefore men both fear and envy women, and see themselves as inferior to women because of this (see *womb envy*)
- Freud claimed that sex and aggression were the two most important drives in human development. Others have stressed psycho-social conflicts (*Erikson*), the need for self-esteem (Kohut) or the need to overcome inferiority (Adler)
- Freud presented an *alpha bias* in his theory, seeing women as morally deficient. Alternative views of female development have stressed the 'different' course of female development rather than the inferiority of females. (See *Gilligan's ethics of cave*.)

Freudian: anything connected with the theories of Sigmund *Freud.*

Freudian slip: any slip-up, either in speech, writing or in memory lapses that betrays the concerns or pre-occupations of the *unconscious* mind. *Freud* believed that these were no accident but were due entirely to the workings of the unconscious. As such, they were a valuable source of insight into this part of the human mind. These are more technically known as parapraxes.

frontal lobe: see *brain*

frustration-aggression theory: an explanation of aggression which states that if a person is blocked (or frustrated) from achieving some goal then this leads to aggression. The original theory stated that:

- frustration always leads to some form of aggression
- aggression is always a consequence of frustration.

Later refinements of the theory stated that the aggression produced by the frustrating event need not necessarily be directed directly at it (there may be very good reasons for this!) but may be *displaced* onto some other object. Later developments of this theory (*cue-arousal theory*) suggested that the expression of aggressive behaviour as a result of frustration depends upon other environmental conditions (or cues).

As an explanation of aggression, the theory has a good deal of intuitive appeal, but only when we can dismiss other possible causes of an aggressive behaviour. For example, I remember being very late for an important meeting because the train I was travelling on broke down. Although I was very angry, it was not a product of the frustration, but rather it was directed at myself for not getting an earlier train.

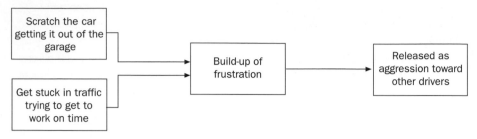

Frustration-aggression theory

functional disorder: a term used for any mental disorder where there is no known organic cause. There is considerable argument over what should be labelled a functional disorder, as there is an assumption by those who adhere to the ***biomedical model of abnormality*** that ultimately an organic cause will be established for all serious mental disorders. Until that happens, the classification functional disorder is given when either sufficient evidence exists for the contribution of social or psychological factors to a disorder, or where the presence of suspected organic influences has not yet been established (e.g. as in ***schizophrenia***).

functions of attitudes: Katz (1960) believed that people hold given attitudes because these attitudes help them achieve certain basic goals. Katz identified four types of psychological function that attitudes meet.

1. *Instrumental* – we develop favourable attitudes towards things that benefit or reward us, e.g. we favour a political party that will advance our lot.
2. *Knowledge* – attitudes provide a meaningful, structured environment so that we can bring order and clarity to our life.
3. *Value-expressive* – attitudes express our basic values, e.g. if you see yourself as environmentally responsible you may develop a positive attitude to wind power initiatives.
4. *Ego-defensive* – some attitudes serve to protect us from acknowledging basic truths about ourselves, i.e. they serve as ***defence mechanisms***.

fundamental attribution error: see *attributional biases*

galvanic skin response (GSR) measures the change in electrical resistance of the skin. The GSR is commonly used as an objective measure of **arousal**, and the principle is commonly associated with the idea of a lie detector. This is also known as the SCR, or skin conductance response.

Ganzfeld: subjects are typically isolated in a red-lit room, with halved table-tennis balls taped over their eyes and earphones playing white noise to cut out sensory information. Sensory deprivation is used so that telepathic messages from a sender in another room can be read more clearly. In later autoganzfeld studies, the procedures are under automated computer control with the receiver in a soundproof, steel-walled and electromagnetically shielded room.

Gardner's theory of multiple intelligences: Gardner (1999) claimed that the traditional view of intelligence as one general underlying factor was far too limited, and that educators have tended to tailor their teaching around a view of intelligence that ignored other less traditional forms of intelligence. He initially proposed a theory based on seven different forms of intelligence, which accounted for a broader range of human potential, and later added an eighth – natural intelligence. The eight forms of intelligence are:
1. Linguistic intelligence
2. Logical-mathematical intelligence
3. Spatial intelligence
4. Bodily-kinaesthetic intelligence
5. Musical intelligence
6. Interpersonal intelligence
7. Intrapersonal intelligence
8. Natural intelligence

gender: a term used where it is considered appropriate to emphasise the psychological characteristics associated with males and females. The term 'sex' is then restricted to biological differences. It is obvious, however, that the biological and psychological characteristics of an individual interact constantly during their development, therefore some psychologists prefer to use the terms interchangeably without any intended differences in meaning between them.

gender bias refers to the treatment of men and women in psychological research and theory such as to offer a view that might not justifiably be seen as representing the characteristics of either one of these genders. It is difficult to offer one all-encompassing definition of gender bias, given that some types of gender bias might appear non-biased to the casual observer. We can usefully classify gender bias in psychological theories as representing either an **alpha bias** (theories that see real differences between men and women, and may represent either an enhancement or undervaluing of one gender compared to the other) or a **beta bias** (theories that ignore or minimise differences between men and women). **Freud's** theory is an example of an alpha bias theory that undervalues women, whilst **Gilligan's** theory of moral development in women is an example of an alpha bias theory that enhances women.

The vast majority of psychological theories might be said to lean towards the beta bias because, in attempting to represent males and females in an objective and unbiased manner, they fail to truly represent the characteristics of (usually) women. Many theories (such as that of **Kohlberg**) are based on a study of males only and therefore might be described as **androcentric**, in that they offer an interpretation of women based on an understanding of the lives of men. Gilligan's theory offers an alternative to Kohlberg's but is based on the lives and priorities of women. In recent years there has been a surge of interest in **woman-centred psychology** in order to counteract psychology's androcentric bias. The use of traditional research methods in psychology has also been biased towards males, and the development of feminist research methods has done much to redress the balance and represent women in a technically more accurate and more favourable manner.

gender constancy: children's understanding of the irreversibility of their sex, which develops in stages roughly between the ages of two and seven years. Some awareness of gender roles emerges in children before the full attainment of gender constancy and, when children attain full understanding of gender constancy, they become increasingly motivated to observe, incorporate and respect gender roles.

gender dysphoria: a condition where individuals experience confusion between their biological sex, their **gender identity** and their **gender role**. They feel that their gender identity does not match the sex that that they were born with, and that somehow they were born into the wrong body. As a result, they may prefer to take on a gender role that is the opposite of the stereotypical image of their sex, and may even prefer to live as a member of the opposite sex. For example, a person with gender dysphoria who was born male may feel more comfortable with a female gender identity and so prefer to dress in women's clothes.

gender identity: our concept of whether we are male or female.

gender role: those behaviours, attitudes and interests that are considered appropriate for one **gender** and inappropriate for the other. Several theorists have proposed biological origins for these differences in males and females, but most psychologists share a belief that differences in the behaviour of males and females are more a product of **socialisation** than biology.

gender schema theory: Martin and Halverson (1981) believed that the key to gender development is the acquisition of information about one's own gender. According to this view, basic gender identity is sufficient for a child to identify him/herself as a boy/girl and take an interest in what behaviours are appropriate for that gender. In order to do this, children develop schemas of gender-appropriate behaviour. These schemas are learned from their observations of, and interactions with, other people. Children are most interested in the schemas appropriate for their own gender (i.e. the in-group). From an early age, children focus on in-group schemas and avoid behaviours that belong to out-group schemas.

gender stereotypes: a set of beliefs about what it means to be male or female. These involve preconceived ideas about male and female differences in psychological traits, attitudes, social relations and occupational interests. The most worrying aspect of gender stereotypes is that to people that have them, all these different parts are interrelated. So, knowing that someone is female (or male) means that we would then also have 'knowledge' about their interests, attitudes and typical behaviours.

gene: a part of the *chromosome* of any organism that carries information in the form of *deoxyribonucleic acid (DNA)*. Genes can potentially last for many generations and are constantly replicated and affected by the process of *natural selection*.

general adaptation syndrome: suggested by Selye (1956), this proposes that there are three stages in our response to long-term stress.
- The alarm reaction during which the sympathetic branch of the *autonomic nervous system* is activated. This increases heart-rate and blood pressure, and releases hormones that maintain and intensify sympathetic activity
- The resistance stage during which, if the stressor persists, the body tries to cope by maintaining the same high level of physiological arousal
- The exhaustion stage, where the body's resources and defence against the stressor become exhausted. Although some aspects of physiological arousal may decline, others (such as the level of adrenal hormones in the blood) do not, and the individual may become more vulnerable to stress-related disorders such as ulcers and high blood pressure.

The model of the general adaptation syndrome has been very influential in showing that a range of different stressors all trigger the same adaptive response. It does, however, have some problems, mostly with the fact that not all people react to long-term stress by developing stress-related disorders, and those who do show many differences in the type of disorder that they develop. This suggests the presence of other physiological or psychological factors that would explain these individual differences.

general factor (g): a general *intelligence* factor that was originally thought to underlie people's performance on different tests of mental ability. This hypothetical factor was first suggested by Charles Spearman, who observed that people that performed well on one type of ability test also tended to do well on other types of test. Correlations between different test results were never perfect, however, so the idea of one single underlying factor gradually gave way to the idea of more specific abilities relevant to different types of test.

generalisability: refers to the ability of the researcher to make a justified extension of their conclusions to a whole category of objects or *population* of people. To be able to generalise out from a specific finding from a *sample* of *participants* to a much wider group requires that both the *sampling* procedures and the nature of the study itself warrants such extension. One such problem concerns the use of volunteers in research. There is sufficient evidence to suggest that volunteers may not be typical of a generally non-volunteering population.

generalisation: the term has a number of meanings in psychology:
- it may apply to the 'broad brush' approach to judging all members of a particular group as being the same (see *stereotype*). For example, thinking that all men are mad about football, or that all Liverpudlians are comedians

- as part of a *classical conditioning* procedure, the term refers to the *participant's* tendency to respond not only to *stimuli* that have formerly produced a *response*, but also to stimuli that are in some way similar to the original stimulus. For example, if an organism is conditioned to respond to a circle, it will also respond (although less strongly) to an ellipse
- as part of an *operant conditioning* procedure, the participant's tendency to produce responses that are similar to the response that had previously been *reinforced.* If you are rewarded for good work in psychology, there is a tendency to also produce good work in other subjects as well.

genetic determinism: a belief that the development of any organism is under genetic control. This may not appear controversial when applied to the behaviour of simple organisms, but is more so when used as an explanation of the behaviour of more complex animals such as human beings. The view that much of human behaviour is also determined by genetic factors has received recent attention through the development of *evolutionary psychology*.

genetics: the study of inherited characteristics (see *gene*) and also of the roles of *genes* during lifetime development.

genome research: research into the genetic basis of human characteristics. The genome is all the DNA that a person possesses, including the genes. Genes carry information for making all the proteins required by organisms. These proteins determine, among other things, how the organism looks, how well it fights infection, and sometimes even how it behaves. The human genome project, completed in 2003, aimed to identify all the 20,000–25,000 genes in human DNA. Knowledge about the effects of DNA variations among individuals can, it is claimed, lead to new ways to diagnose, treat, or even prevent the many disorders that affect us.

genotype: the *genetic* make-up of an individual. The genotype is a collection of inherited genetic material that is passed from generation to generation. Although such material is inherited, it does not necessarily appear in the organism's *phenotype*. Thus, the genotype is best thought of as a set of hereditary factors that influence the development of a characteristic, although they are not necessarily the only factor.

geographical profiling: Using information about where an offender has chosen to commit crimes, geographic profiling attempts to determine where an offender is most likely to reside. An example of a geographical profiling computer programme is 'Dragnet' developed by David Canter of the University of Liverpool, following examination of offences by serious serial offenders.

Gestalt: a German word that literally means 'whole configuration' and which emphasises that the whole (be it the person or a perceptual image) is always greater than the sum of its parts. Thus, the person is seen as being more than just all their component parts, a view that was directly opposed to the ideas of *reductionism*.

Gestalt laws of perceptual organisation: the view that perceptual forms could be experienced through the application of perceptual principles. The brain applies these principles in a way that enables us to perceive unified forms rather than simply collections of unconnected images. Examples of these principles are:

Proximity

The figure is perceived as three groups of two lines rather than six separate lines

Similarity

The figure is perceived as two columns of black dots and two of white dots

Closure

The figure is perceived as a square despite the fact that the 'square' is not complete

Gestalt therapy: a *humanistic therapy* that takes into account all aspects of a person's life and experience, so as to bring about a sense of the whole person, characterised by a sense of self-awareness. People who undergo this type of therapy typically try to protect themselves from perceived threats and therefore do little to actualise their true human potential. Not clinging to past conflicts and feelings is a fundamental requirement to growth. It is an important requirement of Gestalt therapy that clients recognise who they are at the moment, and through this awareness, personal growth becomes possible.

Gibson's bottom-up theory of perception: see *perception*

giftedness refers to individuals who possess some exceptional intellectual ability such as high *intelligence quotient (IQ)*, creativity or some specialised talent such as art, music or science. Recent research into the cognitive processing abilities of intellectually gifted children suggests that they not only encode information more rapidly, but are also highly adept at combining and comparing it with existing knowledge, enabling them to gain many new insights. Creativity in particular appears to be sensitive to the encouragement of others. The parents of highly creative children are more likely to value nonconformity, emphasise intellectual curiosity and be accepting of their child's individual characteristics.

Gilligan's ethics of care: Carol Gilligan published *In a Different Voice* (1982), which challenged Kohlberg's views of moral development as they might apply to women. Using evidence from women's real life moral dilemmas, such as choosing whether or not to have an abortion, she established that women had a different, but not inferior, moral orientation from men. Whereas in Kohlberg's most advanced level of moral reasoning, people are concerned with more abstract issues of justice, the participants in Gilligan's research focused more on relationships and the need to care for others. This suggested a different emphasis in their moral reasoning, and one that would appear inferior if measured on Kohlberg's criteria. Moral development for women is seen as going through these three stages:

- concern for self
- concern for others
- concern for self and others.

The most mature of Gilligan's stages sees the woman as trying to find the right balance between what is right for her and what is right for others. When faced with moral dilemmas such as those used by Kohlberg, males and females are equally able to think in terms both of abstract ideas of justice and also of their concern for the welfare of others. However, female participants' reasoning appeared more oriented to the latter and males' to the former. Gilligan's work opened up a surge of interest in **gender** differences in moral development.

Gould's 'Evolution of adult consciousness': Gould (1978) identified seven age-related stages of adult development. He proposed that, as we move through these stages, we progress from childhood consciousness to adult consciousness, and we do this by facing and leaving behind false emotional assumptions (e.g. 'only my parents can guarantee my safety' and 'there is only one right way to do things'). These assumptions give us an illusion of safety and act as a buffer against anxiety, so can be difficult to relinquish. Gould believed that the 40s were a particularly challenging phase of life as we develop an emotional awareness of our own mortality, a characteristic of the so-called 'mid-life crisis' Once realised, this awareness of our own death is never far from consciousness, and how time is spent becomes a matter of great importance.

Grasha's six learning styles: Grasha and Reichmann (1974) developed the Grasha-Reichmann Learning Style Scales (GRLSS) to determine college students' styles of classroom participation. This model focuses on student attitudes toward learning, classroom activities, teachers, and peers. The authors propose that students naturally select the most productive style from the six described below:

1. *Avoidant students* have high absenteeism, do not enjoy learning, and avoid taking part in activities.
2. *Participative students* are eager to learn and take responsibility for their own learning.
3. *Competitive students* see the classroom as a win–lose situation and enjoy competitive activities.
4. *Collaborative students* work well with others and enjoy cooperative learning and working in groups.
5. *Dependent students* see the teacher as a source of information, want to be told what to do, and will learn only what is required.
6. *Independent students* prefer to work alone and require little direction from the teacher.

Gregory's top-down theory of perception: see *perception*

grief reaction response: a common response to loss, serious injury or impending death. The grief reaction response consists of five stages: denial, anger, bargaining, depression, and acceptance. For example, people in denial may act or think as though they are not dying. Anger may be expressed as a sense of injustice ('Why me?'). Bargaining can be a sign of reasoning with death, i.e. seeking more time. When people realise that bargaining is not working, depression may develop. Acceptance involves facing the inevitable, and may come after discussions with family, friends and medical professionals. Many athletes also go through these stages in response to a serious injury. The speed with which an individual moves through these stages varies widely.

group dynamics: the many different interactions that take place among members of a group. These would include, for example, leader–follower relations and group decision-making. In a looser sense, the term is often used to refer to how well a group of people get on together, and how well they work together.

group polarisation: the tendency for groups to show a shift towards the extremes of decision-making when compared to decisions made by individuals. When individual members of a group are already cautious in their attitude to a decision, they will show a shift toward an even more cautious attitude when they discuss this as part of a like-minded group. When individuals are less cautious before group discussion, they tend to show a shift towards more risky decisions when they are making a decision as part of a like-minded group (see *risky shift*).

group therapy: a term used to refer to the practice of carrying out therapeutic sessions in groups rather than individually. The therapist does not direct in quite the same way as they might in an individual therapy session, but acts more as a facilitator, encouraging group members to identify with each other, and ultimately to help each other. In this way, group members are acting as both client *and* therapist. By listening to each others' experiences and feelings, clients can learn a great deal about their own condition. Some advantages of this approach to therapy are:
- by experiencing the success of others in the group, individuals are given hope that they might also conquer their own problem
- clients come to recognise that they are not the only one with a particular problem, thus making them feel less isolated
- clients are given the opportunity to help others, and experience the positive effects of their role in that help
- positive social interaction is developed, as deficiencies in social interaction are common in many psychological disorders.

groupthink: the name given to the tendency for certain types of groups to reach decisions that are extreme and which tend to be unwise or unrealistic. If the group is a highly cohesive collection of individuals with similar views on the subject under discussion, and they are cut off from alternative opinion, they are more likely to reach this highly polarised form of decision. Group members may ignore or discount information that is inconsistent with their chosen decision and express strong disapproval against any group member who might disagree. The eventual decision then appears to be endorsed by all. The social and political consequences of groupthink may be far reaching, and history has many examples of major blunders that have been the results of decisions reached in this way.

GSR: see *galvanic skin response (GSR)*

habit: a behaviour that has been acquired as a result of experience and is now performed almost automatically. Examples of habits would include behaviours that satisfy psychological cravings (such as a desire for food or nicotine) through overeating and chain smoking. There are many explanations of habits. *Psychoanalysts* explain habits as the expression of *repressed* impulses in the form of habitual behaviour. *Learning* theorists see habits as a form of conditioned behaviour over which the individual has little control. A habit can be learned by the consequences that follow the behaviour when it is produced, but once the habit is firmly entrenched, it becomes self-rewarding and difficult to shift.

habitat: a geographical area where conditions are particularly well suited to a particular species.

habituation: an explanation of learning where the *response* of an *organism* to a novel *stimulus* gradually fades as it becomes apparent that the stimulus is not biologically significant. Organisms first respond to an unusual stimulus by showing some sort of startle reaction (for example, looking up, freezing, running away). After repeated presentations of the stimulus, with no significant consequences for the organism, the response gradually disappears, and the organism is said to have habituated to the stimulus.

hallucination refers to the *perception* of things that are not present. Hallucinations can take many forms, and may involve all the main senses:

- somatic hallucinations give the experience that something is happening inside the body, such as a snake crawling around the stomach
- visual hallucinations involve perceptions of people, objects, colours, etc. that are not present
- tactile hallucinations may be experienced as a tingling sensation, or even the feeling that something is crawling over your body
- olfactory hallucinations involve the detection of odours that no one else can smell, for example, the constant smell of burning or of decay
- auditory hallucinations, particularly hearing voices, is a symptom of many certain forms of *psychosis*, most notably of *schizophrenia*.

hallucinogen: any sort of chemical substance capable of causing *hallucinations*.

halo effect refers to our tendency to allow one specific *trait* or our overall impression of a person to influence our judgement of their other traits. So, if we know that a person is a cold person, we will attribute a number of other associated traits to that person without any knowledge that they are true.

hardiness: a psychological *construct* that is taken to mean resistance to illness, or ability to deal with stress. From studies of highly stressed executives, Kobasa *et al.* were able to identify the characteristics of those who handled stress well from those who did not. Those who reported the fewest illnesses showed three kinds of hardiness:

- they showed an openness to change
- they had a feeling of involvement or commitment to their job
- they experienced a sense of control over their lives.

Kobasa found that the most important of these factors was the first, openness to change. Those who perceived change (such as the loss of their job) as a challenge rather than a devastating personal event, were more likely to interpret the event positively and show fewer signs of stress as a result. The idea of hardiness makes a great deal of intuitive sense, but has been difficult to demonstrate in anything but an indirect way.

hassles: see *daily hassles*

Hawthorne effect: named after the Hawthorne works of the Bell Telephone Company where it was first observed, this refers to the fact that any new method of working may produce positive results when it is first introduced simply because the people affected respond with an initial enthusiasm. This increase in results is, in fact, nothing to do with the change itself, but rather it is caused by the fact that workers feel someone is interested in them and therefore they respond positively to whatever change is being implemented. In the original research, even conditions designed to lower productivity had a positive effect on worker output. This was attributed to the fact that the participants reacted positively to being part of the study. Nowadays the Hawthorne effect is often quoted whenever there is the possibility that a research participant's behaviour is, at least in part, due to the fact that he or she knows they are being studied.

Headstart: a compensatory education programme set up in the United States in the 1960s. The aim of Project Headstart was to provide a period of enrichment which would make good the effects of early deprivation in some of America's poorer children. This was accomplished by providing a period of pre-school nursery education. Headstart failed to provide the significant gains in intellectual and educational development that its supporters had hoped for. To its critics, this was further evidence of the importance of genetic over environmental influences, and a further confirmation of the inherited deficiencies in the groups studied. To those who believed in the principle of Headstart, the failure of the programme was more a consequence of its inability to provide the right sort of experience at the right sort of time. Nowadays the term *Headstart* is used in its more general sense to describe any of a large number of programmes aimed at providing compensatory pre-school education for 'at risk' children. The results of these more contemporary programmes are far more encouraging than the original of the same name.

health-belief model: our willingness to seek medical help or change a health-risk behaviour depends both on the extent to which we perceive a threat to our health and also the extent to which we believe that practising a particular behaviour will reduce that threat. This model offers an explanation why many young people fail to act in a way that would lower their susceptibility to accident or illness – they do not perceive a threat so have no need to change their behaviour. By the same token, many older people do not change their behaviour (e.g. smoking) because they do not believe that changing their behaviour will significantly reduce the perceived threat to their well-being.

health education programmes: are designed to educate people about health and to motivate them to modify unhealthy lifestyles.

health psychology is defined by Matarazzo (1982) as:

> The educational, scientific, and professional contributions of the discipline of psychology to the promotion and maintenance of health, the prevention and treatment of illness, the identification of aetiology and diagnostic correlates of health, illness and related dysfunction, and the improvement of the health care system and health policy formation.

hedonic relevance: the tendency to make a *dispositional attribution* if, as a result of another person's behaviour, we are directly affected in some way. Thus, if someone crashes into *our* car, we are less likely to accept reasons like ice on the road or poor visibility, and more likely to attribute their behaviour to their bad driving or inattentiveness.

hedonism: a belief that all behaviour is, or should be, motivated toward the pursuit of pleasure and the avoidance of pain.

Heinz dilemma: a hypothetical *moral dilemma* where participants are asked to decide what a fictional character should do in response to a number of different conflict situations. The most famous of these involves a husband, Heinz, who must decide whether he should break a law and steal a drug to try and save his dying wife. Responses given to dilemmas such as the Heinz dilemma are usually used to determine at which stage of *Kohlberg's* developmental theory of moral reasoning the person is currently functioning.

helping behaviour: see *altruism (human)* and *bystander behaviour*

hemisphere asymmetries: see *lateralisation of function*

heredity: the study of the biological transmission of *genetic* characteristics from parent to offspring. The term is often used as a contrast to the influence of *environment*, although it is probably the interaction between the two that has attracted the most interest from psychologists.

heritability: the proportion of the variation within a particular characteristic that can be accounted for in terms of inherited factors. For example, on the basis of early *twin studies*, a figure of 80 per cent was commonly quoted as the percentage of IQ that was attributable to genetic inheritance.

heteronomous morality: literally meaning the morality of another. In this stage of *Piaget's* theory of *moral development* (about 5–10 years), children unquestioningly accept the rules of adults. These are seen as unchangeable and require strict obedience. Piaget felt that two things contributed to the child thinking this way about adult rules:

- adults have the power to force compliance, therefore the child must both respect adult rules and also those that enforce them
- young children are still cognitively immature. Their thinking is characterised by *egocentricity,* a belief that everybody thinks the same way that they do. If everybody accepts the rules, then they must be right.

heterosexuality: an attraction to or sexual contact with a person or persons of the opposite sex.

hierarchy of needs: see *Maslow, A*

High/Scope: an educational approach that originated in the US. The main principle is that children are active learners who learn best from activities that they plan and carry out themselves and then reflect upon. In the 1960s, a longitudinal study, the High/Scope Perry Preschool Project, was set up to find out if pre-school education could make a long-term difference to children's wellbeing. This research examined the lives of 123 African Americans from low-income families, who were at high risk of failing school; from 1962 to 1967, 58 received the High/Scope preschool programme and 65 similar children were assigned to a control group. The programme was found to produce lasting benefits for children and their families.

hindbrain: see *brain*

hippocampus: part of the limbic system in the forebrain, the hippocampus plays an important role in *memory*. Damage to this area results in an inability to form new memories, although existing memories remain intact.

histogram: a type of *frequency graph* where the number of scores in each category is represented by a vertical column. For example, the distribution of A-level grades for a particular examination might be as follows:

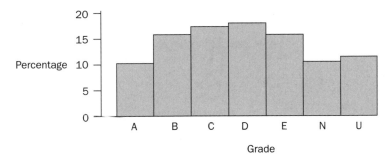

HIV: the human immunodeficiency virus, the virus that can cause AIDS. The virus gradually multiplies inside the body of an infected person, and eventually destroys the body's ability to fight off illness. HIV is transmitted in three main ways:
- through unprotected sex
- by drug users who share their equipment
- from an infected mother to her unborn child.

holism: the view that the parts of any whole cannot be understood except in their relation to the whole; i.e. the whole is greater than the sum of its parts. Holistic therapy refers to a treatment system that focuses on the whole person rather than on specific diseases or disorders, and considers physical, emotional, social, environmental, and spiritual factors.

holistic: refers to any approach that emphasises the whole person rather than simply their constituent parts. An example of this approach is in *Gestalt therapy* where clients are encouraged to develop a sense of 'whole person' self-awareness.

holophrase: a single-word utterance that is characteristic of the language of very small children. Some psychologists believe that these single words function as 'telegraphic' speech patterns, i.e. they are abbreviated sentences that are due to the child's language production limitations. Others believe that they merely represent simple concepts such as possession ('mine') or desire ('want').

home advantage: an often cited effect in sport. The home advantage effect has been noted in many sports, including football, cricket and basketball. These studies have indicated that teams win between 52% and 88% of their home games. Home advantage appears to be a largely psychological phenomenon, particularly when other differences between the two teams are largely insubstantial. One explanation offered for this phenomenon is territoriality. In one study, *testosterone* levels were higher in football players before their home games than before away games. This suggests that the elevated levels of testosterone may be related to a greater innate tendency to defend home territory and display aggressive behaviours to outsiders. Other research suggests the possibility of a home disadvantage, particularly in situations where there is a high audience expectation of success.

homeostasis: the process by which the body maintains a constant internal physiological environment. Through the homeostatic drives, behaviour is directed which initiates drinking, feeding and temperature regulation. For example, a drop in body temperature initiates a variety of processes (such as shivering) which restore the temperature of the body. Homeostasis thus initiates other processes that function in a regulatory manner and which re-establish the initial, optimum condition. This can be considered analogous to a thermostatically controlled central heating system. When the room temperature drops below the setting on the thermostat, the thermostat switches on the boiler which causes hot water to flow through the system raising the temperature of the room. When the room temperature reaches its optimum level, the thermostat switches the boiler off.

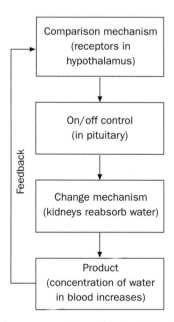

The homeostatic control of the concentration of water in the blood

homing: a term used to refer to the navigation of animals toward a target (normally their home range). Many different animals have been shown to have impressive navigational skills, including fish, birds, bees and even humans. The ability of Polynesian islanders and of Eskimos is legendary in this respect. The best known of the animal navigators are fish and birds. Salmon have been known to travel 2,000 miles out to sea, only to return to the exact stream where they hatched. Arctic terns nest in the Arctic and winter in the Antarctic, and make a round trip of 22,000 miles in the process.

To perform these impressive feats of navigation, the homing animal must not only set off in the right direction, but must also maintain the correct course despite changes in the prevailing weather conditions. A number of navigational cues are used by animals, although exactly how they use them is not completely clear. Many birds make use of the difference between apparent time (as measured by the position of the sun or stars in a particular location) and personal time (as indicated by the animals' internal clock) to estimate position. By comparing the two, they can estimate where they are relative to home, and also how far away. A number of different sense organs are influential in navigational behaviour. Salmon can discriminate between the chemical characteristics of the river in which they were born, even when they are still some considerable distance away from it. Visual landmarks are frequently used in the final stages of homing, particularly to mark out a nest or burrow. Many species are able to head straight for home without any visual landmarks and can navigate successfully in the dark or in dense fog. How they can do that is not completely understood, although the use of the earth's magnetic field is one possible solution. There is still considerable controversy over this suggestion, although it is generally acknowledged that the magnetic field does influence the navigational behaviour of many species of birds.

The importance of effective navigation and of homing behaviour is unquestionable, especially where animals must cover vast distances during migration or when they have been *foraging* in unfamiliar territory. It seems likely, therefore, that this ability has been subjected to the pressures of *natural selection* in that those animals with the most effective navigational skills are more likely to survive and thus pass on a predisposition towards navigation which is then affected by learning in the environment.

homosexuality: a term used to refer either to sexual contact with members of the same sex, or a sexual preference for one's own sex. There has traditionally been a great deal of *prejudice* against homosexuals, and until 1980, the *DSM* classification of mental disorders included homosexuality as a mental illness. The term 'homosexual' is more commonly used for males, with the term 'lesbian' being used for females. The term 'gay' can be used for either.

hormone: see *endocrine system*

hostile aggression: an act of aggression where the intention is to directly harm or injure another person or object.

hothousing: a term used to describe attempts to accelerate the early learning of children. Despite a great deal of interest and involvement in hothousing, particularly in the USA, it has not been the subject of a great amount of psychological research. There is, however, sufficient evidence to suggest that early training can produce significant gains in a number of different areas, including language development. Whether or not the early gains can be maintained into adulthood is not certain, although it is clear that what happens in the years after the enrichment period has a crucial influence on any sustained rate of development. Whether or not hothousing is 'good' for a child is open to debate. Children whose development is accelerated in one area may experience difficulties in other areas of their life, and thus be deprived of many of the experiences that we consider 'normal' in the development of a child. This does not mean, however, that early enrichment cannot be beneficial to the overall development of the child. Informal stimulation at the pace set by the child within a context of fun and enjoyment has much to commend it.

Hovland–Yale model: Hovland *et al.* (1953) discovered that effective persuasion could be achieved by focusing on who says what to whom, i.e. the source (who), the persuasive message (what) and the audience (to whom). Hovland's team identified three major factors that determined the persuasiveness of a message. These were source factors (e.g. experts are seen as more credible than non-experts); message factors (e.g. messages can be more effective if they create a moderate level of fear); and audience factors (e.g. with intelligent audiences, presenting both sides of an argument is more effective).

humanistic psychology: a more recent development in the history of psychology, humanistic psychology grew out of the need for a more positive view of human beings than was offered by *psychoanalysis* or *behaviourism*. Major humanistic psychologists such as Carl Rogers and Abraham Maslow believed that human beings were born with the desire to grow, create and to love, and had the power to direct their own lives. The environment that a person is exposed to and interacts with can either frustrate or assist this natural destiny. If it is oppressive, it will frustrate; if it is favourable, it will assist. Humanistic psychologists also believe that the most fundamental aspect of being human is subjective experience. This may not be an accurate reflection of the real world, but a person can only act in terms of their own private experience. This is probably the biggest problem for scientific psychology which stresses the need for its subject matter to be publicly observable and verifiable. Subjective experience, by definition, resists such processes.

humanistic therapies are based on the idea that psychological disorders are a product of self-deceit. Humanistic therapists try to help clients view themselves and their situations with greater insight, accuracy and acceptance. The fundamental belief of this type of therapy is that clients will be able to fulfil their full potential as human beings if they can achieve these goals. Examples of humanistic therapies include *client-centred therapy* and *Gestalt therapy*.

hygiene factors: those aspects of a job that cause dissatisfaction in workers. These include pay, working conditions and the quality of supervision. According to Herzberg, attending only to these hygiene factors (for example by improving the physical working environment or paying workers more money) would not produce a better motivated workforce. Work satisfaction, and ultimately motivation, is dependent more on the workers' opportunities for responsibility and involvement in the overall scope of the job. Many manufacturers (such as Toyota and Volvo) have adopted job-enlargement schemes to involve workers far more in the whole production process rather than just one small part of it.

hyperactivity: see *attention-deficit hyperactivity disorder (ADHD)*

hypersomnia: recurrent episodes of excessive daytime sleepiness or prolonged night-time sleep. People with hypersomnia are compelled to nap repeatedly during the day, often at inappropriate times such as at work or during a meal. These naps usually provide no relief from symptoms. Patients often have difficulty waking from a long sleep and can feel disoriented.

hypnosis: the induction of a sleep-like state which represents an altered state of consciousness. Modern theories of hypnosis can be classified as either state or non-state theories. State theorists believe that while in the hypnotic state people will act in a way that is quite divorced from their normal way of behaving. For example, they might perform involuntary actions or may display distortion of memory. The reasoning behind this claim is that hypnosis involves special processes that only operate while in a hypnotic state.

Critics of state theories argue that many of the claims of 'unique' behaviours under hypnosis can be dismissed as they can also be achieved in other 'non-hypnotic' states. For example, state theorists claim that hypnotised subjects can exceed the physical and mental abilities of non-hypnotised subjects. With the use of stimulating and task-motivating instructions, however, the same results can be achieved without hypnosis. The success of hypnosis as an analgesic (painkiller) can also be equalled with the use of distraction and other anxiety-reducing techniques.

Non-state theorists argue that the phenomena associated with the hypnotic state can be adequately explained within the normal range of social and *cognitive processes*. During hypnotic induction (where the subject is put into a hypnotic state), it is claimed, a context is created such that hypnotist and subject both play the parts they see as most appropriate. Whilst this is not a claim that allegedly hypnotically induced behaviour is faked, it does offer the suggestion that such behaviours can be explained without resorting to the idea of a special hypnotic state. There is still considerable controversy around the state and non-state issue, and whilst there appears to be little experimental evidence for a unique physiological correlate of the hypnotic state, there are still a number of features of this state whose explanation remains highly controversial.

hypochondria: a type of somatoform disorder (disorders where physical symptoms have no known physical cause, and are therefore linked to psychological problems) whereby the client misinterprets minor physical symptoms as indicating serious illness.

hypothalamus: a small structure at the base of the forebrain which is directly or indirectly involved in a wide range of different behaviours, for example:
- in behaviours related to the internal state of the organism – through its connections with the *pituitary gland*, the hypothalamus controls the secretion of hormones into the bloodstream
- in *arousal* – through its connection with the autonomic centres in the brainstem, the hypothalamus is able to regulate the activity of the *autonomic nervous system*.

hypothesis: a statement of what you believe to be true. The fundamental requirement of any hypothesis is that it can be tested against reality (i.e. is it true or not?) and can then be supported or rejected. To test our hypothesis we first assume that there is no difference between the populations from which the samples were taken. This is known as the *null hypothesis* (H_0). The research hypothesis is often called the *alternative hypothesis* (H_1).

hysteria: a type of psychological disorder where emotionally laden mental *conflicts* manifest themselves as physical symptoms, either in the form of dissociative reactions or conversion hysteria. In the latter case, the underlying conflicts are *unconsciously* converted into symptoms that appear to be physical in origin, but no organic causes are found. Common examples of this type of hysterical reaction include blindness and muscular paralysis.

The term 'mass hysteria' refers to the 'contagious' effects of hysterical reactions among large groups of people. This can be seen at religious gatherings, music concerts or even football matches.

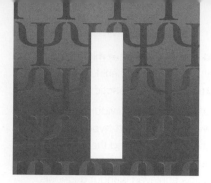

iatrogenic disorder: any abnormal condition that is unintentionally produced by a physician. Examples include the recovery of repressed 'memories' that have been unwittingly planted by the therapist (see *recovered memories*), and *multiple personality disorder (MPD)*. This latter disorder, made famous in Alfred Hitchcock's cult movie *Psycho*, and through films based on real-life cases, like *The Three Faces of Eve*, is claimed by some psychologists to be manufactured during the therapy sessions rather than being a true clinical disorder. Therapists are believed to create the disorder by subtly suggesting the existence of alternate personalities in their clients, or by displaying interest when they display symptoms that suggest dissociation (the separation of one part of their personality from another).

ICD: see *International Classification of Disorders (ICD)*

iconic representation: see *Bruner, J*

id: see *Freud*

identical twins: see *monozygotic twins*

identification: a type of *social influence* which is brought about by a person's desire to be like another person or to be part of a particular social group. It involves adopting the behaviours, attitudes or other characteristics of the other person or the group, not necessarily because this brings us rewards, but because we find it satisfying to be like those with whom we are identifying. We may come to accept and believe their opinions and values, but not with any great depth of commitment, as the motivation to identify is born more out of the desire to be like someone else rather than to accept all that they stand for.

identification with the aggressor: a *Freudian* concept by which the male child attempts to deal with the *castration anxiety* that they experience as a result of their *Oedipus complex*, by *identifying* with the father. As the father is seen as a rival for the mother's affections, the child believes that the father will punish him by castrating him. The child can deflect this potentially disastrous event by integrating his own self with that of the father. The father would not punish the child, as it would be like punishing himself. The term has also developed a more general usage in the psychological literature and applies to any sort of defensive identification with a potential source of punishment. Bruno Bettelheim describes graphically how, in the concentration camps of the Second World War, prisoners would sometimes identify with their captors in a desperate attempt to avoid the terrible consequences that would otherwise befall them.

identity: a person's sense of self, an idea of ourself as a unique being, developed out of the various roles and associations of childhood. In the psychosocial theory of Erik **Erikson**, the development of a stable identity is seen as the major task of **adolescence**.

idiographic: any approach or method in psychology that is concerned with the individual rather than in the development of general laws of behaviour. This approach is normally contrasted with the **nomothetic** approach.

illusion refers to a **perceptual** experience that is not a true representation of the physical event we are receiving through our senses. An illusion is more than a simple case of 'mistaken perception', it is an experience that cannot be predicted by a simple recording of the stimulus itself. For example, in the Müller–Lyer illusion, the line with the outgoing fins 'appears' to be longer than the line with the arrowheads, but it is actually the same length.

In the Moon illusion, a full moon 'appears' larger when it is low on the horizon than it is at its zenith. Despite the fact that we know that the distance between the earth and the moon has not changed (and therefore neither has the size of the moon), the illusion remains a powerful one. Illusions tell us a great deal about how we perceive, particularly concerning the active role that the brain plays in the perceptual process. Illusions also demonstrate the important role of context in perception. This is vividly illustrated in the Ebbinghaus illusion, where the two circles in the centre of the patterns appear different in size simply because of the context set by the size of the circles surrounding them.

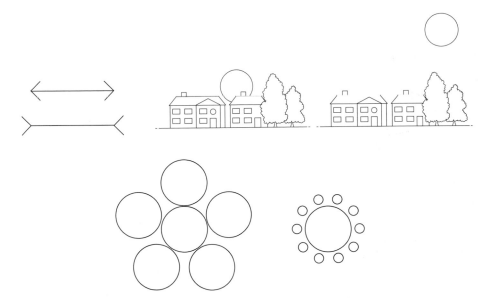

The Ebbinghaus illusion

illusory correlation: occurs when a person perceives a correlation between two events that in reality are not correlated or are correlated to a lesser extent than perceived by that individual. For example, you may meet someone from Liverpool whom you find amusing. Some time later you meet someone else from Liverpool whom you also find amusing. You therefore relate these two events and assume all people from Liverpool must be amusing.

imitation: the copying of another person's behaviour. Evidence suggests that imitation is present in children as young as a few days old. Imitation is clearly a powerful means of learning, and the *reinforcement* provided by parents when their children imitate 'grown-up' actions ensures that children acquire many aspects of their behaviour in this way.

immune system: This is a system of cells within the body that is concerned with fighting against intruders such as viruses and bacteria. The most important part of the immune system are the white blood cells, known as leucocytes; they work to identify and kill foreign bodies (antigens). One of the most important types of white blood cell is the lymphocyte. These develop either as B cells or T cells. One specific B cell is tuned to a specific germ, and when the germ is present in the body the B cell produces millions of antibodies designed to eliminate the germ. T cells (Killer T cells) detect cells in the body that are harbouring viruses, and when they detect such a cell, they bump up against it and kill it. A system called the Major Histocompatibility Complex (MHC) marks all the cells in your body as part of 'you'. Anything that the immune system finds that does not have these markings is definitely 'not you' and is therefore fair game to be attacked.

implicit memory: see *explicit memory*

implicit personality theory: a set of assumptions based on our own experiences about which *personality* characteristics are associated with which others. For example, we may believe that ambitious people are also hard working or that artistic people are unconventional. These 'theories' are referred to as 'implicit' because the person may have no evidence that they have any substance or, indeed, no conscious awareness that they exist. However, they do influence our judgements about other people, and are therefore a powerful influence on our behaviour. Implicit personality theories have the advantage of simplifying the way in which we deal with complex information about the world around us, but as they are merely a set of untested assumptions, they may tell us little of any real value about the people to whom we apply them.

implosion therapy: a technique for ridding a client of *phobias* that requires the client to imagine the feared situation. This causes an 'explosion' of anxiety, but because the explosion is internal (i.e. they are not experiencing it for real, but are imagining it), it is called an implosion. The principle behind this treatment is that the client must be able to experience the feared situation (e.g. imagining themselves caught in a cellar full of rats) in the safe context of the therapy session. As phobics will normally attempt to escape from or avoid the phobic situation, they are denied the opportunity of doing that in this therapy. The therapist describes a fearful situation, then invites the client to imagine it as the therapist has described it. This produces panic, but as the treatment is repeated over and over again, the situation loses some of its power to produce panic, and so gradually the fear subsides.

impression formation: the process by which we form impressions of other people. According to Asch (1946), some pieces of information (called central traits) have a disproportionate influence on the final impression. Other pieces of information (called peripheral traits) have much less influence. The order in which information is received can also play a role in impression formation, with information presented first (the primacy effect) being more influential than subsequent information. Asch also found that a recency effect can emerge, with the last information received being more influential than previous information. Other aspects of impression formation include the positivity-negativity effect. In the absence of information to the contrary, people tend to see others in a positive light. However, if there is any negative information, this assumes a disproportionate influence on impression formation and is more difficult to change in the light of subsequent positive information. Impressions of other people are also strongly influenced by widely shared assumptions about the personalities, attitudes and behaviours of people based solely on their group membership (see **stereotype**).

impression management theory refers to our desire to make a favourable impression on other people. As a result of this, we regulate our behaviour in order to appear in a good light. There are several tactics that we might use to achieve this goal:

- we may dress in a particular way that we feel will be positively evaluated by others. We may, for example, spend a great deal of time and money maintaining a year-round suntan because this delivers the message, 'Look at me, I've got a suntan in January, I must be successful'
- we might ingratiate ourselves to others, either by flattery (by agreeing with them or showing interest in them, for example), or by doing them favours (normally smaller favours than we want in return)
- we may ask others for their advice or their opinion. Many people find this flattering and are more likely to form a favourable impression of us because of it.
- Evidence from studies that have investigated the effectiveness of the above tactics have shown that they do tend to work. Whether they are ethical or not is a different matter.

imprinting: a type of **learning** that takes place during the early part of an animal's life. Imprinting usually takes place soon after hatching (in birds) or birth (in other species). It results in a fixed attachment to another animal (usually the mother) that is difficult to change with subsequent experience. Imprinting often takes place during a specific time period in early development (known as the **sensitive period**) and is characterised by the 'following response' in which the young animal will follow the imprinted object. This type of imprinting is generally referred to as **filial imprinting**. Young animals imprint on particular characteristics of the mother so that they approach only her rather than other adults who may attack them. In **sexual imprinting**, the young animal learns the characteristics (colouration, plumage, etc.) of members of the opposite sex within their own species, a vital task if later courtship and mating is to be successful. In mallard ducks, sexual imprinting is more readily achieved by females, since the males are a bright colour and easy to distinguish from other duck species. Male mallards apparently find the learning task of discriminating their own species more difficult, given the drab colouring of females and their similarity to other species of duck. Animals that are raised with an inappropriate species may sexually imprint on that species, and show a later preference for the foster species over their own. The most persistent cross-species learning, achieved at imprinting, is found in male mallards.

Sexual imprinting does occur most readily to members of an animal's own species, less readily to members of a related species, and least readily to members of an inappropriate species. Some birds who have been hand-reared by humans do sometimes imprint upon them, and as the effects of sexual imprinting are long lasting, this may give them extreme problems for mating with their own species later on. Whether or not mammals show imprinting is more contentious. Lambs and young goats (kids) appear to imprint, and **Bowlby's** theory of **attachment** in human young certainly drew heavily on ideas from imprinting theory and research.

inclusive fitness: a measure of the total reproductive gain of an animal through its own direct descendants (direct fitness) plus the reproductive gain of close genetic relatives (indirect fitness) (see *kin selection*).

independent behaviour: a term used to describe situations where individuals resist social influence. For example, people may feel able to act independently and resist the pressure to conform when in the presence of allies who also resist. Similarly, pressures to obey might be resisted in conditions where the 'victim' could be seen or in the presence of disobedient peers.

independent measures design: see *experimental designs*

independent variable: some aspect of the experimental situation that is directly manipulated by the experimenter in order to see if it causes a change in some other behaviour (the *dependent variable*). For example, allocating participants to either a drug or *placebo* condition (independent variable) in order to measure any change in the intensity of their anxiety (*dependent variable*).

indirect fitness: the reproductive gain that can be achieved by an animal by helping genetic relatives to survive and reproduce. If an individual shares 100 per cent of its own genes, it will share 50 per cent with direct offspring, 25 per cent with first cousins, 12.5 per cent with grandchildren and so on. Thus, if by self-sacrifice an animal can preserve the life (and reproductive capacity) of two cousins and eight grandchildren, it will indirectly have passed on 1.5 times its own genes.

individual differences: an acknowledgement that people differ in their genetic make-up, their life experiences, their emotional disposition, intelligence and so on. Often ignored or minimised in *research* within the *nomothetic* tradition, it is very much the central theme of *idiographic* approaches such as the *case study*. *Humanistic psychology* has, as one of its central beliefs, the idea that all people are unique.

individualism refers to any *culture* where the main type of social arrangement is the nuclear family (parent(s) and children). The term is normally used to contrast with a *collectivist* culture which emphasises more communal relationships and wider kinship groups. The UK is an example of an individualist culture, and China is an example of a collectivist culture.

individuation: refers to our need to be seen as different from other people in some respect, rather than being seen as, or feeling, exactly the same. Although we appear to crave similarity to others in many respects, we do not want to be exactly like them. Most people crave some feelings of individuality. Because of this we may occasionally behave in unusual or bizarre ways. This may risk social disapproval from others, but it reaffirms (to ourselves at least) our sense of individuality. People may also seek individuality because they desire more *control* in their lives. Merely *conforming* to the group norm means that we lose our sense of personal freedom, so the occasional foray into our own individual ways of behaving can maintain the sense of personal control.

inductive reasoning is the process by which general principles about whole populations are drawn based on the findings of research investigations. This is the backbone of all experimental psychology. If we carry out research on a representative sample selected from a given population, we may then develop general principles that apply to the whole of the population of interest.

infanticide refers to the killing of offspring by **conspecifics**. Infanticide has been reported in a number of animals, including lions, rodents and primates. In Hanuman langurs, for example, males that have recently taken over a group will attempt to kill all un-weaned infants so that the females are able to bear their offspring before they, too, are displaced from the group by the next male. Some birds, including hawks and owls, may not commit infanticide directly, but may contribute to it. Their chicks do not hatch out at exactly the same time, therefore one is older and subsequently larger than the other. The younger chick may be harassed by the elder chick, ignored by the parents and will gradually die of starvation. The parents appear to tolerate this, and may even feed the dead chick to the surviving one as food. It is possible that these birds lay two eggs and use one as insurance against failure of the first. In some species, two eggs are laid as a matter of course. In good years, the parents will be able to sustain both, whereas in poorer years, one will die and the parents will not have wasted a great deal of energy and resources trying to maintain it. It appears, then, that some birds use this strategy as reproductive opportunism, just in case it is a good year for resources.

inference: a type of **cognitive process** which involves making a judgement on the basis of available evidence rather than by direct observation of the facts. For example, if we find spilt cream and pawprints in the butter, we might infer that our fridge has been raided by the cat.

inferential analysis: statistical techniques for assessing the probability of chance occurrence of certain differences or relationships in a set of data.

infidelity: men have evolved several different strategies to deter their female partners from committing infidelity (i.e. adultery). These range from vigilance to violence, but all are fuelled by male **jealousy**.

information processing: an approach within cognitive psychology that emphasises how information is gathered, manipulated, stored and retrieved. An example of the information processing approach can be seen in the **multi-store model of memory**. The model proposes that information is processed in a serial manner as it moves from one stage to the next.

information processing approach to intelligence: emphasises the cognitive processes that underlie intelligent behaviour rather than merely quantifying intelligence (the **psychometric approach**). Individual differences in intelligence, therefore, reflect differences in the cognitive operations that people use when solving problems. For example, people differ in processing speed (the speed with which they carry out mental operations such as item identification or retrieval from memory). Processing speed is an important aspect of intelligence and has been found to correlate positively with **IQ**.

informational influence: a type of **social influence** whereby we turn to other people to gain information about what to think or how to act. When we are uncertain of our opinions or the most appropriate way to behave in a particular situation, other people are a valuable source of information. By adjusting our opinions and actions to those around us, we are demonstrating a type of **conformity (majority influence)**. Indeed, informational influence is one of the main reasons why people are willing to be influenced by other people.

informed consent: see *consent*

infradian rhythms occur less often than once every 24 hours, for instance hibernation in small mammals and the human menstrual cycle.

in-group: a reference to any group of which we perceive ourselves to be a member. This might be based on global dimensions, such as race, religion or class, or on more specific localised dimensions, such as friendship or subject choice. This is usually contrasted with the idea of an *out-group* (people who are not of the same group as us) and is characteristic of the 'us and them' classification present in much of our social encounters. Being a member of the 'in-group' carries with it an implicit sense of elitism, and because of this we tend to be biased toward our own group and against members of the out-group (see *minimal groups*).

inhibition: a term with a wide variety of different meanings, but generally taken to mean any process or response that is restrained or otherwise prevented from occurring.

innate: anything that is natural to an organism, existing at birth (or in potential) rather than acquired, a product of genetic factors. The term has two common uses within this definition. The first refers to anything that is universally present among all members of a species and does not have to be acquired (fish, presumably, do not have to learn to swim, therefore swimming is innate in fish). The second use of the term refers to inherited characteristics within an individual that might mark him or her as genetically different from others.

innovation (minority influence): a form of *social influence* which can be attributed to exposure to the minority opinion in a group. In order for a minority to have this influence over the majority, a number of conditions are necessary:
- they must express a clear position at the outset
- they must hold firmly to it despite pressure exerted by the majority to change it
- they must hold a consistent line with each other.

A consistent finding of research in this area is that minority influence is only felt after a period of time. This suggests that a consistently expressed opinion by the minority sets up a number of inter-personal processes that lead to the gradual defection from the majority position. Why does it work?
- according to the *covariation principle* the majority will make a *dispositional attribution* in that they will see the minority as being confident and certain of their opinion
- as the minority opinion continues to be expressed despite the inhibitory pressure of majority disagreement, its impact is increased (the *augmentation principle*)
- this causes the majority to take the minority view seriously. If they are not that confident in their own opinion, they may move in the direction of the minority. If one or more of the majority 'defect' to the minority position, it may set up a 'snowball effect' where the influence of the minority becomes more and more pronounced.

The influence of a minority is especially strong if they are putting forward a position in line with emerging social norms (the *Zeitgeist*) rather than a position opposing them.

insecure attachment: a form of attachment between infant and caregiver that develops as a result of the caregiver's lack of sensitive responding to the infant's needs. It may be associated with poor subsequent cognitive and emotional development. The two major types of insecure attachment are:

- insecure/avoidant – characterises those children who tend to avoid social interaction and intimacy with others.
- insecure/resistant (ambivalent) – characterises those children who both seek and reject intimacy and social interaction.

insight refers to the (often sudden) comprehension of the solution to a problem. The term is also used in **psychotherapy** where a client might be said to achieve insight if they arrive at an understanding of their condition, or the reasons for its existence, that they previously did not have.

insomnia: the inability to get an adequate amount of **sleep**. The difficulty can be in falling asleep (initial insomnia), remaining asleep (middle insomnia), or waking up too early (terminal insomnia). Insomnia is classified as either transient (short term), intermittent (occasional) or chronic when it is constant and long term. Insomnia can either be primary, where it occurs on its own with no known cause, or secondary, where insomnia has a single, underlying medical, psychiatric or environmental cause. Primary insomnia may be a consequence of poor sleep habits (e.g. staying up working too late). Secondary insomnia may be evident in individuals who must work shifts or who are suffering from jet lag.

instinct: a term that tends to defy definition, but is generally taken to mean any response that is natural (i.e. inborn and unlearned) and a characteristic of a given species. Instincts are seen as the motivators for many animal behaviours such as courtship, mating and parental behaviour, although their role in human behaviour is more contentious. **Freud** used the term to refer to **Eros** and **thanatos** (the life and death instincts) which were the underlying causes of many aspects of human behaviour, notably sexual and aggressive behaviours. As a term, 'instinct' is less used by psychology than previously, since the claims made for it have not been substantiated by evidence.

institutional aggression: this 'institutionalised' form of aggression may occur within groups or institutions such as the armed forces, prisons or mental institutions, or between different groups. For example, the 'importation model' of institutional aggression in prisons claims that prisoners may bring their own social histories and violent traits with them into prison and this influences their adaptation to the prison environment. The 'deprivation model' argues that prisoner or patient aggression is the product of the stressful and oppressive conditions of the institution itself (e.g. crowding, fear, frustration). See also **dehumanisation** as an explanation of institutional aggression at a group level.

instrumental aggression: a form of aggression where the primary aim is not to inflict pain on the victim, but to reach some other goal where the aggression is merely incidental. A child who pushes another out of the way to be first in line for Father Christmas's grotto is displaying instrumental aggression.

instrumental conditioning: see *operant conditioning*

intelligence: notwithstanding early attempts to define intelligence in terms of one underlying *general factor (g)*, most definitions stress the ability to function effectively within a given *environment*, which implies the adaptive nature of intelligence. Inevitably, the definition of intelligence becomes intertwined with the term *intelligence quotient (IQ)*, as calculated from performance on *intelligence testing*. Because these tests tend to measure adaptive behaviour within a particular *cultural* context, they are (somewhat inevitably) culturally biased in that it is difficult to measure adaptive and effective behaviour without embedding it in a cultural setting.

intelligence quotient (IQ): a way of comparing the mental age (what a child can do relative to other children of their age) of a child with their chronological age (their actual age). IQ is calculated by dividing mental age by chronological age (and multiplying by 100 to give a whole number). Thus, an eight-year-old child who can accomplish the mental tasks of the average 12-year-old would have an IQ of 150. If the same child could only accomplish the mental tasks of the average six-year-old, their IQ would be 75. The average IQ at any age is always considered to be 100.

intelligence testing involves the construction and administration of tests that measure *intelligence.* Early tests of intelligence such as the Stanford Binet test and more latterly the *Weschler Intelligence Scale for Children* (the WISC) were used to identify specific aspects of a child's mental functioning that might need some special remedial attention. Intelligence tests typically measure several different aspects of a person's intelligence, such as their verbal ability or their arithmetic ability. It is also technically possible to ascertain a more general measure of intelligence (the *intelligence quotient, (IQ)*) from such tests, although the usefulness of this measure is more open to question. Intelligence testing has had a somewhat chequered career, probably reaching its height in the 1960s, when many educational and vocational positions were decided on the basis of the results from these tests. It is rare nowadays to find such decisions being made solely on the basis of intelligence test results, although intelligence testing in a more refined and skill-specific way is still alive and kicking.

intense fandom: a form of extreme fan behaviour toward celebrities, which may result in celebrity worship (see *celebrity (attraction to)*) or, in some extreme cases, stalking behaviour.

interference theory: an explanation of forgetting, when one memory interferes in some way with the memory we are trying to recall. The two main types of interference are *proactive interference* when an existing memory interferes with the thing we are trying to remember, and *retroactive interference (inhibition)* when a more recent memory interferes with an existing memory.

intermittent reinforcement: see *schedules of reinforcement*

internal attribution: see *dispositional attribution*

internal–external scale: a *personality* scale that measures the degree to which people feel that what happens to them is a product of their own skills or intentions, or whether it is due to some other factor that is out of their *control*. For example, people who score towards the external end of the scale might feel that much of what happens to them in life is simply a product of luck or fate. Those who score more towards the internal end of the scale would interpret life success as being a product of skill and hard work.

internal validity: see *validity*

internalisation: a type of *social influence* which is born out of our desire to be right in our opinions and values. If we consider another person both to be trustworthy and also of good judgement, then we are more likely to accept their opinions and values and to integrate them into our own. Over time these become dissociated from their source, and become a stable part of our own cognitive world.

International Classification of Disorders (ICD): a classification system of physical and psychological disorders published by the World Health Organisation. This provides statistics from many different countries so that those who use ICD can reach consensual agreement on the characteristics of the disorders they are treating. ICD–10 (the most recent version at the time of writing) emphasises the patterns of symptoms and the course of the disorders rather than their *aetiology* or their treatment. ICD is not devised for diagnostic purposes, unlike *DSM* which is primarily a manual for clinical diagnosis.

inter-observer reliability: see *inter-rater reliability*

interpersonal attraction: the study of factors and processes involved in the attraction between two people. As such it covers a wide range of different forms of attraction, including friendships, sexual attraction and romantic love.

inter-rater reliability refers to the need to assess the degree to which two or more observers agree on the classification or scoring of the behaviour being studied. The more that observers agree, the higher is the inter-rater reliability.

interrogation techniques: techniques used to question a suspect in order to gain information. Research has shown that some interrogation techniques may lead to *false confessions*.

inter-sexual selection: see *sexual selection*

interview: see *surveys and interviews*

intra-sexual selection: see *sexual selection*

intrinsic motivation: motivation that arises from internal forces (e.g. desire, ambition) that activates a goal-directed behaviour, rather than motivation that arises from external influences (e.g. reward or threat). See *extrinsic motivation*.

introjection: a *Freudian* term which refers to the unconscious taking in of parental values. These lead to the development of the moralistic and idealistic *superego*.

introspection: the process by which a person looks inward at their own mental processes to gain insight into how they work. In this process, *participants* would be presented with *stimuli* (for example, something to be memorised, or a problem to be solved) and they would report what went through their mind while they were carrying out the action. Introspection is not readily accepted as an accurate reflection of the mental goings-on during such activities, because for one thing, only those processes of which the participant is aware will be reported.

introversion: one part of the introversion-extroversion personality dimension associated with the *personality* theory of HJ Eysenck. Introversion is associated with a reluctance to seek the stimulation of social contacts and to be generally more passive and controlled than *extroverts*.

investigator effects: see *experimenter effects*

IQ: see *intelligence quotient (IQ)*

jealousy: an emotion characterised by anger and bitterness when someone thinks another person is trying to take a lover away. Unlike women, men can never be entirely certain that they are the fathers of their children, as fertilisation is hidden from them, inside the woman. As a result, men are always at risk of cuckoldry, the reproductive cost that might be inflicted on a man as a result of his partner's infidelity. The consequence of cuckoldry is that the man might unwittingly invest his resources in offspring that are not his own. The adaptive functions of sexual jealousy for a man, therefore, would have been to deter a mate from sexual infidelity, thereby minimising the risk of cuckoldry. According to the theory of evolved sex differences in jealousy (Buss *et al.*, 1992), women are more likely to experience emotional jealousy, a response to emotional infidelity (i.e. the man falling love with another woman), and the threat of a consequent loss of resources.

jet lag: a term used to refer to the physiological effects of disrupted circadian rhythms that arise from jet travel across different time zones. This is a consequence of the internal body clock (***endogenous pacemaker***) being out of synchronisation with local time and other time-related social customs (***exogenous zeitgebers***). The effects of jet lag are worse when flying west to east (phase advance) than when flying east to west (phase delay).

jigsaw technique: a technique for reducing ***prejudice*** by using a 'common goals' approach. The technique is most often used with mixed-race groups of children. Each member of the group is given the task of finding out information that forms only one part of the lesson to be learned. They then have to communicate that information to the rest of the group. Because each member of the group relies on all the other members in order to complete the task, they should support each other rather than compete with them. Results from studies of this technique support the claim that it leads to increased liking of the children in the group, but shows less evidence that this liking might generalise out to other members of the racial groups concerned.

Jungian: a theory or an idea that might be attributed to the ***neo-Freudian*** theorist Carl Jung (1875–1961). Jungian theory is popularly known for its emphasis on a hypothesised ***collective unconscious***, and makes much of the symbolic nature of dreams.

just world hypothesis: the belief that the world is a fair and predictable place, in which good deeds are rewarded and bad deeds punished. Because of their belief in a natural cause–effect relationship between behaviour and its consequences, subscribers to this view of the world often believe that people who experience misfortune must somehow have deserved it.

kin selection refers to behaviours that, while they may reduce the survival chances or reproductive effectiveness of an individual animal, serve to increase the likelihood of the animal's close genetic relatives surviving and reproducing. The most obvious example of this is in parental care. Parents who feed and care for their offspring are practising behaviours that would be favoured by *natural selection* because they maximise the transmission of their genes to subsequent generations. Offspring are not the only relatives to share copies of genes. The coefficient of relatedness (the *probability* that any two animals will share a gene) is as high for siblings as it is for parents and their offspring. Although the coefficient of relatedness is less for other relatives, it may still benefit an animal to help pass on its genes indirectly by helping all relatives. Kin selection is most often applied as an explanation of altruism among related animals. It is possible for an altruistic animal to pass on more copies of its genes through helping others survive and subsequently reproduce than would be possible from its direct offspring alone. The term *direct fitness* describes the reproductive gain from an animal's own offspring, and *indirect fitness* the reproductive gain from non-descendant genetic relatives. Together they make up the animal's *inclusive fitness*. Kin selection emphasises the importance of this inclusive fitness when deciding whether an animal really does gain or lose by an altruistic act.

kinaesthetics: a term used to describe the feedback from sensations in the muscles or joints. It is, therefore, most concerned with feelings connected with movement.

Klinefelter's syndrome: a condition that occurs in males who have an extra X chromosome in most of their cells (i.e. XXY male). The syndrome can affect different stages of physical, language and social development. The most common symptom is infertility. Because they often don't make as much of the male hormone *testosterone* as other boys, teenagers with Klinefelter's syndrome may have less facial and body hair and be less muscular than other boys. Boys developing these characteristics are often teased at school, which in turn leads to the development of behavioural problems. Many of the problems caused by this condition (excluding infertility) can be alleviated by testosterone replacement therapy.

Kohlberg, L (1927–1987) is best known for his theory of *moral development*, which proposes that there are *universal* stages of moral development, and that moral understanding is inextricably linked to cognitive development. By using people's responses to a series of *moral dilemmas*, Kohlberg established that it was not so much people's decisions about these dilemmas that were insightful about their moral development, but more the reasoning behind the decisions. Kohlberg found evidence for three levels of moral reasoning, with each level split into two stages. He suggested that people went through these stages in a fixed order, and that these stages were universal in all human beings, who, regardless of culture or background, would experience the same direction of development, although many would not achieve the more advanced stages. The two main factors influencing the development from one stage to another are:

- disequilibrium – the child faces a moral issue and notices weaknesses in the present way they reason about it. This may be induced by listening to the views of others
- gains in perspective-taking – as the child grows, they become more able to view issues from the perspective of others. Thus a child at the **preconventional** level may look at an issue very much from the perspective of personal consequences to them, whereas a child at the **conventional** level views an issue more from the perspective of others.

Kohlberg's levels of moral development are as follows:

- The preconventional level: children accept the authority (and moral code) of others. If an action leads to punishment, it must be bad. If it leads to reward, it must be good. There is also a sense in which decisions concerning what is good are defined in terms of what is good for us.
- The conventional level: children believe that social rules and the expectations of others determine what is acceptable or unacceptable behaviour. A social system that stresses the responsibilities of relationships as well as social order is seen as desirable and must, therefore, influence our views of what is right and wrong.
- The postconventional level: here what is right is based on an individual's understanding of universal ethical principles. What is considered morally acceptable in any given situation is determined by what is the response most in keeping with these principles. These are often abstract and ill-defined, but might include: the preservation of life at all costs, and the importance of human dignity.

(See also **Gilligan's ethics of care** for an alternative perspective on moral development in women.)

Korsakoff's syndrome: a type of **amnesia** typically found in chronic alcoholics. In these cases, the client loses their memory for recent events, yet memory for earlier events remains unimpaired. Korsakoff's syndrome has been a source of evidence concerning the nature of short- and long-term memory.

K-strategy: a term from evolutionary biology to describe a type of reproductive behaviour where an animal has few offspring and invests a great deal of energy and resources in the rearing of each. The prime example of this way of doing things is the kangaroo (hence **K-strategy**). This strategy is normally contrasted with the **r-strategy**.

Are you studying other subjects?

The *A–Z Handbooks (digital editions)* are available in 14 different subjects. Browse the range and order other handbooks at **www.philipallan.co.uk/a-zonline**.

labelling theory: a way of understanding the tendency of people to adopt certain styles of behaviour as a direct result of a label that has been applied to them. This uses the **self-fulfilling prophecy** to explain that many people will behave in a seemingly self-destructive way simply because they have been negatively labelled in some way. In education, the use of educational labels such as 'remedial' or 'unintelligent' may produce behaviour that supports that label. In displaying unintelligent behaviour the child effectively justifies the label being used. There is considerable concern over the perils of labelling in mental health. By applying a diagnostic label (for example a general one, such as 'mentally ill', or a specific one, such as **schizophrenic**), we may set up a succession of negative experiences for the person, such as stereotyping by mental health professionals, social rejection and a tendency for the person to see themselves in the same negative way as everybody else does. As with the previous example, diagnostic labels may serve to create self-fulfilling prophecies. Positive effects of labelling may also be achieved. Claims concerning the positive effects of streaming in schools have centred around the belief that application of a positive 'label' (such as 'top group') will cause children to respond more positively and therefore show a higher level of achievement.

laboratory: the term is usually used to denote a room where psychologists can observe behaviour while at the same time maintaining some degree of **control** over the physical environment that might otherwise effect the behaviour of the people being observed.

laboratory experiment: see **experiment**

lack of consolidation: disruption of neural processes that serve to stabilise a **memory trace** after its initial processing. Lack of consolidation disrupts this process and so may interfere with the establishment of newly acquired memories. Research suggests that newly acquired memories are processed during sleep and that this process may contribute to changes in the brain that underlie consolidation of new memories. Sleep-related consolidation of memories, particularly those involving **procedural knowledge**, appears to be impaired in patients with primary **insomnia**.

LAD: see **language acquisition device (LAD)**

laissez-faire: a form of leadership or parenting style that is characterised by a lack of direct **control** and guidance. In the latter example, it amounts to uninvolved parenting, and may border on neglect (see **child rearing styles**).

language: generally accepted as consisting of an agreed set of symbols that enable us to convey meaning and converse with other members of the same **culture** that share the same language. The problem with a definition such as this is knowing how far we can stretch it. Controversies over attempts to teach human language to non-human species have cast doubt over whether such studies have really demonstrated human language or whether the subtleties of language are unique to human beings.

language acquisition device (LAD): a device that *Chomsky* proposed was uniquely human and enabled the human infant to acquire language. This *innate* device allowed young children to infer the rules that govern human speech, and then to use these rules to produce language.

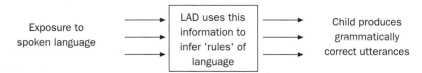

The language acquisition device (LAD)

language development: the study of the acquisition of *language* in human young. To achieve linguistic competence, children must master the four sub-systems of language:

- phonology – the ability to understand and produce speech sounds
- semantics – the ability to understand words and the different combinations of words
- grammar – the ability to understand the rules by which words are arranged into sentences and the rules by which words can indicate tense and gender
- pragmatics – the ability to understand the rules of effective communication such as turn-taking, initiating and ending conversations and so on.

Theories of language development tend to differ in terms of their emphasis on natural or experiential influences. The *behaviourist* perspective, for example, stresses the importance of *conditioning* and *imitation* in the acquisition of language skills. The *nativist* theory of Noam *Chomsky* sees language as a species-specific skill unique to human beings. Of particular importance in this theory is the *language acquisition device (LAD)*, which allows children to understand language and generate grammatically correct language of their own.

latency refers to a period where an organism is, or appears to be inactive. This inactivity is usually started by a particular stimulus and ended by the organism producing a response.

latent learning refers to the fact that if an animal is allowed to wander around (for example) a maze without being *reinforced* for doing so, then later on, when placed in the maze it will learn it faster than other animals with no previous experience. It may appear fairly obvious that this would happen, but prior to this finding it was believed that animals such as rats could only learn if reinforced for doing so. Latent learning meant that they must have formed a mental representation of the maze without reinforcement.

lateralisation of function: the term lateralisation refers to the tendency for certain neural functions to be largely confined to one hemisphere of the brain or the other. For example, language is largely confined to the left hemisphere, and spatial processing confined to the right. Although originally believed to be a characteristic only of the human brain, it now appears that many other species share with humans lateralisation of brain functions. The reason why lateralisation occurs is not yet certain. Two possible explanations are:

- lateralisation has evolved because of functional incompatibility of brain systems. It is possible that two functions (such as language and spatial processing) must be kept apart because optimal performance in one is somehow detrimental to optimal performance in the other. Cues that are important for language are irrelevant for spatial processing, and vice versa

- the 'neural space' of the left hemisphere is mostly taken up with language, therefore other important cognitive functions must be housed elsewhere, in this case the right hemisphere.

lateral thinking: an approach to problem-solving where the person looks at the problem from many different angles in an attempt to find the best solution. This is an alternative to the 'head down, go for the one right solution' approach, and is more likely to establish different paths to the same end result.

law of effect: according to this law (formulated by Edward Thorndike), events in the environment serve to provide rewards for some behaviours but not for others. As a result of this, behaviours that produce 'good' effects are repeated, those that produce 'bad' effects or no effect are not. In this way, behaviours are 'selected' in a manner parallel to the process of natural selection. Appropriate behaviours appear more often, whereas less appropriate behaviours undergo extinction.

law of exercise: the belief that repeated actions of an act make it easier to perform and less prone to error. As an explanation of learning, it does tend to simplify the influence of other factors such as motivation of the organism, provision of *reinforcement* and so on.

Lazarus' theory of appraisal: identifies two stages in the process of *stress* and coping. In a primary appraisal of the situation, individuals must decide whether it is benign, stressful or irrelevant. If they appraise it as stressful, they must decide what to do about it. In the second stage, secondary appraisal, people evaluate the options and decide how best to respond. Both stages involve emotional forecasting, i.e. predicting what feelings the situation is likely to produce (primary appraisal) and predicting the likely emotional impact of each potential response (secondary appraisal).

learned helplessness: the tendency for an organism to give up trying to avoid or escape from an unpleasant stimulus because in the past all their attempts at so doing had been frustrated. In experimental investigations of this phenomenon, dogs would be given electric shocks and prevented from escaping. After repeated shocks the dogs would no longer try to escape, even when a fairly obvious means of escape was made available.

learning: the process of acquiring knowledge which results in a relatively permanent change in *behaviour* or in the predisposition to behave in a certain way. Learning is normally distinguished from other changes in behaviour that might be due to *evolution* (adaptation over generations) or *maturation*, in that it normally occurs as a result of practice or other related experience during the lifetime of the organism. *Behaviourist* views of learning stress the role of *reinforcement* in this process, with learning being seen as a result of certain responses being reinforced and therefore occurring with greater frequency in the future. Some psychologists believe that organisms are *biologically prepared* to learn some things more easily than others, particularly those that are related to survival. *Imprinting* is seen as an example of extreme biological preparedness. Learning is important to organisms that can change their behaviour in this way, because it enables them to adapt their behaviour in order to fit the changing demands of the environment around them.

legislation and health: the introduction of laws aimed at improving health by making certain 'unhealthy' practices illegal. In 2007, legislation came into force that made it illegal to smoke in public buildings in the UK. The primary objective of this legislation was to protect workers and the general public from the harmful effects of secondhand smoke. Nearly a quarter of a million people quit smoking with the help of local NHS Stop Smoking Services between April and December 2007.

lesion: any impairment or destruction of tissue caused by injury or surgical intervention.

levels of measurement refers to the way in which *data* is measured in psychological research investigations. The different levels of measurement simply extract different types of information depending on the amount of information available in the data, and the nature of the measuring instrument being used. The main levels are:

- nominal data – grouped into categories. The scores in each category are described as frequencies. An example would be the number of students from different ethnic backgrounds in a university
- ordinal data – in the form of ratings or ranks. Examples would be attractiveness ratings given by participants to photographs of brides and grooms, or placing those same photographs in a rank order of attractiveness (1st, 2nd, 3rd ...)
- interval data – the measurement scale being used has fixed units of measurement (such as an inch or a second), but the lack of a real zero value means that different scores cannot be taken as proportions of each other, e.g. an *IQ* of 160 does not mean that the person has an IQ twice as high as someone with a score of only 80
- ratio data – like interval data, but zero actually means zero, and proportional comparisons become meaningful. A distance of 2 miles is twice as far as a distance of 1 mile.

levels of processing refers to the theory put forward by Craik and Lockhart (1972) in which they proposed that the attentional and perceptual processing that takes place when something is learned determines how much information about the item is stored in long-term memory. The amount of meaningfulness extracted from a stimulus thus defines its level or depth of processing. At the shallowest level, processing extracts only physical features (such as size or colour) of the stimulus; at the deepest level, it produces information about its meaning. The main assumptions of the theory are:

- the level of processing of an item determines its memorability
- the deeper the processing level, the stronger the *memory trace* and the longer it lasts.

Subsequent research has suggested that the original levels of processing theory was an over-simplification of the way in which memory worked. Craik and Tulving (1975) established that elaboration of processing was a key factor in determining whether an item would be retained. So, if when something was learned, it involved a good deal of processing of the same kind, such as remembering a word embedded in a complex sentence, it would be more likely to be remembered than if the same word was embedded in a simple sentence (less elaborate processing). Other research has shown that stimuli that are distinctive or unique in some way are more likely to be remembered than stimuli that are not. Critics of the levels of processing approach to memory point out that:

- there is a circularity of reasoning involved in the measurement and justification of depth in research. If something is better remembered, this is taken as an indication that it had been subjected to a deeper level of processing. This enhanced processing is then seen as the reason for the better retention performance for that item
- there are problems assessing exactly what level of processing an individual might be using in a particular experimental task. Tasks that are designed to elicit shallow

processing may also involve deeper semantic processing, thus confounding any results that might be obtained
- the levels of processing theory describes what happens in memory rather than explains it. In arguing that depth of processing leads to better long-term memory than shallow processing, the theory fails to explain why this would be so.

Levinson, D J (1920–1994): an American psychologist best known for his book *The Seasons of a Man's Life*. According to Levinson, the human life cycle consists of four different eras. Each era (e.g. early adulthood, middle adulthood) is characterised by different developmental tasks that must be mastered during this period. These eras are linked by periods of transition during which the individual relinquishes tasks of the previous era and embraces the tasks of the next era.

libido: in *psychoanalysis,* a term used to represent energy that comes from the *id*. Originally Freud thought that this was predominantly sexual, although in later writings he changed the meaning of the word to represent it more as a sort of life energy that would drive the individual toward self-preservation and sexual reproduction.

life changes (stress): see *life events*

life events refer to events that necessitate a significant transition or adjustment in various aspects of that person's life. This classification would include events such as widowhood (loss of a husband or wife), divorce, retirement and so on. Because of the potential for major adjustment as a direct result of these events, they are often referred to as 'critical' life events. However, this general classification might misrepresent what is critical to an individual. To some people, divorce is a major stage of transition, and the disruption it causes is extremely traumatic and longlasting. To others, the death of a pet or being passed over for promotion is more traumatic. Note that life events can be things not happening, such as not being promoted, or not getting to university. Psychologists who subscribe to the 'life events model' of development see the changes in adulthood and old age being largely a product of the critical events that we experience and the adjustments we make as a result of those events.

Rank	Life event	Mean value
1	Death of spouse	100
2	Divorce	73
3	Marital separation	65
4	Jail term	63
5	Death of close family member	63
6	Personal injury or illness	53
7	Marriage	50
8	Fired at work	47
9	Marital reconciliation	45
10	Retirement	45
11	Change in health of family member	44
12	Pregnancy	40
13	Sex difficulties	39

Rank	Life event	Mean value
14	Gain of new family member	39
15	Business readjustment	39
16	Change in financial state	38
17	Death of close friend	37
18	Change to different line of work	36
19	Change in number of arguments with spouse	35
20	Mortgage over $10,000	31
21	Foreclosure of mortgage or loan	30
22	Change in responsibilities at work	29
23	Son or daughter leaving home	29
24	Trouble with in-laws	29
25	Outstanding personal achievement	28
26	Wife begins or stops work	26
27	Begin or end school	26
28	Change in living conditions	25
29	Revision of personal habits	24
30	Trouble with boss	23
31	Change in work hours or conditions	20
32	Change in residence	20
33	Change in schools	20
34	Change in recreation	19
35	Change in church activities	19
36	Change in social activities	18
37	Mortgage or loan less than $10,000	17
38	Change in sleeping habits	16
39	Change in number of family get-togethers	15
40	Change in eating habits	15
41	Vacation	13
42	Christmas	12
43	Minor violations of the law	11

The Social Readjustment Rating Scale (Holmes and Rahe)

Thus, developmental change in adulthood is seen as less smooth and continuous than might be proposed by '*life-span*' theorists. Early models of life events saw life events as representing pathological conditions which introduced stress into the person's life. In the Holmes and Rahe 'social readjustment rating scale', **respondents** indicate those events that they have experienced in the previous twelve months, and each is given a score for its potential stress to the person. As a guide, marriage is given a stress score of 50 and death of a spouse the highest score of 100. Note that even Christmas is included as a stressful period which might cause significant hardship (both financial and social). The higher the score, the greater the likelihood of the person suffering some psychological health problem (the commonest reaction appears to be **depression**).

More recent views of the significance of life events have represented them more as processes. Life events do indeed cause an initial reaction of shock and immobilisation (how would the news that you had won £20 million on the National Lottery affect you?), but individuals then have the chance to enter a new period of their life by building upon the experience in a positive and constructive way. Thus, the life event might be integrated into their life rather than dominating it. A widow becomes 'a single woman' and a disabled person becomes 'a person with a disability'. The degree to which a person can both cope with, and grow from, a life event will be determined by the resources available to them. These may be social, such as the presence of friends and relatives in a social network, and personal, such as the person's health, **self-esteem** and psychological **hardiness.**

life-span development: the belief that an individual develops throughout their life. Although not tied to one specific theory, the life-span approach to development does make a number of assumptions:
- the potential for development extends throughout the life cycle
- there is no one optimum route that development must take
- development takes place on a number of different fronts at the same time. We develop socially, intellectually, emotionally and physically. Progression or decline in one of these is not necessarily a sign of a progression or decline in the other three
- this approach emphasises the reciprocal influence of individual and environment. A common metaphor is of a river which is shaped and modified by the terrain through which it flows. In turn, the river exerts its own influence on that terrain.

Life-span developmental theorists include Erik **Erikson** and Daniel **Levinson**. The life-span approach to development can be contrasted with the **life-events** approach.

light adaptation: the process by which the eye adjusts to higher levels of light intensity. The pupil of the eye contracts and the **cones** become operative. At this level of operation, the eye becomes less sensitive to lower light intensities.

Likert scale: an attitudinal measurement scale which measures an individual's agreement or disagreement with attitude statements such as 'psychologists hold the answers to all life's problems'. There are usually five different levels of agreement or disagreement, going from 'Strongly agree' through 'Not sure' to 'Strongly disagree'.

linguistic relativity hypothesis: a theory proposed by Whorf in 1956, whose central idea was that the language that a person speaks has a great influence on the way that they think and perceive. There is a weak and a strong version of the hypothesis. The weak form argues that language affects the way in which we perceive the world around us.
The commonest example for this is the claim that Eskimos have many different words for snow simply because they are able to distinguish more types and characteristics of snow than we are. The strong version proposes that the linguistic differences of different peoples are actually reflected in the ways they represent and think about the world. Hopi Indians and Thais do not, for example, have the same sense of past, present and future in their language

as we have. This is seen as evidence for the rather different way in which they think about time. Intensive research on the claims of this theory have failed to come up with convincing evidence for its main proposition.

lithium: an element found naturally. In the form of lithium carbonate it is used extensively for the treatment of *bipolar disorders* such as *manic-depressive psychosis*. Although the exact way that lithium works is still not known, it is thought that it has a general effect on the neuronal cell membrane, affecting *neuronal transmission*.

Little Albert: a study carried out in 1920 by Watson and Rayner, in which they *conditioned* a nine-month-old child by making a loud noise every time the child played with a rat. After repeated repetitions of this rat/loud noise pairing, the child showed a fear response to rats that *generalised* to other furry animals and even, it is reported, to Father Christmas's beard!

Little Hans: one of *Freud's* most famous *case studies*. Hans was a five-year-old child who feared that if he went out into the street, he would be bitten by a horse. Freud diagnosed this as a symbolic fear, i.e. a fear of something that was represented in the symbol, in this case the horse. This was seen as indicative of the *castration anxiety* experienced by male children as a result of the *Oedipus complex*.

lobotomy: a surgical technique developed in the 1940s in which an incision is made in the frontal lobe of the *brain* to sever the neural connections between the frontal lobe and the lower centres of the brain. Originally thought to be a cure for *schizophrenia*, it proved less than effective in this respect and caused irreversible brain damage instead. Many patients, already debilitated by their schizophrenia were left permanently withdrawn and apathetic by the lobotomy.

localisation of function refers to the belief that specific areas of the *cerebral cortex* are associated with specific physical or behavioural functions.

locus of control: a term used to refer to a person's perception of personal *control* over their own behaviour. It is measured along a dimension of 'high internal' to 'high external'. A high internal perceives themselves as having a great deal of personal control and therefore is more inclined to take personal responsibility for their behaviour, which they see as being a product of their own ability and effort. High externals perceive their behaviour as being caused more by external influences or luck.

long-term memory: that part of *memory* that is concerned with information that is part of the past, as opposed to *short-term memory*, which is more concerned with information from the present or immediate past. There are a number of distinctions that can be made concerning long-term memory: *episodic memory* (memory of the personal episodes in our life) and *semantic memory* (memory of knowledge); *declarative knowledge* (knowing that ...) and *procedural knowledge* (knowing how ...). *Forgetting* from long-term memory is normally due to an inability to retrieve at the time (for whatever reason), although it is likely that some material is lost due to physiological reasons.

longitudinal study: an investigative method where *participants* are studied over an extended period of time (often years). There have been a number of popularised longitudinal studies portrayed on television such as the '7 Up', '7+7', '21 Up', etc. series that followed a group of children from different backgrounds throughout their life in order to document their life changes and experiences. Longitudinal studies can give valuable information about the impact of early experiences on children, as well as the way in which behaviour changes (or stays constant) over time. They are a relative luxury in the investigative repertoire of the research psychologist, given that they take so long and can be expensive to maintain and administrate. The drop-out of participants over the course of the study (the attrition rate) can also minimise the effective conclusions that can be drawn from such studies.

looking deathworthy: research in the US (Eberhardt et al., 2006) has shown that, in murder cases where the likelihood of the death penalty is high, jurors are not influenced simply by the knowledge that the defendant is black, but also by the extent to which the defendant appears stereotypically black. Defendants who are more stereotypically black are far more likely to receive the death penalty than those who are less stereotypically black. This research suggests that, in sentencing decisions, jurors treat such traits as powerful cues to deathworthiness.

Lovaas technique: a form of behavioural therapy, based on the principles of operant conditioning, for children diagnosed with autism or related disorders. The technique consists of an intensive behavioural intervention that breaks down desired skills (such as self-help and language skills) into their most basic components, and rewarding the child's positive performance. Success is promoted through the use of reinforcement of successive approximations to the desired behaviour. Treatment begins as early as possible, usually before the child is five years old and ideally before three and a half years. This is thought necessary in order to teach basic social, educational and daily life skills, and also to reduce any stereotypical and disruptive behaviours before they become established. The home-based programme consists of forty hours a week of intensive therapy on a one-to-one basis for six to eight hours per day, for two or more years.

lowballing: a compliance technique whereby an initial request for compliance is followed by a second request for the same behaviour, but it is now costlier to engage in that behaviour. Individuals tend to maintain their commitment and still comply with the request even though it has become more costly.

lucid dreaming: dreaming while knowing that you are dreaming. Lucidity usually begins when the dreamer realises that the experience is not occurring in physical reality, but is a dream. The quality of lucidity can vary greatly. When lucidity is at a high level, dreamers are aware that everything experienced in the dream is occurring in their mind, therefore there is no real danger: they are asleep in bed and will awaken shortly. With low-level lucidity there is some awareness of dreaming but not enough to realise that other people in the dream are simply dream representations, or that they are actually asleep and safe from harm.

Machiavellian intelligence: an adaptation to social problem-solving in large groups of animals. This form of intelligence enables individual animals to manipulate others in their social group without causing aggression. Among social-living animals, individuals can use behavioural tactics to manipulate those who are not allies into unwitting help. This ability to understand and plan deception appears to be restricted to the great apes, although other primates seem to be able to learn such tactics by watching. Manipulative tricks include the management of attention, in which the target's attention is diverted towards or away from something to profit the agent of deception (the animal doing the deceiving), and 'creating an image' in which deception serves to change how other animals view that individual. For example, one animal might groom another in order to gain access to and steal some resource.

magic number 7 (plus or minus 2): see *digit span*

magnetic resonance imaging (MRI) is a type of non-invasive imaging technique that allows physicians to look into a living brain. A patient lies with their head surrounded by a large magnet, which creates a powerful magnetic field. The brain is then bombarded with radio waves. Molecules in the brain vibrate in response to these radio waves and emit radio waves of their own. These are recorded and analysed by a computer, which then builds a three-dimensional picture of the structures of the brain. MRI images are more detailed than CT scan images and do not subject the patient to X-rays. The amount of detail from a MRI image can show up even very small changes in the brain, such as the loss of myelin around axons.

majority influence (conformity): see *conformity (majority influence)*

maladaptive thoughts: patterns of thinking and behaviour that cause or maintain emotional problems. Maladaptive thinking may be accompanied by irrational beliefs, i.e. beliefs that are held even though they are not true (e.g. 'It is important to be liked by everybody').

mania: an emotional state characterised by intense, but more often than not, inappropriate elation, resulting in hyperactivity, distractibility, excessive talkativeness and disrupted (racing) thought processes. People who suffer from mania nearly always have bouts of depression as well.

manic-depressive psychosis: see *bipolar disorder*

Mann–Whitney U test: a non-parametric statistical test used to detect whether there is a difference between two independent groups on some measure of behaviour.

Marcia's theory: Marcia (1966) interviewed adolescents about their 'identity status' After analysing their answers, he identified four categories of identity development. Adolescents would start at identity diffusion, move through moratorium, possibly via foreclosure, before ending with identity achievement.

- Identity diffusion – adolescent hasn't even started to think about issues such as occupation, politics and attitudes to sex.
- Identity foreclosure – adolescent has prematurely formed an opinion that is not based on his or her own personal consideration (e.g. accepting conventional attitudes toward such issues).
- Identity moratorium – decisions about identity are put on hold while the adolescent 'tries out' various possibilities (e.g. dabbles with different political ideas).
- Identity achievement – adolescent has been through a period of confusion or crisis and has achieved his or her own identity.

Marcia believed that these four 'statuses' are not necessarily sequential, with some adolescents skipping certain stages, but moratorium appears to be a prerequisite for successful identity achievement.

Maslow, A (1908–1970): a *humanistic* psychologist who coined the term 'third force' to illustrate how the central beliefs of humanistic psychology differed from the established approaches of *psychoanalysis* and *behaviourism*. Maslow provided the rather original (at the time) notion that human beings inherit a psychological structure of needs, capacities and tendencies that are essentially good. This was in sharp contrast to the doctrine of *Freudian* psychoanalysis which saw human needs and tendencies as essentially anti-social and in need of the 'training' provided by socialisation. Maslow believed that healthy development involved the actualisation of these capacities and that psychopathology results from the denial or frustration of those needs and capacities.

Maslow is best known for his hierarchy of needs (see diagram overleaf), in which he proposed that basic needs, such as the physiological needs of hunger and thirst, must be satisfied before the higher needs (such as esteem and *self-actualisation*) can be achieved. The specific form that self-actualisation takes may vary from person to person. It may involve the creation of an artistic masterpiece, becoming an acknowledged sportsperson, or even being a good parent. Once self-actualisation is achieved, the *peak experiences* associated with these different areas of functioning become a common occurrence.

Critics of Maslow's approach cast doubts on the scientific *validity* of his claims. His theory is dismissed by some as speculative and inspirational, yet lacking in scientific verification and support. Maslow accepted that although his theory might not be considered successful in a laboratory or *experimental* sense, it had fitted in well with the personal experience of many people and had enabled them to make sense of their lives.

M

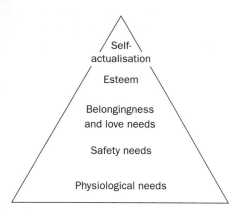

Maslow's hierarchy of needs

massed practice: an arrangement whereby an organism completes a series of *learning* trials without a rest period between each trial. Learning tends to be less effective (i.e. takes more trials) than it is when the trials are more spaced out (*distributed practice*).

matched pairs: see *experimental designs*

matched subjects (participants) design: see *experimental designs*

matching: the term has two main uses in psychology, as a procedure in *experimental design* and as a process of *interpersonal attraction*. In experimental design, it refers to a procedure whereby *participants* in one condition are matched with participants in another in terms of anything that might have an effect on the *dependent variable*. This might be age, sex or many other factors. When used as an explanation of interpersonal attraction, it refers to the tendency for people to select partners who are alike in physical attractiveness, background or education for example.

maternal deprivation: a term made famous by John *Bowlby* who believed that children deprived of maternal care and affection in early childhood would suffer some degree of emotional, social or intellectual retardation in later life. The term 'deprivation' is applied when an *attachment* bond is broken. Bowlby's early work with evacuated children in World War Two led him to believe that prolonged separation from the mother was the cause of the deprivation syndrome. This belief was strengthened as a result of research with rhesus monkeys carried out by Harry Harlow in the 1950s. Harlow showed that young monkeys separated from their mothers shortly after birth and raised in isolation would show irreversible effects later in life. Early studies of children raised in orphanages showed that they too frequently showed signs of adverse social, linguistic and intellectual functioning that were extremely long-lasting. Effects such as this that are due to the non-development of the attachment bond are a product of maternal *privation*. Bowlby's work has clearly had a number of beneficial effects, particularly in the improvements of institutional care of young children, and the gradual increase in fostering as a preferred alternative to institutional care. Many of his claims about the dangers of separation from the mother appear to have been overstated, and the guilt that was felt by generations of working mothers appears to have been largely unfounded.

maternal privation: see *privation*

maturation: the developmental process that moves us towards maturity. The term has been used in this way by most psychologists, but with subtle differences in its finer meaning:
- it may be seen as being purely the biological unfolding or 'ripening' of *innate* tendencies with no assistance from the environment. Walking might be such an example
- the environment acts as a trigger for these innate tendencies, and also determines the direction that they take. Human language is such an example. We need to hear speech before we can produce it, and the speech we hear will determine the language we speak.

mean: the arithmetic average calculated by dividing the total of all scores added together by the number of scores, e.g. $3 + 5 + 6 + 3 + 3 \div 5 = 4$, the mean.

means-ends analysis: a type of problem-solving strategy typically used in computer programs such as the general problem solver. Means-ends analysis selects those behaviours (the means) that shorten the distance between the present state and the desired goal (the ends). If a particular operation has successfully shortened the distance between these two positions, the program moves on to the next step. If it has not, it may try another operation. Often goals are broken down into sub-goals. To achieve fame and happiness, we seek a good job. To get a good job, we go to university. To get to university, we work hard for our A levels and so on. Each operation towards a sub-goal can be evaluated as to whether it moves us closer towards the immediate 'end'. If we find that studying gets us better grades, then we continue with that operation, and that in turn moves us closer to the ultimate goal of fame and happiness.

measure of central tendency: a measurement that provides some sort of typical value in a set of scores. The *mean* is perhaps the most sensitive of the measures in that a change in any single score will change the value of the mean. The *median* and the *mode* would be unaffected however.

measure of dispersion: a measurement of the spread or variability in a set of scores. Although the *measure of central tendency* tells us what a typical score is in a set of scores, it does not tell us how far the other scores are spread around that central score. Measures of dispersion add that information. They vary from the *range*, a rather crude calculation of the difference between the smallest and the largest score, to the *standard deviation*.

media and addictive behaviour: Sulkunen (2007) believes that the media are a rich source of lay beliefs about addictive behaviour, particularly about substance use and abuse. For example, films about drug-users, such as *Trainspotting* (1996) and *Human Traffic* (1999), present scenes of drug competence and enjoyment of the effects, with this enjoyment frequently contrasted with the dullness of ordinary life. In the US, however, guidelines have now been developed for film and television writers concerning media representations of drug-taking behaviour. These recommend that writers should communicate that all illegal drug use is unhealthy and harmful and that addiction should be presented as a disease. Television and the internet have also been identified as media that could potentially be used to provide effective intervention for addictive behaviours, with television increasingly being used to promote healthy lifestyles and behaviour change such as smoking cessation and physical exercise.

media campaigns for healthy living: use of the mass media (e.g. television, newspaper and internet advertising) to try to change the health habits of a society. An example is the healthy eating campaign launched in Scotland in 2009 as part of a long-term commitment to change Scotland's diet and produce a healthier population. A special helpline and dedicated website were set up to offer information and advice on how the nation's health can be changed for the better.

media effects refers to the belief among many researchers and social commentators that the media (principally television and video) are responsible for the development of certain anti-social behaviours among those who are exposed to them. Various mechanisms are proposed to explain this causal relationship. These include the following:

- cognitive priming: children may learn problem-solving *scripts* from their observations of modelled behaviour on television. Frequent exposure to scenes of violence may lead children to store scripts for aggressive behaviour in their memories, and these may be recalled in a later situation if any aspect of the original situation – even a superficial one – is present
- vicarious reinforcement and legitimations: television may inform viewers of the positive and negative consequences of violent behaviour. When violence is justified or left unpunished on television, the viewer's guilt or concern about consequences is reduced
- desensitisation: frequent viewing of television violence may cause viewers to be less anxious and sensitive about violence. Therefore someone who becomes desensitised to violence may perceive it as more 'normal' and be more likely to engage in violence him or herself.

The media effects model has many critics, who question both the research studies that have been carried out to demonstrate effects, and the assumptions that are made as a result of this research. Some of the arguments against a media effects model are as follows.

- Research has discovered that young offenders watched less television and video than their non-offending counterparts, had less access to the technology in the first place and had no particular interest in specifically violent programmes.
- Psychological research into media effects has tended to represent young media users as 'inept and naïve' viewers, and underestimates what children can and do understand about the media.
- The kinds of media violence which are typically condemned by the effects model are limited to fictional programmes. The acts of violence that appear daily on our television screens on news programmes are somehow exempt from this condemnation.

median: the middle value in a set of scores when they are placed in a rank order, e.g. 3, 3, 3, 5, 6. Median = 3.

mediated relationships: relationships that are not face to face, but conducted wholly or in part through some other medium (e.g. internet, telephone). Such relationships can be synchronous (e.g. a telephone call) or asynchronous (e.g. an e-mail or SMS text). In contrast to the synchronicity of face-to-face communication, the asynchronicity of an e-mail or text allows partners more time to reflect upon and prepare their messages at their own pace, thus they may be able to communicate in a more socially desirable and effective manner than is possible in a face-to-face interaction. For face-to-face relationships to be effective, partners must engage in entrainment, i.e. the synchronisation between partners of their activities in order to be physically present at the same time. In a mediated relationship, losing the need for entrainment provides partners with a sense of personal space and control over their relationship.

Mediated relationships are often represented as less 'rich' than face-to-face relationships since they lack the cues associated with non-mediated relationships (e.g. body language, the richness of spoken language). Although in some cases this may lead to *deindividuation*, i.e. increased use of uninhibited behaviours because of relative anonymity, this is not always the case. The SIDE (social identity deindividuation) model (Reicher et al., 1995) challenges the assumption that not being able to 'see' the object of a communication leads people to behave badly. They argue that anonymity may also cause people to act more pro-socially. Mediated relationships also offer possibilities for people who are shy, lack access to suitable others, have lack of time, or have physical handicaps that make developing face-to-face relationships more difficult.

medical model: see *biological model of abnormality*

meiosis: a type of cell division within the body by which the sperm and egg cells are produced. During meiosis, the *chromosomes* divide, with 23 chromosomes going to each of the two gametes (sex cells) that have resulted from this division. The number of chromosomes in each cell is halved in this process.

melancholia: a condition described by the Greeks and Romans, and characterised by a deep and persistent sadness. The condition corresponds most closely to what we now call *depression*.

memory: a term that can be used in many different ways, but most often in one of three ways:
- a mental function by which we are able to retain and retrieve information about events that have happened in the past. When we organise something so that we can remember it or recall it later on, we are said to be using our memory
- the storage system whereby these memories are retained in the brain. Terms such as *short-term memory* and *long-term memory* are used to indicate the time-span of such systems
- the information that we actually remember, i.e. we have a memory of something.

memory for shocking events: see *flashbulb memory*

memory improvement: see *memory-practical applications*

memory-practical applications: research into the processes involved in memory and forgetting has enabled psychologists to develop a number of techniques to understand or improve memory in practical situations:
- in *eyewitness testimony* tasks, research has demonstrated how recall of an incident is subject to a number of distortions and inaccuracies
- memory for medical information – research on what and how medical information (such as advice from doctors and treatment instructions) is remembered has enabled researchers to advise medical practitioners on how to improve communication with patients
- *mnemonic* devices can be used to improve memory on simple tasks such as learning a list of names.

memory trace: the biological representation of an event in memory. This is thought to be biochemical in nature, although an exact biochemical location for a specific memory event has not yet been established.

mental age: a level of intellectual functioning which is appropriate for children of a particular age. When dealing with children of 'normal' *intelligence*, the mental age is equal to the chronological age (the actual age of the child). With children of less than normal intelligence, the mental age is less than the chronological age. For children of above normal intelligence, the mental age is greater than the chronological age.

mental handicap: a general term used for a person who has some form of *mental retardation*.

mental illness: a general term used to indicate that a person's level of psychological functioning is sufficient to warrant psychiatric intervention. The term also implies that the *abnormality* is caused by factors similar to those that might cause a somatic (physical) illness. Opponents of this view of abnormality, such as Thomas Szasz, have argued that whereas the symptoms of physical illness are objective, the symptoms of mental illness are entirely subjective.

mental retardation: defined in *DSM* as significantly below average intellectual functioning along with deficits in adaptive behaviour (ability to care for oneself) and occurring below the age of 18. Using *intelligence* test scores as a judgement of level of intellectual functioning, significantly below average is seen as having a score below 70 (the average is 100). Statistical analysis tells us that approximately 2.5 per cent of people fall into this below-70 category.

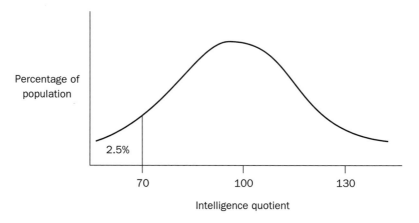

DSM recognises four different levels of mental retardation:
- mild (IQ 55–70)
- moderate (IQ 40–55)
- severe (IQ 25–40)
- profound (IQ below 25)

The causes of mental retardation range from known organic causes to cases where there is no known organic cause. This latter classification is by far the larger one. Developmental theorists stress that a large proportion of cases of mental retardation are a product of motivational deficits. The cumulative effects of social deprivation, a history of failure, and poor or inconsistent *reinforcement* means that many children lack the motivation to perform. An alternative explanation is that some form of brain damage which is too slight to be detected causes mild (the more common) retardation. The environment then either masks or enhances this retardation depending on whether it is enriched or impoverished. Organic explanations of mental retardation include chromosomal abnormalities (such as in **Down's syndrome**) or genetic conditions (such as in phenylketonuria). More recently, environmental hazards such as the lead in petrol engine emissions have been implicated in the onset of mental retardation.

mental set: see **set**

mere exposure effect: an explanation of why people are attracted to each other. This proposes that if we are repeatedly exposed to the same stimulus, we develop a greater attraction to it. The major explanation of this effect comes from **sociobiology**. If animals are exposed to something for the first time, they display negative reactions (such as fear or aggression). Repeated presentations lead to a decrease in these negative reactions. Frequent interactions with others may also increase our judgements of similarity with them, and hence our attraction to them.

metacommunication: literally, communication about communication, whereby one display changes the meaning of the ones that follow. The most familiar example of this is the 'play bow' in dogs. By adopting this posture before play fighting, dogs can communicate to each other that the 'aggressive' posturing that follows is not real aggression, but play.

method of loci: a way of increasing the effectiveness of our memory. To use this method involves memorising a series of different locations (such as rooms in a house or points on a walk) and then imagining one of the items to be remembered in each location. To remember the items, we then mentally walk through the house, entering each room in turn and 'seeing' the item there. For example, to remember the **BPS** ethical guidelines, we might go from the kitchen where we see a very competent and professional cook at work, to the dining room where there is a deceptive clock that always tells the wrong time (keywords are 'competence' and 'deception'). (See also **pegword system** and **mnemonics**.)

midbrain: see **brain**

milieu therapy: a humanistic approach to the treatment of psychological disorders that stresses the role of an institution in the recovery process. It involves the creation of an environment that is conducive to self-respect and individual responsibility, and involves the client in meaningful activity.

Milieu therapy was developed in the light of concerns that institutions cause a deterioration in patients because they are deprived of self-respect, responsibility and the opportunity to engage in meaningful activities. Some institutions, such as the therapeutic community at Kingsley Hall, set up by the **anti-psychiatrist** R D Laing, involve staff and patients as equals, and the social milieu this creates is the central feature of the treatment being given. Some success has been reported for milieu therapy programmes, but predominantly as an additional form of therapy to other types of treatment.

mimicry refers to the resemblance of one animal (the mimic) to another (the model) such that the two are confused by a third animal (usually a predator). These similarities have normally **evolved** because they give some selective advantage to the mimic. There are many different types of mimicry including the following:
- Batesian mimicry – the predator avoids the mimic because of its physical similarity to a more dangerous or noxious model. Although mimics normally mimic other animals, they may also mimic plants and other objects. For example, stick insects resemble twigs that

M

are inedible to the predators that normally prey on stick insects. Although Batesian mimicry has obvious survival advantage value for mimics, its usefulness depends on many other critical features such as the number of mimics relative to models. If the mimics significantly outnumber the models, predators are more likely to encounter them before they encounter an example of the model. As, therefore, their first encounter was not with the noxious model, predators will search for the mimics rather than avoiding them

● Mullerian mimicry – a number of noxious species share similar warning signals. No deception is involved (all are noxious) and all mimics benefit because predators avoid them all. Unlike Batesian mimicry, it is difficult to distinguish which is the mimic and which is the model

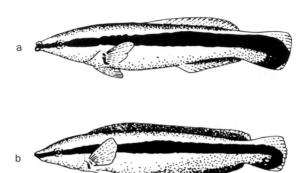

(a) The cleaner wrasse and (b) its mimic the sabre-toothed blenny

● aggressive mimicry – in this type of mimicry one animal mimics another in order to take advantage of a special relationship that exists between the model and other animals. The sabre-toothed blenny mimics the colour and markings of the cleaner wrasse. Unlike the model, however, which cleans larger fish (who benefit from this service and therefore do not attack it), the mimic takes a bite out of the unfortunate 'customer'.

mind: one of the trickiest terms to define, it has several definitions within psychology. It is part of a philosophical belief that the mind is an ephemeral (non-physical) entity if compared to the body, which is a physical structure. The term is used in a more general sense nowadays, such as in referring to the totality of mental processes (such as *perception*, *attention* or intellectual functioning). In this context, an understanding of 'how the mind works' becomes essential in explaining observable behaviour.

mind-body problem: see *dualism*

minimal brain dysfunction: a term used where the patterns of abnormal behaviour demonstrated by children seem to suggest some organic problem but none can be found. Despite the fact that no organic factors are evident, minor brain damage has been proposed in explanations of *attention-deficit hyperactivity disorder (ADHD)*, and *dyslexia* among others.

minimal groups: a classification of group membership where group members might have very little in common, and may experience little or no interaction with other members of the group. Using such experimentally constructed groups, it has been found that even on the basis of such minimal experience, group members identify with their group, and show 'in-group' favouritism and 'out-group' *prejudice* and *discrimination*.

minority influence (innovation): see *innovation (minority influence)*

mirror neurons: neurons that fire both when an individual performs an action and also when observing the same action being performed by another person. They are so-called because they 'mirror' the actions of other people. The exact functions of mirror neurons are still open to speculation, but it is possible that they are important in understanding the actions of others, or for learning new skills through imitation.

misattribution: a wrongful *attribution* of an emotional response to a cause that has not produced it. This is most commonly observed in experimental manipulations, but also appears frequently in real life. An example is the *Romeo and Juliet effect*. Here, the response (attraction between two adolescents) is caused (or enhanced) by the arousal produced by parental disapproval for the relationship.

misleading information: information, e.g. in the form of a leading question, that is provided after an event and therefore may distort people's memories by altering and adding information. Research by Elizabeth Loftus and her colleagues has shown how misleading post-event information can distort people's memories for *eyewitness testimony*, childhood experiences, and even disliked foodstuffs.

mitosis: a type of cell division within the body, whereby cells divide into other cells, each with the full set of *chromosomes*. Each of these cells receives an exact copy of the chromosomes in the original cell. During development, mitosis occurs again and again, until finally the adult organism is created.

mnemonics: devices used to improve memory. Examples of mnemonic devices include the *method of loci* and the *pegword system*. Although mnemonic devices are effective ways of increasing the memorability of fairly simple information, they are limited in their ability to increase the effectiveness of our memory of complex information, and they do not lead to an understanding of the remembered material.

mode: the most frequently occurring value in a set of scores, e.g. 3, 3, 3, 5, 6. Mode = 3.

model: a type of 'mini-theory' that represents a pattern of relationships between different aspects of *behaviour*. For example, the *Atkinson and Shiffrin model of memory* represents the relationship between the different aspects of *short-* and *long-term memory*. The term may also be used to represent a person who has an important function in the *socialisation* of an individual. In this function, they may be described as a 'role-model'.

modelling: a fundamental part of *observational learning*, in which somebody observes another (the model) and then attempts to imitate their behaviour. Modelling is considered to be an influential part of many aspects of the *socialisation* process.

monogamy: a type of mating system where males and females usually mate only with one member of the opposite sex. If a monogamous pair is maintained for one breeding season only, with new partnerships formed for subsequent breeding seasons, this is called serial monogamy. The reasons why monogamy would evolve are different for males and females.

FOR MALES:
- Males are better able to defend individual females. Males may stay with a single female and guard her throughout the breeding cycle. Although *polygyny* may be the ideal mating arrangement for the males of many species, circumstances often make monogamy a more realistic alternative.

- More young survive within a monogamous relationship than would survive if the male had more than one mate.

FOR FEMALES:
- There are no resource advantages in having more than one mate. The selection of the fittest available male helps to ensure survival of the female's *genes*. The maintenance of monogamous behaviour helps to achieve that end.
- They are no better off as the second mate of one male than as the sole mate of another.

monomorphic: when used in the phrase *sexually monomorphic*, it means that there are no discernible differences between the sexes in terms of size, colouration, etc.

monotropy: a claim made by John *Bowlby* that the young child has an innate tendency to become *attached* to one specific individual, and that this attachment is qualitatively different from other subsequent attachments. Evidence no longer supports this idea.

monozygotic twins: meaning one *zygote*, these twins are formed through the splitting of a single zygote (or fertilised egg cell). Generally regarded as being *genetically* identical.

mood disorders: disorders that affect the emotional state of those suffering from them. *DSM-IV-TR* has two major categories of mood disorder, depressive disorders and *bipolar disorders*.

moral anxiety: a *Freudian* belief that people are anxious about the possible punishment that may follow expression of their *id* impulses, rather than following the wishes of their *superego*. As a result of this, many id impulses, including sexual impulses, become associated with anxiety, and are therefore seen as morally wrong.

moral comparisons: attempting to draw comparisons between individuals or whole groups of individuals in terms of their moral reasoning.

moral development: in its most general sense, this term refers to the process by which children come to internalise standards of right and wrong within their society. Psychological explanations of moral development tend to stress either 'moral relativism' (what is right is dependent on the culture being studied, there are no universal standards of right and wrong) or 'moral universalism' (certain *values*, such as the preservation of human life at all cost, are of central and universal importance to all individuals and cultures). As is the case with many areas of psychology, different orientations offer quite different interpretations of moral development:

- *social learning theory* – sees moral development in terms of the child's acquisition of morally acceptable *behaviours* which are learned as a result of direct *reinforcement* and the observation of other important people in the child's life. Expectations of reward and *punishment* then guide the child toward those behaviours that are seen as morally acceptable within that society (note that this is clearly a moral relativist view)
- *psychoanalytic* theory – as a result of the *Oedipal* and *Electra* conflicts, children identify with the same sex parent and internalise their *values* into a *superego*. The superego then acts as both a guide and conscience, inclining the individual toward socially desirable behaviours and steering them away from those that might bring them into conflict with authority figures
- cognitive-developmental theories, such as that of Lawrence *Kohlberg*, see moral development as reflecting the way that children reason about moral issues, which in turn is a

product of their intellectual development. According to Kohlberg this pattern of development would be found in all human beings, and therefore is an example of a moral universalist theory.

moral development and crime: there is some evidence to support the view that delinquents show a lower level of moral reasoning than non-delinquents.

moral dilemma: a hypothetical conflict situation where participants must decide which course of action an actor should take. These dilemmas involve difficult moral choices, such as deciding whether to break a law and save a life, or uphold the law and allow someone to die. Responses to these dilemmas give important insights into the types of reasoning people use when making their moral decisions.

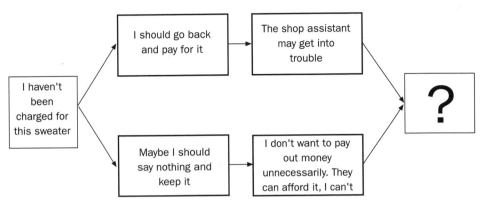

A typical moral dilemma

moral realism: a characteristic of *Piaget's* theory of *moral development*, where children come to accept the rules of adults as inviolable and absolute. One of the main reasons for this way of reasoning about right and wrong is that the child realises the power imbalance between those who make the rules (adults) and those who must obey them (children). This power imbalance is all the more evident because adults have the power to enforce compliance, whereas children do not have the power to resist.

moral strain: the unpleasant sensation experienced when we are obliged to carry out an act we feel to be immoral in order to respond to an order from an authority figure.

moratorium: a term coined by the *neo-Freudian* psychologist Eric *Erikson* to describe a period of *adolescence* when a person experiments with various values and goals in order to establish their own individual identity.

mores refers to those standards of behaviour or customs that are considered appropriate within a society and are therefore expected from its members. These are generally not formalised but are accepted nonetheless by the majority.

morpheme: the minimal unit of speech that carries some meaning. In essence this is the single word, although it can be some part of a word, such as 'un', that only has meaning when used with another word, such as 'couth' or 'lucky'.

morphological features: the physical form of something. It has been suggested, for example, that the morphological features of new-born mammals are such that they cause adults to bond more successfully with them. The Disney corporation has made billions of dollars out of our natural weakness for the cute features of young animals.

motivated forgetting: the inability to recall memories because they have been *repressed*. *Freud* believed that the potential for some memories to cause an individual *anxiety* was so great that they had to be kept out of the conscious mind. The practical and *ethical* problems in testing this suggestion *experimentally* has meant that there is a general lack of support for this explanation of forgetting.

motivation: the most usual definition of this term is to see it as *why* organisms act in the way that they do. Motivation is seen as the internal state of an organism that drives it to behave in a certain way. Explanations of motivation tend to be one of three main types:

- physiological explanations – these emphasise the importance of internal *drives* or needs. For example, an animal that has been deprived of food will experience a hunger drive and will be driven to seek food to satisfy its physiological need. Drive states such as hunger, thirst, temperature regulation and sex are often referred to as 'primary' drives because of their importance to the organism
- behavioural explanations – these rely on drive states that are acquired through *learning*. An example would be the motivational pull of money. We are motivated to work for money because of its acquired association with the primary drives such as hunger and thirst
- psychological explanations – for complex human behaviours, the basic idea of internal drive states pushing us towards specific drive-reducing behaviours is still relevant. For example, the need for *achievement* or the need for *affiliation* or the need for *self-actualisation* are examples of some of the more complex human needs (see *Maslow's hierarchy of needs* for a discussion of this).

motor neuron: a single nerve cell that leads to a receptor site on an effector such as a muscle group.

MRI: see *magnetic resonance imaging (MRI)*

Müller-Lyer illusion: see *illusion*

multidimensional approach to anxiety: suggests that *anxiety* in sport performance consists of two subcomponents: cognitive and somatic (physiological). These two subcomponents are predicted to influence performance differently. Cognitive anxiety is the mental component of anxiety and in sport it is commonly experienced as negative expectations of performing a task and so negative self-evaluation. This produces a negative correlation between cognitive anxiety and performance in that the higher the anxiety, the lower the performance. Somatic anxiety refers to the physiological aspects of the anxiety and is typically experienced as rapid heart rate, shortness of breath, butterflies in the stomach and tense muscles. Somatic anxiety has an inverted U-shaped, curvilinear relationship with sports performance, with lower and higher levels of somatic anxiety being detrimental to performance (see *Yerkes-Dodson law*).

multimodal therapy: a *cognitive behavioural therapy* approach to the treatment of psychological disorders that takes into account all aspects of a disorder rather than focusing on only one area of functioning. The approach, as developed by Arnold Lazarus, sees people as being a composite of seven different dimensions represented by the letters BASIC IB:

Behaviour

Interpersonal relationships

Affective processes

Biological functions

Sensations

Images

Cognitions

For therapy to be effective, Lazarus believed that each of these different areas of functioning must be treated. For example, a problem may be due to the distorted view that a person has about some aspect of the world around them. Treatment would then focus on these thought processes. However, these thoughts may have produced specific coping behaviours which must also be dealt with if the problem is to be fully overcome.

multiple personality disorder (MPD): see *dissociative identity disorder (DID)*

multi-store model of memory: see *Atkinson and Shiffrin model of memory*

mutation: a sudden change in the *genotype* of an organism that is not due to normal patterns of inheritance. During the process of *meiosis*, a *chromosome* may break with the chromosome pairs, joining together in a different arrangement (a process commonly referred to as 'crossing over'). Small changes in *genetic* material may have adaptive value to the organism and are passed on through the processes of *natural selection*. Larger mutations rarely have such adaptive value because they produce changes in the characteristics of an organism that lower its overall level of fitness.

mutualism: a term used in the study of animal behaviour to suggest that two or more animals may co-operate because to do so is beneficial to all of them. A lioness may co-operate with another lioness in the capture of large prey. Both benefit in that the prey is more likely to be caught by the combined forces although there is a cost in that they must share the spoils. Mutualism is likely to develop in situations where the benefits of co-operation outweigh the costs of sharing.

myelin sheath: a layer of fatty material that covers the axons of nerve cells. There are two major functions of this covering. The first is to insulate one nerve cell from another and so prevent the impulses from one from interfering with the impulses from the other. The second is to speed up the conduction of nerve impulses along the axon (see *neuronal transmission*).

My Lai: a massacre of Vietnamese civilians that took place in March 1968, during the Vietnam War. In the course of three hours more than 500 Vietnamese civilians were killed in cold blood at the hands of US troops. At the inquest into the massacre, it became clear that soldiers had carried out the killings on the orders of their commanding officer, Lt William Calley. Calley was subsequently court-marshalled for his part in the massacre, and at his trial found guilty of premeditated murder. Psychologist Stanley Milgram examined the transcripts provided by the soldiers who took part in the massacre at My Lai. He found many similarities between the reasoning of those involved in the killings and the reasoning of the participants in his *obedience* experiments. In both situations, individuals displaced responsibility away from themselves by drawing a distinction between their duty and their personal feelings. In both situations those involved had suppressed their conscience and were simply obeying orders. Milgram believed that My Lai was a powerful real-life demonstration of the dynamics of obedience to authority.

M

narcolepsy: a sleep disorder characterised by sudden and uncontrollable episodes of deep sleep in inappropriate situations. The four main symptoms of narcolepsy are excessive daytime sleepiness, cataplexy (loss of muscular control in response to an emotional stimulus such as surprise or laughter), sleep paralysis (an inability to move the body while still awake), and hypnagogic hallucinations (vivid, dream-like auditory, visual or tactile sensations that occur while falling asleep). Narcolepsy usually begins in adolescence or early adulthood, with about 1 in 2,000 people being sufferers. Explanations of narcolepsy vary, with some pointing to a malfunction in the system that regulates *REM sleep*, and more recent explanations suggesting the influence of a *neurotransmitter* called hypocretin. Hypocretins appear to play an important role in maintaining wakefulness. Research with narcoleptic dogs has found evidence for a mutation in a gene on chromosome 12, which disrupted the processing of hypocretin.

nativism: an approach within psychology (or any other discipline for that matter) that stresses inborn or inherited contributions to behaviour. The argument over whether inherited or acquired characteristics are more influential within a particular area of functioning is referred to as the *nature vs nurture* debate.

natural experiment: see *experiment*

natural selection: that part of Darwin's theory of evolution that explains why some members of a species produce more offspring than others. According to this theory, animals that are well adapted to their environment will leave behind more offspring than those who are less well adapted. Over time, those *traits* that give animals an advantage over others (in respect to survival and reproductive opportunities) will become more numerous in a species. The most effective traits are those which improve the survival chances of the animal or increase its reproductive success. The theory can be summarised as follows:

1. Individuals within any species differ (genetic variation).
2. All organisms have a vast capacity for producing offspring, but the size of populations tends to remain constant. It follows, therefore, that there must be *competition for resources* (such as mates, food and territories).
3. As a result of this competition, some organisms leave behind more offspring than others. These inherit the characteristics of their parents, and evolutionary change thus takes place through natural selection.
4. As a consequence of this natural selection, organisms become better adapted to their environment, better able to find a mate and escape from predators.

naturalistic observation: a type of investigation that has two characteristics: (a) the observer does not attempt to manipulate any aspect of the situation, but merely watches and records; (b) the observations do not take place in the artificial environment of the laboratory, but in the natural settings in which we would normally find that behaviour. There are two main types of observational technique, **participant observation** and **non-participant observation**. In the former, the observer will join in with the activities of a group in order to gain a greater insight and depth of understanding of their behaviour. In such situations, the group members are unaware of the real identity or purpose of the observer. In the latter technique, the observer endeavours to remain unobtrusive and records details of an individual's or group's behaviour, normally without the participants being aware of the observer's presence or the purposes of the investigation. In order to carry out effective observations, investigators must:

- devise appropriate ways of classifying and recording the desired information
- carry out a number of preliminary investigations (**pilot studies**) to make sure that all observers who observe an event would classify and record it in the same way (**inter-observer reliability**)
- the major advantage in these techniques is their ability to explore behaviour in its natural setting without the constraints of laboratory or experimental artificiality
- because observation tends to take place over a longer period of time than in the 'one-off' situation of a typical experiment, greater insights can be obtained into the behaviours of interest
- because there is no control over an independent variable, then it is not possible to form conclusions about cause–effect relationships
- if participants become aware of the observer's presence, they may respond to that presence in that behaviour becomes less natural because of their reaction to an extra feature of the situation, the presence of an observer.

nature vs nurture: a controversy within psychology that is concerned with the extent to which particular aspects of **behaviour** are a product of either inherited or acquired characteristics. Those who subscribe primarily to the 'nature' side of this argument might see some aspect of behaviour (such as the manifestation of **schizophrenia**) as being a product of **genetics**. Those who subscribe to the 'nurture' side of this argument would likewise see the behaviour as being a product of **environmental** influences. The nature versus nurture debate has been at its most controversial when applied to explanations of the differences between individuals, for example differences in **IQ**. When used in this context, psychologists have attempted to determine the proportion of variation that is attributable to one or the other influences.

naughty teddy: the now infamous teddy bear used in McGarrigle and Donaldson's study of number **conservation**. This study produced findings that challenged the original findings of Jean **Piaget**. Piaget claimed that young children would have difficulty understanding that the number of coins in a row would not change despite changes in the row's appearance. Piaget found that if he transformed the arrangement of coins, children would often say that the number of coins had also changed. This was taken as evidence that could not yet conserve number. By using naughty teddy who accidentally changes the layout of the coins, McGarrigle and Donaldson found that far more children answered correctly than in Piaget's original experiment. Findings such as this demonstrate that it is unwise to separate out the competencies of a child and the situation in which they are assessed.

near-death experience: a personal experience associated with impending death, sensations might include feelings of detachment from the body, feelings of levitation, serenity and the presence of a light, which for some has profound spiritual meaning. Near-death experiences mainly occur when a person is close to death or has been pronounced dead but recovers. Estimates suggest that as many as 20% of heart attack survivors report having had a near-death experience. Research has shown that the drug ketamine can produce the classic symptoms of a near-death experience. The administration of ketamine can produce all the features of the near-death experience, including travel through a dark tunnel into light, the conviction that one is dead, out-of-body experiences and mystical states. Because the near-death experience can be induced using drugs, many scientists conclude from this that such experiences can be reduced solely to alterations of brain chemistry.

Necker cube: one of a class of reversible figures that changes its perspective with continued viewing. As the viewer fixates the three-dimensional cube, it spontaneously changes, with the front appearing to change to the rear and back again. Evidence such as this is used to support the top-down view of *perception.*

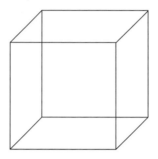

The Necker cube – which is the front and which is the back?

negative reinforcement: the termination of an unpleasant state following a response. If an organism is exposed to an *aversive* situation, and termination of that situation is made contingent upon some response, then we say that the organism is being negatively reinforced every time they produce that response and it ends the aversive situation. For example, many children find that if they go on and on about something, the incessant pleading becomes unpleasant to their parents. By responding to the pleading (giving in), the parents are negatively reinforcing them and the children will be more likely to act in the same way in the future. Negative reinforcement is commonly confused with *punishment*. The best way of distinguishing between them is to consider the effects that they have. Negative reinforcement increases the response that led up to it, punishment decreases it.

negative-state relief: this is the alleviation (relief) of sadness or guilt (negative states) through helping others (which is personally rewarding and thus eliminates the negative state). People learn during childhood that helping others in need is a positive behaviour that will make them feel good about themselves. According to this view, and in contrast to the *empathy-altruism hypothesis*, the motivation for helping someone in need is entirely egoistic, depending on the anticipated emotional consequences. For example, we may see someone standing at the side of the road, thumbing a lift in the pouring rain. If we pass we may feel guilty, but if we stop we can avoid this guilt and feel better about ourselves.

The negative emotions may be present before the opportunity to help arises, or may be aroused by the situation itself. Either way, helping someone in need offers a powerful antidote to whatever negative feelings we may be experiencing. The problem of whether people help others in distress for altruistic or egoistic reasons is not yet resolved. One suggestion is that we are more likely to feel empathy when we feel a close attachment with the person in need. It is possible that this form of altruism has developed as a result of **kin selection**, the tendency to help members of one's own kin because they carry many of the same genes. On the other hand, when we have no particular attachment or relationship with the person in need we may reduce our distress either by helping, or simply leaving the scene of the distress.

negative symptoms: a classification of **schizophrenia** where characteristics that are present in the normally functioning person are absent in the schizophrenic client. Examples would include poverty of speech, flatness of affect and apathy.

negative training stress model: physical training stresses an athlete both physically and psychologically, and so can have both positive and negative effects. The positive effects include being fitter, faster etc. (i.e. positive adaptation). However, too much training can lead to negative training responses such as staleness and burnout (i.e. negative adaptation).

neo-Freudian: a term that is used to characterise a group of Freudian-influenced psychologists who, because of disagreements over some aspects of Freudian theory (such as the importance of sexual urges in behaviour), developed adaptations of this theory which stressed other aspects of behaviour and experience. The best-known of the neo-Freudians are Alfred Adler and Carl Jung.

neonate: a new-born child.

nerve impulse: see *action potential*

nervous breakdown: a non-technical expression which is usually used to indicate the presence of a severe emotional disorder. May also be used (far less accurately) to describe someone who suffers from any of the stress-related illnesses (see *psychophysiological disorder (psychosomatic disorder)*).

neuron: another name given to the nerve cell. The network of neurons and the connections between them make up the *nervous system*. A neuron contains a cell body from which extend the axon and the dendrites. The axons and dendrites of some neurons are surrounded by a *myelin sheath* which gives them a distinctive white appearance (hence 'white matter'). Neurons do not touch each other, but where a neuron does come close to another neuron, a *synapse* is formed between the two. The function of a neuron is to transmit nerve impulses along the length of an individual neuron and across the synapse into the next neuron.

neuronal transmission: the process by which a nerve impulse passes along the length of a *neuron*. The neuron is surrounded by a semi-permeable cell membrane. This membrane allows electrically charged particles to pass through from the inside of the neuron to the outside and vice versa. When the neuron is in its resting state, the concentration of these particles is different between the inside of the neuron and the outside (the resting potential). The membrane is positively charged on the outside and

N

negatively charged on the inside. In this state it is said to be polarised, with the difference of inside to outside measured at −70mv. If this state of equilibrium is disturbed, the membrane changes its electrical state by shifting particles so that the inside of the neuron now becomes positively charged and the outside negatively charged (depolarisation). If sufficient depolarisation takes place, then the change in activity becomes an action potential which in turn affects the next part of the neuron and so on. After an **action potential** has passed, that section of the neuron returns to its resting potential, having first gone through a short state of hyperpolarisation where the electrical difference between the inside and outside of the cell is unusually high, and a further action potential cannot be generated until the cell returns to its resting potential.

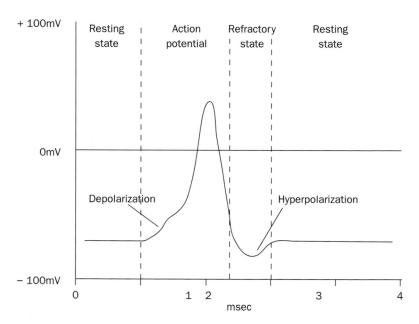

Action potential graph

neuroplasticity: the brain's ability to reorganise itself by forming new neural connections throughout life. Neuroplasticity allows the neurons in the brain to compensate for injury and disease and to adjust their activities in response to changes in environmental demands.

neuroses: a general term used to denote a wide range of disorders characterised by the following:

- unrealistic anxiety accompanied by other associated problems such as **phobias** or **compulsions**
- the neurotic individual retains complete contact with reality
- the disorder tends not to transgress wider social **norms**, although it is recognised as unacceptable to the neurotic individual.

The use of the term **neurosis** has been replaced in contemporary classification systems. In the latest version of the **DSM** classification of mental disorders (**DSM-IV-TR**), the term has been abandoned as a general classification category, and the various categories of disorder that had previously been under its umbrella reassigned to other diagnostic classifications. In the **ICD** system, the term 'neurotic disorder' is used for any long-lasting disorder that is distressing to the individual, where more or less accurate contact with reality remains, and where there is no obvious **organic disorder**.

neurotic anxiety: an idea from psychoanalytic theory which refers to an unrealistic fear of expressing impulses that have previously been **repressed**. **Freud** gave us two possible reasons for this kind of anxiety. His earlier explanation suggested that we would experience anxiety when unconscious impulses (such as sexual or aggressive urges) were blocked (or **repressed**). His later explanation saw neurotic anxiety as being a fear of what might happen if we did express these impulses. We may rid ourselves of this anxiety by either repressing the impulses or distorting reality in some other way to enable us to handle the anxiety that these impulses create (see **defence mechanism**).

neurotransmitter: a chemical that is released by one neuron, crosses the synaptic gap and is then received by special receptor sites on the next neuron. Neurotransmitters such as **acetylcholine** and **dopamine** thus have an important role in the process of **synaptic transmission**.

nightmares: a nightmare is a dream occurring during **rapid eye movement (REM) sleep**. Nightmares result in feelings of inescapable terror or extreme anxiety. They frequently wake the sleeper, who then recalls the content of the dream. Nightmares might be associated with anxiety and trauma but there is also the possibility that nightmares serve a beneficial function. Nightmares may also represent a form of emotional problem-solving, representing a unique opportunity to explore potential solutions to a problem without the risk of adverse consequences. Nightmares may also prepare an individual for negative emotional experiences that are unavoidable. This preparation would result in an improved adaptation to the situation prior to experiencing it in real life.

nominal scale: see **levels of measurement**

nomothetic: refers to any approach or method that deals with the establishment of general patterns of behaviour. The traditional **experimental** methods are generally referred to as being nomothetic as they attempt to establish common forms of functioning that would apply to all members of a **population**. Nomothetic methods are normally compared to **idiographic** methods.

non-conformity refers to situations whereby somebody resists the temptation to conform to the actions of judgements of the majority. Non-conformity is largely explained through the process of 'self-categorisation'. People sometimes describe themselves in terms of their membership of a particular group or category (for example, psychology student, David Bowie fan, or whatever). If this categorisation forms an important part of their **self-concept**, they are more likely to conform due to **normative influence**. If membership of a group does not form an important part of their self-concept, they are less likely to yield to group **norms**.

There are two different types of non-conformity response:
- independence – people who resist group norms and maintain their own independent behaviour, for example those who are not affected by fashion changes
- anti-conformity – characterised by consistent opposition to group norms, for example someone who bucks the fashion trend simply because they want to be seen as different or not part of the group norm.

Not conforming to the majority opinion may also be explained in terms of a person's exposure to the views of a convincing minority position (see *innovation (minority influence)*).

non-experimental approaches: simply any investigative approach that does not qualify by definition as an *experiment*. An experiment is traditionally defined as a procedure when the investigator manipulates some aspect of a situation in order to observe the effects of that manipulation. In the absence of that manipulation an investigation would be considered to be 'non-experimental'. Some types of experiment (such as natural experiments) do not have this direct manipulation as a feature, so are regarded as '*quasi-experiments*'.

Examples of non-experimental approaches in psychology would include the **observational** method and **case studies**. Arguments about which method is best, experimental or non-experimental, are pretty futile, as each offers different advantages to the researcher. Experiments generally offer greater *control* and an ability to make statements about cause and effect.

Non-experimental methods, on the other hand, tend to offer insights derived from more life-like situations, and therefore tend to have a greater *ecological validity*. Non-experimental approaches to research are best seen as one of a range of investigative tools that are available to the research psychologist.

non-participant observation: a type of observational technique where the researcher observes the behaviour of an individual or group without intruding into the situation being studied (see *naturalistic observation*).

non-verbal communication: generally known as 'body language' by non-psychologists, this refers to any aspect of communication that is achieved without verbal or written language. Non-verbal communication may be achieved through posture, facial expressions, gestures, etc.

norepinephrine: a term used in the USA for what we in Europe refer to as noradrenaline.

norm: a generalised expectation shared by most members of a group or *culture* that underlies views of what is considered appropriate within that group. These are sometimes formal and explicit, but are often informal and implicit. We may have norms covering appropriate behaviour in different roles, different situations and so on. Breaking these norms is often followed by sanctions or even exclusion from the group.

normal distribution: refers to the symmetrical, bell-shaped curve that might be produced when a set of scores is represented on a *frequency graph* (see opposite). Many different *variables* are supposed to form a normal distribution when measured in the *population* as a whole. Height and *IQ* are commonly quoted as being normally distributed. In a normal distribution, the majority of scores are clustered around a mid point with the lower and higher scores being less frequent towards the end of the distribution. These 'tails' of the distribution extend in both directions and theoretically never touch the x (horizontal) axis.

normality: defined by some as 'an absence of abnormality', the term is often used in the sense that it portrays an absence of disease, mental disorder or other form of psychological dysfunction. To actually classify something or somebody as 'abnormal' implies a departure from the state of normality. This is not as clear cut as it may sound. The term normality comes from the related term *norm*, yet also implies an evaluative judgement. What is normal

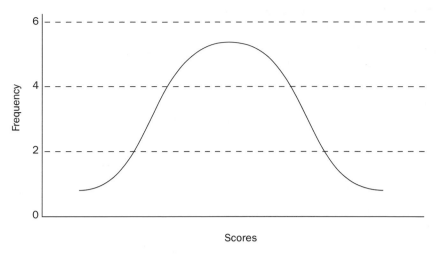

A typical normal distribution

in the sense that most members of a **population** possess the characteristic may not be considered normal if we were to look at the behaviour in terms of its contribution to the overall adaptiveness of the person possessing it. To illustrate the point, if most of the members of a given **population** suffered paranoid delusions, this may be considered normal in the statistical sense, but not normal in the adaptive sense of the word.

normative influence: an explanation of conformity which is a result of people's desire not to infringe group **norms**. Normative conformity often occurs because people want to be seen as part of a group rather than being seen as a deviant from it.

null hypothesis: in testing our *alternative hypothesis*, we first assume that there is no difference between the populations from which the samples were taken. This is known as the null hypothesis (H_0). We make this assumption then calculate the **probability** that our two samples would differ as they did if this were true. If this probability comes out as very low (lower than 0.05) then we reject the null hypothesis and accept, provisionally, the alternative hypothesis (H_1).

NVC: see *non-verbal communication*

obedience: a type of *social influence* whereby somebody acts in response to a direct order from another person. There is also the implication that the actor is made to respond in a way that they would not otherwise have done without the order. The most famous series of experiments in this area was carried out by Stanley Milgram in the 1960s. Milgram found that, if instructed to do so, people could deliver potentially fatal electric shocks to another person as part of a psychological *experiment*. During the experiments, many of his *participants* showed signs of distress and made moves to withdraw, but 65 per cent showed total obedience to the orders of the experimenter that they should continue right to the end. The aim of this research was, in part, an attempt to explain the terrible war crimes carried out during World War Two. What it actually showed was that the tendency to obey an authority figure, even when that involves taking another's life, can be observed in all of us.

There are a number of different explanations as to why people show obedience to authority figures:

1. Authority figures can relieve individuals of the responsibility for their actions. After World War Two, many of the Nazi war criminals excused their behaviour by claiming they were 'only obeying orders'.
2. Authority figures often show visible signs of their authority, such as the wearing of badges and uniforms. These remind people around them exactly who is in charge.
3. Initial requests may well be quite innocuous, but may then be increased to a point where the recipient of the order is pressurised to perform increasingly harmful acts.

It is clear that obedience is a powerful form of influence, but it can be resisted. Research into how individuals resist the influence of an authority figure has suggested the following:

- reminding individuals that it is they who are responsible for their own actions, and not the authority figure
- increasing our exposure to disobedient models
- questioning the motives of the authority figure ('why are they asking me to do this?')
- knowledge of the power of the 'obedience effect' (perhaps through a study of social psychology) can reduce its influence.

obesity: is usually defined in terms of body mass index (BMI). This is calculated by dividing a person's weight (in kilograms) by height (in metres) squared. This yields a figure ranging from normal weight (20–24.9) to clinically obese (30–39.9) and severe obesity (40+). Obesity can also be defined in terms of waist circumference, with weight reduction recommended when waist circumference is greater than 40 inches in men and 35 inches in women. Obesity is associated with a number of adverse health consequences, including cardiovascular disease, diabetes, high blood pressure and cancer. Research has also established a relationship between obesity and psychological problems, including depression, panic disorder and agoraphobia.

Psychological explanations of obesity tend to focus on lack of physical activity (e.g. research has shown a position correlation between the rising incidence of obesity and increased levels of car ownership) and food intake (e.g. Schachter's emotionality theory claims that obese people are more likely to eat when they are upset). Biological explanations of obesity include the role of genetic factors (e.g. body size appears to run in families) and evolutionary explanations. An evolutionary explanation of obesity describes how the tendency to store excess body fat would have been adaptive for our ancestors as a way of dealing with subsequent food shortages.

object permanence: an understanding that objects which are hidden from view continue to exist despite the fact that the child has no physical evidence of their existence. *Piaget* claimed that this was because children under the age of eight months would be unable to create an image of the object when it was out of their sight. This means that to the young child, objects around it, including the mother, seem to mysteriously disappear and reappear. As the child grows older s/he becomes better able to understand not only that things continue to exist when they are out of sight, but also that they may move and thus reappear in a different place.

objectivity: the ability to carry out an investigation and to collect data without allowing personal interpretation or bias to influence the process. If we have to rely on a subjective interpretation of an event (such as 'was that an act of aggression or of playfulness?'), we may find it difficult to maintain our objectivity. Psychologists may choose either to concentrate on actions which are unquestionably relating to the behaviour of interest (stabbing someone in the back, for example, could hardly be interpreted as playfulness) or relying on the shared agreement of more than one observer of the same event (*inter-observer reliability*).

observation: an incredibly general term used to describe any situation where an observer records behaviour that is exhibited by a participant. The term 'observation' may be used as a technique for gathering *data* (i.e. we *observe* somebody doing something) or as the design of a study. It is this second meaning of the term that leads to such a variety of usage. To give a precise definition of the term observation means contrasting it with an *experimental* study. In an observation there is no manipulation of an *independent variable*. There are many different types of study that would be classified as 'observational' under this definition. The table below gives some of the commonest categories:

Controlled observation	Participants are observed in an environment that is, to some degree, under the control of the observer.
Naturalistic observation	Behaviour is studied within its natural context, e.g. children are observed while playing in a school playground.
Participant and non-participant observation	An observer participates in the group being studied (participant) or observes from outside the group and tries not to be intrusive in any way (non-participant).
Structured observation	Observation is guided by the use of specific observational categories, e.g. an event may be recorded every time it happens (event sampling) or by the frequency of its happening within specific time periods (time sampling).

observational learning: see *imitation*

observer bias: the tendency for observers who are aware of the *hypothesis* under test to see and record what might be expected, rather than what actually happens. To guard against this, we can use observers who have no knowledge of the predictions being made.

obsessions are irrational thoughts and images that invade a person's conscious mind and appear uncontrollable to the person experiencing them. Obsessions may take the form of intense and graphic images (such as accidents), ideas (such as the idea that our house is full of germs), doubts (about the future, the past and so on) and fears (for example, about what we might say). Such is the intensity and frequency of these thoughts that the anxiety they produce interferes with the normal functioning of the person who has them. Trying to ignore or dismiss obsessive thoughts creates even more anxiety. One way in which the obsessive deals with this anxiety is by developing *compulsions*.

obsessive-compulsive disorder: a form of *anxiety disorder* characterised by excessive, intrusive and inappropriate *obsessions* or *compulsions.* This is characterised as an anxiety disorder because the sufferer's mind is filled with persistent and uncontrollable thoughts (obsessions) which they attempt to *control* through repetitive behaviours (compulsions). One of the most famous examples of an obsessive-compulsive disorder is Lady Macbeth, who was compelled to continuously wash her hands after the murder of Duncan.

occipital lobe: the posterior part of the cerebral hemispheres in the brain, the main function of which is in the processing of visual information.

occupational psychology: the branch of psychology that deals with human beings at work. A very wide and varied range of interests, including the selection and recruitment of staff, the effect of working conditions on staff performance and psychological well-being, careers guidance and counselling and the study of people in different occupations. Although most people associate occupational psychology with its industrial context, occupational psychologists may be found working in many non-industrial settings as well. Entry to this branch of psychology is normally through a postgraduate degree.

Oedipus complex: a term given by *Freud* to describe the incestuous feelings that a young boy develops toward his mother, coupled with a jealousy and rivalry with his father for the affections of the mother. As the son comes to realise that the father is more powerful than he is, he begins to fear punishment, specifically that his father might castrate him for his incestuous feelings toward the mother. When the *castration anxiety* becomes intense, he *represses* his feelings for the mother and identifies with his father in a process called *identification with the aggressor*. This lessens the chances of being castrated, as the father will no longer see him as a rival. In this way the boy will attempt to emulate his father, and in so doing he will internalise the father's moral standards, and so develop a superego.

oestrogen: a hormone involved in the development of secondary sexual characteristics in the female, and regulation of the menstrual cycle. There are many different types of oestrogen (e.g. oestradiol and oestriol), but they are all known collectively as the oestrogens. Oestrogens are found in both males and females. In females they are made in the ovaries and in males they are made in the testes (albeit in small amounts). They are also made in the adrenal gland in both sexes. Although the levels of oestrogen remain constant in males, they fluctuate in females depending on the phase of their menstrual cycle. Oestrogen has many physical effects on the body (e.g. it affects the balance of cholesterol in the blood), but it also has psychological effects, for example, oestrogen levels can affect how a person feels emotionally.

offender profiling: believed by some to be a 'term of convenience' which refers to attempts made by psychologists to make inferences, based on behaviour at the crime scene, about the likely type of offender. By integrating any such biographical information about the offender with known psychological theory, it becomes possible for the police to eliminate some suspects (thus narrowing the field of investigation) or to pursue new lines of enquiry. Offender profiling has been particularly useful in serious crimes such as sadistic assaults, murder or rape, although it is also used in other 'less' serious crimes such as arson and burglary.

There are significant differences in the way in which offender profiling is used in the USA and the UK. In the former, offender profiling is based more on investigative knowledge of crimes and criminals (i.e. knowledge of who tends to commit particular types of crime), whereas in the latter, analysis of a particular offence is used to draw inferences about why the offender has acted in that way. Offender profiling in the UK builds up knowledge about a criminal from the various traces that he or she leaves during the crimes. For example, particular behaviours during a rape may indicate a particular attitude to women in general. Despite the success stories attached to offender profiling, estimates of its usefulness vary. In a recent survey among British detectives who had worked on cases where offender profiling had been used, it had led to the identification of an offender in less than three per cent of cases, and had 'helped to solve' only 16 per cent of cases.

one-tailed hypothesis: see *hypothesis*

one-tailed test: used in carrying out a test for *significance* in a set of *data* when the researcher is convinced (usually because of previous research evidence) that the results could only go in one direction.

one-trial learning: technically, this is the belief that all learning takes place after only one *trial*, with the associated assumption that more complex learning only appears to take longer because it is broken down into smaller components with each component being learned in a single trial. The term has also been used to describe the rapid learning that takes place when organisms are *biologically prepared* to learn associations that have a clear survival value.

ontogeny: the evolution (i.e. the origin and development) of an individual organism, from conception to death. This can be compared to *phylogeny*, which is the evolution of a species.

open-ended questions: a technique used in *unstructured interviews* and *surveys*, where the questioner asks the *respondent* a question and the respondent can answer in any way that they wish. For example, instead of asking the question: 'Why did you take A-level psychology? Was it:
(a) to make you more popular with the opposite sex?
(b) because you couldn't spell archaeology?
(c) because you liked the look of the teacher?'

the question 'Why did you take A-level psychology?' is asked instead.

These type of questions give a great deal more depth and insight into participants' behaviour, but are difficult to quantify for later analysis.

operant conditioning: also known as instrumental conditioning, this is an explanation of learning normally attributed to Burrhus *Skinner*, where the consequences of a *response* determine the *probability* of it reoccurring in the future. Organisms are seen to operate on their environment, and these 'operants' create an effect in the environment. By manipulating these effects (e.g. in a *Skinner box)*, it is possible to increase or decrease the future probability of the event reoccurring. Any event that increases or strengthens an organism's rate of responding is referred to as a *reinforcer*. Positive reinforcers are those events which, when they follow a response, increase its future probability of occurring. Negative reinforcement refers to the removal of an unpleasant state following a response. For example, many cars have the aggravating habit of flashing a seat-belt warning sign at you until you put your seat belt on. The action of belting-up is thus negatively reinforced. If the consequences of a response cause a decrease in the rate of responding, the organism is said to be punished.

Skinner also believed that organisms learn how to behave in specific circumstances, and that responding in a particular way to one stimulus will bring about a desired consequence, whereas responding in the same way in other circumstances will not. If you watch cars along a main road where there is a traffic camera, you will notice them slowing down as they near the camera, and then speeding up again as it is passed. Once an organism has been reinforced for responding to one stimulus, they can generalise out their responses to other similar stimuli. Years ago, when I used to ride a motorcycle with a white fairing (similar to police bikes), traffic in front would frequently slow down – no prizes for guessing why!

operation refers to the act of carrying out something. The commonest use of the term in psychology is in the performance of a mental or logical act. So, if we are asked to perform some mental arithmetic, we would be carrying out a mental operation.

operational definition: an aspect of effective scientific methodology, operational definitions are precise definitions of the terms used in studies. For example, in an *experiment* to test the effect of *arousal* on performance, we would need to know exactly what sort of arousal and how we would measure it. We would also need to know what type of performance we were suggesting that arousal affected, and how we would measure that. Without these precise definitions, it is difficult to be anything but vague in scientific research, and it makes replication of research almost impossible. One problem with using operational definitions (e.g. how much somebody laughs as a sign of happiness) is that our measurements are always one step removed from the thing we are really interested in.

operationalisation: the process of making a vague concept (such as aggression or liking) concrete and measurable (e.g. level of shock delivered or attraction rating from 1 to 10). This is an important requirement of testable *hypotheses*.

opponent processing: a theoretical position which, when applied to motivation, proposes that whenever an organism functions in a particular motivational state (for example, being fearful), excitation at that end of the 'happiness dimension' will set up inhibitory processes at the other end of this dimension (i.e. relaxed). In order to maintain some degree of motivational normality, when the conditions that produced one state are no longer present, there will be a shift in the other direction. We commonly experience a sense of being 'down' shortly after being in a very happy state.

opportunity sample: see *sampling*

optic chiasma: the point at which the optic nerves from the two eyes meet. The nerves from the inner halves of each retina cross over so that the input from the inner part of the left retina is processed by the right side of the visual **cortex**. The nerve cells from the outer halves of the two retinas do not cross. What this means in terms of visual damage is that damage to the left optic nerve produces blindness in the left eye. Damage to the left optic tract (after the optic chiasma) produces blindness to the right visual field.

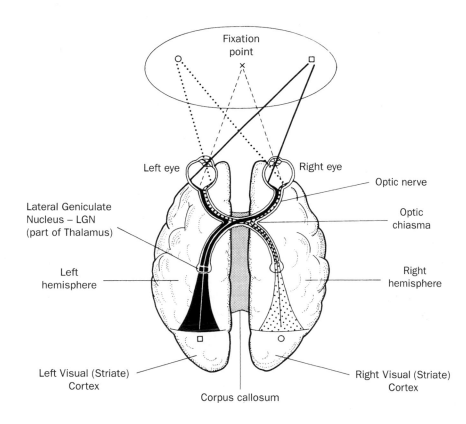

The visual system showing the optic chiasma (from R.D. Gross, 1992, Psychology: The Science of Mind and Behaviour, 2nd edn, Hodder & Stoughton)

optimal level of arousal theory: a theory that postulates that each athlete has his or her own zone of optimal functioning (ZOF), and that the athlete performs best when this level of arousal falls within the ZOF. This theory does not apply only to sportspeople. Zuckerman (1979) believed that, for some people, the ZOF was set very high. These people, referred to as 'sensation seekers', appear to need to involve themselves in extreme sports such as rock climbing, bungee jumping or motorcycle racing. The reason why some people crave extreme sports and others do not can be explained in terms of what they regard as a 'normal' level of stimulation. For people who have a routine, fairly boring life, even a walk or cycle ride adds that extra bit of stimulation. However, for those who fly fast jets, ride police motorcycles or snowboard for a living, 'routine' is slightly different, and a greater level of stimulation is needed to create an optimum level of arousal.

optimal mismatch theory: an educational practice of accelerated learning based loosely on *Piaget's* theory of intellectual development. It works by 'mismatching' the child's present level of competence with a set of problems that are only just out of this present level. If the difference between what they can do, and what is being asked of them is just right (i.e. the mismatch is 'optimal'), then children experience a cognitive conflict and they attempt to discover solutions through their own actions. Programmes based on this idea have been mostly successful with moving children more rapidly through the earlier levels of Piaget's theory, but as critics point out, they are only accomplishing something that would have happened sooner or later anyway, and the strain on teacher resources to accomplish this acceleration does not make it a worthwhile exercise.

order effect refers to the fact that research participants may perform differently on the different conditions in an *experiment* simply because of the order in which they do them. Participants may become tired, more or less tense, hungry, fed up, etc. We normally try to minimise the influence of order effects by ensuring that participants do not all perform the different conditions in the same order.

ordinal scale: see *levels of measurement*

ordinate: when plotting data on a graph, the ordinate refers to information on the vertical or y axis of the graph. In an experiment, the *dependent variable* is plotted on this axis.

organ of corti: a receptive organ in the inner ear which is stimulated during the process of hearing.

organic disorder: any disorder where there is a known physical cause. Early work with sufferers of general paresis (a mental disorder) established the syphilis germ as the physical cause of the disorder. More recent work with schizophrenics has suggested several possible physical causes, including excessive *dopamine* as well as enlarged brain ventricles (indicative of brain damage). Supporters of the *biomedical model of abnormality* claim that most disorders have an organic origin, although few have been incontrovertibly proven.

organism: a term that is often used in psychology (including in this book) to describe both human and non-human animals (it also refers to all living things, but the latter are not really of direct interest to psychologists). The term has its roots in early *behaviourism*, where it was used to indicate that all animals would learn in the same basic way, and so findings from 'lower' animals could be generalised back to humans. Nowadays, the term is more often used to denote an objectivity on the part of the psychologist. Organisms are simply 'units' that respond in some way during a research study.

Origin of Species: the book in which Darwin put forward his general principles of evolution in 1859.

outcome study: a technique for finding out whether a therapeutic intervention has actually worked. For example, one group of people suffering from a particular psychological problem might be given a drug or other form of treatment. They can then be compared to a *control group* who might receive a *placebo*. If the outcome of the former group is more favourable (in terms of their changed behaviour) than the control group, then the change can be attributed to the effect of the treatment.

out-group: those people who are not in the *in-group*, i.e. any individuals who, for whatever reason, are not part of or accepted by the group of people with whom we normally mix.

Because of the tendency to identify readily with the group of which we are a member, the out-group may be picked on or discriminated against (see *minimal groups*).

out-of-body experience (OBE): the sensation of being awake and seeing one's own body from a location outside one's physical body. OBEs have been reported by people while they have been under the influence of general anaesthetic, or when under the influence of drugs. Research has also shown that OBEs can be induced artificially by electrically stimulating a part of the brain called the right angular gyrus.

overcompensation: a Freudian *defence mechanism* in which an individual tries to cover up for a weakness in one aspect of their life by concentrating instead on some other aspect of it. For example, a child may attempt to overcompensate for his lack of physical ability and the resulting feelings of inadequacy by working extra hard at his or her academic work.

over-extension refers to those instances where a word is used to cover objects or situations other than those for which it is normally used. An example would be the tendency for young children to call all men of a certain age 'daddies'.

Aiming for a grade A*?

Don't forget to log on to **www.philipallan.co.uk/a-zonline** for advice.

O

pain management: the various measures and techniques used by people to *control* and alleviate pain. Some of these techniques are used in the short-term management of pain, some in its longer-term control. Examples of pain management strategies are as follows:

- The biomedical model may involve chemical or surgical intervention. Chemical intervention typically involves the use of analgesics such as aspirin, ibuprofen or paracetamol which work on the damaged tissue that is causing the pain. Opiates such as morphine act directly on the central nervous system in the brain and spinal cord by inhibiting pain messages from travelling to the brain. Surgical intervention, used occasionally for short- to medium-term pain relief in the terminally ill, involves making lesions in specific areas of the brain that are known to cause pain in other body areas. Any such relief tends to be temporary, a reminder of the complexity of our sensitivity to pain.
- The behavioural model views pain as a set of behaviours rather than a subjective response. Examples of 'pain behaviours' might include staying in bed, complaining about pain and discomfort and so on. According to the principles of *operant conditioning*, all behaviours become a product of their consequences, and therefore can be changed in the same way. Traditional methods of treatment tend to reinforce pain behaviours - when we are ill we tend to get attention and affection from our family, for example. By changing the consequences of these behaviours (i.e. not reinforcing pain behaviours) and by others using social *reinforcement* to shape more adaptive 'non-pain behaviours' (such as getting up and moving about), the subjective experience of pain may be altered in a more adaptive way. This technique is most useful where people have developed inappropriate methods of dealing with their pain (e.g. over-reliance on drugs or avoidance of remedial treatment) and has helped many people to lead normal lives without the use of pain-relieving medication.

pandemonium: a model of *pattern recognition* associated with Selfridge (1959) in which letters can be recognised by the combination of a number of simpler processing units. The name *pandemonium* (taken from Milton's epic poem *Paradise Lost*, and meaning 'palace of demons') provides a metaphor of 'feature demons' (feature analysing units), each of which provides information about one specific feature (orientation, shape, etc.). In this way, integration (i.e. letter recognition) can be achieved out of chaos (i.e. separate and distinct feature analyses).

panic disorder: classified under *DSM-IV-TR* as an *anxiety disorder*, these often quite unpredictable attacks involve a very wide range of symptoms, including heart palpitations, chest pains, dizziness, laboured breathing, intense apprehension and a feeling of unreality. These short-lived attacks tend to occur frequently, and are sometimes linked to specific situations (for example, on public transport). If these attacks occur consistently in a specific situation, it is probably indicative of a **phobia**; if they are not directly linked to any specific situation, this constitutes a panic disorder. For example, the **DSM-IV-TR** classification lists two types of **agoraphobia**, with and without panic disorder. The former is the more common, as patients who experience panic disorders tend to avoid situations where they might occur, or where they might be embarrassed if they did occur. If this avoidance becomes serious, agoraphobia may be the result. The causes of panic disorders are not clear. There is evidence that they run in families (therefore a **genetic** cause may be possible) and that they are linked in some way to breathing difficulties such as hyperventilation. By activating the **autonomic nervous system**, hyperventilation creates many of the physical responses that characterise panic attacks. Psychological causes stress the 'fear of fear' that sufferers of this disorder typically show. Physical sensations are misinterpreted so that even minor sensations are amplified into something much more serious. People with panic disorders thus experience far more anxiety when they are faced with unexplained and unexpected symptoms of ill health.

Treatment of this disorder has tended to concentrate on **drug treatments**, although more recently psychological therapies have been used with great success. These train patients in relaxation techniques, teach them how to cope with panic attacks, then expose them to attacks in a safe and supportive therapeutic environment. With practice and the support of the therapist, clients learn to re-interpret the physical symptoms that cause panic attacks, and to **control** the attacks should they occur by using cognitive (e.g. a belief that the sensations are harmless) and relaxation techniques.

paradigm: in its most common usage within psychology, this term has two meanings:
- a particular perspective on behaviour that comprises all the attitudes, beliefs and techniques that make up that perspective. Within mainstream science, a paradigm is generally accepted by most who work within that field. For example, within physics, the impact of Copernicus, Newton and Einstein has led to an evolution (or paradigm shift) from the theories developed by one to those developed by the next. Critics of the view that psychology could be considered scientific have argued that there is no one generally accepted paradigm within psychology to which most psychologists subscribe
- a particular experimental procedure, such as the **classical conditioning** paradigm.

paradox: any situation that, taken logically, should not exist. The majority of the so-called paradoxes in psychology arise out of a temporary lack of understanding or through situations that can be readily understood by adopting another level of explanation. An example is the altruism paradox whereby animals that engage in self-endangering behaviour appear to receive no advantage for it, and actually put themselves at a disadvantage in the reproductive stakes. In Darwinian terms, they appear to decrease their fitness. By adopting a different level of explanation (such as **kin selection**), it is claimed that the paradox disappears.

paradoxical sleep: another term used to describe **REM** *sleep*. It was so called because when a person is in this state, the rapid eye movements that give **REM** *sleep* its name make the person appear to be awake. They also have an aroused **EEG** showing that the brain is active, and more so than in wakeful states. Hence the paradox, they appear to be awake, but they are behaviourally asleep.

paralinguistics refers to how something is said rather than what is said. Paralinguistics thus includes facial expressions whilst talking, pauses, tone of voice and so on.

parallel play: a category of social play where children play alongside each other, aware of each other's presence, but not attempting to join in each other's play. This can frequently be seen among young children playing at Lego tables in large department stores. A 'group' of four children can all be building separate models, with no co-operation or apparent interest in the activities of the others. It is thought that children are attracted to the company of other children, but do not yet have either the communicative or social skills to take the situation beyond mere presence.

parallel processing: an explanation of *information processing* where more than one processing operation can be carried out at the same time. Unlike *conscious* processing, which is normally carried out sequentially, this type of processing is typically carried out without conscious input. When reading these words, for example, you are processing for meaning, pronunciation and syntax at the same time. However, more complex operations such as processing conversations can only be achieved one at a time.

paranoid disorder: a disorder in which the client has persistent *delusions* of persecution or jealousy, but does not have the *hallucinations* that accompany *paranoid schizophrenia*.

paranoid schizophrenia: a type of *psychosis* in which the client has an organised system of *delusions* and *hallucinations*. These delusions may be of persecution, or sometimes related to jealousy or exaggerated beliefs about the person's power or importance. Although the thought processes of the paranoid schizophrenic may be deluded, they are not fragmented as in other forms of schizophrenia.

paranormal: any experience that is beyond the range of normal experience and defies scientific explanation (e.g. *extrasensory perception (ESP)*, *psychokinesis (PK)* and *out-of-body experiences (OBE)*).

paraphilias involve sexual attraction to objects and activities that are unusual in nature. These may involve children or non-human objects, or even experiences of pain and humiliation. To be diagnosed as a paraphiliac, the following conditions are necessary:
- the urges or fantasies must be intense and recurrent
- the person must either have acted on them or experienced extreme guilt or other distress about them
- the urges or fantasies must have been experienced for at least six months.

Few people receive a diagnosis of paraphilia, and those who do are predominantly men. As yet, research has revealed little about the causes or treatments of paraphilias.

parapsychology refers to that branch of psychology which is concerned with the explanation of the paranormal (that which cannot be explained in terms of normal sensory experience). These paranormal phenomena include clairvoyance (perception of an object removed from normal sensory experience), precognition (knowledge of future events) and telepathy (thought transference). Explanations of these phenomena attract a good deal of scepticism from mainstream scientific psychologists for the following reasons:
- results from research supporting these phenomena has proved difficult to replicate under controlled conditions
- explanations such as that offered for a form of clairvoyance known as 'distance viewing' (*perception* of objects from thousands of miles away) appear to contradict the general laws of physics concerning the transmission of light

- explanations often conflict with the rest of scientific knowledge. Precognition, for example, presupposes that the future in some way affects the present (in that it becomes known to us). This line of thinking is a reversal of our understanding of the nature of cause and effect
- this branch of psychology unfortunately attracts many fakes who detract from those who make genuine attempts to study this area in an honest and scientifically valid manner.

parasympathetic nervous system: together with the *sympathetic nervous system*, this forms the *autonomic nervous system* of the body. The sympathetic and parasympathetic systems have complementary, although not necessarily opposing, functions. The sympathetic system produces activation in the muscles and glands so that the organism can be in a state of *fight or flight*. The parasympathetic system, on the other hand, deactivates the muscles and glands and restores the organism to a state of calm and relaxation. Although their actions in this *arousal* sequence are complementary (one activates, the other de-activates), there are other times when their different functions means that they are active together. A classic example is the tendency, common among many animals to empty their bladder (parasympathetic action) when physically aroused (sympathetic action).

parental investment (PI): any investment in an individual offspring that increases the offspring's chance of surviving at the cost of the parent's ability to invest in other offspring. A simple illustration of this is the female parent's investment in her eggs. Typically, females produce far fewer eggs than males produce sperm. Eggs contain nutrients, sperm do not. The more nutrients the female puts into her eggs, the fewer additional eggs she can produce. Parental investment can take a number of forms:

- retaining eggs in the body
- transmission of nutrients through a placenta
- building nests and staying with the young
- feeding and devoting time and energy to the instruction of the young.

Because of the greater overall investment of females, males may compete with each other for access to what is essentially a scarce resource - the eggs of females. Females may then become choosy, looking for males that can provide resources (that can then be turned into more eggs) or other benefits. Parental investment can also be found in males. They may:

- establish territories (and thus provide resources)
- build nests
- feed females prior to ovulation
- help in the incubation, feeding and instruction of the young.

In some cases parental investment is greater in the males of a species than it is in the females. In these cases females compete for males, and males become choosy. To recognise this fact, the terms 'mate competition' and 'mate choice' are preferred to the more usual terms 'male competition' and 'female choice'.

parent-offspring conflict refers to a conflict between a feeding parent and its offspring in that the offspring, in trying to maximise its own interests, attempts to manipulate the parent into providing extra resources. The reasons for this conflict appear to be *genetic*. As the parent and the offspring share 50 per cent of their genes, the parent will try to spread resources equally over all their offspring, with whom they also share 50 per cent of their genes. An individual offspring will inevitably try to extract as much food as possible for itself, sometimes to the point that they will attack and kill their **siblings** (see also **infanticide**).

A classic example of parent-offspring conflict is in weaning conflict. A mother will try to wean her offspring off milk, but the offspring will attempt to prolong the suckling period. The period of lactation (during which the mother feeds milk to her offspring) is extremely demanding on the female and she cannot start to replenish her resources for the next litter until she has completed it. It is not, therefore, in her best interests to prolong it unnecessarily. The graph below demonstrates the problem.

In the early period of the offspring's life, the parent gains more by feeding the offspring than ignoring it. As the offspring grows it will reach a point where it can do as well on its own as it can by receiving parental help. The conflict arises over where this point would be. To the parent, given their need to begin the replenishment of resources for the next litter, it would be earlier than it would be for the offspring. The shaded area in the graph below is where the parent will attempt to end feeding and the offspring tries to prolong it. It seems likely that parents will tend to win these conflicts. There are several reasons for this assumption:

- if the offspring has the gene to manipulate its parents successfully, then this gene will be passed on to its offspring, who will, in turn, manipulate their parent. That way, the present offspring wins in the short term, but loses in the long term
- parents are larger and more powerful than offspring, therefore they should be able to resist the offspring's attempts to extract more food. It is possible that the offspring might attempt to deceive their parents by begging more vigorously, but the extra energy this uses may negate the beneficial effect of any extra resources they may be able to gain by doing so.

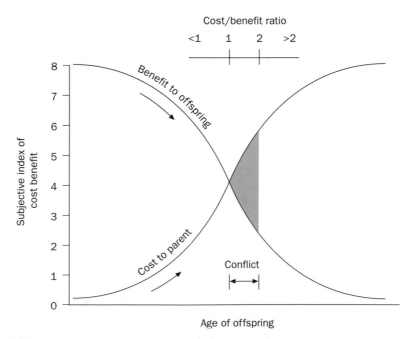

Parent-offspring conflict with changes in ratio of cost to parent/benefit to offspring

parietal lobe: see *brain*

Parkinson's disease: a movement disorder characterised by a continual rapid tremor in the limbs, a lack of sensory-motor co-ordination and a tendency to be exhausted. The condition is thought to be caused by a malfunction in the production of the neurotransmitter *dopamine*.

parsimony: the scientific principle which states that if two opposing theories each explain the same phenomenon and are equally tenable, the simpler of the two is preferred. Applying this principle in psychology is nowhere near as easy as it might be in the physical sciences. For one thing, the evaluation of a theory as 'tenable' is a subjective judgement (and therefore subject to human bias) and also the assessment of a theory as simple or complex may be misleading in itself. To illustrate, *behaviourism*, with its emphasis on observable behaviour, is often valued as being a parsimonious explanation of all manner of things (such as gender role behaviour and mental disorders), whereas *Freudian* psychoanalysis, with its instinctual drives and repressed sexuality, is criticised for being a non-parsimonious of those same areas of functioning. To accept a theory because it is 'simpler' may miss the possibility that the more complex theory might have greater *validity*.

partial reinforcement: see *schedules of reinforcement*

participant: a term used to describe those people who are studied and who contribute *data* in a *research* investigation. The term is now more favoured than the previous term 'subject' which, it was felt, depersonalised the people who took part in studies. The term 'subject' is now used almost exclusively to refer to 'non-human' animals.

participant observation: a type of observational technique in which the observer actively joins in with the activities of the group whilst at the same time recording details of the group members' behaviour (see *naturalistic observation*).

paternal deprivation: a recognition that loss of the father, or being brought up without a consistent father figure might have specific deprivation effects that are not evident in the more usually referred to *maternal deprivation.* Research into children with absent fathers has found some evidence for a range of emotional and social disturbances depending on the nature of the absence.

pattern recognition: a process of visual *perception* which enables us to identify and recognise two-dimensional stimuli (such as words on the page) and three-dimensional stimuli (such as objects in our environment). Various theories have been proposed to explain how we achieve this sort of recognition. These include:
- template theories – incoming stimuli are compared to stored images (templates) in the brain. The stimulus is recognised if a close match can be made
- prototype theories – incoming stimuli are compared to 'typical' images of that class of stimuli. For example, if we were to imagine a house, most Westerners would find that they had a similar image of what a house looked like. Anything that approaches that image, i.e. has similar features, will be recognised as a house.

Pavlovian conditioning: see *classical conditioning*

peak experience: a *humanistic* term referring to an important moment in a person's life when they had felt a profound sense that something wonderful and of great value was happening to them, and as a result felt transformed and strengthened by the experience. This could be while listening to a piece of music, a moment of great creativity, or even from being in love. Abraham Maslow, who coined the term, felt that peak experiences were important in a person's quest for *self-actualisation* in that they:

- allowed a person to view themselves in a more healthy way
- released feelings of creativity, spontaneity and expressiveness
- removed neurotic symptoms
- produced a tendency to view life in general as being more worthwhile.

Pearson's product moment test: a test of *correlation* that requires either interval or ratio data (see *levels of measurement*) which is in the form of related pairs of scores.

peer: as it is used in psychology, the term refers to an individual who is in some way equal to the person with whom they are being compared. This may be in terms of intellect, *ability* or in some other way that implies a direct comparison of equals.

peer group: a social unit of (normally) same-age peers who possess common values and standards of behaviour. Peer groups tend to develop in middle childhood when belonging to a group becomes important to us. In adolescence, the peer group may become more tightly knit as adolescents form themselves into cliques (small groups of good friends) that are often identified by their interests. A more loosely organised group (the *crowd*) may help the adolescent's search for an identity by providing him or her with a label ('first years', the 'scallies' and so on). This is based less on the direct interaction of the clique and more on stereotypes or reputation. The clique and the crowd as peer-group influences both serve important functions. The clique provides a context for the acquisition of important social skills and the crowd offers the adolescent a sort of temporary identity as they go through the process of developing their own (see *adolescence*). Research suggests that the influence of the peer group on the developing values of an adolescent may have been exaggerated; many of the norms and values of the peer group appear to be an extension of those acquired in the home. The importance of cliques and crowds gradually declines in later adolescence as the development of more intimate relationships leads the adolescent into adult life.

peer review: the evaluation of academic work by others in the same field prior to publication. It is believed that a larger group of experts in a particular field will be more likely to find any errors in a research article and will be more likely to make a more impartial evaluation of it than would just the person or group who carried out the research in the first place. A problem with peer review is that it can be slow, with months or even a year or longer being required for submitted articles to be reviewed and published. Some critics also believe that peer review has a built-in bias because reviewers tend to be more tolerant of results that are consistent with their own views and more critical of those that contradict them. In addition, peer review is not particularly effective in detecting fraud, particularly if reviewers do not have full access to the data on which the research is based.

Peer review serves three main purposes:

1. Allocation of research funding – it enables funding bodies such as the Medical Research Council to decide which research is likely to be worthwhile.
2. Publication of research in scientific journals and books – peer review is a means of preventing incorrect or faulty data entering the public domain.

3. Assessing the research rating of university departments – university departments are expected to conduct research, which is assessed in terms of quality (Research Assessment Exercise, RAE), which in turn affects future funding for the department.

pegword system: a way of increasing the effectiveness of our memory by associating those things to be remembered with 'pegs' (such as the locations used in the **method of loci**). A commonly used pegword system involves associating each of a list of items with a peg which rhymes with its position in the list. Thus, one is a bun, two a shoe, three a tree and so on. In this way, the first item is imaged with eating a bun, the second with a shoe and so on. Stories connecting these pegs add to the organisational effectiveness of the system.

perception: the process by which information in the environment is transformed into an experience of objects, sounds, events, etc. Perception is a combination of both the physiological processes involved within the senses and also the processes within the brain which integrate and interpret the sensory inputs from these systems. The two main explanations of perception prioritise the role of one or other of these different aspects of the perceptual process. Direct (or **bottom-up**) theories emphasise the importance of stimulus features in perception. In visual perception, for example, the visual information that reaches the eye is thought to contain sufficient unambiguous information about an object for effective perception to take place with little further processing. For example, if you were to stand in the middle of a straight road or railway track (please don't try this!), you would notice that the parallel lines appear to converge (linear perspective) and the feature detail becomes denser (texture density). This is vital information for the brain to interpret the converging lines and denser texture of the object as being further away from the observer.

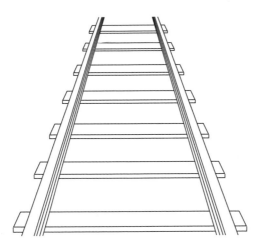

Texture gradient formed by a railway track

An alternative view (the **top-down** view) of the perceptual process sees the eventual product of our perception being 'constructed', that is built up from a combination of stimulus information, expectations and hypotheses (guesswork). The perceptual process involves making sense of all the various bits of information provided by the senses. A key aspect of this view of perception is that because of the role of hypotheses and expectation, perception will be frequently prone to error (see **illusion**).

The former, direct view of perception, is often criticised because it fails to explain those incidences (such as in illusions) where perception is wrong. The fact that perception is usually accurate, however, poses a problem for a theoretical position that emphasises the importance of **hypothesis** and expectation in the perceptual process. Compromise positions, such as that proposed by Neisser (1976), suggest that the relative importance of these bottom-up and top-down processes will be determined by the circumstances in which perception takes place. In most circumstances, perception will be a product of both sets of influences.

perceptual constancy: the tendency for objects to give the same perceptual experience despite the fact that the viewing conditions may change. Commonly quoted examples are *size constancy*, *shape constancy* and *colour constancy*.

perceptual defence: a phenomenon whereby words that have a high degree of emotional content or might be considered 'taboo' are perceptually recognised less easily than words of a more neutral nature. Using a **tachistoscope**, words can be presented to participants for increasing time durations (e.g. 10 msec, 20 msec, etc.) until they recognise what the word is. It is generally found that the **recognition** threshold for the emotionally laden words is higher than for the neutral words (i.e. they are less easy to recognise correctly). This is taken as evidence that **unconscious** defences prevent the person from experiencing this potentially disturbing event. However, this fails to distinguish what might be unconscious defence and what might be a conscious defence, in other words, the social embarrassment at identifying the taboo words to the experimenter.

perceptual organisation refers to the ability of an organism to organise the information that arrives at the senses into a meaningful perceptual experience. Examples of perceptual organisation would include:

- form perception – the ability to perceive figures (as distinct from the background) and patterns
- spatial perception – the ability to judge size and distance within a three-dimensional visual environment
- constancies – the ability to perceive objects accurately despite changes in viewing conditions
- movement – the ability to correctly judge moving objects against a stationary background.

perceptual set: a person's predisposition to respond to particular stimuli in a certain manner, i.e. we perceive what we expect to perceive.

peripheral route to persuasion: a way in which attitude change is achieved when issues are relatively unimportant to the listener or they are distracted from thorough analysis of the speaker's message. In such cases it is not so much the content of the message itself that changes the listener's attitude, but more the peripheral factors such as the status of the speaker (i.e. how much prestige and credibility they have) and the style or form of the message itself (e.g. how the listener comes to be exposed to it and in what form).

permanent memory refers to the belief, shared by many psychologists, that memories are never actually lost, but simply become inaccessible over a period of time. Support for this claim is somewhat sketchy, with research involving *electrical stimulation of the brain (ESB)* and *hypnosis* failing to provide convincing evidence that recall of supposedly lost memories are anything other than vague and often inaccurate representations of patients' experiences.

This is not to deny that all experience may be stored permanently within long-term memory, but so far no conclusive evidence exists to support this assertion.

personal construct: a term coined by George Kelly to represent the way in which a person 'constructs' their view of the world around them. A personal construct is a person's perception about what two objects or events have in common, and which set them apart from a third object or event. For example, you may see two of your friends as dependable and a third as unreliable. You would thus be using a construct of 'dependable versus unreliable' to group those round you into categories. These categories form our personal construction of the world around us, and help us to predict the physical and social environment. Some are shared by others, some are unique to us. Personal constructs can be changed if the person encounters conflicting information, or they may remain stable over time and become a fixed part of the person's *personality*.

personality refers to stable characteristics (*traits*) of a person that underlie consistencies in the way they behave over time and across different situations. It is also assumed that different people will behave in different ways in comparable situations, and that these differences in behaviour are a product of their personality differences. Personality is distinguished from other, more transitory states (such as mood) because of its stability over time. If personality is stable over time, and personality determines behaviour, then it follows that a person should behave in a consistent way on different occasions. A person who is described as an **extrovert**, for example, will act in an extroverted way across a wide range of different situations. Opponents of this trait view of personality suggest that behaviour does not remain consistent over time, but is influenced by the current situation. This situationist view of personality, although able to explain the consistency of behaviour of any one individual across similar situations, has more difficulties explaining individual differences in behaviour in those same situations.

personality disorders are enduring and inflexible ways of thinking about the world or acting in it. Although this may also apply to the enduring characteristics that make up our *personality*, the term personality disorder is applied when these ways of thinking and acting deviate significantly from what is considered appropriate by the rest of society. For example, we all feel a little suspicious of other people at times, but if we were to feel suspicious and distrustful of others far more frequently than perhaps we should, then this could be indicative of a personality disorder. These disorders can be extremely distressing for the person who possesses one, and also for their family and other people close to them. They certainly contribute to an impairment of normal functioning. **DSM-IV-TR** distinguishes ten separate personality disorders which are grouped into three clusters:

CLUSTER A: • odd or eccentric personality disorders, such as paranoid personality disorders – people who display a deep distrust and suspiciousness of others.

CLUSTER B: • dramatic, emotional or erratic personality, such as anti-social personality disorders – people who show a consistent disregard for the rights and feelings of others.

CLUSTER C: • anxious or fearful personality disorders, such as dependent personality disorders – people who have total reliance on others and seem incapable of making even minor decisions themselves.

P

There are considerable diagnostic difficulties with these DSM classifications. One of the major problems is that diagnosis relies more on inferred *traits* rather than actual observable behaviours. It is also difficult to assess when a normal pattern of thought or behaviour might be considered a personality disorder.

personality inventory: a test that is designed to measure personality characteristics. The *Eysenck Personality Inventory (EPI)* based on the personality theory of HJ Eysenck measures personality along the dimensions of neuroticism–stability and *introversion–extroversion*.

person-centred therapy: a humanistic therapy normally attributed to Carl Rogers. Rogers had a very positive view of human nature, and believed that the goal of therapy was not to impose goals on a client and then direct them towards these goals, but rather to let the client decide their own goals, with the therapist acting to support these. The major goal of therapy was thus to provide the right sort of conditions which would return clients to their innate pattern of growth and *self-actualisation*. Therapists refrain from direction or advice but provide, in the form of their own qualities, the right mix of warmth and attentiveness during the therapy session.

Rogers believed the therapist should possess:
- genuineness – they do not hide behind a professional façade, and through their own openness and honesty, provide a model for the client who must express their own feelings and accept responsibility for doing so
- unconditional positive regard – unlike others who withhold affection and regard unless people behave in an acceptable way, the client-centred therapist expresses warmth and acceptance even if they do not approve of the client's behaviour
- accurate empathetic understanding – the ability to see the world through the eyes of the client, to understand how and why the client sees the world the way they do.

Evaluation of person-centred therapy:
- Because of the 'self' emphasis of client-centred therapy, the Rogerian way of evaluating its effectiveness stresses the importance of self-report rather than behaviour change. This in itself poses problems for evaluation, because it is the fact that clients are not in touch with their true feelings that has brought them to therapy in the first place.
- More contemporary forms of evaluation make use of more indirect measurements of functioning, such as physiological measures as well as reports from significant others. Client-centred therapy does seem to provide some help for those who are unhappy, but as Rogers himself warned, it will not help those who are more severely disturbed.

perspective taking: being able to see things from another's point of view.

PET: see *positron emission tomography (PET)*

phenomenology: this is an approach to psychology that emphasises that one's subjective and contemporary experience of an event is an important and influential factor on one's behaviour. We may find it difficult to understand why someone would want to walk across the Antarctic or to spend three days in a bath of baked beans, but that is because we are unable to perceive the world in the way that they do. Only by seeing the world in the same way they do can we really understand why they act in the way that they do.

phenotype: refers to those observable characteristics (or **traits**) of an individual. This is normally distinguished from the **genotype**, which is the genetic information which is passed from generation to generation.

phobic disorders (phobias): a type of **anxiety disorder** where there is a persistent and unreasonable fear of an object or situation. A phobic disorder differs from a normal non-phobic fear in that it is more intense, and there is a compelling desire to avoid the object of the fear. The distress associated with phobic disorders interferes with the normal functioning of a person such that they often find it difficult to lead a normal life. **DSM-IV-TR** distinguishes three categories of phobia:

- **agoraphobia** – a fear of public places
- social phobias – a fear of potentially embarrassing social situations such as having to give a speech or eating in public
- specific phobias – such as a fear of spiders (arachnophobia) or a fear of flying (aerophobia).

Explanations of the possible causes of phobias vary, but it is possible that they may be learned through either **classical** or **operant conditioning**, or through the genetic inheritance of a predisposition to develop a phobic disorder. There are considerable problems with all these explanations, although the effectiveness of **behaviour therapies** in the treatment of phobic disorders lends support to the claim that they were learned in the first place. Phobias can develop at any time of life, although some specific phobias, such as the fear of certain animals, do tend to appear in childhood and disappear without intervention before adulthood. Some psychologists believe that some specific phobias (such as fear of the dark and fear of animals with certain characteristics) are legacies of genuine fears of dangers long past. Natural selection would favour the development of sensitivity to these objects and situations, therefore we have become biologically **prepared** to develop phobic reactions without the normal lengthy exposure necessary for conditioning to take place. Although many phobias disappear on their own, without the need for psychological intervention, those that persist will only diminish with appropriate psychological treatment (see also **agoraphobia**).

phoneme: although often referred to as a speech sound, it is more accurately defined as a unit of sound (or sounds) that has some meaning to those who use or hear it. For example, the phoneme / l / involves more than one single speech sound.

phonic method of reading: a way of teaching children to read that stresses the sounds of letters and letter groups rather than recognition of the whole words themselves.

phylogeny: the evolution and development of a species. See also **ontogeny**, the evolution and development of an individual organism.

physical (physiological) dependence: refers to a dependence on a particular drug which is caused by taking the drug for long periods of time. If the drug is suddenly stopped, the person may suffer severe physiological dysfunctioning associated with **withdrawal**. Examples of drugs that can lead to physical dependence are morphine and heroin (see also **psychological dependence**).

Piaget, J (1896-1980): a Swiss psychologist whose main contribution to psychology was the belief that **intelligence** was the product of a natural and inevitable sequence of developmental stages. He did not suggest that intelligence was simply inborn, but rather that it developed as a result of the constantly changing interaction of the child and environment. Piaget believed that the child went through distinct stages of development. Each stage is characterised by qualitatively different ways of thinking about the world.

During development, the child develops mental structures called **schemas** which enables him or her to solve problems in the environment. Adaptation is brought about by the processes of **assimilation** (solving new problems using existing schema) and **accommodation** (changing existing schemata in order to solve new experiences). The importance of this viewpoint is that the child is seen as an active participant in its own development, rather than a passive recipient of either biological influences (**maturation**) or environmental stimulation.

Piaget had a tremendous influence on psychology for many years, and his ideas have been instrumental in much of the educational thinking of the latter part of the 20th century. His critics have claimed that Piaget underestimated the abilities of young children. Likewise, Piaget's theory is often described as 'anti-educational' in that it describes a sequence of events not readily alterable by education or training.

Piagetian: based on the theories or research of Jean **Piaget**.

pilot study: an initial run-through of the procedures to be used in an **experiment**. By selecting a few **participants** and trying out the experiment on them, we can save time and money on later mistakes. The pilot study is a good way of finding out whether the whole thing is likely to work as we planned it, and also if there are any **floor** or **ceiling effects**.

pituitary-adrenal system: also known as the hypothalamic-pituitary-adrenal axis (HPA), this is the body's slow-acting response to **stress**. When stressors are perceived by the higher centres of the brain, a message is sent to the **hypothalamus**, which releases a chemical messenger (CRF) into the bloodstream in response. On arrival at the pituitary gland, CRF causes it to release a hormone, ACTH, which is transported via the bloodstream to the adrenal cortex. This releases cortisol, which is responsible for several stress-related effects throughout the body, some positive (lower sensitivity to pain) and some negative (impaired cognitive performance). The system is very efficient at regulating itself and, if cortisol levels rise above normal, this leads to a reduction in CRF and ACTH levels, bringing cortisol levels back to normal.

pituitary gland: a part of the **endocrine system**, the pituitary gland produces **hormones** whose primary function is to influence the release of hormones from other glands. For example, gonadotrophins are hormones that are produced by the pituitary and travel through the blood system to the gonads, where they stimulate the release of gonadal hormones such as **testosterone**.

PK: an abbreviation sometimes used in preference to the full term **psychokinesis (PK)**.

placebo: when used in the context of drugs testing, the placebo is a preparation that has no relevant medicinal properties and is given to one group so that the medicinal effects of the real drug can be separated out from the psychological effects produced by people thinking they are receiving it.

play is difficult to define because the criteria used to define it are arbitrary. Mood, excitement and type of activity have all been suggested, but those vary enormously from activity to activity. Observers may only guess at the functions of a particular activity, therefore we might say a child is playing simply because that is how we would classify that behaviour. Common characteristics of play are:

- it is voluntary
- it does not lead to any obvious goal
- it involves repetitions of activities already mastered
- it may be accompanied by 'play signals', such as a special tone of voice or exaggerated movements.

play theories refer to the different way in which theorists explain the nature and function of play. Two examples are:

1. **Piaget** – play is important because it enables the child to practise existing skills in order to consolidate them. As play is mostly fantasy (there are no external goals), it enables the child to achieve a sense of mastery. The child also goes through different stages of play:
   - mastery play – the child repeats activities to consolidate them and develop mastery over them
   - symbolic play – by using the medium of 'make-believe', the child is able to exercise some control over the world around them
   - play with rules – because the child is developing socially, s/he needs to develop rules to ensure co-operation and fair play.
2. **Freud** – through the medium of play the child can:
   - repeat pleasant experiences at will, so s/he has some feeling of mastery and control over life
   - display *defence mechanisms*. Playing with plasticine may be seen as *sublimated* manipulation of faeces, for example
   - master distressing episodes and use play as a means of dealing emotionally with these events.

play therapy: the use of play situations as a form of *therapy*, based on the ideas of *Freudian* theory and later developed by *Erikson*. Play therapy is used in two major ways:

- as a diagnostic tool, in that the behaviour of the child reveals important information about their underlying traits and problems. The play situation thus acts as a *projective test* of the child's emotional problems. This diagnostic use of play therapy is now used mostly by social workers as a means of detecting child abuse, especially sexual abuse, with the use of anatomically correct dolls
- as a form of treatment, in that the play situation allows the child the opportunity to express their feelings and emotions in a fantasy situation. The subsequent emotional release is generally referred to as *catharsis*.

There has been some debate on the reliability of interpretation and some *ethical* controversy.

pleasure principle: the impulsive and pleasure seeking part of our nature that is normally associated with our *id*. We are driven to gratify the desires associated with this principle regardless of their real or moral consequences.

pluralistic ignorance: a term used to explain why people will often fail to respond to an emergency when there are other people around. Social psychologists explain this as an aspect of *social comparison*. When we witness an emergency, we may be unsure what to do, so we rely on the behaviour of others to guide us. If the other people around us fail to react, then our helping behaviour is inhibited. Baron and Byrne (1994) make the point that we are often taught that remaining calm is the most appropriate response to an emergency. As a result, most people pretend to be calm, which is interpreted by others as meaning nothing is wrong and they don't need to react.

polyandry: a type of mating system in which females have multiple mates but males do not. Sometimes individual males mate with a single female and she divides her attention between each of them (classical polyandry). Alternatively, a number of males co-operate to raise the brood of a single female (co-operative polyandry). Polyandry is relatively rare, except for some birds and a few fish species, and occasionally in human societies (such as in Nepal).

polygynandry: a mating system where males and females mate with several members of the opposite sex. The term promiscuity is often used to describe this mating arrangement, but this perhaps suggests that matings are more random than they really are.

For males, the advantages of multiple matings are clear: more matings mean more of their genes in the next generation. The advantages of multiple matings for females are not so clear cut. The following represents some of the possible reasons why females would seek multiple matings:

- they reduce the risks of sexual harassment from *conspecifics.* Female birds that are harassed during the mating period are subject to extreme stress and are more likely to lay eggs that do not hatch
- it introduces sperm competition so that only the most vigorous ones achieve fertilisation
- it reduces the socially disruptive effects of sexual competition among males in social groups
- it may secure the co-operation of several males in the care and feeding of the young and may guard against *infanticide* by non-mating males.

polygyny: a mating system in which successful males gain more than one female, whereas females only mate with one male. The commonest form of polygyny is resource defence polygyny where males gain territories and defend the resources in these territories against other males. The dominant explanation for this arrangement is provided by the polygyny threshold model. Females will settle in a male's territory that is already occupied by another female only if the advantages of so doing are higher than the advantages she might expect from being a *monogamous* partner with a male in a lower-quality territory. If the advantages of being a second female in a good territory (good-quality male, plentiful resources) outweigh the advantages of being a single female in an inferior territory (greater parental assistance from the monogamous male), then the polygyny threshold has been reached and polygyny is preferred by the female.

Other forms of polygyny are:

- female defence polygyny – a male defends a group (harem) of females from other males. This arrangement ensures that males who possess harems have constant access to females and therefore greater reproductive opportunities
- male dominance polygyny – females choose the most desirable males. Males compete to attract the most females.

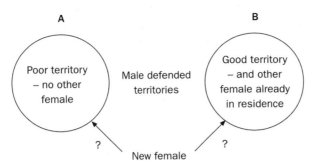

A   B

The polygyny threshold model: a female will choose territory B only if she stands to gain more than being a single female in territory A

Ponzo illusion: an optical illusion where a pair of converging lines distorts the perception of two identically sized lines placed upon it. The Ponzo illusion can be explained in terms of linear perspective. The upper line looks longer because, like train tracks, we interpret the sides of the figure as parallel lines that recede into the distance. Based on this assumption, we interpret the upper line as though it were further away, therefore it must be longer. This is because an object in the distance would have to be larger than an object that was closer to the observer for both to produce retinal images of the same size.

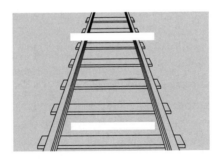

The Ponzo illusion

population: a group of people who are the focus of a research study and to which the results would apply. It is generally inappropriate to study an entire population (for example, all the students in a college or all 16–19 year olds in Liverpool), so a representative *sample* is studied instead.

population validity: is one aspect of *external validity*. Population validity concerns the extent that one can generalise from the *population* studied in the experiment (e.g. male undergraduate students) to other populations.

positive regard: see *unconditional positive regard*

positive reinforcement: the provision of something that strengthens whatever behaviour went before it. Positive reinforcers are normally drive reducers (such as food) or other things that we find attractive or rewarding. In a sense, a positive reinforcer is defined by its consequences. If it has the effect of strengthening a response and thus making it more likely to appear in the future, then it is a positive reinforcer. The strangest things may thus become

203

reinforcing. To some children, being told off by a teacher in front of their peers may be seen as positive reinforcement if it raises the 'street cred' of the person being chastised. Whatever behaviour led to the telling off may then become more frequent.

positive symptoms: a classification of *schizophrenia* where the client has characteristics that are additional behavioural features to normal functioning. Examples would be delusions, *hallucinations* and disorganised thought processes.

positivism: a belief that we should not go beyond the boundaries of what can be observed. To a positivist, science is the single-most important route to knowledge, and only questions that can be approached by the application of the scientific method should concern us. The most obvious psychological development from this positivist approach is *behaviourism*, the study of observable behaviour. A variant of positivism, logical positivism relegated all approaches to knowledge that could not be verified by scientific means to the realm of meaningless emotion and belief. Thus, to a logical positivist, the theory of *psychoanalysis* would be meaningless as a body of knowledge because it could not be verified by observational means.

positron emission tomography (PET) is a way of obtaining images of the functional state of the brain. The procedure usually involves injecting radioactive glucose into the bloodstream. This travels to the brain, where the glucose is taken up into the different brain areas according to their degree of metabolic activity. Parts of the brain that are more active take up more glucose, which in turn emits harmless radioactivity that is analysed by a computer. In this way, maps of the brain can be drawn up that represent the exact areas that are active during specific activities. The technique also allows doctors and researchers to identify regions of the brain that are functioning abnormally in terms of their metabolic activity even if they are structurally intact.

post-conventional morality: see *Kohlberg, L*

post-decisional dissonance: known more popularly as 'buyers' remorse', this is the unpleasant feeling that we may have made the wrong choice between two equally attractive alternatives. Although our reasons for making the original choice between them are likely to have been entirely rational, much of the reasoning that subsequently goes on to reduce the state of dissonance is not. The diagram below illustrates some of the strategies commonly used in the reduction of post-decisional dissonance.

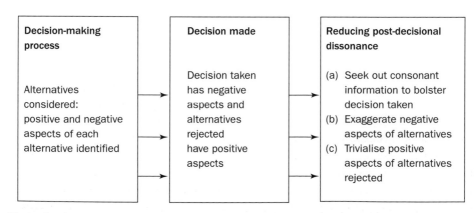

Strategies for the reduction of post-decisional dissonance

post-event contamination: *eye-witness testimony* is vulnerable to 'contamination' from information received after the witnessed event. This phenomenon, also called the 'misinformation effect', has been the subject of extensive research by Elizabeth Loftus and colleagues. They have established that a witness's recall of an event may be influenced by the type of questioning used (in particular the use of leading questions) and by other factors such as the time interval between the witnessed event and the post-event information. One possible explanation for this is that the *memory trace* becomes weaker with time, therefore it becomes easier to fill in the gaps with information from some other source.

post-traumatic stress disorder refers to a distinct pattern of symptoms that develop as a result of some traumatic event (such as an aeroplane crash, kidnapping or rape). The symptoms of post-traumatic stress disorder begin shortly after the event and may last for months or even years. The symptoms include:
- re-experiencing the event – recurring recollections, including dreams and nightmares about the traumatic event
- avoidance – the person tries to avoid anything that is associated with the traumatic event; for example, if they have been in an air crash, they may avoid even watching movies that have aeroplanes in them
- reduced responsiveness – where the person feels a detachment from others and a sort of emotional numbness
- increased *arousal*, anxiety and guilt – people may experience hyperalertness and sleep disturbances. In some kinds of event (such as an air crash), people may experience guilt that they survived where others did not.

In trying to explain why some people suffer from post-traumatic stress disorders and others do not, psychologists have discovered that childhood experiences (such as early abuse or painful parental divorce) may leave some people vulnerable to later *stress*. Although the reasons for this link are not established, it is thought that children may deal with the early trauma by separating themselves from the experience. This becomes a strategy for dealing with trauma in later life.

posthypnotic amnesia: a subject's inability to remember something that happened while they were hypnotised. This is a form of *posthypnotic suggestion* in that the person is told, while under hypnosis, that upon waking they will not remember a particular event.

posthypnotic suggestion refers to a suggestion made while a person is hypnotised that upon waking, they will behave in a certain way. This also implies that the person will not be aware of the source of this suggestion.

power: see *social power*

practice effect: within an experiment, any improvement in performance over the different conditions of the experiment might be attributed not to the *independent variable* under study, but to the learning that takes place when the same task is attempted on more than one occasion. If we were trying to measure how well participants perform a task under two different conditions, we must face the possibility that some of this difference would be inevitable because of the simple fact that they are by now familiar with the task. Provided that the practice effects are not too large, we can compensate for them by ensuring that half of the participants perform the conditions in the opposite order to the others (known as *counterbalancing*). If the effects are large, however, it would be necessary to use different participants in the different conditions of the experiment.

precocial species: animals that can move about, feed and generally look after themselves shortly after birth. Normally contrasted with *altricial species*, the terms refer more to points on a continuum than to distinct classifications. Thus, some animals are better able to look after themselves after birth than others, but both may be described as precocial.

precognition: the ability to forecast future events. Fortune tellers claim to have this *ability*.

preconscious: a *psychoanalytic* term which refers to those thoughts and memories which, whilst not at present part of our *conscious* experience, are nonetheless accessible to it.

preconventional morality: see *Kohlberg, L*

predictive validity: see *validity*

prefrontal lobotomy: refers to a surgical procedure that severs the neural pathways that connect the frontal lobes (see *brain*) from other areas of the brain. This procedure was used extensively until the 1950s after which its use declined and was replaced by the newer drug therapies. It appeared particularly effective with violent mental patients, but produced unsatisfactory side-effects. Lobotomised patients tended to become dull and listless, and many suffered losses in their cognitive capacities (reasoning and memory).

prejudice: as used within psychology, this term means to 'prejudge' somebody on the basis of their membership of a particular category or group. Not all prejudgements are classified as prejudices. Prejudices are specifically those prejudgements which are resistant to reversal when exposed to contradictory knowledge. Prejudice involves more than just having preconceived ideas about another person or group – it involves forming an evaluation of them. Within this definition, prejudice can be either positive or negative, but in the psychological literature, it is normally taken to mean a negative (i.e. unflattering) *attitude* towards that person or group. Prejudice is usually maintained through *stereotyping*, the belief that all members of a particular group share the same characteristics. For example, we may be prejudiced against all supporters of Crabchester Rovers because we believe them to all be pathologically violent thugs. The following explanations are among the many offered for the origins of prejudice.

- personality theories, such as the *authoritarian personality* theory, see prejudice as being one of the consequences of a particular style of upbringing
- cognitive theories – stress the need to categorise people because that simplifies the way in which we see the world around us. This colours the way we interpret events, and this selective interpretation adds weight to our prejudices
- socio-cultural theories – see prejudice as being part of the 'shared wisdom' of a culture. This prejudice may develop because of beliefs concerning competition between groups or may simply be a result of our association with our own group as the '*in-group*' and others as the '*out-group*' (see *social identity theory*).

Prejudice is often confused with *discrimination*, which is a behaviour, whereas prejudice is an *attitude*. A particular prejudice may or may not have a behaviour associated with it. For example, we may possess a prejudice but that might not affect the way we behave towards the object of our prejudice.

Premack principle: see *reinforcement*

preoperational stage: see *Piaget, J*

preparedness: a reference to the fact that organisms are better able to associate certain combinations of stimuli, responses and reinforcers than others. If an animal eats and is then ill, it may develop an aversion to the flavour of the food, but not to visual or auditory stimuli that were present at the same time. If, however, they are given an electric shock while eating and in the presence of a particular visual or auditory stimulus, they will show avoidant behaviour whenever the stimulus is present. This is because food and its flavours are readily associated with illness, whereas sights or sounds are not. Likewise, sights and sounds are more easily associated with pain, whereas food and its flavours are not.

presenting symptom: the symptom that causes an individual to seek medical or psychological help.

primacy effect: a general finding that material presented first to a *participant* is more likely to be remembered than material subsequently presented. In social psychology, it is also used to represent the fact that the first things we learn about a person have a disproportionately higher influence on our impressions of them.

primary reinforcement: see *reinforcement*

principled morality: see *post-conventional morality*

prisoners' dilemma: a hypothetical game scenario that is meant to demonstrate the dilemma of reconciling individual interests and well-being with collective interests and well-being. The game shows how well-meaning people can become trapped in mutually destructive behaviour, when all would benefit from co-operation. There are several variations of this scenario, but all involve a dilemma between selfish self-interest and mutual co-operation. The game examines the story of two police suspects who are thought to be guilty of some major offence. However, the police have only enough evidence to convict each of them for some minor offence. The police need one or both of the suspects to confess and offer each an incentive to confess in private. If one confesses and the other does not, the police will grant the confessor immunity and convict the other of the major offence. If both confess they will be charged with a lesser offence and both will receive moderate jail sentences. If, however, neither confesses, the police will only be able to charge them with the minor offence. The possible outcomes of each decision are shown in the matrix below:

	Prisoner A: Doesn't confess	Prisoner B: Doesn't confess
Prisoner A: Confesses	A: 5 years	A: 10 years
	B: 5 years	B: 0 years
Prisoner B: Confesses	A: 0 years	A: 1 year
	B: 10 years	B: 1 year

The prisoners' dilemma has been used in the explanation of social dilemmas, and of altruistic behaviour, particularly that involving reciprocity. It demonstrates how the collective well-being of a group can be threatened if individuals only take into consideration the individual benefits of their actions.

privation: a term often encountered in the area of *maternal deprivation*, privation refers to the lack or non-development of the *attachment* bond. The term is often used synonymously with the term *deprivation*, although to be technically correct, the latter refers to a loss of the attachment bond rather than its non-development. Conditions that would create privation are fortunately quite rare, although at the time that John **Bowlby** was producing his influential work on the area, the nature of institutional care of young children meant that many were unable to develop satisfactory attachment bonds with a **caregiver**. These children were, according to Bowlby, vulnerable to a much later degree of life stress than normal children.

privileged communication refers to the confidential nature of disclosures between therapist and client. The therapist cannot be forced, except where the information from the client is of an illegal nature, to disclose this information to a third party. If clients did not feel that they could rely on confidentiality in the therapy session, they would not feel able to disclose intimate or potentially embarrassing information, and thus the effectiveness of the therapy session would be decreased.

proactive inhibition: see *proactive interference*

proactive interference: the interference on learning that is brought about by something that was learned in the past. It is described as 'proactive' because it is an effect that will be experienced in the future. If we learn to drive a car with manual transmission, then when we attempt to later drive an automatic, we will find that our manual skills (such as pumping your foot down on the clutch pedal) will have a detrimental effect on our ability to learn the new way of driving. There is also the view among some university academics that statistical skills acquired in A level psychology interfere with the performance of students in degree-level research. The author offers no comment on this point of view.

pro-attitudinal behaviour: a tendency for people to behave in a way that is consistent with their underlying attitudes. If we behave in a way that is contrary to our attitudes (*counter-attitudinal behaviour*), we experience unpleasant feelings that are caused by the cognitive inconsistency of the two events. This relationship between attitudes and behaviour has been formalised in Festinger's theory of **cognitive dissonance**.

probability: a statement of how likely it is that something will happen. This is expressed as a number between 1 (certainty) and 0 (impossibility). A probability of 0.05 is conventionally used in psychological investigations as the appropriate point at which to reject the possibility that results are only differing because of sampling error. The figure of 0.05 is then the probability of the difference (or correlation) occurring if the **null hypothesis** is in fact true.

problem-focused coping: the use of coping strategies designed directly to alleviate the stressful situation itself. These include the following:
- taking control of the stressful situation
- evaluating the pros and cons of different options for dealing with the stressor
- suppressing competing activities in order to deal directly with the stressor.

People typically use problem-focused coping with events that are potentially controllable (e.g. dealing with debt or exam stress) and **emotion-focused coping** with stressors that are less controllable (e.g. dealing with bereavement). Problem-focused coping is generally regarded as the more effective coping strategy, provided the individual has a realistic chance of changing those aspects of the situation that are causing them stress.

procedural knowledge: any form of knowledge to which the person has no conscious access and that can only be demonstrated indirectly through some kind of action. A typical example is riding a bike. Most of us can do it (procedural knowledge) but few can explain how to do it or why we don't fall flat on our face (see *declarative knowledge*).

Prochaska model: Prochaska and DiClemente (1983) based their transtheoretical model of change on the observation that people appear to go through similar stages of change regardless of the type of psychotherapy they are following. The model has two dimensions: the stages of change (an orderly sequence through which people pass) and the processes of change, which refers to the different techniques used. Stages include precontemplation (i.e. not interested in behaviour change), preparation (getting ready to change) and action (the first six months of change). Processes of change include cognitive processes such as dramatic relief (realising the current behaviour can be harmful) and behavioural processes such as reinforcement management (rewarding oneself for positive behaviour). This model has been applied to the prevention of smoking, the promotion of exercise and condom use.

prognosis: when used specifically in clinical psychology, this refers to the expected eventual outcome of any disorder.

projection: this is one of the *defence mechanisms* by which characteristics or desires that are unacceptable to a person's *ego* are externalised or projected onto someone else. For example, a person that has aggressive feelings towards others may find it unacceptable to admit that they have such feelings. They may then be projected onto others such that s/he now feels that they have aggressive feelings towards him or her.

projective test: a type of psychological assessment that presents the person with a set of rather vague stimuli (perhaps shapes or pictures) with the assumption that the person's responses will reflect their unconscious fears and motivations. The best-known example of a projective test is the *Rorschach inkblot test*.

propaganda: an attempt to manipulate opinions through the use of media. Propaganda is probably the commonest example of *psychological warfare*, where it can involve manipulation through radio broadcasts, leaflets and other forms of media. To be considered as propaganda, a message must satisfy three criteria:

- there must be a conscious attempt to manipulate the opinion of others
- only one side of an argument is presented to give the impression that the message carries an unquestionable truth
- the fact that the message has this intention is disguised, so that those receiving it do not recognise it as propaganda.

For propaganda to be effective, the propagandist must consider the aims, target, credibility and means of communication. The effectiveness of propaganda can never be assessed directly, although there are certainly claims to its power. Hitler frequently made reference to the effectiveness of Allied propaganda during World War One, and saw it as one of the main reasons why Germany had lost that war. The relative ineffectiveness of German propaganda in World War One, and of German and Japanese propaganda in World War Two may well be explained by their failure to 'get inside the minds' of their enemy. During the Gulf War, Iraqi propagandists tried to convince American servicemen that while they were fighting in the Gulf, their wives were sleeping with movie stars back home. It is unlikely that this would have been particularly effective, but its credibility was severely lessened by the fact that one of the movie stars mentioned was the cartoon character Bart Simpson!

pro-social behaviour: any act that helps or benefits others, yet may carry some risk or penalty to the person performing it. When one person helps another with no apparent benefit to themselves, we may describe their behaviour as being pro-social. The antithesis of this is that when people set out to harm another in some way, perhaps by acting aggressively toward them, they are said to be displaying *anti-social behaviour*.

pro-social reasoning: the reasoning behind behaviour, based on pro-social, even empathic, rather than egocentric feelings. Eisenberg (1982) has developed a stage theory of pro-social reasoning that shows a clear development in children from self-centred helping for personal gain through to a desire to maintain internalised values and norms of pro-social behaviour. Her stages are as follows:

Level	Description
Hedonistic, pragmatic orientation	Right behaviour satisfies one's own needs – 'I wouldn't share my food because I might be hungry.'
'Needs of others' orientation	Concern for the needs of others is expressed in simple terms, without evidence of perspective-taking or empathy – 'He needs it.'
Stereotypes, approval-focused orientation	Stereotyped images of good and bad people and concern for approval justify behaviour – 'He would like me better if I helped him.'
Empathic orientation	Reasoning shows the ability to take the perspective of others and have empathy for them – 'He is in distress, I must help him.'
Internalised values orientation	Decisions are made on the basis of internalised values and norms, and belief in the dignity, rights and equality of all individuals – 'If I didn't help I would be letting myself down.'

prosopagnosia: also known as face blindness, is a condition in the recognition of faces. Individuals with prosopagnosia can describe a person's face and its expression but cannot recognise whose face it is unless they use other non-facial information such as clothing or voice. Prosopagnosics often have difficulty recognising people even when they have met them many times. In extreme cases, they have trouble recognising even the people they spend the most time with. Most cases of prosopagnosia are due to brain damage as a result of head trauma, stroke and degenerative diseases. Individuals with this form of the disorder (acquired prosopagnosia), had normal face recognition abilities that were impaired as a result of the brain damage. In the second form (developmental prosopagnosia), the inset of the disorder occurs during or prior to the development of normal face recognition abilities, and is usually attributed to the influence of genetic factors.

prototype: generally used to represent something which possesses features which are obviously characteristic of a given category of objects or events. A semi-detached house may be many people's abstraction of the category of objects known as 'houses'. Tree houses and bungalows, although they share the same functions, are rarely seen as typical of this category of object.

pseudoscience: any field of study that masquerades as a science but lacks certain important characteristics (such as the lack of carefully controlled, replicable research and the lack of a theory to explain findings) that typify real science. Much of the research in anomalistic psychology has been dismissed as pseudoscientific for just these reasons.

psyche: taken from the Greek meaning of the word ('essence', or 'soul') and generally taken to mean *mind*.

psychiatrist: a medically trained specialist who can diagnose and treat mental disorders. Psychiatrists' training tends to focus on the *biomedical* approach to psychological problems. Unlike the *clinical psychologist*, the psychiatrist can dispense drugs.

psychic healing: refers to any method used to alleviate health problems by purely mental means. These include faith healing and the laying on of hands (therapeutic touch). In the latter, the therapist moves his or her hands over the patient's body to detect their 'aura', and aims to restore health by realigning the patient's energy field. There are many anecdotal accounts of the success of psychic healing, but few properly controlled scientific studies that have demonstrated its effectiveness. Some of the success of psychic healing may be attributable to the placebo effect.

psychic mediumship: psychic mediums claim to be able to communicate with people in the afterlife or spirit world. One of the best known was Doris Stokes, who brought belief in survival after death to the masses. She made many television appearances and toured extensively. There are many clues that can help a talented medium such as Doris Stokes produce accurate information about someone in the 'spirit world'. A process known as cold reading uses a subject's inclination to find more meaning in a piece of information than there actually is. The willingness of people to elaborate on limited information helps the medium appear to have special powers.

psychoactive drugs: are drugs that alter mood or thought processes. The abuse of these drugs may lead to addiction or, in some extreme cases, death.

psychoanalysis: a term used to describe the *theory* of development associated with Sigmund *Freud*, and the *psychotherapy* derived from that theory. The theory is presented under the *Freud* entry, the therapy discussed here. According to Freud, neurotic problems in later life are a product of the conflicts that arise during the *Oedipal* phase of development. These conflicts may be repressed because the immature *ego* is unable to deal with them at the time. The aims of psychoanalytic therapy are to create the right sort of conditions so that the patient is able to bring these conflicts into the *conscious* mind where they can be addressed and dealt with. Analysts use a variety of techniques to achieve these aims, including:

- free association – the patient is encouraged to speak freely, sometimes while reclining on a couch (an enduring image of Freudian psychoanalysis), and to verbalise anything that comes to mind. In this way the patient may be able to bring content to the surface that has previously been censored by the ego
- resistance – patients may attempt to block discussion by changing the subject quickly, for example, or even neglecting to turn up for therapy. Freud considered these resistances were a valuable insight into uncovering sensitive areas in the patient's unconscious mind
- dream analysis – the analyst attempts to unravel and interpret the symbolic nature of the patient's dreams. The true concerns of the patient are often disguised in their dreams and may be experienced symbolically, i.e. they dream about something that represents their concern, rather than dreaming directly about the concern itself. For example, dreaming about walking up to a crossroads where we must make a decision which way to go may be symbolic of an important life decision that the person must make. The true concerns of the patient are often disguised in this symbolic form to protect the conscious mind from developing full awareness of the underlying concern
- interpretation – the analyst offers interpretations of the patient's thoughts, actions and dreams, and points out their defences. By carefully waiting until the patient himself is about to gain the same insight the analyst can maximise the impact of the interpretation
- denial – related to these interpretations is the problem of the patient's denial. The analyst may well have reason to believe that a patient's denial of an interpretation offered by the analyst is another example of the defensive processes
- transference – this involves reliving the repressed conflict but transferring the repressed feelings (about parents, for example) onto the analyst. This is usually taken to mean that the repressed conflict is near to the surface of the conscious mind, and is encouraged by the analyst.

Evaluation of psychoanalytic therapy:
- The central problem in this evaluation is whether a patient can ever be said to be 'cured' Criteria for assessing cure, some critics believe, have been biased towards psychoanalysis.
- Some research studies have demonstrated that those who undertake psychoanalysis fare little better than those who do not undertake therapy over the same period of time.
- Psychoanalysis appears to benefit only certain types of patient (see *YAVIS*), and is less effective in patients with severe psychopathological problems.

psychoanalyst: someone who has completed specialist postgraduate training in *Freudian* approaches to the understanding and treatment of psychological disorders.

psychodrama: a type of *psychotherapy* in which the individual acts out a particular role or event usually in the company of others who may or may not play a part in the enactment. The idea behind this technique is that the person can express their emotions within the protected and supportive therapeutic context.

psychodynamic: the term has two main uses. It describes any theory that emphasises change and development in the individual, and secondly any theory where *drive* is a central concept in development. Both of these approaches stress the importance of change (i.e. the human organism is seen as dynamic, or constantly changing). The best known of the psychodynamic theories is Freudian *psychoanalysis*.

psychogenic illness: a type of abnormal functioning that is caused primarily by psychological or emotional factors such as worry, work stress or unconscious desires.

psychokinesis (PK): the apparent ability of an individual to influence a physical event without direct intervention. In popular language this is 'mind over matter'.

psycholinguistics: a term with a broad meaning in psychology, referring to the study of anything to do with human *language*. This would include the nature of language, language acquisition, the study of grammar, reading development and so on.

psychological dependence: a term used to describe a reliance on a drug because it makes stressful events more bearable. The term psychological dependence is used where continued use is not required for normal physical functioning (compare with *physical (physiological) dependence*). Dependence is more due to a drive to continue taking the drug because of the way it makes us feel. Marijuana is an example of a drug that may lead to psychological dependence, but not physical dependence.

psychological warfare: the use of psychological knowledge, skills and techniques in conflict situations. Although the commonest examples of psychological warfare have been in the area of *propaganda*, psychologists have also contributed in many other ways, including the following:

- military tactics – including techniques of presenting and interpreting information on the battlefield so that accurate assessment of all aspects of the battle can be dealt with in the most appropriate way. Increasingly, computers can be used for this purpose. Specialists are able to interpret patterns of enemy behaviour in much the same way that statisticians will explore the difference between random and consistent patterns in psychological investigations
- animal training – legends abound about kamikaze dolphins, packed with high explosive and trained to swim up against enemy warships. Whales have been trained to retrieve missiles from depths far in excess of those at which human divers could operate. In the 1940s, *Skinner* demonstrated how pigeons could be trained using *operant conditioning* techniques to sit in the nose cone of a 600 mph missile and guide it in the final stages of its approach on target. Only the fact that more sophisticated mechanical guidance systems were developed stopped this one being taken seriously
- interrogation techniques – focus on destroying the subject's sense of self by turning it against him or her. Interrogators will manipulate the subject's pride and dignity often in ingenious ways (such as refusing access to the lavatory so that he or she is forced to soil him- or herself). The use of sensory deprivation techniques such as social isolation and sleep deprivation have proved effective in breaking some subjects, although such techniques can produce far more constructive clear thinking in others. In those who react badly to this type of deprivation, the negative responses include disorientation, restlessness, hallucinations, apprehension and depression. Sensory deprivation techniques leave no visible scars, so it is almost impossible to prove that they have been used
- special techniques – include the use of broadcasting and leaflets designed to deflate an enemy. In World War Two, the Japanese played Glenn Miller music to American soldiers in order to make them homesick and unwilling to fight. In Vietnam, American helicopters would broadcast confessions from captured Vietcong soldiers even while the battle was still in progress. As it is very important for Vietnamese to die in their homes, leaflets were

dropped reminding the Vietcong of their relatives who had died far away from their homes. The effect of this tactic could be accentuated by using important celebration periods such as the Vietnamese New Year.

psychology: most commonly defined as the 'scientific study of mind and behaviour'. The definition offered by any particular psychologist reflects their own interpretative bias, therefore some would lay more stress on the *mind* part of this definition, others the *behaviour* part. Some psychologists might even offer the view that the study of human behaviour cannot, and indeed should not, be considered a *scientific* discipline.

psychometric testing refers to the practice of measuring psychological factors in a person. It could apply to almost anything, but the commonest examples are in *intelligence*, *personality* and aptitude (see separate entries on *intelligence testing* and *personality inventory*). The history of psychometric testing goes back to the mid-19th century when the tests being used dealt with aspects of intelligence. The use of intelligence tests in particular came under intense attack in the 1960s, when it was claimed that test results were being used to discriminate for jobs and for educational opportunities. This in itself was not a problem, but it was also claimed that test results were being used to bolster *racial discrimination*. In recent years there has been an upsurge in the use of psychometric techniques, particularly in counselling, selection procedures and for clinical *diagnosis*. For a test to be of any use at all, it must have good predictive *validity*, that is it should give an indication how a person would react in some specific situation in the future. The one major problem with many tests (particularly when used in selection procedures) is that people can cheat, or at least present an image in the test that is not an accurate reflection of themselves. Many tests have built in 'social desirability' scales (or lie scales) to check for this. For example, if a *respondent* presents a whiter-than-white image on the social desirability scale (perhaps claiming never to lie or get angry), there may be good reason for doubting their honesty on the rest of the questions.

psychopath: see *anti-social personality*

psychopathology: the study of mental disorders such as *schizophrenia* and *depression*. The term is generally used to refer to the study of mental disorders (such as their *aetiology*). It does not cover the practice of treating mental disorders.

psychopharmacology: the scientific study of the effects that drugs have on behaviour.

psychophysiological disorder (psychosomatic disorder): classified under *DSM-IV-TR* as 'psychological factors affecting medical condition', these are disorders that arise from the interaction of physical and psychological factors. The best known of the psychophysiological disorders are probably ulcers, migraine headaches and coronary heart disease. Ulcers, for example, can be caused by an interaction of physical factors, such as excessive secretions of gastric fluids, and psychological factors, such as environmental *stress*. Coronary heart disease is often a product of the interaction of physical factors such as high cholesterol levels, smoking and lack of exercise, combined with occupational stress and a *type A personality/behaviour* style. The role of environmental stressors in psychophysiological disorders is particularly important. The environment can place demands on us that can be quite intolerable. There are three major types of environmental stressors that might lead to psychophysiological stressors:
- personal stressors – such as bereavement, redundancy or divorce

- background stressors – the ongoing pressures of, for example, living in a high crime area, enduring an unsatisfying job or marriage
- cataclysmic stressors – these are traumatic events or natural disasters that might have long-term effects for a great many of the people affected by them. Many of the people who were present at the Hillsborough football stadium disaster in 1989 experienced psychophysiological disorders for years after the event.

Recent research has established a link between environmental stressors and susceptibility to illness, in particular their effect on the *immune system* (which protects the body from the actions of invading bacteria and viruses). Environmental stressors have also been implicated in 'sudden deaths', where people may die unexpectedly following a major traumatic event. It is not unheard of for people to die at the funerals of close relatives or friends. Treatments for psychophysiological disorders tend to be most effective when they combine psychological interventions (such as *relaxation training* or *cognitive therapies*) with medical treatments for the physical symptoms of the disorder.

psychosexual development: see *Freud, S*

psychosis: a type of psychological condition where an individual experiences a serious loss of contact with reality. Psychotics show impaired or distorted reactions to environmental stimuli, even to the point of withdrawing completely into their own private world where they appear unaffected by the world around them. In some cases the psychotic may experience *hallucinations* or *delusions*.Although psychoses may have a number of quite different origins, including drug abuse, senility or brain injury, the commonest form of this condition is in the form of *schizophrenia*.

psychosocial stages: see *Erikson's 'Eight ages of Man'*

psychosurgery: a surgical intervention which involves the cutting of neural tissue in the brain in order to change a psychological condition. This is a very controversial type of intervention, and one that only tends to be considered when all other methods have failed. There is little evidence that psychosurgical techniques have a significant beneficial effect on behaviour, and they have the very serious drawback that the destruction of neural tissue is irreversible.

psychotherapy: a classification of treatments for mental disorders where the emphasis is on *non*-physical treatments, such as talking about a problem and modifying *behaviour*. Examples of types of treatments that would come under this general therapeutic heading include *cognitive*, *behaviour*, *psychodynamic* and *client-centred therapies*.

psychotropic drugs are drugs that directly affect the brain and alleviate many of the symptoms of mental disorders. Examples of psychotropic drugs would include anti-psychotic drugs which correct confused thinking, *anti-depressants* which elevate the mood of people suffering from depression and anti-anxiety drugs which reduce feelings of tension and anxiety.

puberty refers to the period of development where the person's sex organs become reproductively functional. In girls, this is normally marked by the onset of menstruation. In boys, it is less obvious, but is normally accompanied by the growth of body hair.

punishment: something can be described as a 'punisher' if, when it follows a response, it has the effect of reducing the *probability* of that event occurring again in the future. Punishment is, therefore, the application of a punisher following a response. For example, if a child is scolded every time he feeds his dinner to the dog, eventually he should cease to do so. Punishment may also involve the removal of some desired state, such as not allowing a child out to play because he has been naughty. Punishment appears to be at its most effective when it immediately follows a response. If, after a while, punishment no longer follows that response, the rate of responding tends to return to its pre-punishment levels. The debate over the usefulness, or even desirability of punishment as a technique for changing behaviour has failed to reach any universal conclusions. It does appear that merely punishing undesired responses is not, in itself, a completely effective way of initiating desirable responses. *Reinforcement* of more desirable responses, either with or without the use of punishment, has the effect of increasing the frequency of more desirable responses to take the place of the undesirable ones. Punishment does have some unwanted side-effects, including avoidance and emotional distress as well as modelling appropriate behaviours for the restraint of another's behaviour. It is important to distinguish between punishment (which decreases a response) and negative reinforcement (which increases a response). Both involve exposure to *aversive* stimuli, but in quite different circumstances and with quite different consequences.

A–Z Online

Log on to A–Z Online to search the database of terms, print revision lists and much more. Go to **www.philipallan.co.uk/a-zonline** to get started.

qualitative data: data that cannot be represented in numbers, but rather describes the attributes or properties that an object possesses.

qualitative research has largely developed out of dissatisfaction with the 'number crunching' approach of traditional experimental psychology. It is the belief of those who use qualitative methods that the conclusions that might be drawn from psychological research studies are always context-bound. That is, they cannot really be generalised beyond the context in which they were gathered. Of particular importance in this context-specific view of the research process is the use of language, i.e. 'what does this mean to *you*?'. Qualitative research stresses the interpretation of language (through interviews and diaries, for example) rather than attempting to simply transform it into numbers. In this way the researcher maintains a close focus on what is being said, and the context of expression. *Case studies* may be used so that one person can be studied in depth using this time-consuming approach. Many feminist researchers have turned to qualitative methods because they felt that quantitative methods essentially dehumanise the research process, and that many of the issues that most concern feminist psychology could best be served by the use of qualitative research methods.

quantitative data: data that can be counted or expressed numerically, that can be manipulated and statistically analysed and that can be represented visually in graphs and charts.

quasi-experiment: a type of experiment where the experimenter does not directly influence the allocation of participants to the conditions under study, but makes use of divisions that already exist in terms of the conditions of interest. If a researcher is interested in the effects of two different methods of teaching reading to primary school children, s/he may either directly allocate children to the two different methods (a true experiment) or may choose to study existing groups that are taught in the different methods concerned (a quasi-experiment). Both enable the researcher to make decisions regarding the effectiveness of the different methods, but the conclusions drawn from the quasi-experiment must be more speculative because of the decreased *control* over other possible influences.

questionnaire: see *surveys and interviews*

quota sampling: see *sampling*

racism: a type of categorisation which is applied to individual members of a particular race. Definitions vary in their nature and intent, but broadly fall into two main types:

- socio-economic definitions – racism is regarded as the 'culturally sanctioned, rational responses to struggles over scarce resources'. Because of the social power of many white people over their black counterparts, this is normally of more social benefit to whites than it is to blacks
- ideological definitions – the division of people into 'racial' categories and the accompanying attribution of invariant characteristics to all members of that category (i.e. all white people are …, all Afro–Caribbeans are …, all Asians are …) The application of these invariant characteristics to all members of a particular race is not in itself racist, but it is the implication that these characteristics in some way imply social worth that is so socially divisive.

random allocation refers to the way in which experimenters divide *participants* into the different experimental conditions so that there is no *bias* in the distribution of participant characteristics.

random sample: see *sampling*

randomisation: a way of minimising *order effects*. The order in which participants tackle conditions is determined by random selection.

range: a measure of dispersion within a set of scores. It is calculated by subtracting the lowest score from the highest and gives an idea of the spread of the scores. The range is a rather simple descriptive statistic and is only really of any value when the scores are fairly closely bunched. If they are not, then it gives the impression of a uniformly even distribution of scores across the range when this is not the case.

rank theory of depression: this theory proposes that *depression* is an adaptive response to losing rank in a status conflict and seeing oneself as a loser. According to this theory, such a response is adaptive because it helps the individual adjust to the fact that they have lost and must now occupy a subordinate position in the *dominance hierarchy*. The purpose of the depression is to prevent the loser from risking further injury by continuing the conflict, and to preserve the relative stability of the social group. In defeat, an involuntary process comes into operation which both prevents the individual from continuing to compete, but also reduces his level of aspiration. This involuntary process results in the loss of energy, depressed mood and loss of confidence, which are typical characteristics of depression.

An important contribution of rank theory is that it offers an explanation of how depression might have evolved; it emerged as the yielding component of a status conflict between two individual animals. This yielding following defeat is important for two reasons. First, it ensures that the loser really does yield and does not make any attempt at a comeback, and second, it shows the winner that they really have won so that they break off with no further damage to the loser. In this way social harmony is restored.

When humans interact together the question of dominance may not arise initially. However, after working or living in close proximity for some time, conflict may arise, perhaps over leadership of the group or over access to resources (such as promotion). Over the course of time, the depressive response may also become triggered by other situations that do not necessarily involve the loss of rank, but involve a loss of some other sort (perhaps the ending of a close relationship). In such circumstances a response that has been selected by **natural selection** because it is adaptive is activated in such situations that make it psychologically maladaptive. The growing acceptance of rank theory has led some to suggest a distinction between two different types of depression; defeat depression, caused by a failure to achieve desired goals, and deprivation depression, caused by the loss of **affiliation**.

ranks means putting a list of scores into a rank order from first to last. For example:

Name	Test score	Rank
Bob	16	3
Jane	8	5
George	21	1
Daisy	19	2
Rob	11	4

rapid eye movement (REM) sleep refers to those periods of sleep which are characterised by eye movements and dreaming. In adults, REM sleep alternates with other periods of sleep (non-REM sleep) over a 90-minute cycle. REM periods may last up to an hour, although the average **duration** is around 20 minutes. As the person drifts into sleep, they go through a number of different stages, each deeper than the one before. After about 45 minutes, the pattern reverses, and the person approaches the **EEG** state normally associated with wakefulness. As they reach that level they do not wake, but enter REM sleep. This period is normally accompanied by an increase in heart rate and blood pressure, and faster and more irregular breathing patterns. It is during this state that dreaming is most likely to take place. As the night passes, REM periods become longer and closer together. The exact function of this type of sleep is still not known, although it is generally accepted that whatever the function, it has something to do with dreaming.

rating scale refers to the assessment of a person or behaviour along some scale. For example, schools often give ratings for effort and achievement in particular subjects when writing progress reports:

Science:	Effort	Achievement
Chris	1	A
Sarah	4	D
Pauline	2	B
Tracy	1	B
Adam	2	C

ratio scale: see *levels of measurement*

rational-emotive therapy: a type of *cognitive-behavioural therapy*. This is based on the theory that many prolonged emotional reactions are based on the unrealistic beliefs that people may repeatedly state to themselves. For example, they may convince themselves that they are worthless or that nobody likes them. A common irrational belief is that we must be competent at everything we do. By evaluating everything on this basis, we are frequently met by disappointment and failure. The aim of rational-emotive therapy is to address these irrational beliefs, and encourage the client to think about them in a more rational manner. The main steps of this approach are:

- the client is persuaded to examine their beliefs rationally
- the therapist then guides the client into changing their irrational thinking to more realistic ways of viewing the world
- these new ways of thinking must then be made part of the client's everyday life. Clients are frequently given 'homework' where they must try out these new and constructive thinking processes.

rationalisation: one of the *Freudian defence mechanisms*, it is an attempt to explain our behaviour to ourselves and others in ways that are seen as rational and socially acceptable, rather than irrational and unacceptable. For example, we may hide a rather immature need to eat off a particular plate or drink from a particular cup by explaining that we 'don't want to catch someone else's germs'.

reaction formation: a *Freudian defence mechanism* whereby a person displays a behaviour that is the exact opposite of an impulse that they dare not express or acknowledge. An example would be a man who deals with his homosexual feelings by displaying outward hostility towards homosexuals.

reaction time: the time taken between a stimulus (a light, sound or whatever) and the participant's response to it. There are many different types of reaction time measurements. The commonest are the simple reaction time, where the participant has to make a single response to the appearance of a single stimulus, and the choice reaction time, where there is more than one stimulus and more than one associated response. The reaction time in this instance is the time taken from the onset of a stimulus to the participant choosing and making the appropriate response.

reactivity: changes in the behaviour of people being observed that are due to the fact that they know they are being watched. The term refers to the fact that participants react to the presence of an observer and change their behaviour in one of a number of ways such as showing off, showing evaluation apprehension or trying harder, for example.

realistic anxiety: a state of *anxiety* that occurs whenever we perceive ourselves to be in real danger. In such situations (for example, we are about to be run over by a bus), our ego hustles us into action in order to protect ourselves from being harmed.

realistic conflict theory: if members of one group believe that their interests can only be satisfied at the expense of some other group, then prejudice and hostility may develop between the groups concerned. For example, in a study of 30 tribal groups in East Africa (Brewer and Campbell, 1976), the vast majority rated their own group more favourably than other groups, and displayed more bias and hostility towards other groups that were geographically closer than those further away. This finding is consistent with realistic conflict theory as groups in close proximity with each other would be more likely to be involved in disputes over territory and access to scarce resources such as water and grazing rights.

Realistic conflict theory has a number of advantages over other explanations of prejudice. Particularly important in this respect is its ability to explain the 'ebb and flow' of prejudice over time or different social contexts; this can be attributed to changes in the political or economic relations between the groups concerned. There are, however, a number of problems with the theory which means it is unlikely by itself to provide a complete explanation for all forms of inter-group hostility and prejudice. For example, research has shown that competition does not even appear to be necessary for in-group favouritism to develop. It appears that people will favour their group over another merely as a result of being categorised in that group rather than another (see *minimal groups*).

reality principle: an aspect of *Freudian* theory, whereby we become aware of the demands of the external environment, and act in such a way as to constrain the demands of the *id* within the limitations of the situation. For example, if we are driven towards seeking sexual gratification by our *id* (which operates according to the *pleasure principle*), our *ego* must temper its need for immediate gratification until a more appropriate opportunity arises.

recall: in its simplest definition, the retrieval of information from memory. Being asked to remember the chemical symbol for gold would be an example of recall. (It is Au, by the way.)

recapitulation: the seemingly crazy notion that we recreate the ancestral past of our species (our *phylogeny*) in our own individual development (our *ontogeny*). Thus we are seen as going through a number of different stages of development, both within the womb and after birth, that bear a passing resemblance to our evolutionary past.

recency effect refers to the fact that when a list of words is recalled, those presented at the end of the list are more likely to be recalled than those presented in the middle of the list (see *serial-position curve*). In social psychology, the term is used to refer to the fact that one person's impressions of another will be coloured by their most recent information about them.

receptor: has two major meanings within psychology. A receptor may be a specialised cell (e.g. in the eye) that responds to sensory stimuli, or it may be a site on the surface or interior of a cell that binds with substances such as hormones, neurotransmitters or drugs.

recessive gene: a term used in *genetics* to represent the fact that the genetic information relating to a particular *trait* may be suppressed by the action of a dominant gene and therefore may not appear in the *phenotype.* It is usual to suppose that such traits as represented by recessive genes will only appear in the phenotype if both parents contribute the recessive gene.

recidivism: a term that refers to persistent legal offences. If someone persistently gets into trouble with the police, they might be described as a recidivist.

reciprocal altruism: an arrangement where one organism (the altruist) helps another organism at some cost to itself, and the 'favour' is returned at a later date (i.e. can be reciprocated). Normally the benefits to the recipient are far greater than the costs to the altruist, therefore the arrangement is beneficial to both parties. Reciprocal altruism does require certain ecological conditions to develop, namely:

- low dispersal rate (so that animals have the opportunity for future meetings and thus reciprocity)
- long life span (for the same reasons)
- ability to recognise altruists (to reciprocate) and cheats (to apply sanctions for defection).

Obviously within this arrangement there would be a temptation for some animals to cheat (to accept favours but not to return them). If cheating became common, then eventually every animal would be trying to cheat and therefore reciprocity would break down. The fact that it does not suggests that animals are able to 'police' it. The 'tit for tat' explanation proposes that each animal would simply follow the other animal's last response. So, co-operation would be followed by mutual co-operation (reciprocity) and cheating (defection) would be followed by mutual defection. Tit for tat is effective because it is retaliatory (punishes cheats) and also conciliatory (forgiving). In this way, animals do not miss out on the benefits of future co-operation.

recognition: apart from its obvious meaning, it is generally used in the context of *memory* research. Recognition procedures normally involve presenting *participants* with a number of alternatives of which one is the right solution.

reconstructive memory: an explanation of how fragments of stored information are reassembled during recall, and the gaps are filled in by our expectations and beliefs to produce a coherent narrative. The reconstruction principle states that remembering the past occurs in the context of the present. When we try to recover a memory, we begin with information supplied by the retrieval cue, combine this with what we can recover from the *memory trace*, and then fill in the gaps. We may make inferences based on our expectations, beliefs and prejudices, or we may simply turn to our fund of general knowledge.

recovered memories: a fairly recent phenomenon in which adults recover early *repressed memories*, often of some form of sexual abuse. The event or events which have led to these repressed memories are seen as causing whatever problem (such as *depression* or *eating disorder*) the person is being treated for. Due to a change in climate in which reports of early abuse are more commonly believed than disbelieved, many people have 'discovered' during therapy that they have been abused in childhood and have brought legal action against their abusers. This has caused a storm of protest, both emotional and legal, from those who have been accused of the abuse. Opponents of what is sometimes called 'false memory syndrome' suggest that these memories are not real memories, but have been unintentionally planted by the therapist. They claim that therapists actively look for signs that some sort of abuse has occurred and conduct the therapy accordingly, with implicit or even explicit encouragement of the client to uncover their repressed memories of the 'event'. There are a number of reasons why clients may succumb to the creation of these memories. These include:

- suggestions by an authority figure (the therapist)
- long delays between the event and the memory
- plausibility of the suggestion
- repetitive discussions in therapy of the alleged events.

reductionism: a belief that the subject matter of psychology can more properly be explained within the framework of the physical sciences. Under these terms there is no need to resort to complex psychological or sociological explanations of behaviour when it can be more than adequately explained at a biochemical or physiological level. In the sense that biochemistry and physiology are more established than psychology and sociology, this has an immediate intuitive appeal. Examples of this type of reductionism include biochemical and physiological explanations of **schizophrenia** as well as **sociobiological** explanations of **aggression** and human sexual behaviour. An example of **experimental** reductionism is provided by the laboratory study of what might be considered complex social behaviour. Studies of **bystander behaviour** and **obedience** might give us insights into some of the factors involved in these behaviours but may not tell us much about an individual's behaviour outside of the restricted environment of the laboratory. Arguments in favour of reductionist explanations of behaviour are as follows:

- because of the perceived higher status and respectability of the physical sciences (physiology, chemistry, etc.) reductionist explanations often appear more attractive and 'certain' to the lay person
- reductionist explanations can be more easily verified (or falsified) than more complex physiological explanations, therefore may be seen as more scientifically valid.

Some arguments against reductionist explanations of behaviour are:

- many psychologists believe that the quest for a single causal explanation for human behaviours is futile. To speak of mental disorders only being a case of physiological dysfunction ignores the possible contributions of social and cultural factors
- adopting reductionist explanations of behaviour often distracts attention away from other levels of explanation. To dismiss human aggression as 'an inevitable aspect of human nature' means we are less likely to explore socially constructive ways of reducing it.

reflex has a number of meanings in psychology, ranging from the technical (an **innate** behaviour that occurs without conscious thought or planning and does not vary from situation to situation) to the non-specific (an act which is performed 'on impulse'). In **classical conditioning**, the reflex is unlearned association between certain stimuli and their appropriate responses. Salivation to the presence of food in the mouth is referred to as the salivary reflex.

refractory period refers to the period following an **action potential** when a particular segment of a nerve cell cannot be stimulated.

regression: in **Freudian** theory, this is a **defence mechanism** whereby an individual attempts to avoid current anxiety by retreating to the behaviour patterns of an earlier age.

rehearsal refers to the repetition of something in order to maintain it in the **short-term memory**. We use this technique when trying to remember something temporarily, like a round of drinks or the telephone number of a taxi firm. It is a very shallow **cognitive process**, and the **memory** is usually lost once the rehearsal stops.

reinforcement refers to the process by which a response is strengthened. If an event follows a response and as a direct result of that connection causes the response to be repeated more often in the future, we say that the response has been reinforced. Reinforcement can be **positive** – a response is followed by something the organism wants or needs – or **negative** – a response is followed by the removal of something unpleasant. In both these examples, the reinforcement strengthens (or reinforces) a particular response tendency and makes it more likely to occur in that situation in the future. Neutral stimuli (events that are not particularly significant to the organism) can be paired with *primary reinforcers* (such as food) and thus become *secondary reinforcers*. The best-known example of a secondary reinforcer is, of course, money.

If a secondary reinforcer controls a variety of different responses, it is referred to as a 'generalised secondary reinforcer'. Thus, money can be used to reinforce lots of different responses. Secondary reinforcers may be more effective in the experimental situation because their effectiveness depends only on the perception of receiving them, rather than on the biological feedback from the body that would be necessary for more biologically significant reinforcers such as food. Reinforcers do not have to be things or events, they can also be activities, which are themselves rewarding for the organism performing them. The *Premack principle* states that a more desirable activity (such as watching the telly) can be used to reinforce a less desirable one (such as finishing a lab report). Once a response has been conditioned through reinforcement, it can be maintained through the use of partial (or intermittent) reinforcement (see *schedules of reinforcement*). Organisms that are reinforced only intermittently take longer to stop responding (*extinction*) following termination of the reinforcer than organisms that are used to a full reinforcement schedule. An obvious and familiar example of this is the dreaded fruit machine. Because they pay out only intermittently, we continue to play them for longer than if they continuously paid out then dried up completely.

reinforcer: literally, anything that reinforces. The concept of a reinforcer is by necessity circular. We only know that something is a reinforcer if we know that because of its presence, the future *probability* of a response reappearing is increased. Praising a child for good work may be an obvious example of a reinforcer, but if the praise makes the child embarrassed in front of their friends, they may not try to produce good work in future. In this example, the praise has not reinforced, but it has had the opposite effect, it has acted as a *punishment*.

relative deprivation is the perceived discrepancy between what people feel they have a right to expect (e.g. a good education and comfortable standard of living) and what, given current social conditions, they estimate they are realistically capable of attaining. This is accentuated by comparing our own status to that of others who we feel are in a more favourable social position. Supporters of this theory claim that frustration due to perceived relative deprivation can incite aggression. Relative deprivation will be felt most keenly in modern industrialised societies where the life opportunities and comparative wealth of certain sectors of those societies may be markedly and visibly different to the conditions enjoyed by less privileged groups within these societies.

Relative deprivation can be of two distinct types:
- egoistic relative deprivation: experienced if an individual feels deprived relative to other similar individuals. If our colleagues all seem to be better off than we are, we may well feel deprived in comparison to them
- fraternalistic relative deprivation: experienced when members of one group compare themselves to members of another group. If one group feels that they are worse off than the other, feelings of relative deprivation may arise.

Egoistic and fraternalistic relative deprivation have quite different outcomes, with inter-group conflict being a consequence of the latter.

relaxation training can take many forms but the commonest involves tensing and relaxing each muscle group in turn. The aim of this procedure is to highlight the contrast between the feelings we have when tense and those we have when relaxed. Eventually it becomes possible to relax muscles without having to tense them first. Relaxation training is an important aspect of *systematic desensitisation* where the feelings of relaxation and the anxiety towards the feared object are incompatible so that eventually the client is able to relax in its presence.

reliability: if a finding can be repeated, it is described as being reliable. Within this general meaning of the term, it is also used more specifically within psychological assessment and research:

- for a research finding to be reliable, it must be shown to exist on successive investigations under the same conditions (*replication*)
- for a *psychometric* assessment to be reliable, it should have both internal and external reliability. Answers to a *questionnaire* or inventory may be checked to see if *respondents* answer all questions in the same way or if they contradict themselves. This is a measure of internal reliability. Responses may also be checked over a period of time to see if there is stability of measurement over time. If *respondents* give the same responses or obtain the same scores consistently over time, then the measure is said to have external reliability.

REM sleep: see *rapid eye movement (REM) sleep*

repeated measures design: see *experimental designs*

replication refers to whether a particular finding can be repeated with different people on different occasions. We are more likely to trust a *research* finding if it can be shown not to be a 'one-off'. Replication of a particular finding by other psychologists is vital in establishing a scientific theory.

representative sample: a group of participants that accurately represent the *population* under study. The sample may reflect the gender and age distributions of the underlying population, as well as any other characteristics that, in the opinion of the investigator, might affect the outcome of the study. If the sample taken failed to adequately represent the population, it would be inappropriate to draw any conclusions from the sample that might meaningfully apply to the population (see *sampling*).

repressed memories: see *recovered memories*

repression: a term attributed to *Freudian* theory, it refers to the expulsion from the conscious mind of thoughts and memories that might provoke anxiety (primary repression), or the process by which hidden *id* impulses are blocked from ever reaching consciousness (primal repression). It is important to note that within Freudian theory, repressed memories are not deactivated, but they continue to affect a person's behaviour, although mostly in disguised or symbolic forms (such as dreams or neurotic behaviour).

research: a general term given to any attempt to study a problem through the collection and/or analysis of *data*. Psychologists more usually use the term to refer to an investigative process such as the *experiment* or the *case study*. See also the special use of the term *research* in the 'Examiners' terms' section of this book.

resistance: although the term is also used in its general sense within psychology (resisting some influence or a reluctance to follow orders), it is used in a specialist way within *psychoanalysis*. Here it is taken to represent the process whereby thoughts and memories that are in the *unconscious* mind are prevented from reaching the *conscious* mind. Also within psychoanalysis, the term is used to refer to the way in which the *analysand* offers resistance to the interpretations offered by the *analyst*.

respondent: literally, one who responds, although the term more usually applies to someone who answers questions as part of a *survey* or *interview*.

response: a term with very wide usage but most often used in its technical sense, i.e. the reaction of an organism to, or in the presence of, some *stimulus*.

response bias: a tendency to respond in one particular way to a test item. This may be due to a 'trigger' in the question ('Don't you agree that ...') or a desire to appear to possess socially desirable behaviour ('Do you ever smack your children ...').

restoration accounts of sleep: these include the model put forward by Oswald (1980). He suggests that the high level of brain activity seen in REM sleep suggests a process of brain recovery during this period, while an increase in the body's hormone activities during slow-wave sleep (SWS) reflects restoration and recovery in the rest of the body. Horne (1988) proposes that, in humans, 'core sleep', consisting of about three non-REM/REM cycles, is essential for normal brain functioning, while any additional cycles are not and he refers to them as 'optional sleep'. During core sleep the brain recovers and restores itself after the activities of the day. Both Oswald and Horne agree that REM is any additional cycles are not essential for brain repair and this is supported by the high proportion of REM seen in the new-born baby, where it makes up 50 to 60 per cent of sleep time. The difference between the two approaches lies in the proposed functions of slow-wave sleep. As total sleep deprivation produces few obvious effects on the body, it is possible that body restoration is not the purpose of sleep. Horne suggests that this may well occur during periods of relaxed wakefulness, leaving core sleep to provide for the brain.

restorative justice: encourages those who have caused harm to acknowledge the impact of what they have done and gives them the opportunity to make reparation to the victims of their wrongdoing. For example, criminals and their victims may be brought together to consider what happened and what can be done to put it right.

restricted code: a type of speech code formulated by Bernstein (1962) and characterised by short, direct and context-dependent speech patterns (for example, 'Do as I tell you' or 'Get off it'). These are fairly simple phrases which are readily understood in context, but less well understood out of context. For example, 'Get off it' presumably makes sense to the child to which it is directed, but less sense to somebody else. Restricted code may be used as a shorter and more rapid form of communication between peers, and may rely heavily on shared meanings shown by the use of incomplete sentences. Married couples may frequently use the restricted code when conversing with each other because their shared experiences and understanding mean that it is unnecessary to spell out their meanings and intentions in great detail. By contrast, the *elaborated code* uses less direct and colloquial speech and is not context-specific. Sentences are more complex and contain less dependence on the context, so that the content can be more easily understood by another listener. Bernstein believed that the use of restricted code language disadvantaged those children who relied totally on it. Formal education, he believed, is conducted in the elaborated code, therefore children who could match their own language code with that of the educational system were at an advantage. Bernstein does not dismiss restricted code as 'inferior', but describes it as having 'directness and vitality'.

reticular formation: a complex network of *neurons* and cell nuclei which occupies the central part of the brain stem. Often referred to as the reticular activating system because of the part that it plays in *arousal.* Recent research suggests that the reticular formation has an important influence on sleep, attention, movement and various cardiac, respiratory and circulatory reflexes.

retina: the light-sensitive part of the eye. The retina contains the visual receptors, *rods* and *cones*, and is involved with the initial processing of visual information before it is passed via the optic nerve to the brain.

retrieval: the recall of information from long-term memory. Retrieval of information is dependent on three factors:
- context-dependency – recall depends on replicating the context in which the memory was originally encoded
- state-dependency – recall is better when the person is in the same physical or psychological state as when he/she first learned the information
- cue-dependency – recall is improved by the presence of cues or associations that relate to the memory.

retrieval failure: proposes that forgetting from long-term memory is not because the material is lost but because it is difficult or impossible to access (see *retrieval*).

retroactive interference (inhibition): an explanation of forgetting based on the fact that over time, new memories interfere with existing ones. This interference effect is increased if there is considerable similarity between the new memory and the existing one. Research into this type of forgetting is relatively uncommon nowadays, although there is some research interest in the area of *eyewitness testimony*, which has established that memories can be distorted by subsequent questioning about the event.

retrograde amnesia: the inability to *recall* events leading up to whatever caused the amnesia. Horse riders who have fallen heavily often report being unable to remember the events shortly before the fall.

retrospective study: literally a 'working backwards' in order to establish what, in a person's previous experience, may have contributed to their present condition. John *Bowlby's* study of juvenile delinquents established that many had experienced prolonged separation from their mothers in early childhood. Retrospective studies do suffer from a number of limitations, such as distorted memories and an inability to accurately separate out one causal event from the multitude of other factors that might have contributed to the condition observed.

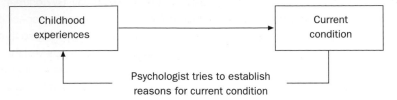

A retrospective study – the research process is to establish what possible forces in earlier experience might have been responsible for the current condition

reversibility: a logical skill whereby a child can mentally go through a series of steps and reverse these steps and arrive back at the original situation. For example, in *conservation* of volume tests, the pre-logical child may state that the volume of a liquid has changed when it is poured into a different-shaped container. The operational child, on the other hand, is able to mentally carry out the transformation then mentally reverse it, correctly stating that the volume cannot change when it is physically transformed.

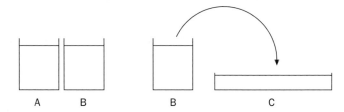

Conservation of volume: The liquid from container A is poured into container B, but the operational child correctly reasons that the process can be reversed, in which case the volume must stay the same

reward: any event which is pleasurable or satisfying to the organism receiving it (for example, food to a hungry animal, social approval to a child). The term is often used synonymously with the term *reinforcement* to indicate that rewards tend to make powerful *reinforcers*. When this is the case, the terms tend to be confused, together with the assumption that something is only a reward for the organism if by applying it after the organism has responded in some way, it has the effect of increasing the future *probability* of that response occurring.

reward/need satisfaction: a theory of the formation of relationships that explains attraction in terms of the rewards that people provide or the needs that they satisfy. We enter into relationships because the presence of some individuals is directly associated with reinforcement (operant conditioning), which makes them more attractive to us. Rewarding stimuli produce positive feelings in us, and punishing stimuli produce negative feelings. The sorts of thing we find rewarding tend to reflect our unmet needs (the need for company, financial security or an attractive partner). If each partner meets the other person's needs then mutual attraction occurs. As well as liking people with whom we share a pleasant experience, we also like people who are associated with pleasant events (classical conditioning). The balance of positive and negative feelings is important in relationship formation. Relationships where the positive feelings outweigh the negative feelings are more likely to develop and succeed, whereas relationships where the negative feelings outweigh the positive are likely to fail.

right to withdraw: under the *BPS code of ethics*, researchers are obliged to inform research participants that they have the right to withdraw at any time and that any data by which they might be personally identified be destroyed. This right to withdraw at any time is not affected by the receipt or offer of any financial or other inducements for participation.

risky shift refers to the finding that people tend to make riskier decisions when working as members of a group than they would when making the same decisions as individuals. Some studies, however, have shown that groups may also show a shift to caution. On average, groups will polarise (show accentuated judgements) toward the attitudes held before the group decision is reached. Thus, if group members, on average, favoured a risky decision prior to the group discussion, then the overall group decision will be a more pronounced shift in the direction of increased risk. Alternatively if, on average, group members had favoured a more cautious decision prior to discussion, then the overall group decision would tend to favour a move to an even more cautious position. In this way, groups tend to polarise the views and attitudes of their members.

ritalin: a drug whose action resembles that of the amphetamines. It has been controversially used in the treatment of children suffering from *attention-deficit (hyperactivity) disorder (ADHD)*.

rites of passage: a term normally used to represent the ritual by which children pass into adulthood. In some societies, this takes the form of a formalised ceremony. In Westernised societies, the term is used in a far more general sense to refer to the period of *moratorium* which is characteristic of *adolescence*.

ritualisation: as used in animal behaviour, this term refers to the gradual modification and exaggeration of some behaviour into a stereotypical display that serves some clear communicative function. This communicative function becomes more obvious and less ambiguous over generations. An example of a ritualised display can be seen in the courtship displays of many birds. These have often started their life with quite different functions (such as feeding or preening behaviours) but have become exaggerated into their present state over many generations and now serve as a courtship display.

Robbers Cave: a famous social psychological experiment carried out in 1954 by Sherif and Sherif. A group of 22 twelve-year-old boys came to the Robbers Cave State Park for summer camp. The researchers split the boys into two groups of 11 boys each, breaking up existing friendships wherever they could. The two groups chose names for themselves, the 'Rattlers' and the 'Eagles'. Hostility between the two groups was quick to develop, escalating to a point where the activities designed to produce tension between the groups could not be continued safely. To reduce hostility, the researchers introduced tasks that required cooperation between the groups. These including solving a water shortage problem and mending a broken-down camp truck. These collaborations meant that the hostility between the two groups gradually subsided, and at the end of the experiment the two groups had successfully integrated into one larger group (see *realistic conflict theory*).

robustness: a quality attributed to statistical tests that can still function effectively in the calculation of *probability* despite the fact that assumptions surrounding their use have been compromised.

rods (and cones): a type of receptor cell found in the *retina* of the eye. Rods are more active under dim light conditions, whereas cones are more active in good light conditions. Species that are more active at night tend to only have rods, whereas those that are active only during the day lack rods and have only cones. Species that are active both day and night (such as humans) have both rods and cones. Individuals who lack rods (or have rods that don't function) suffer from night blindness, and cannot see properly in dim light.

Rogers, Carl (1902–1987) is best known for his views about the therapeutic relationship. These views revolutionised the course of therapy. He took the, then, radical view that it might be more beneficial for the client to lead the therapy sessions rather than the therapist; as he says, 'the client knows what hurts, what directions to go, what problems are crucial, what experiences have been buried' (Rogers, 1961). Rogers developed 'client-centred' (later re-named 'person-centred') therapy, which was a non-directive therapy, allowing clients to deal with what they considered important, at their own pace. This method involves removing obstacles so the client can move forward, freeing him or her for normal growth and development. By his use of non-directive techniques, Rogers assisted people in taking responsibility for themselves. He believed that the experience of being understood and valued gives us the freedom to grow, while pathology generally arises from attempting to earn others' positive regard rather than following an 'inner compass'. Rogers recorded his therapeutic sessions, analysed transcripts of them and examined factors related to the outcome of therapy. He was the first person to record and publish complete cases of psychotherapy.

Rogers' view of education saw schools as generally rigid, bureaucratic institutions which are resistant to change. Applied to education, his approach becomes 'student-centred learning' in which children are trusted to participate in developing and to take charge of their own learning agendas. His attitude to examinations in particular would, no doubt, find a most receptive audience in many students:

> 'I believe that the testing of the student's achievements in order to see if he meets some criterion held by the teacher, is directly contrary to the implications of therapy for significant learning.'

role: the pattern of behavioural rights and obligations that accompanies a particular social position and which the person is expected to learn and perform. For example, a person may have a role as teacher, father, friend or confidant. Each of these roles carries with it expectations of how it should be most appropriately carried out. Sometimes these may be prescribed within a relationship (e.g. doctor/patient; teacher/child), sometimes they may be determined only after negotiation between the parties concerned (e.g. leaders/followers; husband/wife).

role conflict: a situation where an individual occupies two *roles* at the same time, and the expectations of those roles are incompatible. For example, in the American Psychological Association's code of *ethics*, psychological therapists are forbidden to enter into dual relationships with their clients (become both professionally and emotionally involved with them). The expectations associated with these two roles are seen as being incompatible.

romantic love: a type of personal commitment characterised by intense attraction and emotions. This is normally contrasted with companionate love, which is a type of affection we feel for those with whom our lives are deeply intertwined. Romantic love may be a more fleeting state, whereas companionate love may develop out of an earlier phase of romantic love and tends to be longer lasting.

Romeo and Juliet effect refers to the increased attraction that two people feel for each other when they are forbidden from seeing each other by parents or others acting in a parental role.

Rorschach inkblot test: a type of *projective test* consisting of ten bilaterally symmetrical inkblots. These are presented to the participant who is asked to state what he or she sees. The responses that the participants give are indicative of various characteristics such as emotional responsiveness and personality. Part of the fascination with the Rorschach test is that for many, it symbolises what psychology is all about – the ability of trained professionals to tell us something about ourselves that we would never otherwise have been able to work out for ourselves.

r-strategy: a term from evolutionary biology that describes animals that have many offspring but invest little or no parental care in them. As a result of this strategy, the time period between one set of offspring and the next can be very short, thus maximising the breeding success of the animal. This strategy is normally contrasted with the *K-strategy*.

Rubin's vase: an ambiguous figure that demonstrates our ability to switch between figure and background, giving two separate interpretations of these figures as either two faces or a single vase.

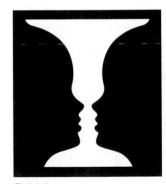

Rubin's vase

231

SAD: see *seasonal affective disorder (SAD)*

Sally-Anne test: a false-belief test used to test for the development of ***theory of mind*** in children. A child is shown a scene with two dolls (Sally and Anne), a basket and a box. Sally places a marble in her basket and leaves the room. While she is out of the room, the second doll, Anne, removes the marble from Sally's basket and puts it in the box. The child watches all this taking place and is then asked the question 'where will Sally look for the marble when she returns?'. A child who possesses a theory of mind will say that Sally will look in the basket because that is where she put the marble. This child realises that Sally has a false belief (i.e. the marble is not really there) but that her belief is true as far as she is concerned (i.e. she has no knowledge of its having been moved). Children with no theory of mind will say that Sally will look in the box for the marble because they will not understand that Sally's belief about the whereabouts of the marble would be any different from their own.

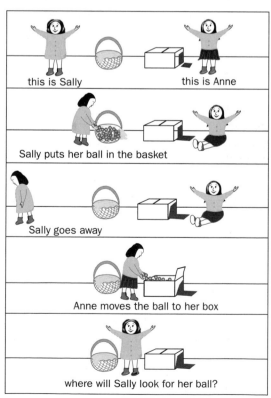

this is Sally   this is Anne

Sally puts her ball in the basket

Sally goes away

Anne moves the ball to her box

where will Sally look for her ball?

The Sally-Anne test (source: www.asperger-advice.com/sally-and-anne.html)

sample: a group of people that take part in a research investigation and are presumed to be representative of the *population* from which they have been drawn. Because of the constraints of time, money and practicality, psychologists can hardly ever study the whole population, and therefore are forced to sample from it using one of the *sampling* methods.

sampling refers to the process by which research psychologists attempt to select a representative group from the *population* under study. As an entire population tends to be too large to work with, a smaller group of participants must act as a representative sample. In an attempt to select a representative sample and thus avoid sampling bias (the over-representation of one category of participant in the sample), psychologists utilise a variety of sampling methods, such as:

1. Random sample – each member of the population under study stands the same chance of being selected.
2. Stratified sample – the composition of the sample reflects the composition of the population, e.g. 30 per cent males, 70 per cent females in the population determines that the sample shall contain a selection of 70 per cent females, 30 per cent males.
3. Quota sample – the researcher selects a quota of people roughly in proportion to their occurrence in the population (e.g. a quota of different age groups).
4. Opportunity sample – roughly a case of selecting whoever is available at the time at that location.

satiation: in its more common usage, this refers to the state in which an organism is no longer motivated by its need for something because the need has been satisfied. A hungry rat is motivated to respond in any way that brings the reward of food, but when it is no longer hungry, it will not respond with the same urgency, if at all.

scaffolding refers to the way in which adults may begin an instructional interaction by using direct instruction, but gradually withdraw their involvement in recognition of the child's developing mastery of the task. This term, coined by Lev *Vygotsky* in his developmental theory, emphasises the social context of children's learning.

scanning techniques: refer to non-invasive techniques used for gaining detailed cross-sectional or three-dimensional images of the brain. These include CT (*computed tomography (CT)*), MRI (*magnetic resonance imaging (MRI)*) and PET (*positron emission tomography (PET)*).

scapegoat theory: an explanation of *discrimination* based on the idea of *frustration-aggression theory.* It proposes that when we strive for personal goals (such as becoming rich or getting a new job), this causes the arousal of psychic (mental) energy. If we are frustrated from reaching this goal, the psychic energy remains activated and we are in a state of disequilibrium that can only be changed through aggression. As the legitimate targets of our aggression are normally unavailable (our teachers, the gas board, etc.), we *displace* all the frustration-produced aggression onto a convenient alternative. This can be a person, a group of people, an animal or even an inanimate object. History has conveniently provided scapegoats so that in times of economic frustration, aggression in the form of active discrimination can be directed against what are seen as 'legitimate' targets. Anti-Semitism in 1930s Germany can be seen as an example of scapegoating, as Jews were blamed for the decline of the German economy. In the deep south of America, Negroes were used as scapegoats for the frustration of a failed cotton crop. The worse the crop, the more Negroes were lynched.

S

scattergram: a graphical representation of the *correlation* between two sets of measurements (for example, between IQ and total number of A level points achieved). The more the points on the scattergram are clustered around some definite pattern, the stronger is the correlation. In a linear correlation (where the points go in only one direction), a direction of bottom left to top right represents a positive correlation, whilst a direction of top left to bottom right indicates a negative correlation.

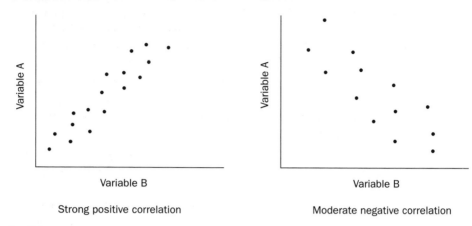

| Strong positive correlation | Moderate negative correlation |

Scattergrams

schedules of reinforcement: these are different ways of delivering a *reinforcer* with the aim of maintaining a person's present rate of response. According to **operant conditioning** theory, individuals who acquire a new behaviour might typically receive a reinforcer every time they perform the right response (continuous reinforcement). This ensures rapid acquisition of the behaviour being reinforced. Once the rate of response reaches a certain level, it is more appropriate to switch to a schedule that presents the reinforcer only some of the time. This is more like the way in which reinforcers might be available in real life, and is likely to maintain the response rate for a much longer period. If we played the National Lottery every week and won every time, we would, no doubt, become lottery addicts and would spend much of our time filling out lottery tickets. If our success suddenly ended and continued to desert us for a few more weeks, we would probably stop buying tickets. If, however, success was occasional, our interest would be maintained over a much longer period. In this way, full reinforcement is most influential in the acquisition stage of a response, partial reinforcement in the maintenance stage.

Reinforcement schedule	Example
Full (continuous)	Every example of the desired response is reinforced
Fixed interval	A reinforcer is delivered at fixed time intervals provided a response occurs during that time
Variable interval	A reinforcer is given, on average every so many seconds, but the interval is varied so that it is not predictable.
Fixed ratio	A reinforcer is given every so many responses, regardless of time intervals.
Variable ratio	A reinforcer is given on average every so many responses, but the actual number varies for each presentation of the reinforcer.

schema: this has two major meanings in psychology:

- in social psychology, it refers to a store of information about previous experiences that is used to evaluate future experiences and make decisions about them. For example, you are asked to attend an all-night party at a friend's house. Your previous experience of all-night parties (sleeping on the floor, long walks home and hangovers) convinces you they are to be avoided. The schema both organises our experience of events, and also influences the way we perceive future events of the same type
- in *Piagetian* theory, a schema is an organised structure of knowledge or abilities that change with age or experience. We have physical schema (such as bike-riding schema) and mental schema (such as multiplication and division schema).

schizoid is often used to describe *schizophrenia*-like symptoms, yet without a diagnosis of schizophrenia being made. More accurately, it is a shortened form of the schizoid personality disorder, which is characterised by emotional coldness and isolation, and an inability to form close relationships with others.

schizophrenia: a serious mental disorder that is characterised by severe disruptions in psychological functioning. Schizophrenics may experience a variety of disturbing and frightening symptoms such as:

- thought disturbances – schizophrenia produces a kind of reasoning that appears obscure and incoherent to others. Schizophrenics may also suffer from *delusions*, unwarranted interpretations of events that have no basis in reality
- perceptual disturbances – a tendency to perceive the world around them differently to others, including the experience of *hallucinations* and an inability to recognise the emotional states of others
- emotional disturbances – some schizophrenics display no emotions at all, others may display inappropriate emotional reactions
- motor disturbances – meaning that sufferers may display unusual physical actions such as giggling and laughing, or standing immobile for hours at a time
- disturbances in social functioning – an inability to maintain social relationships with others, together with poor social skills, means that schizophrenics tend to lead a poor-quality life.

Schizophrenics can be divided into those with negative symptoms, and those with positive symptoms. Positive symptoms refer to the presence of something that is normally absent (such as hallucinations). Negative symptoms refer to the absence of something that is normally present (these include apathy, absence of emotion, etc.). The complex origins of schizophrenia create a good deal of argument among *psychiatrists* and psychologists. Some of the main explanations of causes are as follows:

- genetic explanations emphasise the inheritance of a genetic vulnerability toward schizophrenia for certain individuals. Whether this vulnerability develops into the disorder depends on whether the home environment is supportive or stressful (the *diathesis-stress paradigm*)
- biochemical explanations emphasise the role of the *neurotransmitter* dopamine in the onset of the disorder (see *dopamine hypothesis*)
- increasing medical evidence suggests that schizophrenia may be related to damage to specific areas of the brain. In particular, schizophrenics have enlarged brain ventricles (cavities within the brain), which may be due to damage in other areas of the brain around them.

The major treatments for schizophrenia are the **anti-psychotic drugs** that eliminate many of the symptoms of schizophrenia (but are ineffective in around 30–40 per cent of schizophrenics), and **psychotherapies** such as **insight** therapy and **family therapy**. A controversy exists over whether schizophrenics should be treated within institutions or within the community. Despite the promise of community care, many schizophrenics go through cycles of hospital admission, discharge into the community and then readmission back into hospital (the 'revolving door syndrome'). A lack of adequate support within the community may also result in schizophrenics experiencing long bouts of unemployment and homelessness.

schizophrenia in remission: a diagnostic label that refers to the fact that a client has had periods of schizophrenia, but at the time the diagnosis was made, was free of schizophrenic symptoms. There is considerable disagreement among mental health professionals concerning how long a client has to remain free of all schizophrenic symptoms before this diagnostic label is finally dropped.

schizophrenogenic family: a term given to a family that has poor communication patterns and high levels of conflict among its members. The idea of a schizophrenogenic family has been implicated with the development of **schizophrenia**, particularly in adolescents, who seem particularly vulnerable to the stress that develops in such family atmospheres.

science, psychology as: the belief that the behaviour of human beings is similar in all relevant aspects to the subject matter of other sciences. Human behaviour is therefore seen as being no different from other naturally occurring phenomena in that the following assumptions apply:

- determinism – all behaviour is seen as being caused (see **free will vs determinism**)
- predictability – if behaviour is determined, then it should be possible to predict future events
- **control** – if behaviour is predictable, then it raises the possibility that it might be controlled.

Problems with the view of psychology as science:

- systematicity – science assumes a coherent body of knowledge. This is fine in principle, but the complexity of the subject matter, together with the difficulties of investigating it, present problems for psychology in this respect
- reflexivity – both observer and observed are members of the same species, therefore it is difficult to maintain an objective, distanced perspective on the subject matter
- generality – scientific laws are seen as being generalisable across space and time, whereas psychological explanations are often restricted to specific times and places. For example, many of the findings from research into **conformity** and **obedience** in the United States in the 1950s and early 1960s have been attributed to the particular social climate of the US at that time
- testability – much of the subject matter of psychology is unobservable, therefore cannot be accurately measured. It is probably true to say that of all the sciences, psychology is the most inferential. That is, there is a far bigger gap between the actual data obtained in research investigations and the explanations that are put forward to explain it. A case in point would be **Freud's** theory of psychosexual development, where many of the central ideas are neither testable nor falsifiable.

scientific fraud: the violation of the codes of scholarly conduct in professional scientific research. The most famous example of fraud in psychology is probably the case of educational psychologist Sir Cyril Burt. At the time of his death in 1971, Cyril Burt was an extremely influential member of his profession. Within months however, psychologist Leon Kamin reported on a number of flaws in Burt's IQ research involving monozygotic twins who were reared apart. Kamin suspected the data might be fraudulent, but simply concluded that they were of little scientific merit. The first public accusation of fraud against Burt came in 1976 from Oliver Gillie, medical correspondent of the *Sunday Times*. Gillie set out to find two of Burt's named research assistants, Margaret Howard and Jane Conway. Despite a thorough search, he was unable to locate either, and concluded that they were fictitious names that Burt had credited with his own work. Subsequent critics went further, accusing Burt of making up most of, if not all, his data to further the hereditarian position in the IQ debate.

The field of anomalistic psychology has also had its fair share of accusations of scientific fraud. Paranormal researcher J. B. Rhine reported that at least 12 of the researchers in his lab had behaved dishonestly in seeking to gain significant results, including his personal assistant Walter Levy, who had tampered with the equipment he was using to record ESP in rats.

scientific method refers to the use of investigative methods that are objective, systematic and replicable. It is objective in that researchers do not let preconceived ideas or biases influence the collection of their data, and systematic in that **observations** or experiments are carried out in an orderly way. Measurement and recording of **empirical** data are carried out accurately and with due consideration for the possible influence of other factors on the results obtained.

It is replicable in that all observations can be repeated by other researchers with the same results. If results are not replicable, then they are not reliable and cannot be accepted as being universally true. The research process is not restricted to empirical observation, but also necessitates the use of reason to explain the results of these observations. The development of scientific **theories** and the constant testing and refining of these theories through further observation completes the scientific cycle.

PROS: • because of its reliance on objective and systematic methods of observation, knowledge acquired is more than just the passive acceptance of facts
• if scientific theories no longer fit the facts, they can be refined or abandoned. This means that scientific knowledge is self-corrective
• because scientific methods rely on a belief in determinism, they are able to establish the causes of behaviour through the use of methods that are both empirical and replicable.

CONS: • by concentrating on objectivity and **control** in observations, scientific psychologists create contrived situations that tell us little about the way people act in more natural environments
• the cause and effect view of behaviour which is explored using scientific methods is not universally shared by all psychologists. If human behaviour is not subject to the laws and regularities implied by scientific method, then predictions become impossible and these methods inappropriate.

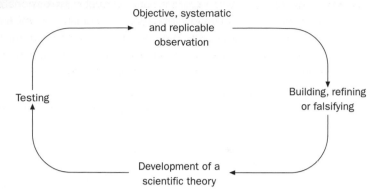

The scientific cycle

script: an internalised representation or 'story' about what typically happens in a specified situation. Scripts are a type of ***reconstructive memory*** where the child fuses together many different instances of the same sequence of events and thus develops a generalised script of what generally happens, and consequently, what he or she might expect to happen in future. If we were to ask a young child what happens when we go to church, he might tell us: 'We go in, sit down, then we stand up and listen to a man talking, then we say a prayer and go home'. At first scripts are restricted to a few acts, but become more elaborate with age. Children rely on scripts to organise and interpret everyday life, and will often use them as a frame of reference to aid in the understanding of stories that other people tell to them. They have special significance when children are asked to testify as witnesses (see ***children as witnesses***).

seasonal affective disorder (SAD) is a type of mood disorder in which mood episodes are related to changes in the seasons. For people who suffer from SAD, the winter may trigger the onset of a severe depression, together with a general slowing down, tendency to sleep a lot, and overeating. When summer comes, SAD sufferers become elated, more active, and thinner. Although the exact mechanisms of SAD are still uncertain, it appears to be linked to the secretion of melatonin, a hormone that has an important role in the regulation of sleep. Light suppresses melatonin secretion whereas darkness stimulates it. SAD sufferers are thought to have abnormally high thresholds for melatonin suppression, therefore need much higher levels of light to ward off the depressive effects of their melatonin.

second messengers are molecules created in the post-synaptic cell by the action of ***neurotransmitters*** binding to receptor molecules. This creates a chemical reaction and produces the second messengers which initiate an ***action potential*** in the post-synaptic cell. The action of second messengers is short lived as they are rapidly broken down by enzymes in the cytoplasm of the post-synaptic cell.

secondary memory: another term for ***long-term memory***

secondary process: a ***psychoanalytic*** term used to describe the mental functioning that takes place in the ***conscious*** mind, and which is rational, logical and oriented toward reality. This is normally contrasted with primary process functioning which tends to be irrational, impulsive and linked more to the pursuit of pleasure and the avoidance of pain. The former is associated with ***ego*** functioning, the latter with ***id*** functioning.

secondary reinforcement: something that does not itself have the power to *reinforce* behaviour, but acquires that power through its association with something else. Money is an obvious secondary reinforcer because through money, we can obtain many of the things we want or need. We learn very early on in our development that we can obtain these things with money so it becomes an acquired or 'secondary' reinforcer.

secondary sexual characteristics: genetically determined characteristics that are not concerned with sexual reproduction, but are nonetheless different between the sexes, such as body hair or voice pitch.

secure attachment: a particular type of attachment bond that may be established between any two individuals (usually the mother and infant). The fundamental assumption in attachment research on human infants is that consistently sensitive responding by the parent to the infant's needs results in an infant who demonstrates secure attachment, while lack of such sensitive responding results in *insecure attachment*. Secure attachment is related to healthy subsequent cognitive and emotional development.

sedative: a class of drugs that produce drowsiness and diminished sensori-motor skills by depressing *central nervous system (CNS)* functioning. There is a gradual build-up of tolerance to these drugs, so that larger doses are needed to produce the same effect, and this may lead to drug dependence.

selective attention: see *attention*

selective breeding: a technique whereby animals can be mated in order to produce offspring with specific characteristics.

selective optimisation: the suggestion that older people seek to maintain their intellectual abilities by concentrating their resources on things they can still do well.

self: a sense of personal identity and an experience of a person's uniqueness. The word is used in many different ways in psychology, including:
- an inner force that controls and directs the person
- the totality of all personal experience (synonymous with 'individual' or 'person')
- as personal awareness or *consciousness*
- as an end point of personal development (see *self-actualisation*).

The term *self* is often used as a prefix to a number of other psychological terms (e.g. *self-esteem, self-fulfilling prophecy*). In these cases, its meaning is given subtle changes by the term to which it is attached.

self-actualisation: a term that has two meanings. Firstly, it may be used in a motivational sense, i.e. the motive to realise one's full potential. Secondly, in the *personality* theory of Abraham *Maslow*, it is the final level of development. When a person has satisfied all the more basic needs such as the physiological and safety needs, they may move to higher levels of functioning. These are characterised by a rising above the pressures of our environment, rather than simply coping with them. Self-actualised people have an acceptance of who they are despite their faults and limitations, and experience a drive to be creative in all aspects of their lives.

self-awareness: is the state of being, or ability to be, consciously aware of oneself. There is considerable debate over which species have this capacity. One line of argument is that it is restricted to the humans and other great apes.

self-concept: literally, the way we view ourselves. We may experience a sense of individuality (being different from others) as well as a sense of inter-dependence (belonging and association with others). Different **cultures** tend to emphasise the importance of either individuality or inter-dependence within the individual. **Individualist** cultures such as the UK, USA and Australia stress individualism in their socialisation, whereas more **collectivist** cultures such as China and Japan foster a sense of inter-dependence in their members. The self-concept has two related aspects, **self-understanding** and **self-esteem**.

self-disclosure: the tendency to disclose increasingly intimate information about ourselves as we get to know someone better. At the beginning of a relationship, self-disclosure tends to be about superficial details such as hobbies or taste in music. As the relationship becomes more intimate, so does the nature of the disclosure, and we disclose details of our fears, things that are important to us, as well as details of our sexual preferences. Self-disclosure is more likely when we trust someone else not to laugh at our revelations, or to reject us because of them. We must also trust the other person not to pass on these details to a third party. Mutual self-disclosure is seen as an important ingredient in **interpersonal attraction**.

self-efficacy is a term referring to the belief that we can perform adequately in a given situation. When applied to health, self-efficacy beliefs are important in shaping unhealthy behaviours into more healthy ones. For example we may choose not to diet because we believe that for us, dieting will not work or we will not be able to keep to the strict regime. Self-efficacy may also be based on our observations of others' performance ('If she couldn't do it, what hope do I have?') or on our observations of our own emotional states ('I wouldn't be very good company, I'm a bit down at the moment').

self-esteem: the value we place upon ourselves. As children explore their abilities they may come to think highly or not so highly of themselves depending on their success and the success of others around them. In early childhood children tend to judge themselves in four main areas:

- cognitive competence – ability to solve problems and achieve
- social competence – ability to get along with others
- physical competence – what they can and can't do: run, play football, etc.
- behavioural conduct – are they a 'good' boy or girl?

With age, these domains of self-esteem become more differentiated as we form judgements of our attractiveness to the opposite sex, our humour, our adequacy as a partner and so on. Some views of the development of self-esteem see it as being a product of perceptions of our competencies in all these different areas. As some of these are more important than others (it may not bother us, for example, that we judge ourself as unattractive or of low athletic ability), we tend to weight the importance of each judgement rather than just adding them all together. Alternative views of self-esteem development believe that it is the judgements of others that become the basis for our own self-evaluation.

self-fulfilling prophecy: a belief that things often turn out just as we predicted because people act in such a way as to bring about our prophecy. Thus, informing a student that they will fail an examination may set up processes within the student such that they believe that failure is inevitable, work less hard and eventually fail, thus fulfilling the original prophecy.

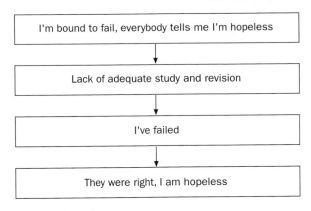

The self-fulfilling prophecy in action

self-perception theory suggests that our attitudes and other self-characterisations are shaped by our observations of our own behaviour. Thus, if we find ourselves stopping to tickle every stray cat we come across, we might see ourselves as a pet lover. Similarly, if we never seem to have much success with the opposite sex, we perceive ourselves as unattractive to others.

self-recognition (animal behaviour): the ability for an animal to recognise that a reflection (for example, in a mirror) is, in fact, an image of itself. With human beings, some experience with a mirror is necessary before they realise that they are looking at an image of themselves. This appears to also be the case with chimpanzees who, after a few days of getting used to a mirror will use it for the same sort of things as do young children (e.g. inspecting their bottoms, removing mucous from their noses etc.)! There are also reports of similar self-recognition behaviour with orang-utans, dolphins and gorillas. Other species, such as monkeys and gibbons, fail to recognise themselves in a mirror, and domestic cats, dogs and parrots all react to their image as if it were another animal.

The reasons why some species appear able to recognise themselves in mirrors and others not remains a mystery. One possible reason is that self-recognition is confined to those species who can use the information that is provided by mirrors. This is unlikely given that some species that cannot self-recognise in mirrors are still able to use mirrors to help them find things that are otherwise hidden. Other explanations revolve around the belief that self-recognition is confined to species that have self-awareness. This capacity for self-awareness is assumed to be confined to the great apes (chimpanzees, orang-utans, gorillas and humans). However, although plausible, the suggestion that a chimpanzee is self-aware, yet a monkey is not, assumes characteristics of the mental states of individual species that are beyond the bounds of scientific enquiry.

self-serving attributional bias: a tendency to attribute successful outcomes to *dispositional* factors and unsuccessful outcomes to *situational* factors. If we do well in something, we may well feel this success is due to our own ability or effort. If we do badly, we may externalise the blame onto some other factor (like bad luck or dodgy textbooks). There are a number of reasons why the self-serving bias might occur:

- cognitive explanations stress the fact that if we expect to succeed, we are more likely to relate success to our own efforts and externalise failure as being due to some other cause

- motivational explanations stress the need to feel good about ourselves and preserve a positive **self-esteem.** The self-serving bias allows us to preserve our sometimes fragile sense of self-worth
- impression-management explanations see the self-serving bias operating because of our need to project an impression of competence and hard work. Failure may threaten this preferred image, therefore is externalised.

Classic examples of the self-serving bias can be found every Monday in the sports pages of the national newspapers. Football teams frequently lose because of poor refereeing, indifferent support or the state of the pitch, but rarely because they weren't good enough or didn't try hard enough!

selfish gene theory: an important *sociobiological* theory that is normally associated with the biologist Richard Dawkins, it proposes that any behaviour of an organism is specifically 'designed' to maximise the survival of its *genes*. A consequence of this idea of the 'selfish gene' is that survival of an individual organism may be of secondary importance to the survival of its genes. Thus, many examples of self-endangerment or of apparent *altruism* can be more easily understood by taking a 'genes eye view' and estimating the benefits of such behaviour to the genes of an individual animal. Many such actions often facilitate the survival of a particular gene line because they enable other organisms that share a proportion of the altruist genes to survive as a direct result of its actions (see *kin selection*).

semantic differential: sometimes referred to as Osgood's semantic differential, after Charles Osgood who developed it, this is a technique used to evaluate the meaning of particular concepts to the participants taking part. Participants rate the meaning of each of the words along a number of polar dimensions such as weak–strong, dirty–clean, etc. In this way people's attitudes to specific objects can be assessed on different levels (such as positive or negative).

semantic memory: see *episodic memory*

senescence: the period of old age. As with *adolescence*, there is no one agreed age period that can be classified as senescence, but rather the term is used in a general way to describe those years when the developmental tasks of adulthood give way to a different set of tasks and priorities in old age. The term is preferred to the equivalent term *senility* because of the (false) belief that it is accompanied by an inevitable deterioration in all levels of functioning.

senile dementia: see *dementia*

senility: see *senescence*

sensation: refers to the stimulation of a receptor (such as the eye) rather than the experience of (for example) seeing, which is referred to as *perception*. Some psychologists argue that it is impossible to separate these two processes, claiming that we cannot experience sensation without first interpreting or recognising it. Others claim that the amount of information in the sensory data creates the perceptual experience itself (see *direct theories of perception*).

sensitisation: an organism becomes more sensitive to a particular stimulus or class of stimuli. When used as an explanation of learning in non-human animals, it refers to an increased response to stimuli that are highly relevant and frequently repeated, such as attacks by predators. If a fox were to attack a group of chickens, and carried one off amid much struggling and distress, the other chickens in the group would develop an increased alertness and escape behaviour at the future appearance of a fox.

sensitive period: a term that has gradually replaced the related term *critical period*. It refers to a period in the development of an organism when it is psychologically and physiologically best able to develop a particular response. It is used in all sorts of different areas, such as the development of *attachment* bonds, the development of *language* and so on.

sensori-motor stage: see *Piaget, J*

sensory handicap: having a disadvantage in terms of one of the primary senses such as vision or hearing. Thus, blind or partially sighted people are said to have a sensory handicap. Those who have such a disadvantage often experience a double handicap: the handicap itself and the disadvantageous attitudes of the rest of society towards them. The term 'disability' or 'impairment' is more often used nowadays.

sensory nerve: see *afferent neurons*

separation anxiety: the term has two major uses in psychology. In *psychoanalysis*, it refers to the anxiety that a child feels with respect to the possible loss of the mother. In *attachment* theory, it refers to the unrealistic and often excessive worries that the child feels when they are apart from the primary caregiver. If excessive, these may develop into various forms of social withdrawal or refusal to go to school.

serial-position curve: a graphical representation of what happens when participants are asked to recall items from a list. Typically they recall more items from the start of the list (the *primacy effect*) and the end of the list (the *recency effect*), with those items in the middle of the list being the ones that are most likely to be lost.

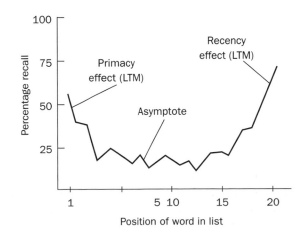

A serial-position curve

serial processing: a type of *information processing* where information is processed in a series of stages. Most consciously processed information is processed in this way.

seriation refers to the child's ability in understanding relationships of position in both space and time. Thus, the child would be able to place objects in order of height or length, and also in terms of when events occurred in time. Creating a personal time line (what has happened to them and when it happened), for example, is one of the first steps in children learning the concept of history. Seriation is important in that it enables the child to solve transitive inference problems. For example, if a child has to work out the relation between two sticks of different sizes (without seeing them) s/he may employ a third stick that is intermediate in size between the other two. If the child is told that stick A is longer than stick B which is longer than stick C, then it follows that stick A must be longer than stick C. To be able to solve this type of problem, the child must store all the information about the various relationships between A and B and B and C to be able to deduce the relationship between A and C. **Piaget** claimed that children would not be able to do this until the concrete-operational stage of intellectual development.

serotonin: a **neurotransmitter** that normally produces an inhibitory effect. It has a role in the regulation of mood, where it produces relaxation, and in the **control** of aggressive behaviour. Drugs such as LSD that inhibit serotonin action by blocking the receptor sites may increase dreaming, and may even produce hallucinations when the person is awake. Serotonin is involved in the action of **anti-depressant** drugs.

set: apart from its common usage (a collection of ...), its main use in psychology is to refer to any tendency to respond in a certain manner. There are many different sets in psychology, including:

- perceptual set – the tendency to perceive things in a certain way. Food invariably looks more appealing when we are hungry
- motor set – a tendency to perform an action in the same way despite conscious intentions to change
- functional set – a tendency to see and use objects in only one way

Although the effects of set tend to limit the variety of our responses in all of the above examples, their effect is usually only temporary, although the tendency does reoccur.

sex differences: a term used to refer to commonly observed differences between males and females. These can be classified as either primary (associated with reproduction), secondary (biological, but not associated with reproduction) and differences of mental, emotional or behavioural characteristics. It is in this latter use of the term that the greatest controversy lies. When sex differences are found in these areas, there is often a temptation to interpret them as being caused by some underlying biological difference and to see them as stable **traits** rather than products of **socialisation**. It is because of this faulty interpretation that so many of our **gender stereotypes** arise.

sex-linked trait: any **genetically** determined characteristic that is associated more with one sex than the other. An example of a sex-linked trait would be the better performance of men over women in tests of spatial ability. A genetic explanation of this has placed the **gene** for high spatial ability on the X **chromosome**, where it is recessive (i.e. it can be overruled by a different gene on the other chromosome). If the other chromosome is a Y chromosome (giving XY, the male chromosomes), then it cannot overrule genes on the X chromosome. If the other chromosome is an X chromosome (giving XX, the female chromosomes), the recessive gene will only be expressed if it is present on both chromosomes, otherwise it will be overruled. This explanation is also offered for other sex-linked traits such as colour-blindness and haemophilia.

sex-role learning: see *gender role*

sex-role stereotype: see *gender stereotypes*

sex stereotypes: see *gender stereotypes*

sexism: technically, a *prejudice* towards people based on their sex. This may be based on the prejudiced person's *attitudes* or beliefs about members of that sex, which is then used to justify their prejudice. In its more general usage, the term refers to a *discrimination* against members of one sex by members of the other (in employment, stereotypes or language). Although this could apply equally well to discrimination against either sex, it is normally used to refer to discrimination by men against women.

sexual dimorphism: differences between the sexes in regard to features such as size, plumage, coat and colouration. Species that are sexually dimorphic typically have developed their different characteristics for quite different reasons, females for camouflage against predators (*natural selection*) and males for the purpose of attracting females (*sexual selection*).

sexual identity: see *gender identity*

sexual imprinting: a form of attachment to members of the same species (usually birds) by which the young learn the characteristics of *conspecifics*, later to be used as the basis for the selection of sexual partners. To many birds, this learning experience takes place during a *sensitive period* of their development, and once formed is thought to be more or less irreversible. The need for sexual imprinting appears particularly strong for *sexually dimorphic* species, where the drab colours of the females make accurate discrimination between females of different species difficult for the male. Males, on the other hand, tend to be brightly coloured and it is easy for the females to discriminate between different species without the need for the learning provided by sexual imprinting. In cases of misplaced sexual imprinting, birds will later attempt to mate with the species with which they were raised (the foster species) rather than their own.

sexual monomorphism: refers to the fact that for some species there are few discernible differences between the sexes with regard to size and colouration.

sexual orientation is a term which implies that our choice of sexual partners may be determined by factors outside of our conscious *control*. Recent evidence suggests, for example, that there are slight differences in the hypothalami of homosexual and heterosexual men. The term is not used universally, with many people choosing to use the less deterministic term *sexual preference*.

sexual preference: a term which is used to refer to the preferred sex of one's sexual partner. As such, it acknowledges the fact that few people are completely *heterosexual* or *homosexual*, but do have a marked preference for one sex over the other.

sexual reproduction refers to the process by which the male and female sex cells are brought into union and a new organism created. The main advantage of sexual reproduction is that it introduces genetic variability by producing new organisms that may be better adapted to a changing environment or the pressures imposed by co-evolving predators.

sexual selection: the selection within nature of *traits* which are solely concerned with increasing an animal's mating success. It works in two ways:

- favouring the development of traits in one sex (usually males) that enable animals to compete directly against each other in order to gain access to, and matings with, the other sex (*intra-sexual selection*)
- favouring the development of traits in one sex that enables animals to attract members of the other sex (*inter-sexual selection*).

Competition as a result of sexual selection is at its greatest when there is a large difference in parental investment between the sexes (when one sex invests more than the other in raising the young) and where the ratio of males to females is imbalanced. Typically, males invest less than females (although this is not always the case), therefore are more likely to compete to obtain as many matings as possible. Males can thus increase their mating success by mating with as many females as possible. To this end, males may evolve elaborate weaponry and *rituals* for fighting, as well as less conspicuous forms of competition such as guarding their mates and replacing the sperm of other males. If, as is the case in most species, the female invests more heavily in caring for the young, she must select males for the resources they can provide or the genetic benefits they might bestow on their offspring. The two major explanations of how genetic benefits may be acquired through sexual selection are:

- males provide traits (such as plumage or other adornments) that are passed on to offspring thus making them 'attractive' to females (Fisher's 'sexy son' *hypothesis*)
- the conspicuous characteristics shown by some males (i.e. the handicap) may be a good indicator of survival ability or of disease resistance.

The elaborate display of the peacock – designed by sexual selection

shadowing: commonly used in studies of *attention*, this involves listening to and repeating back more or less simultaneously a message that is presented in one ear.

shape constancy refers to the tendency to perceive the shape of a familiar rigid object as maintaining that shape despite differences in the position from which it is viewed. A common example of this is when we see a door opening in front of us. The door appears to maintain its rectangular shape despite the fact that the actual visual image changes from a rectangle to a trapezoid.

shaping: the way in which a complex response can be built up by *reinforcing* simpler responses that gradually move closer and closer to the eventual desired response. At the start of a shaping procedure, a response that in some way resembles the desired response, but in an incomplete form, is reinforced every time it occurs. When that response is consolidated, reinforcements are given only when that response is given in a way that moves one step closer to the desired response. That response is then consolidated and so on. In this way, through successive approximations to the end behaviour, the organism can be shaped into producing behaviours that were not originally part of its behavioural repertoire.

short-term memory refers to the belief that *memory* can be divided into two distinct systems, one short term, and one long term. The short-term memory store is assumed to have a limited *capacity*, with material being lost after a few seconds. Material can re-enter the short-term memory through the process of *rehearsal* (repetition) until it is either lost from memory (forgotten) or selected to be transferred to the long-term memory. An example of a memory model that makes this distinction between short- and long-term memory is the *Atkinson and Shiffrin model of memory*.

sibling: a term used to refer to one's brother or sister.

sibling rivalry: a common belief that there is inevitable rivalry between children for parental affection and other resources. It has its origins in *psychoanalytic* theory, with each child wanting to monopolise the mother's love. Research has established that first-born children often feel jealousy toward younger children, but this jealousy typically diminishes toward the end of the younger child's first year.

sign language: a form of gestural communication used by the deaf. *American Sign Language* (Ameslan) has been used extensively in studies of *animal language*.

sign stimulus: a specific aspect of an organism that causes a strong response in another animal. Sign stimuli are normally specially evolved structures, colours, smells or calls that trigger a specific behaviour (such as aggression, parental behaviour or mating behaviour) in *conspecifics*. Research has demonstrated that responsiveness to sign stimuli can develop even in socially isolated animals.

signalling refers to any behaviour where one animal manipulates the sense organs of another in such a way as to change the behaviour of the second animal. The first animal is then said to have communicated with the second animal. There are two main schools of thought concerning communication:

- signals allow their sender to manipulate the behaviour of the receiving animal. Being able to do this gives the sender an evolutionary advantage. For example, animals might send false messages that either lure prey to them or enable them to escape from predators (see *mimicry*)
- both sender and receiver benefit in an act of communication. The selective forces acting on both sender and receiver are probably pushing in the same direction, i.e. towards the *evolution* of an efficient mutual signalling system. 'Honest' communication would be vital in courtship, parent–offspring interaction, and the variety of different forms of social interaction.

There are many different sensory channels through which a signal can be passed from one animal to another. These include:

- vision – for example, plumage, posture and colour are all aspects of visual display that can be used to convey information concerning courtship, threat or sexual receptiveness. Visual displays are of little use in surroundings other than open countryside, or in the dark
- sound – this might be used, for example, in alarm calls, distress calls, mating calls. It has the advantages of being able to travel for long distances, through thick vegetation, and can also be heard in the dark. Sound tends to travel better in water than in air, and low-frequency sounds can travel very long distances. Such sounds are much in evidence in the signals of humpback whales
- pheromones – chemical signals which are released by one animal and picked up by the receptors of another animal whose behaviour is then influenced. As well as being effective in the dark and in undergrowth, chemical smells have the added advantage of being relatively long lasting. It is common for many animals to mark out their territory using scent in this way, and to communicate with potential mates (e.g. as in moths).

significance: see *statistical significance*

simultaneous conditioning: a procedure used in *classical conditioning* where the unconditioned (UCS) and the conditioned stimuli (CS) are presented at the same time rather than one (the UCS) preceding the other, (the CS) as is more usual.

single-blind control: an *experimental* procedure used where *participants* do not know the *independent variable* being manipulated or which of the conditions they are in. The purpose of a single blind procedure is to minimise the possibility that participants might alter their behaviour in order to produce what they believe is the most appropriate response.

single-subject (participant) experimental design: also known as n = 1 research, this involves using only one participant instead of a group of participants in an *experimental* study. Such a technique can be useful for a number of reasons:

- it can provide useful early feedback about the action of the *independent variable*, and enables the experimenter to check the procedures to be used in the major study
- it has clinical usefulness when trying out a therapeutic technique. For example, a client can be tested under one condition (A) then under another condition (B). By testing again under condition (A), it should be possible to drop performance back to the level found in the original condition (A). By employing ABAB designs, it can be ascertained whether any improvement is due to the technique being used or to some other factor such as time or *order effects*.

situational attribution: a term used when we reach a conclusion concerning our own or another person's behaviour, that the behaviour was caused by factors outside the direct *control* of that person. A situational attribution is being made when we decide that a behaviour has been caused by, for example, the difficulty of a task, chance factors such as luck, or a whole host of other external influences (see also *dispositional attribution*).

size constancy: the tendency to still perceive familiar objects as being closer to their actual size rather than the physical size registered on the retina of the eye.

skewed distribution: a distribution of scores which, when plotted onto a graph, forms a distribution which has the majority of scores clumped toward one end or another. For example, if a test used in an *experiment* is too easy, most participants will do well (the *ceiling effect*) and the distribution this produces will be negatively skewed. If a test is too difficult, most participants will do badly (the *floor effect*) and the distribution this produces will be positively skewed.

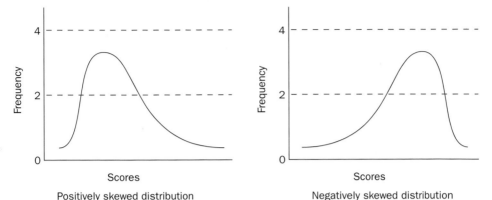

| Positively skewed distribution | Negatively skewed distribution |

Illustrations of positive and negatively skewed distributions

skill: the *ability* that a person has to carry out some task smoothly and competently in order to achieve some end result.

Skinner, B F (1904–1990): one of the founding fathers of *behaviourism*. Skinner's great belief was that we could explain behaviour without the need for unobservable mental processes. Skinner is primarily known for his work on *operant conditioning* whereby the consequences of an organism's responses determine their future reappearance.

Skinner box: named after the *behaviourist*, B F Skinner, this is a small, enclosed cage which has two essential features: something that the animal must manipulate (such as a bar or a disc) and a mechanism for delivering the *reinforcers* after the animal has done so. Variations on the basic theme of the Skinner box included a floor which could be electrified, lights for presenting other *cues*, and so on. The purpose of the Skinner box was to investigate and ultimately demonstrate the various mechanisms and procedures of *operant conditioning*.

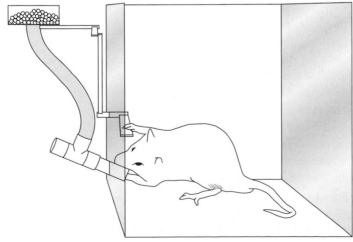

Skinner box

sleep is a behavioural state of warm-blooded vertebrate mammals defined by characteristic changes in posture, raised sensory thresholds, and distinctive electrographic signs (changes in physiological activity). Sleep can be subdivided into two major phases. These are non-rapid eye movement (NREM) and *rapid eye movement (REM) sleep*. NREM sleep can be further subdivided into four stages. These are referred to as slow-wave sleep. The waking, alert EEG is characterised by relatively high-frequency, low-amplitude beta waves. Once we are in bed and relaxed, these beta waves are replaced by alpha waves of higher amplitude but slower frequency. See figure below.

- As a person starts to fall asleep they enter Stage I sleep. This is characterised by irregular low-frequency theta waves. Our heart rate slows down, our body temperature drops and our muscles relax.
- Shortly after this, the person enters Stage II sleep. The EEG pattern is irregular during this stage. It has some periods of theta activity but these are punctuated with short bursts of activity about two to five times a minute (sleep spindles), and sudden, sharp waveforms (K-complexes) about every minute or so.
- After a further 15–20 minutes, Stage III sleep is entered, characterised by high-amplitude delta waves with a frequency of 1–4 Hz. There are still some spindles seen, but delta waves become more prominent and the person moves into Stage IV sleep.
- Stage IV sleep is very similar to Stage III sleep except that the percentage of delta waves increases and the number of spindles decreases. These delta waves are now 150–250 mV in amplitude. Our heart rate and body temperature are now at their lowest.
- After about 45 minutes (90 minutes after the onset of sleep), the EEG becomes gradually more desynchronised (irregular) and eventually theta waves similar to those seen in Stage I sleep are present. The EOG (electrooculogram) record shows that the eyes are darting back and forth and the EMG (electromyogram) is completely silent (the person is paralysed) apart from occasional brief twitchings of the hands and feet. This stage is called *REM sleep*.

These stages of sleep cycle several times during an average night. The whole cycle lasts about 90–100 minutes and as the night progresses more of the cycle is taken up with REM sleep. Also the amounts of Stage III and IV sleep decrease as the night wears on.

The exact functions of sleep are still open to debate. Adaptive theories (see *ecological accounts of sleep*) suggest that we sleep in order to remain inactive at times when it might be fruitless, or indeed dangerous, to continue our waking activities. During the hours of darkness our vision is too poor to enable us to search for food or for mates. Thus the energy expended in such searches might outweigh the benefits gained. Our poorer vision would also make us easier prey for predators. However, for some animals sleeping poses its own dangers and yet these animals continue to sleep. The Indus dolphin cannot stop swimming and so it takes its total seven hours of sleep a day in large numbers of 4–60 second naps. Porpoises switch off one half of their cortex at a time, with the remaining side allowing them to stay alert to any danger. If sleep were merely adaptive then one would have expected it to have been selected out in such animals.

A number of the features associated with NREM and REM sleep suggest that they might serve as restorative phases of the sleep–wake cycle (see *restoration accounts of sleep*). During NREM sleep there are decreases in blood pressure, heart rate and respiratory rate. There is also a release of growth and sex hormones from the pituitary. Thus during this time the body may rest and restore somatic tissue.

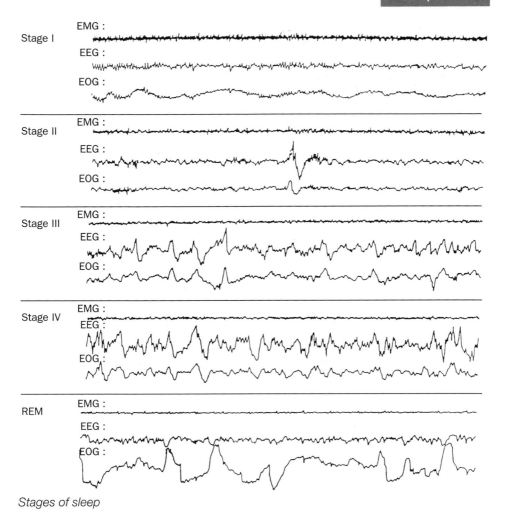

Stages of sleep

sleep cycles: see *rapid eye movement (REM) sleep*

sleep disorders: the most well known sleep disorder is insomnia. However, there is no single definition of insomnia as the amount of sleep people require is very variable, and self-reports of sleep periods can be very unreliable. A fairly common form of sleep disorder is sleep apnoea. This occurs when a person falls asleep and then ceases to breathe for a period of time. During a period of sleep apnoea the level of carbon dioxide in the blood rises and stimulates chemoreceptors. This causes the person to wake up gasping for breath. Narcolepsy is a disorder of REM sleep that is characterised by sleep at inappropriate times. The primary symptom is the sleep attack, which is an overwhelming urge to sleep. Another symptom of narcolepsy is cataplexy where a person's muscles will become paralysed, and they will suddenly drop to the floor, conscious but paralysed. Narcoleptic patients tend to skip the slow-wave stage of sleep and go straight into REM sleep.

sleeper effect refers to the fact that many persuasive messages or ***propaganda*** do not have an initial effect, but any change in behaviour of the person exposed to these messages may take place after a period of time. The term is also used in a much more general context to refer to any delayed effect that might arise as a result of some intervention. For example, some of the children who went through the pre-school *Headstart* programme in the USA in the 1960s showed little improvement at the time, but were later more successful at high school when compared with a *control* group of children who had not been through the programme.

sleepwalking: a sleep disorder whereby a person walks or carries out another activity while still asleep. Sleepwalking (also known as somnambulism) typically occurs in deep sleep (stage 3 or stage 4) early in the night. When people sleepwalk they may look as though they are awake (e.g. eyes open) but they are actually asleep. They may get up and walk around, or even carry out complex activities such as making a meal or even driving a car. An episode of sleepwalking may be very brief, lasting just a few seconds or can last for 30 minutes or longer. In adults, sleepwalking may be caused by a number of factors, including sleep deprivation, alcohol abuse and emotional stress. Among children the causes of sleepwalking are less clear, although it can occur in response to fatigue or anxiety. It also appears to run in families so may well have some genetic influences. Sleepwalking usually gets less frequent as children get older and, although it does not usually indicate a serious underlying disorder, it can be a symptom of other disorders.

Smartie tube test: an example of a *false-belief test*. A child is shown a Smartie tube and asked what it contains (the usual answer is 'Smarties' or 'sweets'). However, the experimenter has substituted a pencil for the sweets, which they then reveal to the child. The child is then asked the question 'What would your friend say was in the tube?'. Children under the age of four wrongly attribute the knowledge they have to other children and answer that they would say there was a pencil in the tube. Children over the age of four correctly answer that their friend would get it wrong and say there were Smarties in the tube. The child is then asked a supplementary question 'What did you think was in the tube?'. The younger children then answer 'a pencil', even though they had previously said the tube contained Smarties, thus failing to acknowledge their own past false belief.

social categorisation: the ordering of the social environment by an individual in terms of social categories, i.e. groupings of people in a manner that is meaningful to that individual (e.g. British, non-British, white, black). Intergroup discrimination (i.e. 'us versus them' or 'ingroup versus outgroup') is the consequence of these categorisations.

social change: occurs when a society as a whole adopts a new belief or way of behaving that then becomes widely accepted as the norm (see *innovation (minority influence)*).

social cognition refers to the role played by cognitive factors in our social behaviour. Social cognition is a major approach within social psychology, and focuses on the way in which our thoughts are affected by the immediate social context, and in turn how our thoughts affect our social behaviour. The approach can be summarised as follows:
- people have a limited *capacity* to process information about the social world, and will take cognitive short-cuts (such as *stereotyping*) in order to minimise the load on this limited processing capacity
- we develop *schemata* that represent our knowledge about ourselves, others and our roles within the social world. Once we have formed these schemata, they bias the way in which we process information and form judgements about ourselves and others
- we are less likely to rely on these schemata when the cost of making a wrong judgement is high or when we are aware that our schematic processing may be inaccurate

- schemata become more complex and organised over time, and also harder to change
- social cognition is criticised for placing too much emphasis on the cognitive aspects of social behaviour, and ignoring other important factors such as emotional factors. The decisions we make may occasionally make no sense when judging them against cognitive criteria, but may reflect a particular emotional state (such as happiness, sadness or anger).

social comparison: a social psychological theory which claims that we use other people as a yardstick in order to evaluate our own attitudes, emotions and behaviour. Uncertainty how to behave or what to think in a situation will have us looking at others to see how they are behaving, or what they are thinking in order to adjust our own behaviour to what appears to be the consensus. People may use social comparison for a number of reasons, such as:

- evaluation – how good are we at something compared to others, or is our response appropriate?
- improvement – comparing ourselves to someone who is better at a particular skill enables us improve our own efforts
- enhancement – we may compare ourselves to others who are less well off than us, in order to convince ourselves that we are not so bad after all.

social complexity and human intelligence: individuals who best deal with the demands posed by other individuals in a social group (e.g. being able to obtain resources without inciting intragroup aggression) would be more successful at increasing their reproductive fitness. The concept of **Machiavellian intelligence** suggests that the evolution of human intelligence was primarily driven by the need to manipulate others within a social group for an individual's own ends. The meat-sharing hypothesis suggests that, for our ancestors, meat was an important source of saturated fat, and so was vital for survival. Stanford (1999) believes that strategic sharing of meat within social groups paved the way for human intelligence. Meat could be used to forge alliances and persuade females to mate, particularly as males did most of the hunting. Stanford believes that strategic meat-sharing required considerable cognitive abilities, as males had to recognise individuals and keep a running score of debts and credits.

social constructionism arose out of criticisms against earlier views of human behaviour which were based around the idea of a rational, self-sufficient individual. Social constructionists argue that we cannot understand human behaviour from this viewpoint. Human beings are a product of their cultural and personal histories, and of their immediate social contexts. The importance of the individual rather than the social being is seen as a bias towards Western cultures which are heavily individualistic in nature. Rather than restrict research to trying to establish patterns of individual behaviour, social constructionists believe that we should study the relations between people that produce this inner world of subjective experience. This has also meant a move away from traditional experimental methods of research, with their emphasis on **quantitative data**, towards methods that provide more **qualitative data.**

social contexts of pathways into crime: an examination of common factors in the background of delinquents that might serve as an explanation of their drift into crime. These include the influence of delinquent youth groups (youths who associate with antisocial peers show more aggressive and egocentric personality traits and are less likely to

S

embrace positive social values). Other factors include family risk factors (e.g. children born to young mothers are at more risk of antisocial behaviour and early initiation into smoking and illegal drugs) and educational risk factors (e.g. bullying and truancy). The causal relationship between delinquency and truancy, however, is not clear, as it is also likely that delinquency might lead to truancy rather than the other way round. A number of studies have shown that children who grow up in disadvantaged neighbourhoods with poor living conditions and high rates of unemployment have an increased risk of involvement in crime.

social control: a view of psychology that believes that scientific psychology provides insights into how the behaviour of individuals can be manipulated within a social setting. The possibilities are, in theory at least, almost endless. The use of *reinforcement* techniques, or persuasion and *propaganda* all offer the psychologist opportunities for controlling the behaviour of others. In a sense, the ultimate aim of scientific psychology might be seen as the exercise of social control although the idea is not one that many psychologists would feel happy with. The idea of social control rises many ethical and political issues, particularly in the treatment of *abnormal behaviour*. (See also *ethics/ ethical issues*.)

social desirability: either behaving in a way that would bring social approval from those around us or responding to some measure of *personality* that requires self-evaluation in such a way that we present ourselves not as we actually are, but in a way that we feel displays more socially desirable characteristics.

social dilemma refers to a situation where we must make a decision whether to do something that benefits ourselves, at least in the short term, yet because such selfish actions tend to have some social consequence, we may lose in the long term. In the novel *Catch 22* by Joseph Heller, Yossarian is asked, in response to his request to be grounded from active duty, 'How would it be if everybody felt that way?' to which he replies, 'Then I'd be a damned fool to feel any other way'. This belief that everybody will act selfishly often spurs people to be 'pre-emptive' and show their own selfishness first. Even when we do not believe that other people will act selfishly, we may choose to do so ourselves in the belief that one person acting like that will not make much difference. With everybody reasoning in the same way, selfishness becomes rife and resources are stripped. This is sometimes referred to as the 'tragedy of the commons' in reference to the overgrazing of animals on common land. Each commoner grazed just a few more animals than he was allowed so that eventually the common was ruined for everybody. These sort of social dilemmas can be seen every day, at motorway roadworks, in supermarkets during food shortages and so on.

social disengagement theory: see *disengagement*

social distance scale: a series of statements that are concerned with the preferred social distance between the *respondent* and some other person or group. The respondent is presented with a list of, for example, different ethnic or national groups and asked to indicate which of a set of statements best describes their feelings towards them (for example, would admit X to close kinship by marriage; would admit Y to my street as neighbours; would exclude Z from my country). By scoring the scale, it is possible to obtain a measurement of *prejudice* against any specified group. The scale is by now rather out-dated, and does invite an obvious *response bias* as the respondent, being aware of the negative connotations of prejudice, tries to mask their own from the researcher.

social exchange theory claims that much, if not most, of our social behaviour is influenced by the expectation that our actions towards others will be reciprocated in some way. Relationships are based on a mutual exchange of benefits. If we do something to help a friend or colleague, we may expect nothing in return at the time, but there is an unstated assumption that should the position be reversed, we could expect like behaviour in return.

social facilitation and inhibition (SFI): an improvement in performance on some task due to the presence of others (social facilitation), or an impairment in performance due to the presence of others (social inhibition). This can either be due to the presence of a passive audience (the **audience effect**) or the presence of others who are performing the same task (the **co-action effect**).

social identification: the process by which an individual's **self-concept** is based on a perception of belonging to a social or cultural group.

social identity theory proposes that when we categorise ourselves and others, we develop conceptions of 'us' (the **in-group**) and 'them' (the **out-group**). This leads to social comparison with the out-group, and because of the need to provide ourselves with a positive social identity, an inevitable development into social competition. Tajfel's work on minimal groups showed how easy it is for people to develop a need to see their own group as 'better' than another group. There are three components of social identity theory – categorisation, identification and social comparison:

1. **Categorisation:** We categorise objects and people in order to understand them. We use social categories like black, white, student or socialist because they are useful. If we can assign people to a category then that tells us things about those people. Similarly, we find out things about ourselves by knowing what categories we belong to.
2. **Identification:** We identify with groups that we perceive ourselves to belong to. Part of who we are is made up of our group memberships, i.e. sometimes we think of ourselves as group members and at other times we think of ourselves as unique individuals. This varies according to different situations, so that we can be more or less a group member, depending upon the circumstances. What is crucial is that thinking of ourselves as group members and thinking of ourselves as unique individuals are both parts of our self-concept. The first is referred to as social identity, the latter is referred to as personal identity.
3. **Social comparison:** The basic idea is that a positive self-concept is a part of normal psychological functioning. To deal effectively with the world we need to feel good about ourselves. In order to evaluate ourselves we compare ourselves with others. We can gain self-esteem by comparing ourselves with others in our group, and we can also see ourselves in a positive light by seeing ourselves as a member of a prestigious group. People also choose to compare their groups with other groups in ways that reflect positively on themselves. People are motivated to see their own group as relatively better than similar (but inferior) groups. Groups tend to choose dimensions that maximise the positive status of their own group. For example, groups which perceive themselves to be of high status on particular dimensions (e.g. more technologically advanced) will choose those as the basis of comparison. Groups of low status may choose alternative dimensions to preserve their own self-esteem as part of the social comparison process. For example, people from some Middle Eastern Islamic countries might regard their country as inferior to the West in terms of economic and technological advancement but might regard their way of life as being morally superior.

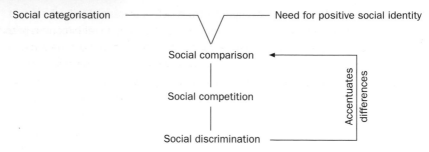

Diagrammatic representation of social identity theory

social impact theory: a theory of *social influence* proposed by Bibb Latané (1981). The influence of an audience on our performance of a task depends on the number of people, their immediacy and their status. So, the influence of others is greater when there are more of them (number), they are closer to us (immediacy) and they are of high status.

social influence: refers to the various processes (such as majority and minority influence) by which a person's attitudes, beliefs and behaviours are modified by the presence or actions of others.

social inhibition: see *social facilitation and inhibition (SFI)*

social inoculation: a device used in persuasive communications. When attempting to persuade an audience to change their attitudes or behaviour (for example their voting behaviour), a speaker might warn them of the arguments of others, thus decreasing the impact of future messages contrary to the existing one (i.e. they are 'inoculated' against its effect). Politicians use this trick a great deal: 'They may tell you they are a party of lower taxes and reduced employment, but...'.

social isolate: somebody who has few, if any, interpersonal ties with other people.

social learning theory: the basic assumption of this theory is that people learn not through direct *reinforcement* but through the observation of *models*. Learning is achieved by observing the behaviour of models then mentally rehearsing the actions they display. The observed behaviours can then be *imitated* and the cycle is complete. This does assume, of course, that the person is able to reproduce the observed behaviour. We may marvel at the football skills of Steven Gerrard or Fernando Torres, but most of us would find it impossible to reproduce them. Social learning theory is able to explain many more complex social behaviours (such as *gender role* behaviour and moral behaviour) than models of learning based on simple reinforcement.

social loafing refers to the tendency for some people to expend less effort in a group task than they would when carrying out the same task individually. Social loafing is most evident in additive tasks, i.e. those tasks where the contributions of each group member is combined into a group product. In such situations it becomes difficult to identify the contributions of any one individual so people socially 'loaf'. Simply believing that others are likely to loaf means that we are likely to loaf also. According to *equity theory*, we aim to receive out of a situation something roughly equivalent to what we put in. If we feel that others are not working as hard as we are, we will then adjust our own output to match theirs.

social meaning: the meaning given to an event or situation by the shared understanding of those who experience it. People who experience an event (for example, racial *discrimination* or some aspect of social behaviour that might be perceived as an emergency) will arrive at an understanding of the event through the shared attitudes and beliefs of the group (*social representations*) or perhaps by comparing their reactions to the reactions of others in a situation. For example, you may come across someone slumped across the pavement. Everybody appears to be ignoring them and continuing on their way. Each person experiencing this event uses the reactions of others to gauge whether what they are seeing really is an emergency. If no one is seen to react, then it is not perceived to be an emergency, and you also pass by, a process known as *pluralistic ignorance* to indicate that the social meaning given to an event is often inaccurate because of our reliance on the attitudes and behaviours of others.

social needs: those needs which are focused on some aspect of social behaviour, such as the need for affiliation, the need for approval or the need for power.

social norms: a way of thinking or behaving that is considered appropriate and proper within a particular society, and that most members of that society adhere to. Compliance with the social norms of a society may lead to acceptance by societal members, non-compliance to rejection.

social phobia: see *phobic disorders (phobias)*

social power: refers to the influence that one person has over another, whilst remaining relatively immune to the same effect in return. There are several different forms of social power, although any one individual (the agent) might display all of these types at the same time in their relationship with another (the target):
- coercive power – the ability to administer punishment on others
- reward power – the ability to give rewards
- expert power – the target believes the agent has superior knowledge or ability
- legitimate power – the target believes the agent has the authority to make decisions and direct the target's behaviour
- referent power – the target identifies with or is attracted to the agent.

social psychology: '... an attempt to understand and explain how the thoughts, feelings and behaviour of individuals are influenced by the actual, imagined or implied presence of others' (Allport, 1985).

social representations refers to the way in which ordinary people represent the world around them. Knowledge is first presented by specialists, (such as psychologists, politicians or journalists) but is then passed around from non-specialist to non-specialist (the rest of us) until we have reached some kind of consensual understanding, a popularised representation of the original information. In this way, people can turn the unfamiliar into the familiar, and the complex into the more easily understood. These social representations rapidly become established as unquestioned common-sense explanations which enable people to understand the world around them. Once constructed, these representations acquire a force of their own, and they impose themselves on us in such a way that we find it hard to resist them. Social representations thus provide an established order so that we can interpret and understand our social world, and also function effectively within it. Although psychology can provide many of the technical explanations of behaviour, lay people can offer popularised views of the same events. Thus, explanations of *prejudice*, *mental illness* or *AIDS* abound within popular culture and have developed in an almost casual interactive way through our social interactions with others. In order to study and measure social representations, researchers have turned increasingly to *qualitative research*.

social schemas: are mental representations of social knowledge based on previous experience. They offer us summaries of our social world such that we can categorise new information more easily and process it more quickly. They tell us, for example, what to pay attention to and what we might ignore. Social schemas are an example of top-down processing in social cognition. As such they influence what is remembered in a social situation (consistent information is remembered, inconsistent information is forgotten) and also influence our judgements of people in the process of impression formation.

social skills training: a form of behaviour therapy used to help individuals who have difficulties relating to other people.

socialisation: the process of acquiring the knowledge, *values* and social skills that enable the individual to become a member of their society and behave appropriately within it. Although the term socialisation refers to a life-long process, in that individuals are constantly learning and adapting their skills, it is more usually used to refer to the period of childhood and *adolescence*.

sociality in non-human animals refers to the tendency for some animals to live in groups. Animals live in groups for a number of reasons:
- increased vigilance – the presence of other animals means that predators are more likely to be detected
- group defence – group-living animals can defend themselves more effectively against predators
- foraging advantages – group members may be able to gain information about feeding sites from the behaviour of other group members
- sociality gives rise to communities which often reduce the need for competition, especially between males. The alpha male has a dominant position once a 'pecking order' of seniority is adopted. Hierarchies of status also occur in female groups of animals such as chickens or baboons.

Group living also has disadvantages for animals, including:
- increased competition for resources – may result in more aggression as animals compete for food, nest sites or mates, etc.
- increased risk of parasitism and disease – with closely packed animals there is a greater opportunity for the spread of parasites, either directly through contact, or indirectly through nests and other surfaces.

socially sensitive research is defined as any studies in which there are potential social consequences or implications, either directly for the participants in the research or the class of individuals represented by it. The essence of this definition is that much of what we study in psychology has a social impact. Research about the genetic basis of criminality, for example, has a potential for profound social consequences (e.g. compulsory genetic testing, false imprisonment of genetically influenced criminals). The sorts of investigations that would come under the heading of socially sensitive research would include research into racial differences, gender-related abilities, sexual orientation and so on. Not only does this type of research have implications for the people that take part, but also for the wider social group that they represent. If, for example, researchers carried out research that demonstrated differences in the mathematical abilities of boys and girls, this might well have implications far beyond the very small percentage of participants that had actually been tested. This may take the form of lowered expectations for one sex compared with the other, self-fulfilling prophecies, occupational discrimination and so on.

A major concern in the interpretation and application of research findings in psychology is that they may be used for reasons other than those for which they were originally intended. Some of the controversies that arise from socially sensitive research can be attributed to poorly designed or executed studies or inappropriate interpretations of the findings. Although other scientists would be aware of these problems, the media and the public might not, and thus poor studies might shape important social policy to the detriment of those represented by the research.

Psychologists could avoid the controversies associated with this kind of research by restricting their research interests to those areas that attract very little attention from the media and from peers outside of their special area of interest. This is not really the answer, as much of the research that takes place in socially sensitive areas has important and potentially beneficial effects for certain sections of society (e.g. exploring patterns of behaviour that increase the risk of HIV-infection or investigating the educational underachievement of specific groups). What we should be most concerned about, however, is the possibility that the results of such research might also offer the possibility of abuse and discrimination or, as Sieber and Stanley (1988) suggest, '… offer some scientific credibility to the prevailing prejudice'.

sociobiology refers to the use of evolutionary ideas to explain the social behaviour of animals.

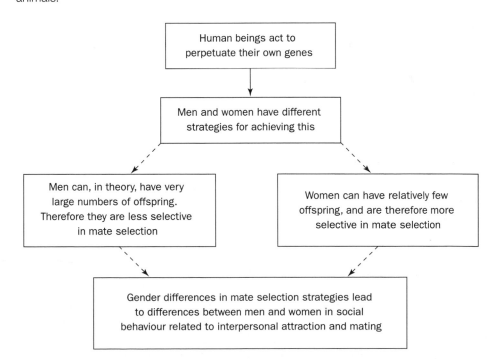

Evolutionary ideas in sociobiology

Ideas central to sociobiology include the following:

- strategies – a strategy is one of a number of possible courses of action that might be taken by an animal. Strategies that are subject to genetic **control** (such as parental care or altruistic behaviour) are thus subject to the laws of **natural selection**. Those which contribute to increased **inclusive fitness** are thus more likely to become established in the behavioural repertoire of a species
- evolutionarily stable strategies – a strategy may be described as an ESS if it becomes widespread in a population and resists invasion by other alternative strategies. It is an optimum strategy dependent on the circumstances in which it is used. For example, the use of and response to appeasement displays may become widespread in that they confer advantages on both parties in a dispute. A victorious animal that does not respond to an appeasement display by breaking off from a fight risks further injury and a decline in reproductive fitness.

The central problem of sociobiology is to provide an acceptable explanation for **altruism biological**.

sociograms: a graphical representation of relationships in a group. Developed by Moreno as a technique to provide juvenile offenders with a more positive 'prison' experience, it requires people to respond to a series of questions such as: 'On an outing, who would you most like to sit next to?'. From the responses given by all members of the group, a network can be drawn up that indicates friendship links, stars (frequently chosen people) and isolates (those that are rarely or never chosen).

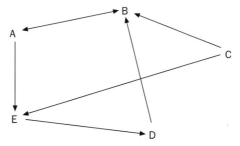

A typical sociogram: B is the most selected, C is an isolate

solvent abuse: the inhaling of fumes from domestic and industrial products leading to an intense feeling of intoxication. These products include solvent-based adhesives, paint thinners and removers and dry cleaning agents. The most common technique used is inhaling the fumes from a plastic bag placed over the face. A feeling of intoxication kicks in almost immediately, with some users experiencing hallucinations. The effects are short lived, resulting in the prospect of repeated abuse.

somatic treatments: an approach to the treatment of mental disorders that utilises physical and chemical methods. The somatic (or biological) approach to treatment is linked to the **biological model of abnormality**. For example, if a disorder can be explained in terms of an excess or deficiency of a particular chemical, then it makes sense to try to alter that state through the use of drugs. **Drug treatments** are the most widespread example of the somatic approach. **Electroconvulsive shock treatment (ECT)** has also been used effectively in cases of severe **depression**. It is not the case that a belief in the biological causes of a disorder necessarily warrants a biological treatment. Psychological treatments may be used instead of or in conjunction with biological treatments.

somatotype: meaning body type, this term was most often used in the context of the historical constitutional theory, where it was used to link together body type and *personality* or body type and propensity for *mental illness*.

spatial memory is the ability of animals to form a mental image or map of its familiar area or home range. The exact nature of such an internal representation is not known although it is generally believed that the *hippocampus* plays an important role in this respect. It is possible that this form of memory operates quite differently in different species. Birds which rely heavily on stored food (e.g. Clark's nutcrackers) have better spatial memory than those which are less reliant on food storage (e.g. scrub jays). The volume of the hippocampal regions in species with highly proficient spatial memories tends to be greater than those with less proficient memories, reinforcing the apparent relationship between the hippocampus and spatial memory.

Spearman's rho: a *correlation* which can be calculated from two sets of ranked *data*. Spearman's correlation is most likely to be used with ordinal data (see *levels of measurement*) and produces a mathematical figure (the *correlation coefficient*) between +1 (a perfect positive correlation) and −1 (a perfect inverse correlation). A correlation of 0 indicates no relationship.

Spearman's two-factor theory of intelligence: Spearman claimed that individuals who do well on one test of intelligence (IQ test) tended also to do well on others, and those who did poorly on one test also did poorly on others. He proposed two factors that together could explain why this was the case:
- specific abilities (s) – individuals performed consistently well (or badly) on specific aspects of intelligence, such as vocabulary and mathematical intelligence, but not on other aspects
- general intelligence (g) – what explained the positive correlation between different test performances and the specific abilities that make up these tests, was a general intelligence (or g) that determined performance on all types of intelligence test.

species refers to a category of organisms that share similar *genetic* characteristics and are able to breed among themselves. It is fairly certain that less than half of the insect species in the world have been identified yet. Their *genetic* characteristics remain to be investigated.

species-specific behaviour: any *behaviour* that is common to all members of a species and appears in similar situations. An example may be the specific courtship displays of different *species*.

speciesism: a term used to demonstrate that *discrimination* against non-human animals is logically parallel to other forms of discrimination such as *ageism* and *racism*. All of these involve the classification of all members of a particular group on the basis of what are often purely arbitrary characteristics. This 'label' is then used to justify the discrimination that follows. In this way we may excuse our use of other species for our own ends because we assume that, as 'non-human' species, they cannot expect the same moral considerations that we, as human beings, would justifiably expect. This concept is often quoted by those who are against the idea of *animal research* on ethical grounds.

specific phobias: see *phobic disorders (phobias)*

spiral curriculum: the main principle of this method is that the key concepts of any discipline can be taught in some form to children at any level. Concepts that are initially introduced in simple form at primary school level can then be further explored, developed and extended in increasingly sophisticated ways as the child matures and develops. Although children may not fully understand or remember their initial experiences, the idea is that they will take in some of the information, which will then act as a basis for later learning.

split-brain studies refers to studies derived from cerebral commissurotomies (or split-brain operations). This operation, performed in certain forms of severe epilepsy, involves cutting the corpus callosum, and effectively separating the two hemispheres of the brain. Through this operation the epilepsy could be confined to one hemisphere and therefore its effects could be reduced. Very few of these operations have been carried out, but they have provided valuable insights into the working of the two hemispheres and the corpus callosum that connects them. In right-handed people, speech is located in the left hemisphere. If the hemispheres are isolated from each other through cutting the corpus callosum, information presented to the right hemisphere cannot be commented on because the speech centre is in the left hemisphere. These studies have suggested that the role of the corpus callosum is to let each hemisphere be aware of the activities of the other. The right hemisphere controls visuo-spatial activities, and the left hemisphere can reflect upon these activities through speech.

split halves reliability: a method of assessing the internal consistency of a test. By splitting the items of a test randomly into two halves, or into odd- and even-numbered questions, the participants' performance on the two halves can be compared. If they perform the same on the two halves then the test is reliable, in other words, all parts of the test appear to be performing in the same way.

spontaneous recovery refers to the reappearance of an extinguished *conditioned* response. If a conditioned response is no longer *reinforced*, it will no longer be produced by the organism. Following a rest period, however, the response can spontaneously reappear.

spreading-activation model: a theory of memory based on the networks of associations that connect different bits of information. Each piece of information within a network is called a node, which may be in the form of images, smells, memories, emotions, etc. For example, the word dog may be linked associatively with characteristics such as barking, makes the house untidy or even with the emotion of fear, which may be based on an idiosyncratic episodic memory of being bitten by a dog in childhood. According to spreading-activation theory, activating one node in a network triggers activation in closely related nodes, i.e. it spreads activation to related information stored in memory. This spreading activation does not have to start with a word, but may be triggered by a thought, an image or even a smell.

SQ3R method: a type of study technique that emphasises the need to Survey material, Question the issues in that material, Read it thoroughly, Recite the main points, and finally Review the information once more.

SSRIs: Selective Serotonin Reuptake Inhibitors – block the transporter mechanism that re-absorbs the neurotransmitter serotonin into the presynaptic cell after it has fired. As a result, more serotonin is left in the synapse, prolonging its activity and making transmission of the next impulse easier, thus reducing the symptoms of depression. The best known of these drugs is Prozac (fluoxetine).

stage theories: the idea that, as we develop, we go through a series of discrete stages during which we learn or respond in different ways. Examples of stage theories are Freud's psychosexual theory and Kohlberg's theory of moral reasoning. Usually development proceeds from a less mature to a more mature stage, but it is a characteristic of many stage theories that people occasionally revert to less mature stages in certain situations.

stalking: a form of conduct that places people in fear for their safety. Stalking involves repeated and persistent attempts to impose unwanted communication and/or contact on another person, e.g. through telephone calls, e-mail, and by approaching and following the target person. Some stalkers develop a love obsession with another person (e.g. a coworker or a celebrity), and many suffer from delusional thought patterns that prompt their behaviour. As many stalkers of this type are unable to develop normal personal relationships through conventional means they develop fantasy relationships instead, inventing fictional stories with their unwilling victim in the lead role as their love interest. Most stalkers, however, have had some previous relationship with their victim (either personal or romantic) before the stalking behaviour began. Research suggests that stalkers have a range of motivations for their behaviour, from reasserting power over a partner who rejected them, to the quest for a loving relationship.

standard deviation: a statistical measure of the variation in a set of scores. The standard deviation gives a researcher an idea of how spread-out a set of scores is around the *mean* value. Standard deviations with N values (the number of scores) of less than 25 can be biased, so need to be corrected in order that generalisations back to the parent population can be made.

standardised instructions: a set of instructions used in an *experiment* that are consistent in style, content and delivery across all conditions and *participants* of the experiment. As the instructions are often the only verbal interaction between the experimenter and the *participant* during the experimental session, it is important that what is said is the same for everyone, otherwise it adds another possible *variable* that can influence behaviour. Standardised instructions may be written down or presented on a computer monitor to ensure complete similarity across all participants.

standardised procedures refers to a fixed set of rules and procedures used in the administration and scoring of either an *experiment* or a *psychometric test*. It is important that standardised procedures are adhered to, as even the smallest variations may have a greater impact on participant performance than the researcher is able to predict.

standardised tests are tests that attempt to measure an individual's performance compared to a *population* of similar individuals (for example 11–16-year-old schoolchildren or undergraduate students). These tests enable researchers to establish *norms* of performance which are representative scores for members of that population. In this way, once a test is standardised it can be given to any number of people whose performance can then be compared to the norms of the rest of the population in order to determine their present level of functioning.

statementing: the 1981 Education Act requires local education authorities to identify children who have special needs, and to make additional educational provision to meet those needs. The formal assessment (or statement) of these special needs is usually made by a team of professionals, including educational psychologists. It is estimated that approximately 2 per cent of children in England and Wales have the special needs identified by the Act.

statistic: a mathematical calculation which reflects the characteristics of a *sample* of behaviour or of the selected *participants* in a study. As used in psychological research, a statistic such as the *mean* or *standard deviation* that is calculated from a sample is generally assumed to represent the underlying characteristics of the *population* from which the sample has been drawn.

statistical infrequency: any behaviour that is statistically infrequent is regarded as abnormal. Most human characteristics (including personality traits and behaviour) fall within a normal distribution, with most people clustering around the middle of the distribution (i.e. the norm), and fewer and fewer towards the edges. Any characteristic that is statistically rare according to this distribution is considered abnormal.

statistical significance: in a statistical significance test we assume that the *null hypothesis* is true and calculate the *probability* of a difference occurring if this is so. If $p < 0.05$ we reject the null hypothesis and assume there is a real difference between the populations from which the two samples have been drawn. At this point we accept that something else is causing the results, although because of the nature of psychological research this 'something else' is not always that certain. The fact that something is 'statistically significant' tells us that it is unlikely to have been caused by chance, but does not necessarily tell us that the result is of any particular significance.

stereoscopic vision: the perceptual experience of a three-dimensional image through the combination of two different views of the same scene from the two eyes.

stereotype: a fixed, often simplistic generalisation about a particular group or class of people. As people are essentially 'cognitive misers', they form stereotypes about others so that there is a greater predictability in the behaviour of those around us. These stereotypes are often negative and unflattering, and may underlie *prejudice* and *discrimination*. Stereotypes may not necessarily be false assumptions about the target group, as they often contain a 'grain of truth'. A stereotype must be a widely shared set of beliefs, thus further reinforcing the fact that some degree of accuracy is often evident. Stereotypes may change over time, but those who hold them are often reluctant to abandon them.

Sternberg's triarchic theory of intelligence: a theory of intelligence that describes three different forms of intelligence.
- *Analytical intelligence* – the ability to combine the most appropriate mental 'components' when applying intelligence to a problem. Metacomponents act as the overall executor of intelligent behaviour, recognising and determining the exact nature of a problem, developing strategies to solve it and monitoring their effectiveness. Performance components are the cognitive processes that are involved in actually solving a problem and knowledge-acquisition components are used to acquire and learn new material by sifting out relevant from irrelevant information.
- *Practical intelligence* – the ability to make a 'considered' response to a problem dependent on the context in which the problem occurs, judging which response is likely to be the most appropriate in that situation.

- *Creative intelligence* – helps an individual identify when a problem is a new one, and so requires intelligent behaviour to solve it. It also helps to identify when the person has so much experience of a particular problem that an automatic response is more appropriate.

stimulus: a difficult term to define, yet one that lies at the very centre of the field of scientific psychology. Stimuli typically have the following characteristics:
- they have some physical reality (such as a sound or a smell)
- they must be capable of stimulating the sensory organs of the *organism* receiving them
- they should stimulate some response from the organism
- they are predominantly external in origin, but may, within limits, originate from within the organism.

Examples of stimuli that would satisfy these criteria include environmental events such as heat or noise, and bodily feelings such as pain or discomfort.

stimulus discrimination: an aspect of *classical conditioning* where an organism responds to one stimulus whilst losing the tendency to respond to similar stimuli. In other words, the organism discriminates between significant and insignificant stimuli, continuing to respond to the former while ignoring the latter. Discrimination is achieved when generalised stimuli undergo *extinction* – they do not signal the coming of anything particularly important. On the other hand, the original conditioned stimulus is associated with the unconditioned stimulus from time to time, so does not undergo extinction. For example, dogs will often perk up when they hear a particular engine sound because it is followed by the appearance of their owner. Other engine sounds will be ignored as the dog learns to discriminate between their owner's engine and the engine sounds of other people's cars.

stimulus driven processing: see *bottom-up* processing

stimulus generalisation: an aspect of *classical conditioning* whereby an organism not only responds to the conditioned stimulus, but also to stimuli that are similar to the conditioned stimulus. The more similar the stimulus to the conditioned stimulus, the stronger will be the response. Stimulus generalisation is an important aspect of learning in the wild, because it enables an organism to respond to other potentially significant stimuli. For example, if an animal learns which sights, sounds or smells signal the presence of a predator, it must also learn to respond to slight variations of these stimuli as well. In this way the organism builds in a 'safety factor' which helps it to survive.

stimulus-response learning: a term used to describe any type of learning which involves an association between a *stimulus* and a *response*. The production of the latter is thus governed by the presentation of the former.

storage: the process of retaining information in sensory memory, *short-term memory* or *long-term memory*. Sensory and short-term memory have limited storage that is only temporary, whereas storage in long-term memory is both permanent and unlimited.

storm and stress: a view that *adolescence* is a time of intense conflict in an individual's development. Originally attributed to Hall (1904), it is the view that an adolescent cannot truly pass into adulthood without first experiencing a turbulent period of change. This view has had a lasting influence on both popular culture and some of the older psychological theories of adolescence (e.g. *Erikson's* psychosocial theory of development).

strange situation test: a procedure designed to test the quality of the *attachment* bond between mothers and their infants (see the diagram below).

S

265

Mother   Stranger

The strange situation has three phases, with the infant's reactions being noted in each of the phases:
1. Reaction to a stranger when in the presence of the mother.
2. Reaction when left alone with the stranger.
3. Reaction when re-united with the mother.

Results of the strange situation test typically show four patterns of reaction:
- securely attached infants explore when the mother is present and react positively to the stranger. When left by the mother they are upset, but are soon calmed when the mother returns. Approximately two-thirds of children at one year are securely attached by this description
- anxious/avoidant infants do not attempt to interact with the mother when with her, nor do they appear particularly upset when left with the stranger. When the mother returns, the infant may not make any attempt to get close to her
- anxious/resistant infants appear to be anxious even when with the mother. They are upset when she leaves and cannot be consoled by the stranger. When the mother returns, they attempt to get close to her, but resist her attempts to comfort them
- disorganised infants typically show confused behaviour and do not appear to be able to initiate any effective coping behaviour either during the separation or on the mother's return.

stratified sample: see *sampling*

stress may be defined in a number of different ways:
- as a stimulus – stress may be seen as characteristics of the ***environment*** (time stresses, job stresses, for example). These are known as 'stressors'
- as a response – stress is seen as a person's response to these characteristics (a stress reaction)
- as a 'lack of fit' between the person and his or her environment (the transactional view of stress) – the person experiences stress when the perceived demands of their environment are greater than their perceived ability to cope.

An important aspect of this last view is that stress is a product of the imbalance of the perceived demands and a person's perceived ability to cope rather than the actual demands and the their actual ability to cope. There may well be a real difference between demands and ability, but if this is not realised by the individual, they do not experience stress.

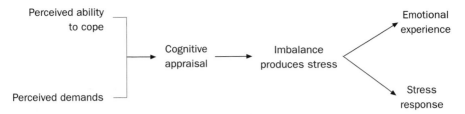

The transactional view of stress

Stress has wide-ranging effects on the individual, including the following:
- subjective effects – such as fatigue, apathy and lowered *self-esteem*
- behavioural effects – such as excessive drinking, loss of appetite and restlessness
- cognitive effects – such as hypersensitivity to criticism and concentration difficulties
- physiological effects – such as increased blood pressure, breathing difficulties and increased blood glucose levels
- health effects – such as coronary heart disease, ulcers, headaches and migraines
- organisational effects – such as job dissatisfaction, poor work relations and absenteeism.

stress inoculation therapy: a form of cognitive behavioural therapy developed by Meichenbaum (1985) specifically to deal with stress. Meichenbaum claimed that, in order to deal effectively with stress, individuals should develop a way of coping before the problem arises. He suggested that people could inoculate themselves against the 'disease' of stress in the same way that they could inoculate themselves against infectious diseases. There are three phases in stress inoculation:
1. Conceptualisation – the client is educated about the nature and impact of stress.
2. Skills acquisition – coping skills are taught and practised in the clinic and then in real life.
3. Application – clients are given opportunities to apply the newly learned coping skills in different situations, which become increasingly stressful.

stress management: the different ways in which people attempt to cope with stress. There are two broad categories of coping strategies:
- the first involves attempts to change our relationship with the stressful environment. Examples of this category would include escaping from the stressful situation, or preparing ourselves for situations that we anticipate will be stressful. This might involve thinking ahead about a situation and its likely impact, thereby preparing ourselves adequately for the event
- the second category of response research involves 'palliative' strategies that attempt to soften the impact of the stress once it has occurred. Examples of this category include denial, by which we refuse to acknowledge all or some of the threat in the situation, and intellectualisation, by which we detach ourselves emotionally from the situation.

Other coping strategies, including various relaxation techniques, may be appropriate in some or all cases. However, the use of such strategies may delay the direct reaction that we need to solve the problem that is causing the stress. This is also true of another way of coping, escaping via the use of alcohol, tranquillisers, or other drugs.

There are some stressors for which no clear solution exists, for example, caring for the chronically ill. In such situations, softening the impact of stress may be the only way for us to cope. If stress is long-term or particularly severe, marked emotional changes may take place. If the coping strategies we employ do not work, we may regard the situation as one for which there is no solution and increasingly see ourselves as unable to **control** the events of our lives. Hopelessness and helplessness are both likely to give rise to feelings of **depression**, and may even lead to suicidal thoughts.

The effectiveness of each of these strategies is determined by many other factors, some of which are listed below:

- **previous experience:** once we have experienced a particular stressful situation, we are usually able to cope better with it if reoccurs. The experience provides us with knowledge about the situation and makes it more predictable. For example, the second visit to a dentist is usually easier than the first
- **information:** information about an impending stressful event allows us to make preparations that will ease the impact and intensity of our reactions to the stress. It is well known, for example, that describing surgical procedures and typical post-operative reactions, including pain, to patients can often aid recovery
- **individual differences:** some people try to protect themselves from the full impact of the stress by denying, playing down, or emotionally detaching themselves from the situation. Providing information to these people may actually increase their stress levels, rather than decreasing them
- **social support:** not surprisingly, the impact of stressful events is affected by our social systems. Response to stress can be eased by support from either the family or the community. For example, studies have shown that women who have close, confiding relationships are less likely to develop stress-related psychiatric disorders
- **control:** the degree to which we believe we can **control** a situation has an important impact on the degree to which that situation is likely to cause us stress. Research has shown that the most harmful and distressing situations are those in which we feel entirely helpless, believing that nothing we can do will significantly alter the outcome.

stressors: see *stress*

subconscious: this term is used in a number of different ways, although the common thread is that all refer to a stage or level that is just outside of conscious awareness. In **psychoanalytic** theory it refers to a level through which material must pass before it reaches the conscious mind. The term **preconscious** is sometimes used in preference to this term. Neither should be confused with the term **unconscious** which has an altogether different meaning in psychoanalysis. Cognitive psychologists might also use the term to refer to a state where memories are not active in the conscious mind, but are able to be brought into awareness at any time.

subculture: a 'culture within a culture' that retains many of the characteristics of the parent culture, but also has a number of special characteristics of its own. For example, within any culture, there may be a number of subcultures such as 'youth', 'delinquent' or 'football hooligans'.

sublimation: a *Freudian* defence mechanism whereby a person expresses sexual or aggressive energy in ways that are perceived as being more acceptable to society. Thus, many activities, from dancing, humour, art, music or even love itself, may all be seen as the sublimated gratification of sexual or aggressive energies.

subliminal perception: a controversial and not altogether widely accepted view that the behaviour of human beings can be influenced by stimuli presented below the threshold necessary for them to be perceived. Research findings on this phenomena have been inconclusive as to its existence, but there is sufficient concern over the possibility that it really does work to declare the use of such techniques in advertising and propaganda as highly unethical.

substance abuse: a pattern of behaviour where a person relies excessively on a particular substance (e.g. alcohol or opioids such as heroin) and allows it to dominate their life. Regular use of some substances may change the body's response to that substance and establish a maladaptive pattern of behaviour aimed at satisfying the body's craving for the substance concerned. Because of their loss of **control** over their need for the substance, and the fact that it occupies such a central part of their lives, substance abusers may seriously damage their personal relationships as well as their physical health. Prolonged use of addictive substances such as nicotine and heroin, may lead to a person becoming **physically dependent** on that substance.

summation: literally, an adding together, either in statistics, where a set of scores are added together, or in physiology, where the intensity of a stimulus is increased due to the combined effect of more than one sensory input.

superego: in **Freudian** theory, that part of the **personality** that deals with the moral and the ideal. Whereas the **id** is concerned with instant gratification of its desires, the superego is more concerned with whether behaviour is morally acceptable. The superego develops out of the **Oedipus complex**, and is largely an internalisation of the attitudes, values and rules of the same sex parent. It has two parts, the ego ideal, which are the standards of good behaviour that we aspire to, and the **conscience**, which stops us from engaging in behaviour that is considered wrong. Through making us feel proud and satisfied when we fulfil our ego ideal, and guilty and ashamed when we offend our conscience, the superego gradually develops into a powerful influence on our behaviour. It is always in **conflict** with the id, however, and the conflicting demands of these two hypothesised structures must be arbitrated by the third part of the personality, the **ego**.

superordinate goal refers to a higher and more important goal than that normally pursued by individuals within a group. Research often shows that **prejudice** between groups can be reduced, at least temporarily, if both groups are involved in pursuing a common goal. For example, in times of war, many social prejudices would be put aside as people join forces against a common enemy.

superstitious behaviour is behaviour that is maintained by some coincidental relationship between a **reinforcer** and the behaviour. If a reinforcer happens at the same time or shortly after an unrelated event, we may forge a superstitious relationship between the two events even though there is no genuine connection. Thus, the wearing of 'lucky underwear' or the bizarre spitting and boot-tapping behaviour of American baseball players can be attributed to some previously coincidental co-occurrence of the behaviour and some desired outcome.

surface structure: see **deep structure**

surveys and interviews are techniques where investigators make use of **questionnaires** to obtain information about a particular area. Surveys are generally remote, in that respondents (people who complete the questionnaires) do not have an interviewer present, whereas interviews involve face-to-face interaction between the interviewer and the respondent. The investigator first defines an area of interest such as people's attitude to television violence, and designs questions that will elicit information relevant to that topic. Interviewers are specially trained to deliver questions in a **standardised** way, that is without bias or encouragement to **respondents** to answer questions in a certain way. If interviewers cannot develop an appropriate rapport with their interviewees, then questions may not be answered in an open and honest manner.

PROS:
- both of these techniques allow investigators to focus their attention on very specific areas of interest
- surveys tend to be a more economical method to use than interviews, and have the additional benefit of greater anonymity for the respondent
- interviews, particularly unstructured interviews, allow the interviewer to extract more information from the respondent and to clarify anything about the questions that might be confusing.

CONS:
- respondents may attempt to 'fake good' in that they may give answers that put them in a favourable light
- as mentioned above, interviews are less economical than surveys and, because of a lack of anonymity, may produce artificially bland responses
- questionnaires may contain questions that are leading or ambiguous, and in the interests of easier marking, less searching than might be the case in a face-to-face interview.

survivor guilt: a deep sense of guilt that is experienced by those who have experienced and survived some catastrophe which claimed the lives of others. It was first evident in survivors of the Holocaust in the Second World War, but has been seen subsequently in the survivors of natural disasters such as floods and earthquakes or other tragic events such as the Hillsborough disaster in 1989 (when 98 Liverpool supporters lost their lives). Part of this sense of guilt is caused by the belief among survivors that they did not do enough to save others who died, and part derives from the pervasive feeling that compared to those who died, those who survived were unworthy to do so.

symbiosis: a relationship between two animals where each animal derives benefit from the arrangement. A common example of a symbiotic relationship can be found in the behaviour of the cleaner wrasse, a small reef-dwelling fish. The cleaner wrasse cleans the parasites off larger predatory fish, which make no attempt to eat the cleaner. Both animals profit from the arrangement: the smaller fish obtains food and the larger fish is cleared of parasites that would otherwise cause it considerable harm. Symbiotic relationships are not recognised as being mutually beneficial by the two participating animals. Each has evolved a behaviour that is advantageous to itself. The fact that the other animal also benefits has led biologists to label the relationship symbiotic.

symbolic representation: see *Bruner, J*

sympathetic nervous system: see *autonomic nervous system*

sympathomedullary pathway: one of the two main ways in which the body responds to stress. Immediate stressors activate the sympathetic branch of the *autonomic nervous system*, which prepares the body for fight or flight by releasing noradrenaline into the bloodstream. Changes include increased heart rate and blood pressure and the mobilisation of fat and glycogen in the bloodstream. Neurones of the sympathetic nervous system also travel to the adrenal medulla, which, when activated, releases adrenaline into the bloodstream. This has widespread effects within the body, for example boosting the supply of oxygen to the brain and muscles and suppressing less important functions such as digestion.

symptom: in its general usage within psychology, this is some event which is taken to indicate the existence of an underlying disorder.

symptom substitution is the idea that if neurotic symptoms are eliminated without the underlying causes being treated, the person will merely exhibit the neurosis in other ways and through other symptoms.

synapse refers to the gap between the end of the axon of one *neuron* and the dendrite of the next. It is referred to as the synaptic cleft or synaptic gap.

synaptic transmission refers to the process by which a nerve impulse passes across the synaptic cleft from one *neuron* (the presynaptic neuron) to another (the postsynaptic neuron). As an *action potential* reaches the end of one neuron it causes small sacs (the synaptic vesicles) to open and release *neurotransmitter* substances. These neurotransmitters flood across the synaptic cleft. When they reach the dendrite of the next neuron, they bind with a special receptor site. Depending on the receptor sites that are activated, this may produce an excitatory or inhibitory effect. If it is an excitatory effect, it means that the cell is more likely to fire; if it is an inhibitory effect, this means that the cell is less likely to fire. Inhibitory synapses are vital because they prevent us from being overwhelmed by excitatory impulses or by low-level information. The likelihood of the receiving cell firing is also determined by the number of receptor sites that are stimulated. The more receptor sites, the more likely it is that the cell will fire. This, in turn, is determined by the number of transmitters released by the presynaptic neuron, which is influenced by the frequency of impulses arriving at the synaptic vesicles that manufacture and release these transmitters.

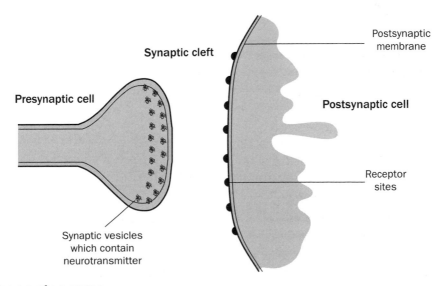

Diagram of a synapse

systematic desensitisation: a type of *behaviour therapy* which is designed to reduce the anxiety that an individual feels when in the presence of a particular feared object. In this procedure, a client is first trained to relax, then exposed to graded stages of anxiety-provoking situations. The idea is that the relaxation inhibits any anxiety that might be elicited by the object. The person is gradually exposed to the feared object, first through imagining it and then moving into actual physical situations involving the feared object.

Do you need revision help and advice?

Go to pages 298–312 for a range of revision appendices that include plenty of exam advice and tips.

tables: a way of presenting a collated summary of data collected in a research study. A table should always be able to stand independently of text, i.e. be interpretable without reference to the text, but should also be accompanied by text that tells the reader how it should be interpreted.

tabula rasa: literally meaning 'blank slate', this refers to a belief popularly attributed to *behaviourism* that all human behaviour is infinitely plastic, and therefore is ultimately explainable in terms of the experiences that an organism goes through rather than any *genetic* predispositions or characteristics that the organism possesses. This approach is probably correct in assuming that some aspects of behaviour (such as social *roles* or attitudes) are almost entirely determined by cultural variables, but are on less solid ground in refusing to acknowledge that other aspects of behaviour are influenced and patterned by genetically determined characteristics.

tachistoscope: a piece of laboratory equipment which enables an experimenter to present visual stimuli to *participants* for varying time durations and at different illumination intensities. Depending on the complexity of the machine, stimuli can be exposed for anything from 1 msec to over 1 minute.

tardive dyskinesia: a syndrome that is sometimes experienced as a side-effect of anti-psychotic drugs. It is characterised by involuntary movements of the tongue, lips, jaw and other facial movements.

taste aversion refers to a type of learning where an organism forms an association between feelings of sickness and (usually) a particular food. As a consequence of this learned association, the organism avoids that food in the future. This learned association violates the usual principles of conditioning in that it is formed after only one experience of the food–sickness combination, and is extremely resistant to *extinction*. Most organisms show 'bait shyness', a hesitancy to sample new or unusual food. If a food is toxic in some way, they must learn to avoid such foods in order to survive. Organisms that can make such rapid associations are more likely to survive and pass on their genes to the next generation. This behaviour is shaped by *natural selection*, and is seen as an example of *biological preparedness*.

teaching styles: refers to the preferred tactics used by individual teachers to impart knowledge to their students. Teaching style may be classified in broad terms in these four main ways with the teacher acting as:

- formal authority who delivers knowledge to a largely passive audience
- demonstrator or personal model for learning

- facilitator who encourages and assists students to learn for themselves
- delegator who shifts the responsibility for knowledge gathering to the students.

telegraphic speech refers to the shortened sentences (resembling telegrams) that characterise children's speech patterns from around 18 months to two years. Examples of telegraphic speech, such as 'doggy chase pussy cat' do show the rudiments of early grammar, and can be quite creative, given that many of the sentence constructions will never have been heard from adults. Telegraphic sentences tend to leave out the 'functor' words, that is the articles and prepositions, containing only the 'important' nouns and verbs. Young children who are able to generate only short utterances will tend to emphasise what for them are the meaningful words in a sentence, and de-emphasise the less important spacing words such as 'the', 'and' and 'under'

telepathy: the transmission of thoughts from one person to another without any verbal or other type of communication taking place. Telepathy is what some people refer to as 'mind-reading'.

temperament: part of a person's general nature that is characterised by their tendency toward particular types of emotional reactions or moods. It is generally acknowledged that temperament has a strong genetic influence because of the similarities within families, and the individual differences shown by new-born babies in their reaction to a range of different *stimuli*.

template theories: see *pattern recognition*

temporal lobe: see *brain*

territoriality: the tendency of animals to defend a particular geographical area from other members of their own species. Territories are important to their owners for two main reasons:
- territories provide material benefits such as food resources and nesting sites. If food becomes scarce within a territory, however, an animal may abandon it and search elsewhere
- territories give their owners *control* over a resource (such as a place to breed) that is needed by females, therefore females are more likely to choose males with territories as mating partners.

Some territories have no resources and are used merely as a place where a male can display to a female. These display grounds (or leks) enable a female to assess males on a number of criteria, including the centrality of their territory in the lek (better quality males normally occupy more central sites in the lek). Territories can be defended in a number of ways. Long-range signals such as scent markings and vocalisations may serve to keep *conspecifics* away from the territory, whereas *agonistic* gestures such as threat displays are used for closer encounters.

testosterone: a *hormone* produced by the testes in the male (although small amounts of testosterone are also produced by the ovaries in females). This is responsible for many characteristics of 'maleness' such as the development of the *secondary sexual characteristics*. Testosterone has also been implicated in *aggression* and in *dominance* behaviour in non-human animals.

test-retest reliability: see *reliability*

thalamus: part of the *forebrain*, the thalamus transmits nerve impulses which travel up sensory pathways to the appropriate areas of the *cortex*. The thalamus also has an important role in memory. Damage can produce *anterograde amnesia*, an inability to learn new information. Damage to the thalamus can also cause tremors (jerky movements) while at rest, although these are absent when the client is carrying out an intentional movement.

thanatos: a *Freudian* term which represents the death *instinct*. This is characterised by *aggressive* behaviour and a general rejection of things pleasurable.

thematic apperception test (TAT): a type of *projective test* in which people are shown ambiguous pictures and asked to tell a story about them, including what had led up to the event in the picture, what was going on, what the characters were thinking and how the story would end. In a normal person, the TAT can reveal concerns and personality characteristics, as well as their motivation for power, achievement and affiliation. In a clinical client, the test can reveal their underlying emotional problems.

theories of crime: theories that attempt to account for the onset of criminal behaviour. These include the following:

- Biological theories – explain crime in terms of genetic transmission (criminal behaviour appears to run in families), biochemistry (e.g. low levels of brain serotonin) or neurology (e.g. some criminals show clear evidence of brain dysfunction).
- Personality theories – Eysenck (1964) believed that certain personality types were more inclined towards crime. These were neurotic extraverts, whose personality predisposed them to sensation seeking and impulsivity and were therefore more likely to carry out acts of antisocial behaviour.
- Psychoanalytic theories – Freud believed that a poorly developed superego would result in poor control over antisocial impulses and a lack of guilt, which would lead to a greater likelihood of unacceptable behaviour. Bowlby's maternal deprivation hypothesis proposed that disruption of the attachment bond between the mother and child during the early years might lead to 'affectionless psychopathy' and later deviance.
- Social learning theories – criminal behaviour is learned through association with other people, and this learning includes techniques to carry out specific crimes (e.g. stealing cars or shoplifting) as well as specific attitudes toward criminal behaviour. See also *social contexts of pathways into crime*.

theory: a collection of general principles which serve as an explanation of established facts and observable data. For example, a psychologist who observes a consistent tendency for people to select marriage partners on the basis of physical attractiveness might generate a theory of interpersonal attraction that will be able to explain these findings. *Scientific* theories can be tested for their accuracy through *hypothesis* and further data collection. It is an essential characteristic of a scientific theory that it is amenable to such rigorous testing. In its simplest form, a theory can be seen as an honest attempt to explain a particular body of knowledge. In this more liberal sense of the word, a number of psychological theories that fail the criteria for 'scientific' theories are nonetheless regarded as 'theories'.

theory of mind: an understanding that other people possess mental states that involve ideas and views of the world that are different from our own. Children typically develop a theory of mind around four years of age. Absence of this ability has been implicated in *autistic disorder (autism)*. Many of the difficulties associated with autism (such as difficulties in communicating or in developing interpersonal relationships) might be explained in terms of an absence of a theory of mind. An often-quoted theory of mind problem that is correctly solved by most four-year-olds but incorrectly solved by children with autistic disorder is demonstrated in the *Sally-Anne test*.

theory of planned behaviour: a person's intention to carry out a particular behaviour is only possible if they believe they have some behavioural **control** over the behaviour in question. For example, some people refuse to diet or exercise because they believe that they have no control over their weight. Their likelihood of future success in a particular behaviour, therefore, will be determined by past experiences ('It hasn't helped before') or perceived obstacles ('I won't have the willpower to keep it up'). If the individual has favourable attitudes and subjective norms (see **theory of reasoned action**) towards a particular behaviour, the likelihood of them actually performing the behaviour in question increases with the degree of perceived control. The importance of behavioural control has been highlighted in areas such as weight loss, reducing problem drinking and looking for a job.

theory of reasoned action: a theory that explains why sometimes **attitudes** are good predictors of a person's behaviour, and sometimes they are not. This theory suggests that specific attitudes (e.g. toward Children in Need) are far more likely to be related to specific behaviours (e.g. pledging money) than might be general attitudes toward 'charity'. Specifically the theory suggests that the tendency to engage in a specific behaviour is determined by a person's intention to do so. I may feel myself generally charitable, but may never actually donate anything. However, I may feel that this particular charity is extremely worthwhile, and may therefore resolve to pledge ten pounds during the evening broadcast. A second aspect of the theory is the concept of a 'subjective norm' which proposes that a person's intention to act in a certain way is influenced by what he believes important others feel he should do. So, if the information that a person has about a particular behaviour is itself mediated by what others think about it, this produces a positive or negative subjective norm for that behaviour. If we are aware that people who are important to us think that giving money to charity is a 'good thing to do', we are more likely to have a positive attitude towards it, and are more likely to act consistently with that attitude.

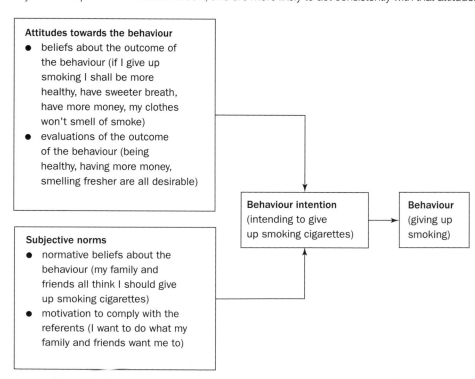

Theory of reasoned action

therapeutic community: a therapeutic situation where a person's total social environment is used to help them overcome some psychological disturbance. This is based on the assumption that it was the person's former social environment that led to the disturbance in the first place.

therapy is the name given to any process that helps people to overcome their psychological difficulties. A broad distinction may be drawn between **psychotherapies** (that tend to involve discussion or action) and **somatic treatments** (medical or biological intervention).

thinking: a mental manipulation of ideas, memories, symbols, etc. The term encompasses a number of different types of activity (such as creativity, intellectual functioning and problem solving), each of which could be said to involve thinking. All the different types of thinking have the following in common:
- thinking is symbolic (it uses words and images)
- thinking is not directly observable, but is inferred
- thinking involves the manipulation of some identifiable content.

third force is a term sometimes used to describe the **humanistic** perspective in psychology. Humanistic psychology developed as an alternative to the psychoanalytic and behaviourist perspectives, and was therefore considered a 'third force'

Thorndike puzzle-box: an early piece of laboratory apparatus used to study learning. It consisted of a wooden 'cage' into which an animal (typically a cat) was placed. The animal could see a food reward on the outside of the box, but could not get to it until it had discovered a way to escape (by manipulating a mechanism inside the box). As escape was followed by reward, the animals learned quickly and eventually were able to work the mechanism immediately without any wasted irrelevant behaviours. This is seen as evidence of **trial-and-error learning** and was the forerunner of Skinner's **operant conditioning**.

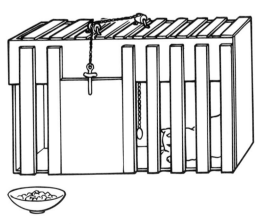

Thorndike puzzle-box

thought disorder: a general term that refers to any disturbance of thought or speech that might be symptomatic of a mental disorder. Thought disorders are, for example, a **symptom** of **schizophrenia**, where they may be experienced as incoherence in thought and speech patterns, or as delusions.

three mountains test: a *Piagetian* task in which children are shown a model of three mountains, each of which has a feature that distinguishes it from the others (see diagram below). The child then stands to the side of the model, and watches as a doll is positioned at some point around the mountains. If **pre-operational** children are asked to select a photograph that shows the doll's view of the mountains, they are unable to do so, picking instead the view that they have. This is taken as an indication of the pre-operational child's **egocentricity**.

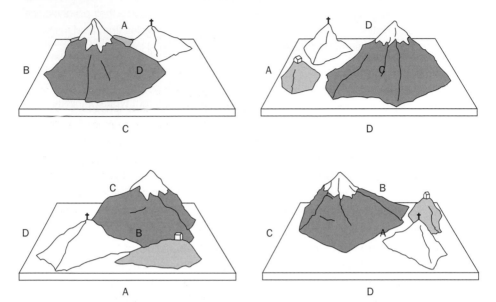

The three mountains test

Thurstone's multifactor theory of intelligence: Thurstone argued against the existence of one underlying general intelligence, proposing instead seven primary factors that make up intelligence, namely word fluency, comprehension, numerical computation, spatial skills, associative memory, reasoning and perceptual speed.

time sampling: involves brief periods of **observation** such that a number of individuals can be observed. For example, if we had to observe a group of ten people over a one-hour period, we might observe each person for ten 30-second time samples, and build up some idea of the frequency and consistency of specific behaviour patterns.

tip of the tongue phenomenon: a term used to refer to the feeling that we know a particular word, yet are unable to retrieve it. Research has established that when participants feel that they know something yet cannot retrieve it, they are usually able to recognise the word immediately it is presented.

token economy: a type of **behaviour modification** programme based on the principles of **operant conditioning**. Token economies have been used in many different settings and for many different disorders, including severely regressed **schizophrenics** and **autistic** children. There are three aspects of a token-economy programme:
1. Patients are rewarded for desirable behaviour (such as self-care) by being given tokens.
2. The more patients perform these desirable behaviours, the more tokens they receive.
3. These tokens can then be cashed in for items or activities that the person really wants (such as sweets or trips to the seaside).

tolerance refers to the way in which the body adjusts to the continued use of certain drugs so that larger and larger doses of the drug become necessary in order to produce the same effect.

top-down processing: explanations of perceptual processing which rely on previous experiences, expectations or the context in which perception takes place.

trace decay: see *decay*

tragedy of the commons: a term originally attributed to Garrett Hardin and refers to dilemmas that involve multiple individuals each seeking immediate benefits from limited resources. The dilemma is based on the belief that many big problems are caused by the sum of the solutions to many smaller problems. The tragedy of the commons gets its name from a historical right of farmers to graze a set number of cattle on common land. If 100 farmers graze one cow each and the common can sustain 100 cows maximum there is no problem. However, if one farmer chooses to graze one extra cow ('after all, just one extra won't make much difference') and the others follow, the common becomes overgrazed and unfit for use. As a result, everybody suffers because of their attempts to increase their own self-interest in a co-operative arrangement. The tragedy of the commons is an example of a *social dilemma* and has been applied to many problems of our contemporary society, most notably over-population and the exploitation of the earth's resources for short-term profit.

trait: a term used to refer to a hypothetical structure that might account for any enduring personal characteristics that a person might have. For example, if a person is always buying things without appearing to think too carefully about their purchases, we may say they have the trait of impulsiveness. Similarly, if someone is nearly always late for things, we may describe them as lacking the trait for punctuality. In the study of genetics, the word may also be used to describe any inherited characteristic (such as eye colour).

trait and state anxiety: 'state' anxiety is the intense anxiety state we experience when something causes us to feel temporarily anxious. For example, we might experience this type of anxiety if a dog runs out in front of our car when we are driving. When the moment passes (and the dog is safely on the pavement again), the anxiety retreats and we feel normal again. Trait anxiety refers to the relatively stable individual difference between individuals in that some individuals have a tendency to become more anxious than others in situations that are likely to provoke anxiety.

trait theories of personality assume that people possess enduring characteristics (*traits*) that determine their behaviour across different situations and across time. Some psychologists use the idea of traits in a more conservative way, choosing merely to infer their existence through observation of patterns of similar behaviours. For example, if someone is persistently late for appointments, we tend to say that they have the trait of unpunctuality.

transfer of training refers to the way in which we might transfer skills learned in one situation to a second, related situation. Thus, learning to play tennis may introduce a range of co-ordination and racket skills that would then transfer to similar games such as squash.

transference: a term used in *psychotherapy* to describe the way in which patients may recreate feelings and conflicts from their life (most notably early feelings towards their parents) and transfer them to the therapist.

trauma: a term that is used either for a physical injury caused by an external force, or a psychological injury caused by an emotional event.

traumatic: an event that is capable of causing either a physical or psychological injury.

trial: a commonly used term in experimental psychology, it refers to a single unit of experimentation where a stimulus is presented, an organism responds and a consequence follows. In *conditioning*, learning is said to take place after a number of such trials.

trial-and-error learning: a view of learning originally put forward by Edward Thorndike, this proposes that responses that do not achieve the desired effect are gradually eliminated, and those that do are gradually strengthened.

triangular theory of love: Sternberg (1988) describes love as consisting of three components:

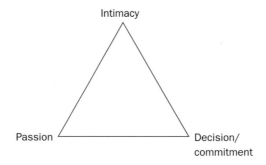

- intimacy: the closeness each partner feels to the other and the strength of the bond that binds them together. Partners high in intimacy like, value and understand their partners
- passion: based on romantic feelings, physical attraction for and sexual intimacy with the partner
- decision/commitment: represents cognitive factors such as acknowledging that one is in love and has a commitment to maintaining the relationship.

According to this theory, 'true' (i.e. consummate) love is achieved when all three components are achieved.

Consummate Love = Intimacy + Passion + Commitment (i.e. a balanced triangle)

Relationships can become unbalanced if there is too great an investment in one component rather than the others, or if one component is missing as in the following examples:
- Romantic Love = Intimacy + Passion
  (i.e. no commitment, as in a holiday romance)
- Companionate Love = Intimacy + Commitment
  (e.g. a marriage where partners are committed to each other, but where the passion has disappeared)
- Infatuation = Passion alone
  (passionate, obsessive love for another, without intimacy or commitment).

t-test: a statistical test used with parametric data to find out if there is a significant (i.e. real) difference between the mean scores of two different groups in an experimental study.

Turing test: a test to determine how closely computers could mimic human thought. Turing suggested that if a human was conversing through typed questions and answers with another person and at some point unknown to the first person, the second was replaced by a computer, would the first person notice that the switch had been made? If they did not, then the computer would have passed the Turing test and could be said to be capable of human thought.

Turner's syndrome: a genetic condition that affects only females, and which can cause a range of physical, emotional or educational disabilities. This syndrome occurs when one of the two X chromosomes that are found in females is completely or partially missing. There are two characteristics that occur in almost all cases of Turner's syndrome, i.e. being shorter than the average height and a lack of development of the ovaries, with the result that such women are infertile. The other characteristics of Turner's syndrome vary greatly but most girls and women with this condition are able to lead relatively normal and healthy lives.

twin studies refers to studies where *monozygotic* and *dizygotic twins* are studied in order to assess the relative contributions of *genetics* and *environment* on the development of some characteristic. In some of the more famous tests of *intelligence*, monozygotic and dizygotic twins have been studied both reared together and reared apart. Typically such studies tend to find great similarities in intelligence for monozygotic twins, and these similarities are most pronounced when they have been brought up in the same environment. Similarities for dizygotic twins are not so pronounced, and significantly the *correlations* for dizygotic twins reared together tend to be less than for monozygotic twins reared apart. In concordance studies, other individuals of known genetic similarity (father/son or first cousins, for example) can also be studied in an attempt to ascertain the role of genetics in the development of a particular behaviour (such as *schizophrenia*).

two-factor theory of emotion: emotion is seen as having two components or 'factors': physiological arousal and cognition. When we experience physiological arousal, we must then use cognition (i.e. reasoning) to explain this feeling. This is usually achieved by looking at the context in which we are experiencing arousal and other things that are going on at the same time. Thus, arousal may lead to feelings of intense pleasure in some situations and intense fear in others.

two-process theory of memory: see *Atkinson and Shiffrin model of memory*

two-tailed hypothesis: also known as a 'non-directional' hypothesis, this predicts that there will be a difference (or correlation, or association) between two sets of scores, but does not predict the direction that those results will go. So, we may predict that there will be a difference in performance between a group of people (the experimental group) receiving the *independent variable* and another group (the *control group*) who do not, but unless we actually say which group is likely to perform better, the hypothesis is two-tailed.

two-tailed test: when testing for *statistical significance*, a two-tailed statistical test is used when there is a possibility that results may occur in either predicted direction (as demonstrated in the *two-tailed hypothesis*). A *one-tailed test*, on the other hand, is only used when the researcher is convinced that the results could go in one direction only. For example, in testing the effect of alcohol on driving ability, it would be unusual if alcohol enhanced driving ability, therefore a one-tailed test would be appropriate. On the other hand, if a researcher wanted to analyse the effects of eating hamburgers on driving ability, the results would be less certain, so a two-tailed test would be more appropriate.

type 1 error: an error made following statistical analysis if the *null hypothesis* is rejected when there is still a good chance that it might be true. There are a number of reasons for making a type 1 error, but the commonest is through the adoption of a significance level that is not stringent enough, for example, choosing to reject the null hypothesis at the p (**probability**) = 0.10 level rather than the more customary p = 0.05 level. In this case, the probability of chance causing the results (or of some other explanation not catered for by the **alternative hypothesis)**, is 0.10, or 1 in 10. That is considered unacceptably high, and to reject the null hypothesis on those grounds would be considered an error of optimism, or a type 1 error.

type 2 error: an error made following statistical analysis if the **null hypothesis** is retained when there is a good chance it is false. The commonest reason for this type of error is if the significance level adopted is too stringent, for example choosing not to reject the null hypothesis at the customary p = 0.05 level, and holding out until the 0.01 level instead. In this case, the **probability** of chance causing the results might be considered low enough at the p = 0.05 level, therefore to insist on a p = 0.01 level might be seen as unnecessarily stringent and an error of pessimism (a type 2 error).

type A personality/behaviour: also referred to as Type A behaviour, this refers to a set of personality characteristics that, when present together, increase the risk of stress-related heart disease. People with type A personality are characterised by a constant feeling of working against the clock and a strong sense of competitiveness in everything that they do. Research into the heart disease/type A connection has been contradictory, with several studies providing evidence for the relationship in the USA, but not in the UK. Recent studies have found greater links with heart disease when the characteristics of anger and hostility are also present. There have been a number of attempts to explain type A personality in physiological terms, although none of these has been conclusive. Type A people do appear to be as physiologically aroused when at rest as when carrying out a stressful task. It does appear that type As do not find stressful tasks as stressful as we think they do. This might be the secret of their success.

Time pressure

Always working against the clock
Doing two or more things at once
Irritation with slow-moving traffic or queues
Impatience with others
Agitation when forced to do nothing

Competitiveness

Always playing games to win
Very self-critical
Measuring success as material productivity

Anger and hostility

Feelings of anger both towards the outside world and sometimes towards the self

---

Type A behaviour patterns. Originally only the first two categories were emphasised. Addition of the Anger and hostility component increases the association with heart disease

type B personality/behaviour: a behaviour pattern associated with people who approach life in a more relaxed manner, appear free of hostility and aggression and who are not highly competitive in their work. Research suggests that such individuals may have a lower risk of stress-related heart disease.

type C personality/behaviour: describes individuals who are cooperative, unassertive, unexpressive of negative emotions (such as anger) and overly compliant with external authorities. This is in direct contrast to the type A individual. The development of such a behavioural style is hypothesised as being the consequence of genetic dispositions or family interactions whereby children learn to cope with the challenges of life by placing the needs of others ahead of their own. Although this way of coping may be successful to a degree, the chronic blockage of the individual's own needs and feelings may have serious consequences, including a greater vulnerability to cancer.

type theories of personality are ways of classifying people in terms of a limited number of psychological types. Unlike some other classifications of **personality** (such as **extroversion**), type classifications are 'all or nothing'. That is, a person is either one type or another, there is no mixing of categories. An example of a type theory would be Sheldon's constitutional theory.

ultradian rhythms have a frequency of more than one complete cycle every 24 hours. For example, we go through the different stages of sleep several times during a single night's sleep.

unconditional positive regard: a term from humanistic psychology which refers to the full acceptance of a person regardless of whatever he or she may do or say. Unconditional positive regard is a key component of *client-centred therapy*.

unconditioned response: the commonly used term for what Pavlov referred to as the unconditional reflex, it refers to any response that is consistently produced by an organism whenever an *unconditioned stimulus* is present. Pavlov's original theory emphasised the important role of these unconditioned reflexes, but later behaviourists widened the use of the term to include a whole range of innate behaviours and also behaviours that had previously been established through learning and were now an established part of the organism's repertoire.

unconditioned stimulus: any stimulus that consistently elicits an *unconditioned response* from an organism. In Pavlov's original research on *classical conditioning*, the unconditioned stimulus was the presence of food in the mouth, and the unconditioned response was salivation. The response of salivation was made in anticipation of receiving food (the unconditioned stimulus).

unconscious: in the literal general sense, a lack of *consciousness*. In *psychoanalysis*, the term is used to refer to that part of the *psyche* that contains *repressed* ideas and images, as well as primitive desires and impulses that have never been allowed to enter the conscious mind. Content that is contained in the unconscious mind is generally deemed to be too anxiety-provoking to be allowed in consciousness, therefore is maintained at an unconscious level where, according to *Freud*, it still manages to influence our behaviour (see *psychoanalysis*).

unconscious motive: a term used by *Freud* (among others) to emphasise that not all motivation is conscious and rational. Much of our behaviour, according to Freud, is a product of factors outside our conscious awareness. These may operate under the guise of defence mechanisms or in other symbolic ways.

understudied relationships: the majority of psychological research into interpersonal relationships has stressed the nature of heterosexual, voluntary and impermanent relationships in the Western world. More recently, social psychologists have begun to explore the tremendous amount of diversity in human relationships, including gay and lesbian relationships, *mediated relationships* and the importance of individual and cultural diversity in forming and shaping human relationships.

unfalsifiable: if a *theory* or *hypothesis* cannot be disproved by *data*, it is described as being unfalsifiable. This means that the theory or hypothesis has no scientific value since it cannot be used to make predictions. An unfalsifiable hypothesis will produce data which may or may not support the prediction. If it does not, the hypothesis still holds true, therefore the whole exercise is pointless.

unipolar depression: see *depression (major)*

unipolar disorder: see *depression (major)*

universal: any underlying characteristic of human beings that is capable of being applied to all members of the species despite differences of experience and upbringing.

unstructured interview: a type of interview in which the interviewer asks questions spontaneously, rather than sticking to scripted questions. This allows the interviewer to pursue issues that arise during the interview. In this way, the interview is guided by the responses given by the respondent (person being interviewed).

uplifts: the negative effects of *daily hassles* can, to some degree, be offset by the more positive experiences that we have every day (e.g. a compliment or letter from a friend).

utilitarianism argues that what is ethically acceptable is that which produces the greatest pleasure and happiness (relative to pain and suffering) for the greatest number of people. According to this argument no one person's happiness is more important than any other's. Peter Singer's book *Animal Liberation*, published in 1975, extends this utilitarian argument to include all sentient (capable of sensation) creatures. His 'principle of equality' holds that *all* such creatures have an equal interest in avoiding pain and suffering.

A–Z Online

Log on to A–Z Online to search the database of terms, print revision lists and much more. Go to **www.philipallan.co.uk/a-zonline to** get started.

validity refers to the confidence that we may have that a test, measurement or *experimental* manipulation is actually doing the job it has been designed to do. This very general term is used in many different ways within psychology. Within an experiment, it is possible to assess:

- *internal validity* – was the observed effect really a product of the experimental manipulation? In Milgram's *obedience* to authority studies, conclusions regarding the effect of authority would have been invalid if the participants had not believed they had really been giving electric shocks
- *external validity* – even if the experiment has worked, the results may not apply to other people and to other situations. Social psychology experiments are often criticised for their reliance on American undergraduates and their use of the laboratory as a context for the research (see also *ecological validity*).

When testing the validity of a test or measurement, we assume that it is measuring (or testing) what was intended. There are a number of ways of testing this:

- face validity – does the test appear to measure what it is supposed to be testing? For example, a test of *intelligence* may clearly appear to be just that (high face validity) or may be disguised as something else (low face validity)
- content validity – is the test a fair representation of the area of interest? A-level examination papers are checked carefully to ensure that the questions are an appropriate test of the skills and knowledge of A-level psychology students
- concurrent validity – a test might be validated against an existing measure. For example, a new test of intelligence can be compared with a test of known validity. If participants perform the same on the new test as they would on the existing test, then the new test also has validity
- predictive validity – does the test predict or forecast later performance on some other criterion? Tests used for selection purposes should have good predictive validity
- construct validity – does the test accurately measure some underlying construct, e.g. does an intelligence test actually measure intelligence? If it does, then it should influence people to perform on intelligence tests according to their level of underlying intelligence.

valium: the trade name for diazepam, one of the benzodiazepines, anti-anxiety drugs that cause a decrease in nervousness and anxiety and an overall calming effect. As well as possible side-effects such as drowsiness and general slowing of cognitive functioning, this class of drugs also causes tolerance (higher doses become necessary to produce the same effect) and dependence (attempting to stop using them can lead to **withdrawal** symptoms) if taken over long periods.

values: those aspects of **behaviour** that are important to individuals within a **culture** or may be shared by most members of that culture. Examples of common values in Western cultures include honesty, fair play and freedom of expression. If these values are ignored or rejected by an individual, other members of the culture may define these transgressions as anti-social or as **abnormal behaviour.**

variable: literally anything whose value is free to change. Thus, in a test of intelligence, intellectual ability is the variable; in an experiment to test the effects of loud music on mental arithmetic, the loudness of the music is the variable. Variables are usefully divided up into **independent variables**, **dependent variables** and **extraneous variables** when used in an **experimental design**.

variable interval reinforcement: see *schedules of reinforcement*

variable ratio reinforcement: see *schedules of reinforcement*

variance: a measure of dispersion in a set of scores. That is, it gives us some indication of the amount of variation in those scores. The bigger the variance, the more the scores are spread around the **mean** rather than all being clustered around one central score.

ventro-medial hypothalamus: when this area of a rat's brain is **lesioned**, the rat will show abnormal appetitive behaviour. In the first phase after lesioning, they will develop hyperphagia (over-eating) and will typically become obese. In the second phase, they will eat only easily obtainable and appetising food.

vicarious learning: a term generally used to indicate that **learning** has not been a product of direct experience, but rather one's observation of another's experience. For example, if we were to observe a friend withdrawing his hand in pain from a hot pipe, we would be unlikely to put our own hand on the pipe, having learned vicariously that the pipe was hot.

vicarious reinforcement: the tendency to imitate behaviour that we have seen reinforced in someone else rather than as a result of our own behaviour being reinforced. For example, a child may observe smokers in its peer group being treated as more mature by other members of the group, so imitates their behaviour in order to gain the same reinforcement.

visual cliff: an apparatus used to test an infant's perception of depth (see diagram overleaf). A pane of thick glass covers a shallow drop and a deep drop. The underlying surfaces of both deep and shallow sides are covered with the same chequered pattern. Children of six months and older will not venture over the 'deep' side, and this is taken as an indication that the child can perceive depth.

visual constancy: see *perceptual constancy*

volunteer bias: the belief that **participants** who volunteer for a research investigation may differ in significant ways from non–volunteers, therefore constituting a non-representative **sample**. Some psychologists believe that this volunteer bias makes generalisation to a non–volunteering population inappropriate.

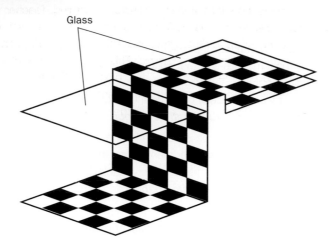

Glass

Visual cliff

volunteer sampling: a self–selected sample of individuals who volunteer to take part in a study rather than being selected randomly or systematically by the researcher. Although this is a convenient method of obtaining participants, and in some sensitive areas of the study the only feasible method, it represents a biased sample. See also **volunteer bias**.

vulnerability to addiction: factors that increase an individual's vulnerability to *addiction* include self-esteem (low self-esteem may cause people to engage in self-destructive behaviours in order to escape self-awareness), attributions (many 'addicts' attribute their behaviour to forces outside their control) and social context (e.g. imitating the behaviour of those with whom they have the most contact).

Vygotsky, L (1896-1934): Lev Vygotsky was a Russian psychologist who believed that cognitive development was founded on social interaction. According to Vygotsky, much of what children acquire in their understanding of the world is the product of collaboration with others. He constructed the idea of a *zone of proximal development* which are those tasks which are too difficult for a child to solve alone but which s/he can accomplish with the help of adults or more skilled peers. As a result of shared dialogues with these helpers, who provide hints and instructions as well as encouragement, the child is able to internalise the 'how to do it' part of the task as part of their inner or private speech. This can then be used by the child on later occasions when they tackle a similar task on their own. Vygotsky introduced two explanatory concepts on how this could be accomplished:
- intersubjectivity – two people (i.e. the child and the helper) begin a task with different levels of skill and understanding. As each adjusts to the perspective of the other, the helper has to translate their own insights in a way that is within the grasp of the child, and the child develops a more complete understanding of the task
- scaffolding – refers to the way in which the support offered by a helper gradually decreases as the child becomes more skilled in the task. As the helper withdraws, the child assumes more of the strategic planning and eventually gains the competencies to master similar problems without the aid of an adult or more knowledgeable peer.

Vygotsky's theory has profound implications for classroom learning. Teachers guide, support and encourage children, yet also help them to develop problem-solving strategies that can be generalised to other situations. The role of expert peers is stressed in the Vygotskian approach, 'co-operative learning'. This symbolises the whole spirit of Vygotsky's approach to development – children learn best not when they are isolated, but when they interact with others, particularly with competent others who can provide the guidance and encouragement to master new challenges.

Do you need revision help and advice?

Go to pages 298–312 for a range of revision appendices that include plenty of exam advice and tips.

Wada test: a technique for anaesthetising one hemisphere of the brain at a time in order to determine which hemisphere is responsible for language. The technique involves the injection of a short-acting anaesthetic (sodium amytal) into the carotid artery serving one hemisphere, then a short time later repeating the procedure for the other hemisphere. If the participant's language skills remain intact (e.g. they are still able to converse with the researcher) with one hemisphere anaesthetised, then this indicates that for that person language must be controlled by the non-anaesthetised hemisphere.

WAIS: see *Weschler Adult Intelligence Scale*

Walden Two is the title of a novel written by American behaviourist B.F. Skinner in which he lays out his visions of a utopian society based on the principles of *operant conditioning*.

Watt's funhaler: part toy, part medical device, the funhaler uses *positive reinforcement* (a hooting whistle and spinning disks) to make it easier and more fun for children with asthma to take their aerosol asthma medication. Watt found that the funhaler produced a 60% increase in compliance among preschoolers.

weapon-focus effect refers to the tendency for people witnessing an armed robbery to focus more on the weapon than the person carrying it. This limits the effectiveness of their *eyewitness testimony* when later questioned about the incident.

Weber's Law is a law of psychophysics which states that the amount by which a stimulus must change in order for that change to be noticeable (the just noticeable difference) is a constant proportion of the strength of that stimulus. Thus, stronger stimuli would need to be increased by greater amounts than would weaker stimuli before they are perceived as different.

Wernicke's aphasia: also called sensory or receptive aphasia. Caused by damage in Wernicke's area in the *brain*, this leads to a problem in the processing and comprehension of speech input, although speech production is relatively unimpaired. See also *Broca's aphasia*.

Wernicke's area: a region in the temporal lobe of the *brain* important in the interpretation of speech and reading.

This area contains the 'word analyser' which holds the sound patterns of words essential for converting speech sounds into words. If damaged, this processing cannot take place and sounds cannot be identified as speech. See *Wernicke's aphasia*.

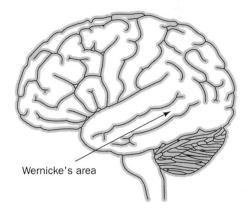

Wernicke's area

Weschler Adult Intelligence Scale: this is an *intelligence test* which provides measures of adult intelligence under the headings verbal intelligence and performance intelligence. Each of these areas is further divided into specific ability areas so that specific deficiencies within an individual can be assessed.

Weschler Intelligence Scale for Children: a version of the WAIS that measures IQ in children aged from six to 16 years.

white matter refers to neural tissue in the form of densely packed bundles of myelinated nerve fibres (nerve fibres covered by a *myelin sheath*), typically found in the brain and spinal cord. In the brain, white matter is found on the inside, with the grey matter (neuronal cell bodies) on the outside. This arrangement is reversed in the spinal cord.

Whorf, B L: (1897–1941)see *linguistic relativity hypothesis*

widowhood: a period of adjustment following the death of a spouse. The initial process normally involves a period of grieving followed by a gradual process of acceptance and adaptation. Women appear to adjust better than men to the death of a spouse, and older people appear to adjust better than younger people.

Wilcoxon rank sum test: a non-parametric statistical test which uses data at the ordinal level of measurement and tests for differences between two sets of unrelated data. An alternative to the *Mann–Whitney U test*.

Wilcoxon signed ranks test: a non-parametric statistical test which uses data at the ordinal level of measurement and tests for differences between two sets of related data.

WISC: see *Weschler Intelligence Scale for Children*

wish fulfilment: a *Freudian* term which refers to any gratification that is achieved through activation of an image of the desired object. For example, a hungry infant may gratify his or her need to feed by imagining the mother's breast when the mother is absent.

withdrawal refers to the symptoms that arise when a person stops taking a drug that they have been taking frequently. Specific withdrawal symptoms depend on the drug being used but typically are experienced as opposite to the effects of the drug itself. The physiological system appears to have adapted to the actions of the drug so that withdrawing the drug or even reducing its dosage disturbs the functioning of the system.

W

Withdrawal symptoms are suppressed quickly by administration of the drug to which the person is addicted. This provides an explanation of why most drug addicts maintain their habit, to avoid withdrawal symptoms.

within subjects design: see *repeated measures design*

witness confidence: refers to the common-sense assumption that a witnesses' confidence in their own eye-witness testimony is correlated with the accuracy of that testimony. Research that has tested the validity of this assumption has yielded mixed results, with some studies finding a positive relationship between confidence and accuracy, some finding no relationship, and others even finding a negative relationship between the two.

wolf children or feral children are children who have been found living in the wild, and whose behaviour led people to believe that such children had been brought up by wild animals. It was believed that these children would provide great insights into various aspects of development such as language acquisition. Evidence surrounding such cases was inevitably sketchy and anecdotal, and it also remained a possibility that these children were originally abandoned because they were retarded or disturbed in some way. This meant that their usefulness as case studies for normal development was severely limited.

woman-centred psychology: rather than merely taking over or adapting old forms of psychology, some feminist psychologists hope to create a psychology of their own which, through addressing specifically female aspects of subjectivity and experience, will empower women. Woman-centred psychology is, in part, a reaction to the *androcentric* bias evident in much of traditional psychological theory and research. See *woman-centred therapy*.

woman-centred therapy: such therapies are based on the belief that there are important and fundamental differences in the psychological make-up of men and women that are not merely due to the influence of sex-role socialisation. The goals of such therapies are to emphasise the positive value of feminine characteristics such as caring and empathy, and to help clients trust their own perspectives of their experiences rather than seeing their femaleness as a deficit.

womb envy: a concept normally attributed to Erik *Erikson*, whereby a man attempts to compensate for his inability to create and nurture life within his own body by trying to accomplish and create within the external world.

women and depression: a startling trend for women to be far more vulnerable to *depression* than men. In fact more than twice as many women are diagnosed as suffering from *unipolar depression* than are men. There are a number of possible explanations for this statistical anomaly, although none is more readily accepted than the others:

- the artefact *hypothesis* – there are no sex differences in depression, but women are more likely to seek medical help for depressive symptoms. More men turn to alcohol to deal with their depressive symptoms, a fact supported by the finding that male alcoholics outnumber female alcoholics by 2 to 1
- chromosomal explanations (the X-linkage hypothesis) – depression is caused by a *mutation* on the X *chromosome*, with the result than females (XX) are more likely to develop depression than males (XY). Depression is *correlated* with other X

chromosome abnormalities (such as colour blindness), but family pedigree studies have failed to support this explanation.

- *psychoanalytic* explanations – see the female being more prone to depression because of her life-long penis envy that develops as a result of the **Oedipal stage.** Because of her sense of loss and the resulting feelings of inferiority, the female remains vulnerable to depression throughout her life
- sociocultural explanations – the female is 'born to fail' either as a housewife who feels undervalued and unrewarded, or as a working woman who bears the double burden of work and family responsibilities
- learned helplessness explanations – women are more prone to depression because they feel they have less *control* over their lives than do men. This perception of lack of control leads to feelings of helplessness which in turn leads to depression.

word recognition threshold is the minimum exposure of a word necessary to recognise and identify it. The threshold is calculated as the point at which the word can be correctly recognised 50 per cent of the time when presented *tachistoscopically*.

working memory: a model of memory originally formulated by Baddeley and Hitch (1974) and updated by Baddeley (1986). This proposes that:

- the concept of a *short-term memory* store should be replaced by that of a working memory system
- this would have a more functional role, being concerned with both the active processing and the temporary storage of information
- working memory is seen as a complex, multi-component system rather than a single unitary store.

The system is seen as having three separate components. These are the central executive, the phonological loop and the visuo-spatial sketchpad (see diagram overleaf). The central executive is seen as an attentional system, allocating attention to different inputs and monitoring the operation of the other components. The phonological loop is sub-divided into the articulatory *control* system, where information is rehearsed in a speech-based form, and the phonological store, which holds speech input for a brief period of time ($1\frac{1}{2}$ – 2 secs). Because of their functions, these two sub-components are known as the 'inner voice' and the 'inner ear' respectively. The visuo-spatial sketchpad deals with visual input, which can be either direct (via the visual sensory register) or retrieved from long-term memory in the form of visual images. As different tasks use different components of working memory, it is possible to combine complex tasks (such as reading or problem solving) with articulatory suppression tasks (such as rehearsal) without disruption of performance. The major advantage of this model is that it deals with the short-term storage and the active processing of information within the same theoretical framework. Its greatest problem is that the most important component, the central executive, is the one we know least about. The working memory model also fails to explain how the role of the central executive might change as a result of practice. More recently, Baddeley introduced the concept of an episodic buffer. This provides a temporary storage space where information from long-term memory and from the visuo-spatial and phonological subsystems can be integrated and made available for conscious awareness*.*

W

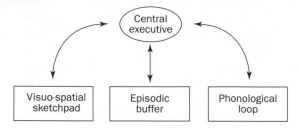

The working memory system

working through: a term used in *psychoanalysis* which refers to the process of confronting repressed conflicts during the analytic session. As part of this process, the *analysand* reinterprets memories and feelings and attempts to overcome their negative effects.

workplace stressors: some aspects of our working environment (such as work overload or impending deadlines) that we experience as stressful, and which cause a stress reaction in our body. There are a number of characteristics of the working environment that are commonly reported as being 'stressful' and therefore would constitute a workplace stressor. These might be divided into physical stressors (such as noise, length of working day and inherent danger) and psychosocial stressors (such as relationships with co-workers, organisation of work, and role responsibility). Each of these two broad types of workplace stressor has the potential to cause a stress reaction, and thus affect physical and psychological health. Whether they do or do not have this effect depends on many other factors, including an individual's ability to cope and available social support.

Wundt, W (1832-1920): German physiologist and psychologist who founded the first laboratory for experimental psychology in Leipzig in 1879. Wilhelm Wundt stressed the use of scientific methods in psychology, particularly through the use of *introspection*. Although the value of introspective reports was dubious, this approach did stress the need for precise subjective observations that contrasted with the poorly controlled observations of earlier studies in related fields. Although Wundt is generally regarded as the founding father of experimental psychology, he did not believe that it was applicable to all areas of human behaviour. Wundt's main contribution was to present psychology as an independent scientific discipline, equivalent in many ways to more traditional 'scientific' disciplines such as anatomy and physiology. Although Wundt's background and training was in these disciplines, he did not believe that human behaviour was reducible to them.

X-Z

X chromosome: together with the *Y chromosome*, this carries the *genetic* information that determines the sex of an organism. Males have an X and a Y chromosome, females two X chromosomes.

xenophobia: a fear of strangers or strange places, although this is popularly recognised as a fear of foreigners.

XXY syndrome: also known as Klinefelter's syndrome. This affects males who are born with an extra *X chromosome*. People with this disorder typically have underdeveloped male genitalia and pronounced feminine characteristics, such as the development of breasts.

XYY syndrome: a *chromosomal* abnormality where there are three sex chromosomes. People who possess this abnormality are males who are of above average height with typically low levels of fertility. There used to be considerable interest in the possible links between this condition and aggressive behaviour, although this has never been proven.

Y chromosome: see *X chromosome*

YAVIS: stands for Young, Attractive, Verbal, Intelligent and Successful, and is sometimes used as a criticism of *psychoanalysis* being able to benefit only those clients who possessed these qualities. Few studies appear to support the first three of these suggestions, although as well as the latter two suggestions there is evidence that psychoanalysis also works best with those clients who are highly motivated and have a positive attitude towards therapy.

Yerkes–Dodson law: the belief that performance on most tasks will increase as the person becomes more *aroused* until a point where any further increases in arousal produce a decrease in performance (see diagram overleaf). The optimum level of arousal will also be influenced by the nature of the task. Simple, well-rehearsed tasks will have a higher level of optimum arousal than more complex, less well-rehearsed tasks (see also *audience effect*).

zeitgebers are external cues that help animals to maintain their *circadian rhythms*. The most important zeitgeber for most animals is light. Receptors in the brain are sensitive to changes in light levels during the day and use this information to synchronise the activity of the body's organs and glands. The sensitivity of our bodily rhythms to zeitgebers is adaptive so long as external stimuli change only gradually. Sudden changes in zeitgebers (such as when we cross time zones in air travel) mean we cannot adjust our bodily rhythms quickly enough, and for a while our physiological activity (such as the sleep–waking cycle) is desynchronised. This desynchronisation of the body's physiological rhythms from the external world gives rise to the feelings of tiredness and disorientation known as jet lag. After a few days the body and the external world re-synchronise, and we are again in tune with the external world and its zeitgebers.

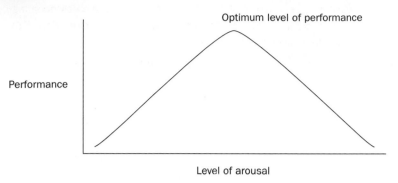

The Yerkes–Dodson law

Zeitgeist: literally, the spirit of the times. This refers to the ideas, trends and **values** that are dominant in a culture at a particular point in history. In social psychology, the Zeitgeist is seen as a counter influence on people's behaviour to the influence of significant individuals in history. For example, the 1960s are commonly recognised as a period of great social, political and ideological upheaval, quite apart from the influence of significant social leaders such as Martin Luther King and Malcolm X.

zener cards: a pack of cards that are typically used in research into **extrasensory perception (ESP).** There are 25 cards in the pack, five of each of a square, circle, star, plus sign and wavy lines design.

zero tolerance: the principle that acting quickly against small crimes will help to reduce bigger crimes as well. It is assumed that allowing a 'climate of disorder' to develop invites escalation in the levels of crime. The presence of graffiti and abandoned cars in a community suggests that there already exists a sense of lawlessness and thus lowers inhibitions in those already predisposed towards crime. Zero tolerance policies have been effective in the US, where there has been a steady decrease in both minor and serious crimes in cities that operate such a policy. Senior police officers are more cautious about the introduction of such practices in the UK. They argue that the success of zero tolerance in the USA has been largely due to the significant increase in the number of extra police officers operating in cities that have initiated zero tolerance regimes, together with the simultaneous development of better co-operation between local communities and the police. An example of the latter is the 'Combined Forces Asian Investigative Unit' operating in Toronto, Canada. This collaboration between the Asian community of Toronto and the Metropolitan Toronto Police Force has led to a decrease in crimes reported in the Asian community for the last five years. Critics of zero tolerance also fear that such a policy may lead to the targeting of certain minority groups and the possibility of subsequent riots.

zone of proximal development: a term from the developmental theory of Lev **Vygotsky** which refers to the range of tasks that children cannot yet accomplish on their own, but can do with the help of adults or other children. This is an important idea in Vygotsky's theory because it emphasises that children's knowledge develops through their experience of adults guiding them toward a more sophisticated solution to a task. This is accomplished by means of co-operative dialogues between adult and child which become internalised as part of the child's own private speech. In the future, the child is able to use this internalised dialogue to accomplish the same task by him or herself.

zygote: a fertilised cell produced by the union of a sperm and an ovum.

X
Y
Z

Psychology revision lists

Using A–Z Online

In addition to the revision lists set out below, you can use the A–Z Online website to access revision lists specific to your exam board and the particular exam you are taking. Log on to **www.philipallan.co.uk/a–zonline** and create an account using the unique code provided on the inside front cover of this book. Once you have logged on, you can print out lists of terms together with their definitions, which will help you to focus your revision.

On the pages that follow, we have listed revision terms for the AS and A-level examinations for the three main awarding bodies:

- AQA (Specification A), see pages 299–302
- AQA (Specification B), see pages 303–306
- OCR, see pages 307–309

This is to help you use this handbook as effectively as possible. On the website, we have set out revision lists for other examination bodies which may provide the psychology exams at your school or college, including:

- Edexcel
- Cambridge International Examinations (CIE)
- Welsh Joint Education Committee (WJEC)
- Scottish Higher
- International Baccalaureate (IB)

AQA (Specification A) revision lists

AS Unit 1 Cognitive psychology, developmental psychology and research methods

Cognitive psychology

Cognitive interview
Eyewitness testimony
Memory
Memory improvement

Misleading information
Multi-store model of memory
Working memory

Developmental psychology

Attachment
Bowlby, J
Day care
Disruption of attachment

Insecure attachment
Privation
Secure attachment

Research methods

Aims
British Psychological Society (BPS)
Case study
Codes of practice
Content analysis
Correlation coefficient
Demand characteristic
Ethics/ethical issues
Experiment
Experimental designs
Extraneous variable
Hypothesis
Interview

Investigator effects
Measure of central tendency
Measure of dispersion
Observation
Operationalisation
Pilot study
Qualitative data
Quantitative data
Questionnaire
Reliability
Sampling
Validity

AS Unit 2 Biological psychology, social psychology and individual differences

Biological psychology

Cognitive behavioural therapy
Daily hassles
Emotion-focused coping
Life changes (stress)
Pituitary-adrenal system
Problem-focused coping

Stress
Stress management
Sympathomedullary pathway
Type A personality/behaviour
Workplace stressors

Social psychology

Compliance
Conformity (majority influence)
Independent behaviour
Informational influence
Innovation (minority influence)

Internalisation
Locus of control
Normative influence
Obedience
Social change

Individual differences

Cognitive behavioural therapy
Deviation from ideal mental health
Deviation from social norms
ECT

Failure to function adequately
Psychoanalysis
Psychopathology
Systematic desensitisation

A2 Unit 2 Topics in psychology

Biological rhythms and sleep

Apnoea
Biological rhythms
Endogenous pacemakers
Evolutionary explanations of sleep
Exogenous zeitgebers
Insomnia

Jet lag
Narcolepsy
Restoration accounts of sleep
Sleep
Sleepwalking

Perception

Bruce and Young's theory of face recognition
Cross-cultural research
Gibson's bottom-up theory of perception

Gregory's top-down theory of perception
Nature vs nurture
Prosopagnosia
Visual constancy

Relationships

Parental investment (PI)
Parent-offspring conflict
Reward/need satisfaction

Sexual selection
Social exchange theory

Aggression

Aggression
Deindividuation
Infidelity

Institutional aggression
Jealousy
Social learning theory

Eating behaviour

Anorexia nervosa
Bulimia nervosa
Dieting

Eating disorder
Obesity

Gender

Androgyny
Biosocial approach to gender development
Gender dysphoria

Gender role
Gender schema theory
Kohlberg, L

Intelligence and learning

Brain size and intelligence
Classical conditioning
Ecological demands and human
intelligence
Gardner's theory of multiple intelligences
Information processing approach to
intelligence
Intelligence

IQ
Machiavellian intelligence
Operant conditioning
Psychometric testing
Self-recognition (animal behaviour)
Social complexity and human intelligence
Social learning theory

Cognition and development

Bruner, J
Kohlberg, L
Mirror neurons
Perspective taking
Piaget, J

Pro-social reasoning
Sally-Anne test
Theory of mind
Vygotsky, L

A2 Unit 4 Psychopathology, psychology in action and research methods

Psychopathology

Depression
Diagnostic and Statistical Manual (DSM)
Obsessive-compulsive disorder
Phobic disorders (phobias)

Reliability
Schizophrenia
Validity

Media psychology

Celebrity (attraction to)
Cognitive consistency theories
Cognitive dissonance
Elaboration–likelihood model
Hovland-Yale model

Intense fandom
Media effects
Self-perception theory
Stalking

The psychology of addictive behaviour

Addiction
Media and addictive behaviour
Theory of planned behaviour

Theory of reasoned action
Vulnerability to addiction

Anomalistic psychology

Anomalous experience
Coincidence
Deception
Ganzfeld
Near-death experience
Out-of-body experience (OBE)
Paranormal

Pseudoscience
Psychic healing
Psychic mediumship
Psychokinesis (PK)
Scientific fraud
Superstitious behaviour

Psychological research and scientific method

Chi-squared test of association
Inferential analysis
Mann–Whitney U test
Objectivity
Probability
Replication

Science, psychology as
Significance
Spearman's rho
Type 1/type 2 errors
Wilcoxon rank sum test
Wilcoxon signed ranks test

AQA (Specification B) revision lists

AS Unit 1 Introducing psychology

Approaches

Autonomic nervous system
Behaviourism
Biopsychology
Cognitive psychology
EEG
Genotype
Humanistic psychology

Localisation of function
PET
Phenotype
Psychoanalysis
Psychodynamic
Social learning theory
Twin studies

Gender development

Androgen
Androgyny
Freud, S
Gender identity
Gender schema theory

Klinefelter's syndrome
Nature vs nurture
Sex-role stereotype
Social learning theory
Turner's syndrome

Research methods

British Psychological Society (BPS)
Case study
Codes of practice
Content analysis
Correlation coefficient
Counterbalancing
Ecological validity
Experiment
Experimental designs
Hypothesis

Independent and dependent variables
Interview
Observation
Pilot study
Qualitative data
Quantitative data
Questionnaire
Sampling
Scattergram
Tables

AS Unit 2 Social psychology, cognitive psychology and individual differences

Social psychology

Attribution
Attributional biases
Authoritarian personality
Competition for resources
Compliance
Defiance of authority
Function of attitudes
Impression formation

Informational influence
Internalisation
Normative influence
Prejudice
Social facilitation and inhibition (SFI)
Social identity theory
Social schemas
Stereotype

Cognitive psychology

Ambiguous figures
Autobiographical memory
Decay
Depth perception
Displacement
Distortion illusions
Forgetting
Gestalt
Gibson's bottom-up theory of perception
Gregory's top-down theory of perception
Interference theory

Levels of processing
Long-term memory
Müller-Lyer illusion
Multi-store model of memory
Perceptual constancy
Perceptual set
Ponzo illusion
Repression
Retrieval failure
Working memory

Individual differences

Agoraphobia
Anxiety disorder
Autistic disorder (autism)
Central coherence deficit
Cognitive therapies
Cold-parenting
Failure of executive functioning
False-belief test
Flooding

Lovaas technique
Obsessive-compulsive disorder
Phobic disorders (phobias)
Sally-Anne test
Smartie tube test
Social phobia
Systematic desensitisation
Theory of mind

A2 Unit 3 Child development and applied options

Child development

Attachment
Bowlby, J
Distributive justice
Gilligan's ethics of care
Insecure attachment
Kohlberg, L
Maternal deprivation
Moral comparisons
Moral dilemma

Piaget, J
Privation
Pro-social reasoning
Scaffolding
Secure attachment
Strange situation test
Superego
Vygotsky, L

Cognition and law

Anti-psychotic drugs
Bipolar depression
Depression
Face recognition
False memory debate
Family dysfunction

Flashbulb memory
Labelling theory
Post-event contamination
Repression
Schizophrenia
Seasonal affective disorder (SAD)

Stress and stress management

Autonomic nervous system
Biofeedback
Cognitive therapies
Denial
Emotion-focused coping
Endocrine system
Hardiness
Locus of control
Problem-focused coping

Rationalisation
Regression
Repression
Stress
Stress management
Systematic desensitisation
Type A personality/behaviour
Type B personality/behaviour
Type C personality/behaviour

Substance abuse

Addiction
Aversion therapy
Physical (physiological) dependence
Prochaska model

Social inoculation
Solvent abuse
Substance abuse

Forensic psychology

Anger management
Behaviour modification
Custodial sentencing
Geographical profiling

Offender profiling
Recidivism
Social skills training
Theories of crime

A2 Unit 4 Approaches, debates and methods in psychology

Approaches in psychology

Autonomic nervous system
Behaviourism
Biopsychology
Central nervous system (CNS)
Classical conditioning
Computer analogies
Erikson's 'Eight ages of man'
Free will vs determinism
Freud, S
Holism

Humanistic psychology
Maslow, A
Observational learning
Operant conditioning
Psychoanalysis
Psychodynamic
Reinforcement
Rogers, Carl
Social learning theory
Vicarious reinforcement

Debates in psychology

Free will vs determinism
Holism
Idiographic
Nature vs nurture

Nomothetic
Peer review
Reductionism
Science, psychology as

Methods in psychology

Chi-squared test of association
Correlation coefficient
Ethics/ethical issues
Experimental designs
Generalisability
Hypothesis
Inferential analysis
Levels of measurement
Mann–Whitney U test
One-tailed test
Pearson's product moment test
Probability

Qualitative data
Quantitative data
Reliability
Sampling
Significance
Spearman's rho
t-test
Two-tailed test
Type 1 and Type 2 errors
Validity
Wilcoxon rank sum test
Wilcoxon signed ranks test

OCR revision lists

AS Unit G542 Core studies

Approaches

Behaviourism
Biopsychology
Case study
Cognitive psychology
Developmental psychology
Ecological validity
Ethics/ethical issues
Experiment
Individual differences

Longitudinal study
Observation
Psychoanalysis
Psychodynamic
Qualitative data
Quantitative data
Reliability
Social psychology
Validity

A2 Unit G543 Options in applied psychology

Forensic psychology

Anger management
Brain dysfunction and crime
Cognitive interview
Cognitive skills programmes
Criminal thinking patterns
Differential association hypothesis
Disrupted families
Ear acupuncture
E-FIT

False confessions
Interrogation techniques
Kohlberg, L
Looking deathworthy
Moral development and crime
Restorative justice
Social contexts of pathways into crime
Weapon-focus effect
Witness confidence

Health and clinical psychology

Biofeedback
Bipolar disorder
Cognitive behavioural therapy
Cognitive rational non-adherence
Cognitive therapies
Daily hassles
Dysfunctional behaviour
Fear arousal and health
Health-belief model
Legislation and health
Life events
Locus of control

Maladaptive thoughts
Media campaigns for healthy living
Phobic disorders (phobias)
Rational–emotive therapy
Schizophrenia
Self-efficacy
SSRIs
Stress inoculation therapy
Systomatic desensitisation
Watt's funhaler
Workplace stressors

Psychology of sport and exercise

Achievement motivation
Body image in sport
Burnout and withdrawal
Coaching effectiveness training
Contingency theory of leadership
Home advantage

Multidimensional approach to anxiety
Self-efficacy
Social loafing
Trait and state anxiety
Yerkes–Dodson law

Psychology of education

Ability grouping
Advanced organisers
Attribution
Bruner, J
Cognitive styles
Differentiation
Discovery learning
Emotional intelligence
Empathy
Erikson's 'Eight ages of man'
Flanders' interaction analysis
Freud, S
Gilligan's ethics of care

High/Scope
Humanistic psychology
Jigsaw technique
Kohlberg, L
Learned helplessness
Learning
Maslow, A
Piaget, J
Rogers, Carl
Spiral curriculum
Stage theories
Vygotksy, L
Zone of proximal development

A2 Unit G544 Approaches and research methods in psychology

Research methods

Chi-squared test of association
Correlation coefficient
Counterbalancing
Ethics/ethical issues
Experiment
Experimental designs
Extraneous variable
Hypothesis
Inferential analysis
Levels of measurement
Mann–Whitney U test
Measure of central tendency

Measure of dispersion
Population
Probability
Questionnaire
Sampling
Significance
Spearman's rho
Tables
Type 1/Type 2 errors
Wilcoxon rank sum test
Wilcoxon signed ranks test

Approaches, perspectives, methods, issues and debates

Behaviourism
Biopsychology
Case study
Cognitive psychology
Developmental psychology
Ecological validity
Ethics/ethical issues
Ethnocentrism
Experiment
Free will vs determinism
Holism
Individual differences

Longitudinal study
Observation
Psychoanalysis
Psychodynamic
Qualitative data
Quantitative data
Reductionism
Reliability
Science, psychology as
Social psychology
Validity

Examiners' terms

One of the problems faced by students in examinations is making sure that they are doing exactly what the examiner wants them to do. In all A and AS level examinations the different skill requirements in questions are elicited by specific action or 'command' words. *Describing* when you should be *discussing* and *evaluating* when you should be *considering* are common examples of not understanding the precise instructions in a question. Knowledge of the terms used in examination questions and of their precise meanings is essential if all that hard work is not to go to waste.

analyse/critically analyse: show understanding by examining the different components of a topic area (an AO2 term). For example, a theory might be analysed by looking at the degree to which it is supported by evidence, whether its propositions can be tested empirically, and whether it is logically consistent (i.e. does it contradict itself?).

applications: actual or possible ways of using psychological knowledge in an applied or practical setting. For example, knowledge from memory research has been applied in helping people to understand medical information.

apply: use an idea, principle, theory or law in relation to a given problem or issue.

assess/critically assess: a considered appraisal of an area through a review of the strengths and weaknesses of the information presented (an AO2 term). This term is used in much the same way as we might use it in everyday language. An examination will assess *you* in terms of your strengths and weaknesses in psychology.

compare: give an account of the similarities between two (or more) items or situations, referring to both (all) of them throughout.

compare and contrast: consider both the similarities and the differences between two items or situations. This can be quite tricky to do well, as it involves developing an overview of each theory (or subject) and being able to show where they are similar and where they are quite different. In comparing the psychoanalytic theory of moral development with the social learning theory, they are similar in that they are both examples of moral relativist theories (i.e. what is right is determined by the rules of the society of which the person is a member). On the other hand, the former explanation sees moral development being governed largely by inevitable emotional conflicts within the child, while the latter sees it as being a product of learning opportunities.

concept(s): an idea or group of ideas that might be used as the basis for a psychological *theory*.

consider: show knowledge and understanding of the topic area (an AO1 term). Just stringing together a list of relevant information may demonstrate knowledge, but rarely shows any real understanding. This is achieved not only by what is presented, but also by the way in which it is presented, in other words how the arguments are developed and the choice of appropriate material to answer the question.

contrast: give an account of the differences between two (or more) items or situations, referring to both (all) of them throughout.

critically consider: show knowledge and understanding of the topic area, as well as its strengths and/or weaknesses (an AO1 + AO2 term). This is essentially the same as *consider* but also asks for a critical stance to be taken towards the material. There are many different ways of doing this, but some of the more common strategies are to present counter arguments (for example 'although Freud said this, Eysenck claimed that ...') or to examine the validity of the research evidence that is being used to substantiate an argument.

criticise: evaluate in terms of the strengths and/or weaknesses of the topic area (an AO2 term). Students often feel that criticise means 'have a go at', and find it difficult to accept that criticise also means 'say what is good about ...'. Although most students can offer negative criticisms of Freud and Piaget, few could discuss the positive and very valuable contributions that they made to our understanding of child development.

define: explain what is meant by a particular term (an AO1 term). For example, 'Give a definition of perception'. Definitions (sometimes elicited by the words 'what is meant by ... ?') do not have to be textbook definitions, but can be your own, provided that they offer a clear and reasonably concise account of the term in question.

describe: show knowledge of a topic area (an AO1 term). As with *consider* above, it is difficult to earn high marks for the descriptive content of a question without also demonstrating understanding. In a sense, this is asking you to 'tell me what you know about ...'. It is always followed by the content requirement in a question, such as 'describe two theories' or 'describe research findings'.

discuss: describe and evaluate a topic area (an AO1 + AO2 term). This is an example of a word that has a quite different meaning in psychology examinations than it does in everyday language. It is important to note that the term asks you not only to *describe* a prescribed content area, but also to *evaluate* that material. For example, 'discuss research evidence relating to divided attention'.

distinguish between: consider the differences between two topic areas (an AO1 + AO2 term). A term not unlike *compare and contrast*, but restricted to demonstrating only the differences between areas.

empirical: refers to almost any form of investigation where the aim is to collect some form of data. This term is often used to illustrate the quantitative side of psychological research and is seen as an essential ingredient of the scientific method in psychology.

evaluate/critically evaluate: make an informed judgement as to the value of an argument, theory or piece of research (an AO2 term). Your evaluation may well take the view that this is actually a spectacularly good argument or theory, but more typically, evaluation tends to be critically negative. For example, social psychology research is often accused of having little practical value because of the unrepresentative sampling methods used in its research (a bias towards American undergraduates).

evidence: material that might be drawn from either *theories* or investigations and is used to support or contradict an argument or theory.

examine: provide a detailed descriptive account of a topic area. Can be used synonymously with *describe*.

explain: show understanding of a topic through coherent and intelligible explanation (an AO1 term). Invites more than just simple definition. This *A–Z Handbook* is based on the definition/explanation format required by these sort of questions.

findings: the outcome of a research investigation. Examiners often use this term when they want to stress the need for you to *describe, assess, evaluate* or whatever, the results of an investigation.

how? describe the procedures or methods used by a researcher or researchers to investigate a particular behaviour and gain their results.

insights: perceptions from *theories* or investigations that enable us to understand or appraise a topic area. Psychologists may achieve these insights in many different ways, so the examiner is giving you quite a wide brief to bring in relevant material from theories, research studies or just plain good psychological thinking.

methods: the different ways that research investigations can be carried out. For example, we talk of experimental methods, non-experimental methods, etc. It is a useful skill to be able to critically examine the methods used in any piece of research that you encounter because it allows you to offer critical comments later on.

model: a term that is used synonymously with *theory*, although it may refer to something that is less elaborate or complex.

outline/state: offer a summary description of the topic area (an AO1 term). This still implies that you should demonstrate understanding, but the content does not have to be elaborated in quite the same detail as might be expected in a *describe* question.

quality of written communication (QOWC): an assessed skill in AS and A2 examinations. For maximum marks you should be able to express ideas clearly and accurately, show evidence of good grammar, punctuation and spelling, and appropriate use of specialist terminology.

research: the process of gaining knowledge, by either an examination of appropriate *theories* or through *empirical* data collection. Note that this is the AQA (A) definition of the term; other examination boards tend to see research as a process of gathering information through psychological investigations.

state: give a specific name, value or other brief answer without further explanation.

studies: *empirical* investigations.

theory: a set of interrelated ideas or principles that can be used to explain observed phenomena (see separate entry for *theory* in main text).

to what extent? consider the merits or otherwise of an argument or concept. Opinions and conclusions should be presented clearly and supported with appropriate evidence and sound argument.